KIPLING'S JAPAN

YOUNG KIPLING

This woodcut of 1890 or 1891, based on a studio photograph,
is a fair likeness of Kipling at the period of his visits to Japan.

KIPLING'S JAPAN
Collected Writings

edited by

HUGH CORTAZZI

and

GEORGE WEBB

THE ATHLONE PRESS
London, and Atlantic Highlands, NJ

First published 1988 by The Athlone Press Ltd
44 Bedford Row, London WC1R 4LY
and 171 First Avenue, Atlantic Highlands, NJ 07716

British Library Cataloguing in Publication Data
Kipling, Rudyard, *1865–1936*
[Selections]. Kipling's Japan: collected writings.
1. Japan. Description & travel, 1889–1892 – Personal observations
I. Title   II. Cortazzi, Hugh, *1924–*
III. Webb, George, *1929–*
915.2'0431'0924

ISBN 0–485–11348–1

Library of Congress Cataloging in Publication data
Kipling, Rudyard, 1865–1936.
Kipling's Japan.

1. Kipling, Rudyard, 1865–1936 — Journeys — Japan.
2. Japan — Description and travel — 1801–1900.   3. Authors,
English — 19th century — Biography.   I. Cortazzi, Hugh.
II. Webb, George, 1929–   .   III. Title.
PR4856.A34   1988   828'.803 [B]   88–22348
ISBN 0–485–11348–1

Printed in Great Britain at the University Press, Cambridge

Contents

Part Two: 1892

Appendices

Maps

Samples of texts

(all following page 37)

Illustrations

PLATES

Preface

Collaboration between the two editors of this book was very logical. It had its origin in 1985 when one of us (Hugh Cortazzi) was preparing the groundwork of the book which would appear in 1987 as *Victorians in Japan*: his voluminous source material of course included parts of Kipling's *From Sea to Sea* and *Letters of Travel*. When the other of us (George Webb) then delivered a lecture before the Royal Society for Asian Affairs on 'Kipling's Japan', one of its themes was that Kipling's original commentary on Japan was more extensive than the edited texts in those two books suggested, and that, seen as a whole, it was a remarkable picture well worth further scrutiny.

Talking it over, we discovered that we had much common ground, though our points of vantage were not the same. It was plain to us at the outset, and became more so as we proceeded together with our usefully stereoscopic view, that what Kipling had said about Japan called for a full-scale study. Everything that he had written on the subject was highly readable, much of it constituted an interesting commentary on contemporary world events or on Kipling's own development, and some of it had been out of print for a century and was virtually unknown. One of us was well placed in the field of Japanese studies, the other in the field of Kipling. Our subsequent co-operation has repeatedly highlighted, at least to us, the value of this balance.

Our twin introductions which follow, Hugh Cortazzi's on Japan, George Webb's on Kipling, will set the scene. The first describes what late nineteenth-century Japan was like, and how it appeared to foreign visitors. The second describes what late nineteenth-century Kipling was like, and how his account of this foreign country came to be written. On what he made of Japan, he speaks for himself. It comes across strongly and lucidly, expressed in his inimitable style, with much praise and some criticism. At its worst it is good but hurried journalism; at its best it is very fine writing indeed; it is intermittently variegated with a sprinkling of memorable verse.

ix

He went to Japan as a self-confessed globe-trotter. Most globe-trotters' accounts of their visits to Japan in the nineteenth century were superficial and of no permanent value. Kipling's was different. A great Japanologist of the day, Basil Hall Chamberlain, in the 1901 edition of *Things Japanese*, paid tribute to his depiction of Japan. It was 'excellent . . . the most graphic ever penned by a globe-trotter, – but then, *what* a globe-trotter!'

Another authority, Lafcadio Hearn, a man of letters who had fallen in love with Japan, and who did much to make that country better appreciated in the West, also thought highly of Kipling's writing. In one of his *Japanese Letters* published in 1911, he praised the 'compressed force in the man's style', a quality reminiscent of the Norse writers, which made him 'a giant in all things compared to me'. He particularly admired the sensitive description (which we reproduce in Letter One of 1892) of the great Buddha at Kamakura.

For all that, some of Kipling's judgements unavoidably lacked depth. His knowledge of Japan, particularly on first arrival, was obviously limited; his prejudices were strong; his view of the Japanese, despite respect for their artistry and affection for their charm, was also patronizing. However, his descriptions were vivid, his observation acute; with his intuitive feel for people, his retentive eye for places and his powerful command of words, he provided evocative pictures of Japan as he saw it. They amount to much more than an album of verbal snapshots: they have unity. Anyone interested in Japan or in Kipling will find his accounts worth reading.

As we explain in the Introduction on Kipling, and more fully in the 'Note on the Texts', we have gone back behind *From Sea to Sea* and *Letters of Travel* to the original newspaper texts from which the relevant parts of those books were derived. This has led us to resuscitate a great deal of interesting prose, and some verse, which did not deserve oblivion. We have also dug up other items, such as a speech and a poem, which were unconnected with the newspaper articles and were in effect unknown. In short, we are setting out substantial new material.

We are also providing a considerable volume of accompanying comment and annotation. We did not lightly undertake this, but as we proceeded we became more convinced of its necessity. The point is explained more fully in our 'Note on the Notes' on page 26. In short, we believe that our accompaniment vindicates Kipling's powers of observation, illuminating both the writer and his subject. A few specialists may not need our commentary: but for the general reader we trust that it will prove not an encumbrance but an enhancement of the record.

Acknowledgments

During two years while this book was taking shape we were helped in various ways by many people – more than can be readily named and listed here, grateful though we are to them all.

Among individuals to whom we are particularly beholden for assistance or encouragement are Professor Charles Beckingham, Dr John Clark, Mr Philip Mason, Professor Tetsuro Nakasuga, Mr Neil Pedlar, Professor Thomas Pinney, Professor Andrew Rutherford and Mr Yukio Shimanaka. On a slightly more institutional basis, we are likewise obliged to Mr John Burt at Sussex University Library; Mrs Irene Pollock at the Guildhall Library; Miss Helen Webb, Librarian of the Athenaeum Club; Miss Sara Hodson at the Huntington Library, San Marino, California; and staff at the National Maritime Museum, San Francisco. We have received attentive help in various quarters of the British Library – from Mr John Huddy (Map Library); Miss Jeanette Sweet (Newspaper Library); Mr Andrew Cook and Mr Hedley Sutton (India Office Library and Records). We are also grateful to Sir Michael Wilford, Chairman of the Royal Society for Asian Affairs; Mr R.A. Longmire, Editor of *Asian Affairs*; Mr Edwin Trout of the Royal Geographical Society; Mr Julian Wiltshire, the Administrator at Bateman's; National Trust staff for their customary helpfulness over use of previously unpublished material; and the Secretary of the Tokyo Club.

We would be ungracious if we did not acknowledge, with much appreciation, that our wives have aided and abetted our labours; and that our secretaries (Mrs Margaret O'Malley and Mrs Jennie McIntosh) have efficiently helped us to handle our paperwork. Our publishers have encouraged us throughout, and they join us in acknowledging the help of the British Petroleum Company plc, Midland Group and the Tokyo Club in the publication of this book. Finally, if we could, we would thank our author, the late Mr Rudyard Kipling, who is more than a *sine qua non*: his entertaining and provocative accounts of bygone Japan have been a pleasure to study and a privilege to edit.

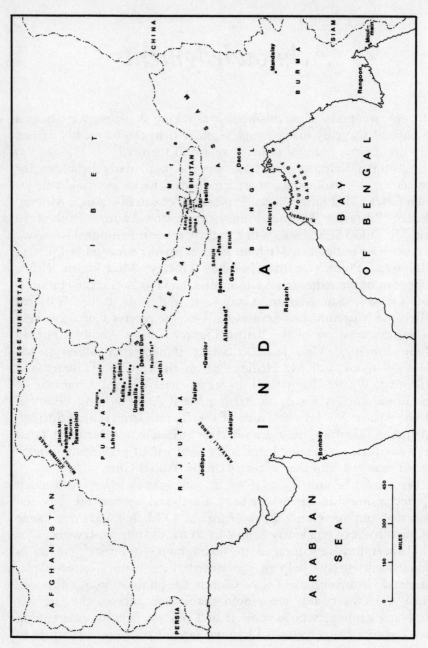

LATE NINETEENTH-CENTURY INDIA: *principal places mentioned in this book.*

Verily Japan is a great people. Her masons play with stone, her carpenters with wood, her smiths with iron, and her artists with life, death, and all the eye can take in. Mercifully she has been denied the last touch of firmness in her character which would enable her to play with the whole round world. We possess that – we, the nation of the glass flower-shade, the pink worsted mat, the red and green china puppy dog, and the poisonous Brussels carpet. It is our compensation.

Rudyard Kipling
Kyoto, 1889

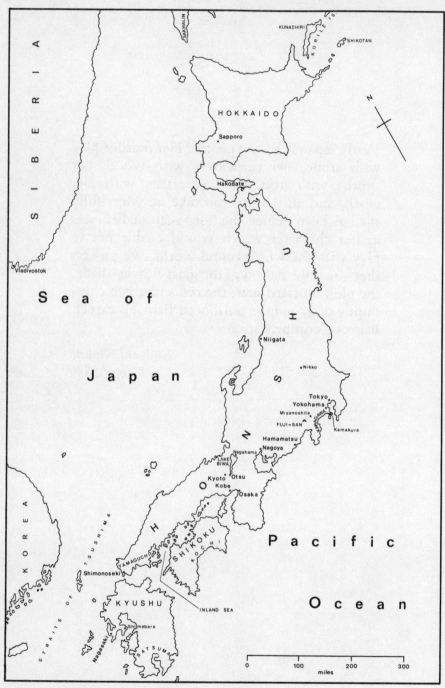

JAPAN: *principal places mentioned in this book.*

Introduction 1
THE JAPANESE SCENE

Japan has changed much more than Britain in the period of almost a century since Rudyard Kipling first visited it in 1889. In the thirty-odd years before that, the country had undergone a revolution which had totally transformed the fabric of society. Nevertheless, in 1889 Japan was still in a transitional stage, between the feudal society which existed when Commodore Perry's famous 'Black Ships' of the US Navy arrived off the coast in 1853 and the modern industrial state we know today.

The Tokugawa period of Japanese history lasted from 1600, when Tokugawa Ieyasu defeated his rivals at the battle of Sekigahara, until 1868 when the so-called Imperial Restoration was effected. This marked the beginning of the Meiji era. *Meiji*, meaning 'enlightened government', was the name given to the era which lasted up till the death in 1912 of the Emperor whose given name was Mutsuhito but who is normally referred to as the Meiji Emperor. Tokugawa Ieyasu had had himself proclaimed *Shogun*, or military ruler, and had established his capital at Edo (renamed Tokyo in 1868). During the Tokugawa era the Emperor and the court were left to stagnate in Kyoto. They had neither power nor wealth.

The Christian community, which had grown up in Japan following the arrival of the first Portuguese Jesuit missionaries in 1549, was subjected to an increasingly ruthless persecution by the authorities in the final years of the sixteenth century, mainly for political reasons and in order to ensure the hold of the new feudal regime of the Tokugawa in Kyushu, where the principal Christian communities were. The persecution culminated in a rebellion and subsequent massacre at Shimabara in 1638. The remaining Europeans were expelled, except for a handful of Dutch traders who in 1641 were transferred to the small island of Deshima, in Nagasaki bay in Kyushu, where they were held in a state of virtual imprisonment. The Dutch merchant colony on Deshima remained the one small window between Japan and the rest of the world for over two centuries.

The Tokugawa rulers enforced a strict feudal regime. Lords

– *Daimyo* as they were called in Japan – who were regarded as loyal to the Tokugawa were given fiefs in strategic places throughout the country, to counterbalance those whose loyalty could not be relied upon so firmly. All the Daimyo, whether *Fudai* (that is, on whose loyalty the Tokugawa thought they could rely) or *Tozama* (literally 'outer', whose loyalty to the Shogun was more in doubt), were forced to spend half their time in Edo, and had to leave their children there as hostages when they visited their fiefs. An effective system of spies, and guard-posts or barriers on the main routes, ensured compliance with these rules.

The feudal society was rigidly divided into four classes: *samurai* or fighting men, farmers, artisans and, last and lowest, merchants. This was the so-called *shi-no-ko-sho* system. The merchants were held in particular contempt by the *samurai*, who were trained to show a disdain for money. In fact, however, they often had to borrow money from the merchants: the growing indebtedness of the *samurai* was one of the many factors which by the nineteenth century had weakened the hold of the Tokugawa Shogunate – or *Bakufu*, as it was generally called.

Even Japan could not stand totally still for over two hundred years. The peace which the Tokugawa had enforced had encouraged the development of internal trade, travel and the arts. By 1853 the system was creaking, and if the regime was to survive change was imperative. The arrival of western forces and merchants knocking at Japan's closed doors acted as the catalyst for an era of radical change amounting to a major revolution.

The first treaties with the west in 1854 did not provide for trade relations, but the door had been unlocked. The Bakufu did all it could to stop it from being opened further, but in 1858 had to give in to pressure from the western powers led by the Americans. New treaties were signed with the United States, Britain, France, the Netherlands and Russia, which provided for the opening of a limited number of ports for trade, as well as granting extra-territorial rights to the five powers over their own nationals in Japan.

The first three Treaty Ports were Nagasaki (in Kyushu), Hakodate (in Hokkaido) and Yokohama (near Edo or Tokyo). The treaties actually specified Kanagawa rather than Yokohama, but this lay on the *Tokaido*, the main route from Edo to Kyoto, and the Japanese authorities rightly feared that this would increase the danger of trouble between the hated foreigners and *samurai* who were constantly travelling along this route. They accordingly managed to push the foreigners a little further away to Yokohama, where they built a couple of wharfs and prepared the ground for a settlement. Yokohama had the advantage, from the Japanese point of view, of being fairly easily sealed off by guarding the bridges over the canals and the swamp which surrounded the settlement on the landward side. Kobe – adjacent to the town of Hyogo, – Osaka, Niigata and Edo – or Tokyo as it became in 1868 – were opened to trade in 1868/69. To travel outside the Treaty Ports a foreigner needed a special passport, which he had to obtain through his country's diplomatic or consular representative. In the early days these were difficult to obtain, but by the time of Kipling's visits they could be procured without any real problem.

At first, life in Japan for the foreign traders and diplomats was tough, and murders were frequent. Such attacks, and interference with western shipping, quickly led to conflicts with the Daimyo of Satsuma (now Kagoshima prefecture in southern Kyushu) and of Choshu (now part of Yamaguchi prefecture in western Honshu). British forces bombarded Kagoshima in 1863 and Shimonoseki in 1864. Satsuma and Choshu, together with some of the other Tozama Daimyo in western Japan, led the opposition to the Tokugawa. They adopted the slogan *Sonno-Joi* ('revere the Emperor, expel the barbarian'). The young *samurai* who dominated these fiefs soon realized their need for western arms, and instead of expelling the foreigners turned to toppling the Bakufu. In a brief civil war in 1868 this objective was accomplished. The young Emperor Mutsuhito, better known by his reign name of Meiji, was no longer to be a mere priestly ruler at his court in Kyoto, but the sovereign power in the land. The real power, however, in accordance with Japanese tradition, remained in the hands of his advisers.

The capital was moved from Miyako or Kyoto (both meaning 'capital') to Edo, renamed Tokyo ('eastern capital'). The chief objective of the young *samurai* who dominated the new regime was summed up in their slogan, *Fukoku-kyohei,* meaning 'a rich country with a strong army'. They were determined to modernize Japan and establish it as a significant power, initially in the far east but also, in due course, in the world. With some justification they feared western colonialism and economic imperialism. They had the awful example of western exploitation of China always before them. Above all, they resented the 'unequal treaties'; they considered extra–territoriality and the other provisions limiting Japanese sovereignty shameful.

The new leaders moved very quickly. The old and rigid feudal class structure was abolished. The *samurai* were forbidden to wear their traditional two swords. Fiefs were abolished; compensation, which took the form of meagre pensions for the Daimyo and *samurai*, was soon commuted into inadequate capital sums. A new and more modern system of central and local government was established by decree, and every effort was made to adopt western forms in everything from dress to the legal system. The introduction of universal compulsory education was a high priority, as the leaders recognised that education was the key to both prosperity and strength.

They also realized the need for an effective industrial base. In the absence of an indigenous banking system and normal entrepreneurial opportunities and skills, the Government had to take the initiative in setting up financial institutions and basic industries. Because of Japan's lack of trained manpower large numbers of foreign experts were employed by the Meiji authorities, until Japanese replacements could be trained, either in Japan or abroad. British engineers, for instance, were employed not only to build but also to run the first railways, which began to operate in the early 1870s between Yokohama and Tokyo, and then between Kobe, Osaka and Kyoto. Other British experts, such as Richard Brunton, were engaged to set up the lighthouse system, to develop telegraphs, and to teach engineering, science and other subjects.

The Meiji government was a small self-appointed oligarchy. Inevitably, in a period of such extreme change enforced by arbitrary methods, resentment and opposition were aroused against the new regime. This culminated in the so-called *Seinan* ('south-west') war of 1877, also referred to as the Satsuma rebellion. This was suppressed, but the oligarchs realized that there had to be some kind of safety-valve for the new western-educated élite. Their views were voiced in the large number of newspapers which mushroomed in Japan in the 1870s and 1880s. Many of the writers of these journals were irresponsible, if only because they had no opportunity to exercise responsibility. The government reacted by applying strict controls and censorship. But the demand for some kind of parliamentary institution to represent popular views required a response. The new leaders needed popular acquiescence at least, for their continuing programme of reforms. They no doubt also considered that a constitution and parliament would help to establish Japan's claim to be recognized as a civilized modern state, and would make it easier to persuade the western powers to accept revision of the 'unequal treaties'. But they had no interest in, or wish for, really democratic institutions; those, they feared, might weaken Japan and halt the revolution which they were enforcing.

In 1882 Ito Hirobumi (later Price Ito) went on an eighteen-month visit to Europe to study European constitutions. He knew what he was looking for, and went first to Berlin and Vienna. Ito also visited London, but he did not find current British theories of parliamentary government appropriate for Japan. The constitution which Ito and other Japanese leaders drew up, with the help of two German jurists, was based on Germanic models and was authoritarian in character. Many powers were reserved for the Emperor, who was declared 'sacred and inviolable'. He alone could declare war and conclude treaties. He was the supreme commander of the armed forces. He could, on his own authority, adjourn or prorogue the Diet, which was to consist of a House of Peers and a House of Representatives elected on a strictly limited franchise. Even the budgetary powers of the lower house were circumscribed: the government was permitted by the Constitution to continue with the previous year's budget if the new one was rejected. The so-called Meiji Constitution was promulgated on 11 February 1889, a few weeks before Kipling's arrival in Japan.

The first elections to the House of Representatives were held in July 1890. From the start the Diet was racked by factionalism, and the lower house had to be dissolved in December 1891 after the new budget had been rejected. The next elections in February 1892 were marked by violence and intimidation. Matsukata Masayoshi, the Prime Minister, was forced to resign in June of that year, at the time of Kipling's second visit, but Ito was not appointed to succeed him until August. This was the political crisis to which Kipling refers in his letters of 1892 from Japan. In view of his misgivings about democracy as a panacea, one might have thought that he would see some merits in an authoritarian constitution such as Japan had just adopted. But he did not understand the background, and saw only the instability reflected by Japanese political behaviour at that time.

The new leaders, in their pursuit of power, had realized from the outset that Japan could not rely solely on the old *samurai* class for defence. Conscription was introduced in 1872: all men on reaching the age of twenty, irrespective of class or origin, were made liable to serve in the armed forces. French, and later German, methods of training were adopted for the army, while the Royal Navy was taken as the model for the Japanese navy.

Japan's foreign trade in these early days was largely in the hands of the foreign merchants in the Treaty Ports. Although the Americans had been the first to force open the door of Japan, they were soon displaced by the British, who in the last three decades of the nineteenth century provided the biggest element in the foreign trading community. The next largest community was the French, although there was always a significant American element, and by the time Kipling arrived American tourists were beginning to visit Japan in considerable numbers. The main British and foreign merchant colony was in Yokohama. The second most important centre was Kobe. There were also small foreign communities in Tokyo, Nagasaki, Osaka and Hakodate. Nagasaki had been particularly important in the 1860s when the Tozama Daimyo were seeking western arms and ships, but by the time of Kipling's visit in 1889 its importance had declined.

The British communities in Yokohama and Kobe lived in a colonial style. They were inclined to treat the 'natives' with at best condescension. If they bothered to learn any Japanese it was usually a form of pidgin Japanese which came to be called the 'Yokohama dialect'. The *Hongs*, as the leading merchants were termed, maintained large establishments and by the time of Kipling's visits many had grand mansions on the Bluff, the hill near Yokohama's Bund (embanked quay) and harbour. They had retinues of servants and enjoyed their own exclusive clubs. They were enthusiastic about their sports, especially horse racing which, dating from beginnings in the early 1860s, had become an important institution for the community. They delegated much of their work initially to Chinese *compradors* (intermediaries) who, as Kipling noted, were regarded as more reliable than Japanese; but these were gradually replaced by Japanese equivalents who were termed *Banto*. The merchants knew little about Japan, and most were not interested in things Japanese, although they all bought souvenirs or 'curios' specially produced for the foreign market.

The foreign market of course included tourists, whom the Japanese accepted as a useful source of income, and as a necessary evil on the path towards the acceptance of Japan in the world at large. Kipling, like other tourists, was also tempted by Japanese curios; a number of items which he must have bought on his two visits to Japan are preserved in his home at Bateman's in Sussex. They include a lacquer casket, a lacquer *inro* (medicine case), an ivory *netsuke* (toggle), a small ivory carving of the Buddha, an ivory bezique marker decorated with a monkey, a Buddha in a black lacquer *zushi* (case), and a pair of carved guardian deities in another *zushi*. All these pieces are light and were easily transported. None was a genuine antique at the time, or of any great value, but they were typical of the sort of items which would appeal to the more discriminating tourist.

At the time of Kipling's visits, western appreciation of Japanese art was limited, and the British tended to be attracted by the decorative elements. The French had become enthusiastic about Japanese prints, which had so much influence on the work of the Impressionists and Post-Impressionists. American art historians were among the first to recognize the value of Japanese painting. Japanese sculpture and Japanese architecture had not yet made much impression, except on the American Edward Morse (1838-1925), who became an enthusiastic advocate of Japanese styles. Many of the wares made for the foreign markets were tawdry and of poor quality, but they appealed to the growing mass markets of Europe and North America.

If the merchants travelled outside the foreign settlements, they rarely ventured far into the 'interior'. They preferred relatively convenient and semi-westernized resorts like Miyanoshita, near Hakone, where the Fujiya and Naraya hotels were accustomed to western visitors – and to their distaste for Japanese food. The traveller who ventured off the beaten track was advised to take with him a supply of his own food, especially Liebig's Extract of Beef, to enable him to keep body and soul together! He was also warned that he would need plenty of Keating's Powder to prevent him from being devoured by the fleas which frequented Japanese inns in those days. Another problem for the tourist was the Japanese bath: his prudery was shocked by Japanese nonchalance about nudity, and he did not like the idea of sharing his bath with others. Kipling, too, found the Japanese bath not to his liking, but he did appreciate the Japanese food he was given, from his first experience in a Nagasaki 'tea-house'. The tourist was inclined to call any Japanese restaurant or inn a 'tea-house': that term could also be used to cover places of assignation.

Towards the end of the century, with the arrival of European and American globe-trotters in increasing numbers and with the development of Japan's railway system, more tourist resorts became accessible and more western-style hotels were made available. As a result, Japan became better known in Europe and North America. Many of these globe-trotters described their experiences, and included in their books drawings or photographs of this 'exotic' country. The initial railway boom of the 1870s had stretched Japanese resources to the full, and there was a pause before the second phase, which lasted from the late 1880s into the beginning of the twentieth century. As Kipling records, the railway from Kyoto to Tokyo was completed only in 1889.

In *From Sea to Sea* Kipling refers to Reed's *Japan*, meaning the two volumes of *Japan: its History, Traditions and Religions: with the Narrative of a Visit in 1879* by Sir Edward Reed. These are preserved among the books in Kipling's study at Bateman's, and we can assume he read them. However, as a tourist, Kipling did not have the time or inclination to study Japan in any depth, and like other visitors to Japan he found Japanese religion puzzling.

Shinto (literally 'the way of the gods') has many forms, and includes elements of animism and ancestor-worship. It was the indigenous cult of the Japanese before the import of Buddhism from China in the sixth century. A Shinto shrine is marked by a simple gateway called a *torii*. Japanese Buddhism is of the Mahayana type: there are many different sects including Amidist, Tantric and Zen schools. Both religions existed side by side, and the Japanese generally adhered to both religions. Buddhist temples might have Shinto shrines in their grounds, while Shinto shrines might have small Buddhist temples within their precincts. At the time of the Meiji restoration the two religions were officially separated, but the distinction remained blurred, especially at Nikko.

Treaty revision was the dominant theme in Japan at the time of Kipling's visits. Every effort was made by the Japanese to persuade the treaty powers that, with the new constitution, a new criminal code and model prisons, it was right and proper that extra-territoriality should be given up and Japan be treated on a basis of equality. However, the powers were understandably reluctant to concede their privileged status, and their attitude provoked – or was used as an excuse for – anti-foreign demonstrations. The British were eventually induced to take the lead in accepting revision, and a new treaty with Britain was concluded in 1894 – though it only came into force in 1899 when a new civil code had been adopted. In 1889 and 1892, during Kipling's two visits to Japan, treaty revision would have been in the mind of every educated Japanese he met. His awareness of this, and his reaction to it, come across, with a host of other impressions, in the Letters from Japan that we present in this book.

Hugh Cortazzi

Introduction 2
RUDYARD KIPLING

Viewed now in retrospect, it was a striking conjunction: young Kipling on new Japan: the emergent writer commenting at brilliant length on the emergent nation. No other man of English letters spent so long there and described so vividly, sensitively and provocatively what he saw.

If Kipling's two visits were made during a remarkable stage in the modern history of Japan, a time of galloping westernization and unsettling change, they were also made at a remarkable stage in the unfolding of his own career. When he landed at Nagasaki in April 1889, aged twenty-three, he appeared to be no more than a cocksure young journalist from India, travelling eastward home. To be sure, he had behind him over six years of assiduous newspaper work, first on the *Civil & Military Gazette* at Lahore, then on the *Pioneer* at Allahabad, and had collected the best of his writing into several slim books: in India, therefore, many British readers would recognize his unusual name, associating it with powerful and evocative short stories and briskly clever verse. In the wider world, however, he was utterly unknown, and during his first visit to Japan – four weeks of eager sightseeing which he exuberantly wrote up for the *Pioneer* as he went along – he attracted no attention whatsoever.

By April 1892, when he came back to Yokohama for two more months in Japan, he was famous. His early Indian writings had now attracted a vastly wider public, and he had since written much more. The strenuous style and exotic content of his work were so original as to grip the imagination of the English-speaking world. The peak of his great popularity was still some years off; he had produced only a fifth of the ultimate output of his lifetime; most of what he is now remembered for was as yet unwritten; he was still only twenty-six; but he was someone of consequence, and when the Tokyo Club held a formal dinner in his honour they applauded him as a celebrity they were proud to see.

Fortunately, sudden success had not spoilt him. He avoided rather than courted personal publicity. He was too humorous and too individual an author to resemble an establishment figure. He wrote

9

not so much to preach as to entertain, or to fulfil an inner compulsion. However, the transformation of his position since 1889 had affected the way he now described Japan. Gone was the light-hearted reporting style of his first visit with its exhilaration and exaggeration, dashed off in copious haste for the readers of the *Pioneer*. His letters of travel now went to *The Times*, addressed less frivolous themes and were loftier in tone. Also he now found more cause for anxiety about the Japanese, and said so with devastating frankness. For Japan, too, had not stood still in the three years he had been away. 1892 was proving a politically unstable year, and the chronic national objection to the 'unequal treaties' was growing strident. Faced with this uncertainty and prejudice, Kipling could don a mantle that he relished, as champion of the expatriate abroad. In some outspoken passages of his reports to *The Times* the vexed question of extra-territoriality and foreigners' rights found eloquent if one-sided expression.

'Kipling on Japan' is thus worthy of both literary and historical attention – and not less so for being so inherently surprising a subject. Most people, including many who have read a lot of Kipling, are unaware that he ever went to Japan. Even his biographers have almost ignored his visits there. True, years after they first appeared in newspapers, his various Letters from Japan were re-published in book form. But there, buried amid miscellaneous collections of his journalistic reports, heavily cut, unexplained, increasingly out of date, they languished. They were inevitably overshadowed by the great bulk and compelling readability of his more literary writing. Today they are among the least regarded of his works. They deserve to be exhumed and presented afresh as period pieces of great piquancy: at the same time the reader deserves an explanation of how they came to be written, and why Kipling went to Japan in the first place.

*   *   *

Rudyard Kipling was born in Bombay in 1865, the son of talented parents. His father, an artist of some distinction, was Professor of Architectural Sculpture in a school of art in Bombay. After five and a half contented early years in India the boy was placed in England with, in effect, a foster-family, and spent the next five and a half years at Southsea, separated from his parents. The arrangement now seems unthinkable but was then not uncommon: it was felt that European children who stayed too long in India suffered in health. However, for Kipling the experience proved deeply unhappy and left scars.

Next he was sent, much more successfully, to a minor public school in Devon; his years there were later fancifully and memorably described in *Stalky & Co*. Apart from the earlier desolate period at Southsea, Kipling's boyhood did much to turn him into a genuine aesthete. In England the relatives and friends of both his parents included some highly cultivated people, such as his uncle Edward Burne-Jones, from whose influence the boy gained much. He grew up with a well-stocked and unconventional mind and some familiarity with the artistic world and its values. For years he had not only read voraciously and retentively, but had himself shown signs of precocious literary talent.

In 1882, at sixteen, he rejoined his parents, now in Lahore, and became assistant editor of the *Civil & Military Gazette*. His work during the next few years on that paper, and then with the *Pioneer*, not only imposed the invaluable discipline of handling deadlines but also, as his skills matured, gave him column space for the prose and verse that poured from him throughout that creative period. The flow was such that even after discarding much that he considered inferior, there was enough material to be collected into a book of verse in 1886, *Departmental Ditties*, and another of short stories in 1888, *Plain Tales from the Hills*, and later that year six more volumes of short stories, *Soldiers Three*, *The Story of the Gadsbys*, *In Black and White*, *Under the Deodars*, *The Phantom 'Rickshaw* and *Wee Willie Winkie*. He also travelled widely for his newspapers, and wrote up his travels with bravura for publication in them.

So much intensive effort was a tour de force, but it took its toll. His health suffered from the climate, and in 1888 his doctor advised against another hot season in India. By that time he was independently deciding to abandon the routine of a provincial newspaper, to leave the *Pioneer*, and to seek his fortune as a writer in London. With guidance from the firm of Thomas Cook he arranged to travel there by way of Japan and the United States, an extravagance which he calculated he could just afford.

In parting from the *Pioneer* he reached a financial settlement which included a contract to write articles for it en route; he also raised some money by selling to the *Pioneer* his rights in his Indian books (which he bought back in late 1892); and he had managed to save something from his salary of seven hundred rupees a month. Cook's basic charge, from Calcutta eastward to Liverpool, was some eleven hundred rupees. As for extras, Kipling would later be able to write from experience, when he was about to sail from Yokohama to San Francisco, that a man can do himself well from Calcutta to Yokohama, stopping at Rangoon, Moulmein, Penang, Singapore, Hong Kong, Canton, and taking a month in Japan, for about sixty pounds ... But if he begins to buy curios, that man is lost.

When he took ship from Calcutta in March 1889, unmarried, unknown abroad, suddenly liberated from the unforgiving deadlines of his profession, he rejoiced in having no fixed programme. After years of overwork, the prospect of freedom was attractive, and was not marred by the obligation to write an account of his travels, since, as he said at the end of his life, 'Mercifully, the mere act of writing was, and always has been, a physical pleasure to me.' He had arranged to go, at least as far as San Francisco, in company with friends, a British scientist at Muir College in the University of Allahabad called Professor S. A. Hill and his American wife Edmonia (or 'Ted') Hill. His relationship with the Hills was a close one, and for several months he had lived as a paying guest with them at Belvedere, their bungalow at Allahabad – which, incidentally, provided the setting for 'Rikki-Tikki-Tavi'.

It had almost certainly been the Hills who prompted him to take that eastward route home, though the idea of taking it together perhaps followed later. On Christmas Day 1888 Kipling had addressed to them an affectionate and graceful written tribute of thanks for their hospitality in Allahabad. It took the form of a poem of seventeen stanzas (now collected by Andrew Rutherford in *Early Verse by Rudyard Kipling*). In it he wished them a happy journey back to America by way of Rangoon and Yeddo (Tokyo), in terms that made it clear he did not himself expect to be with them –

> All good encompass you from East to West
>   Till utmost East becomes the West extreme,
> What time you take your giant pleasure-quest
>   To lands whereof I dream.
>
> For you shall China's wave take softer mood,
>   And Yeddo yield her choicest 'broideries,
> And Halcyons hastening from their haunts shall brood
>   O'er North Pacific seas ...
>
> Rangoon shall strew her rubies at your feet,
>   New skies shall show uncharted constellations,
> And gentle earthquakes in Japan shall meet
>   Your rage for observations.

Evidently, before long it was agreed that they should travel together, and in the event, as they dropped down the Hooghly from Calcutta on 9 March 1889, it was as a contented party of three.

Into the vivid record of travel which Kipling almost immediately started to compose, to be sent back in instalments to the *Pioneer*, the figure of 'the Professor' would continually and pleasantly be intruding. Sadly, a year later, back in India, he was dead. Meanwhile, in Kipling's sprightly narratives of far eastern sight-seeing, he was very much alive, and his laconic comments, whether or not true to Aleck Hill's real character, served as an astringent foil to the author's unabashed enthusiasm.

On his whole seven-month journey back to Liverpool in 1889, Kipling wrote and despatched thirty-nine of the Letters that had been agreed in his contract with the *Pioneer*. Twelve of these were written in Japan in about twenty-six days, representing a much greater intensity of production than the rest. What he could not know was that shortly after reaching England in October 1889, with a vision of the world immeasurably broadened by his travels, he would make his literary mark, and do so with an éclat that would remind the critics of the arrival of Dickens half a century earlier. Had Kipling known at twenty-three that by thirty he would be among the world's most famous living writers, he would have had to take a less casual view of these travel sketches. As it was, he wrote them in haste, as items of ephemeral journalism, and though there are indications in private correspondence that he thought seriously of turning them into a coherent book, he did no more towards that end than he did for the mass of uncollated newspaper pieces which he had left behind unclaimed in India. He enjoyed composing these vignettes of his voyage, and he valued them enough to be resentful later when he found evidence of slipshod editing at the Allahabad end, but he was curiously neglectful of his own interests. He kept a carbon of most of what he wrote in this series of Letters, but he did not even secure the copyright of the text.

Not till ten years later, when American book piracy had taught him the folly of such prodigality and the need to control his own property, did he resurrect the 1889 travel sketches and lump them in with some earlier Indian pieces he had written as a special correspondent and publish the heterogeneous assortment under the general title of *From Sea to Sea* (1899). As he explained in a stiff little preface:

I have been forced to this action by the enterprise of various publishers who, not content with disinterring old newspaper work from the decent seclusion of the office files, have in several instances seen fit to embellish it with additions ...

He himself, so far from adding to the text of the 1889 travel sketches when he eventually assembled it in *From Sea to Sea*, cut it very heavily. He made scores of deletions, removing thousands of words. Though some of the changes are minor, others are substantial, cutting entire paragraphs. For some reason which is by no means self-evident, he lifted out one whole Letter, the one that covers his journey from Kyoto to Nagoya. The justification for these cuts is sometimes apparent, as when an error is corrected, or an Indian provincialism is removed, or some trivial or captious remark is appropriately deleted. However, there are very many occasions where the cut seems unnecessary and the loss of text is to be regretted. In all such cases, and in others where we have not hesitated to use our judgement arbitrarily, we have restored the text from its shorter book length to its original newspaper length. It is true that the writing is of uneven merit which betrays the speed with which it was produced. It is true that its young author was often opinionated, sometimes wrong and occasionally shrill. But it is also true that the Letters as a whole are engrossing – fresh, perceptive and vibrant with energy.

As an acute observer with a noticeable leaning to the dogmatic, Kipling ventured a few predictions about Japan's future, and seemed to think that more might be heard of the Japanese infantry. In the main, though, his guesses were no closer than anyone else's to the extraordinary destiny that actually awaited the country. It is not for forecasts but for contemporary description that his vivid accounts are readable today, and this particularly applies to the 1889 series, which are episodic, anecdotal, amusing, essentially the first impressions of a delighted tourist who was endowed with hyperactive curiosity and a thirst for detail. Japan, which at first he kept comparing with the India he had just left, struck him as an utterly surprising place – inhabited by a people unlikely to be suited to the international arena they were so keen to enter, yet apparently moved by some mysterious and disconcerting motivation. Their manners were seemly, their children enchanting, their craftsmanship extraordinary, their sense of style and beauty very developed – but their passion for modernization was misconceived. All these assessments, and many more, had the freshness of initial ideas not yet subsumed by afterthought nor overlaid by conventional opinions locally absorbed.

A few years later, that distinguished commentator on Japan

Lafcadio Hearn, who greatly admired Kipling, keenly regretted failing to commit his own first impressions of the country to paper, as he admitted in *Glimpses of Unfamiliar Japan*:

> I could not, in those first weeks, resign myself to remain indoors and write, while there was yet so much to see and hear and feel . . . Even could I revive all the lost sensations of those first experiences, I doubt if I could express and fix them in words. The first charm of Japan is intangible and volatile as a perfume.

Fortunately for us, Kipling's self-discipline, perhaps inculcated by his exacting Indian experience, rose to the challenge of Japan at first sight, with a closely written record.

Readers of this book are now offered, among other unfamiliar items, something that has been unavailable since it went in instalments to purchasers of the *Pioneer* almost a century ago. They will find not the amputated text as served up in *From Sea to Sea* but the original, as published by the newspaper, virtually in its entirety. They are also offered, between Letters Six and Seven of 1889 where it chronologically belongs, the one short story Kipling wrote about Japan, 'Griffiths the Safe Man'. Compared with some of the magnificent stories he had already written such as the best among *Plain Tales from the Hills*, it is a minor piece, yet not without interest.

To turn from his first impressions of Japan in 1889 to what he wrote about that country three years later is to note the alteration that has already been mentioned and explained. The obscure Indian journalist had blossomed into a household name. To his earlier titles had been added *Barrack-Room Ballads*, *The Light that Failed*, *Life's Handicap* and *The Naulahka*, and he was working on stories for *Many Inventions*. A major article about him in *The Times*, as early as March 1890, had expressed the hope that this phenomenon would not 'write himself out': in 1892 there still seemed no fear of that, and he was perhaps in less of a hurry.

Recently married in London, with an American wife who was already pregnant by the time he reached Japan, he was now content to spend weeks in and around Yokohama, quietly enjoying the most attractive season of the year. He was neither hastening on to somewhere else as on his previous visit, nor bent on seeing all he could in a short time. His further plans seem to have been vague, but they included a projected trip to Samoa to see Robert Louis Stevenson, and probably a westward drift round the world and back to England or to his wife's people in Vermont. His success to date, his ability to write as they went and to sell what he wrote, ensured financial stability - or appeared to until his bank suddenly crashed, which turned the young couple rather ignominiously back on their tracks, from Japan to America.

It would be twenty-eight years before he troubled to re-publish, among a varied assortment entitled *Letters of Travel* (1920), the newspaper reports he had written from Japan in 1892. There, in that little-read volume, they have lain ever since, largely unregarded. Here, now, in Part Two of our book, we present them as they should be presented, with the accompanying poems which were sent variously in 1892 to *The Times* or to the other two newspapers to which he sent those reports from Japan, the New York *Sun* and the *Civil & Military Gazette*. They are verses which add significantly to the impact of the prose they were designed to accompany, but they are also well worth reading in their own right, especially the superb 'Buddha at Kamakura' and 'When Earth's last picture is painted'.

Part Two of this book has become a compendium of prose and verse, all related to the visit of 1892. The biggest items are the Letters to *The Times* and other papers, now supplemented by the poems sent to those papers but excluded from the text in *Letters of Travel*. Also placed in Part Two are a speech Kipling made at the Tokyo Club, which has escaped the attention of his bibliographers; some verses, 'To the Dancers', that he wrote for a social occasion and never published; an important poem, 'The Rhyme of the Three Sealers', on which we have uncovered some unsuspected background; and a fragment of the autobiography that he wrote at the end of his life.

All in all, Kipling's writings on Japan remain extremely readable, and taken together have a satisfying unity – the enchanted mood of 1889 balanced by the more sober reflections of 1892. The material cried out to be presented as a whole, and that is what we have done. The full accompaniment of explanation that we have provided is designed to bridge the real gap in awareness that most readers will encounter, given what is now almost a century's lapse of time and topicality.

George Webb

A Note on the Texts

The main purpose of this book is to collect into one volume the considerable quantity of material that Kipling wrote about Japan, for the most part while he was in that country. Hitherto, the interested reader could find a good deal of it in two of Kipling's more neglected books, *From Sea to Sea* and *Letters of Travel*. However, only a specialist or bibliographer would be likely to realize the serious incompleteness of the Japan-related sections of those two books: there are many significant pieces missing, out of print, inaccessible and virtually unknown.

This incompleteness does not seem to have troubled Kipling, and it does not appear that Japan, once he had finally departed from it, occupied his thoughts to any great extent. We, however, can see that with the passage of the years what he wrote about Japan wears well – yet is very little recognized and read. There is, therefore, now a strong case for a comprehensive text, derived in the main from the original newspaper articles which preceded by many years the shortened versions as these appeared in book form, and also fleshed out with miscellaneous related items of various provenance. This comprehensive text we now present.

The process whereby we assembled it, though not particularly intricate, requires some explanation, which we provide below, for convenience, under five headings:- (A) The Japan Letters of 1889; (B) The Japan Letters of 1892; (C) Other texts; (D) *Lettres du Japon* – an item which it would be mistaken not to mention, but which we found no reason to draw upon except for pictures; and (E) *Letters from Japan*, published in Tokyo.

(A) THE JAPAN LETTERS OF 1889

Kipling's lengthy book *From Sea to Sea*, which was not published till 1899, was a collection of miscellaneous newspaper work ten or more

17

years old. Its full title was *From Sea to Sea and Other Sketches*: the 'Other Sketches' were purely Indian material, all written before Kipling sailed from India with the Hills in March 1889, and therefore outside the purview of this book. The rest, 'From Sea to Sea' proper, is the record of the journey to England in 1889, in the form of a long series of 'Letters' which Kipling posted back to India as he travelled away from it. The *Pioneer* in Allahabad duly published them one by one between April 1889 and April 1890, under the heading 'From Sea to Sea'. They appeared anonymously but there was no mystery as to their authorship.

However, two-thirds of the 'From Sea to Sea' series are unconnected with Japan. They relate either to the preceding stages of the voyage home (Calcutta to Hong Kong) or to Kipling's later wanderings in North America, and they too are quite outside the purview of this book. Only some twelve and a half out of thirty-nine Letters of 1889 are Japan-related and therefore concern us – though they have much in common with the other Letters in their textual development, which can be conveniently if loosely outlined in three chronological phases, as follows.

Phase 1: the holograph manuscript

Having every intention of writing substantially en route, Kipling carried with him on his journey to England two black leather-bound 'manifold-books', large notebooks interleaved with carbon. In these books he drafted the texts of some – unfortunately not all – of his Letters for the *Pioneer*, together with various other sketches and stories some of which were later published. The idea was that when he posted an original item to India he would retain the carbon in the book for his own use. Whether or not something went wrong with the idea, it is a surprising fact, and uncharacteristic of Kipling, that he did not keep the two books but later presented them to Mrs Hill, who with her husband Professor Hill had accompanied him as far as San Francisco. Eventually they were acquired by the famous Huntington Library at San Marino, California, and that is where they are now.

We have consulted them but not in close detail. Obviously they are valuable source material for the texts: for instance, they can sometimes provide a check on the apparent misreading, in Allahabad, of a hastily written word in Kipling's often difficult handwriting. However, where they differ more substantially from the version that appeared in the *Pioneer*, it has to be remembered that Kipling may have made late changes in the original manuscript before despatching it, and that those changes may not be reflected in the carbon.

Phase 2: the newspaper version

The thirteen Letters from or concerning Japan appeared in print irregularly, some three to six months after they had been written. In every case they appeared first in the *Pioneer*, and shortly afterwards in the *Pioneer Mail & Indian Weekly News*. This latter was not an independent production but a special issue of the *Pioneer*, advertising itself as 'published on the night of despatch of the Overland Mail via Bombay and Brindisi' and containing 'the greater part of the India news and original matter of six issues of the *Pioneer*'.

In the *Pioneer* the Letters about Japan appeared on the following dates in 1889:– 30 July, 16 August, 1 and 24 September, 1 and 11 and 19 and 26 October, 2 and 9 and 16 and 20 and 23 November. Issues of that period are not now easy to find, but access to them in microfiche can be arranged through major research centres such as the India Office Library and Records in London, a part of the British Library, and we examined them there.

For day-to-day purposes we had in our possession a copy of *From Sea to Sea* that had an unusual history. It had been the property of an American bibliographer of Kipling, Admiral L. H. Chandler, who in 1925, while making a detailed comparison between the book text and the newspaper text held at Harvard University, 'grangerized' the book by writing in the amendments or inserting typed slips. Unfortunately, Chandler's amendments were themselves marred by numerous errors and omissions, but we owe him a debt: only when we saw the great mass of important differences between the newspaper and book versions that Chandler's bulging 'grangerized' volume revealed did we realise the scale of textual discrepancy, which has served as a main stimulus in producing our book.

As for the text that the *Pioneer* printed, it was unhappily far from perfect. The editors of the newspaper were no doubt entitled to edit Kipling's Letters as they came in, and they must be presumed to have done so and probably to have corrected some slips. But they were also themselves responsible for letting in far too many stupid blemishes and mistakes, some of which are so obvious that they cry out from the page. We know from unpublished letters by Kipling that when he had returned to England in late 1889 and began to get hold of the *Pioneer* articles, he was furious about the standard of editing that these revealed. 'Undiscriminating slashing' was one stated cause of contention: another must have been the sheer number of avoidable mistakes. It makes the reader wince to find *nasty* for *tasty*, *groves* for *grooves*, *honked* for *hooked*, *drene* for *dune*, *China* for *Chinaman*, *slogs* for *clogs*, *Tukko* for *Nikko*, *Kusile* for *Kurile*, *act* for *art*, and many other disfigurements which could have been prevented with a little trouble.

Phase 3: the book version

Kipling's irritation at that time was presumably compounded by the fact that he was for a while seriously considering turning the whole 'From Sea to Sea' series into a book. On his detailed intentions in this regard, very little is known, but he seems to have contemplated using Professor Hill's photographs (an album of which is also to be found in the Huntington Library) to illustrate the written text. In 1891 Macmillan, in a catalogue of forthcoming publications, listed something called *The Book of the Forty-Five Mornings* by Kipling: it is thought to reflect that project, but it came to nothing, and the matter lapsed.

Eventually, however, his hand was forced by American piracy of his Indian newspaper work. Writing to Mrs Hill in July 1899 he spoke of 'one or two firms' which had 'sent a man out to India to dig up as much of my old work as he could'. Kipling's reaction was to produce *From Sea to Sea*, which appeared in 1899 in the USA and in 1900 – with slight textual variants – in England. (Further slight changes can be found in later editions.)

Very little evidence has survived to explain the editing principles which underlay what Kipling did to the *Pioneer* text when modifying it for inclusion in *From Sea to Sea*. We do know, from the letter to Mrs Hill mentioned above, that he had tried to work at the revisions he considered necessary, while recovering from his serious illness of early 1899. We also know that he had a lifelong tendency to prune his drafts rather than to amplify them. We can safely assume that by 1899 he would have been inclined to regret some of his more effusive and exuberant writing of ten years earlier. A combination of these factors may well account for many of the cuts he now imposed. However, we have no certainty about detail, and cannot even be sure that Kipling was personally responsible for all the changes made. Many of the slighter changes made perfect sense, in some cases correcting obvious error, in others replacing ambiguity or obscurity by clarity, or tactfully deleting expressions of criticism which he had come to regret. Nevertheless, many of the deletions imposed in 1899 cannot be explained on any such principle – except perhaps the pursuit of brevity. Indeed, much that was worth retaining was cut out, thousands of words in scattered passages long and short, including an entire Letter (which we now present as Letter Seven of 1889).

Our confidence that many of the cuts of 1899 were unfortunate and should be restored should not be mistaken for some sort of pietism. We are not asserting that every scrap of hasty writing subsequently discarded by a writer of Kipling's great stature ought to be preserved in deference to some imagined principle of scholarship. Rather, it is our view that what Kipling wrote about Japan proves itself, almost a century later, to be resoundingly worth reading *in toto*; and that it is a pity for us today, given all we know about the later Kipling and the later Japan, to be deprived of the opportunity that readers of the *Pioneer* had in 1889, of seeing in full what the one had to say about the other. We have, therefore, put back nearly all the material that Kipling or his editors took out, and what we present is a great expansion of the version that appeared in *From Sea to Sea*.

Still, in our handling of this we have been necessarily arbitrary. Since Kipling's holograph manuscripts sent to Allahabad have not survived, and since the *Pioneer* text is plainly imperfect, we cannot pretend to have restored in all cases the true original; nor, where Kipling has corrected an obvious error, have we seen it as in any way our role to undo his correction. It was absolutely not our aim to produce a scholiast's text, pedantically particularised, with each minute emendation italicised and every dubious iota flagged. Basically, we have merely restored almost all the deleted material unless in our judgement there was good reason, such as error, not to. In very small details we have not hesitated to edit: for instance, in correcting or standardising faulty or inconsistent spelling, notably of Japanese words or place names; or in rendering a few abbreviations in full; or in making one or two other minimal modifications too slight to enumerate. This approach we believe – and we think Kipling the newspaperman would have concurred – falls comfortably within the routine prerogative of editors and in no way diminishes the integrity of Kipling's text.

(B) THE JAPAN LETTERS OF 1892

The background to Kipling's coverage of Japan three years later, in 1892, is less obscure – or at least involves less evidence – and may be summarised as follows.

Phase 1: the holograph manuscript

We assume that no holograph of what Kipling wrote for newspapers, from Japan, in 1892, survives. We have certainly seen none.

Phase 2: the newspaper version

The Times was now the leading recipient of the travel Letters in this series. The five Letters from, or relating to, Japan in 1892 appeared in *The Times* on the following dates:– 2 and 30 July, 13 and 20 August, 23 November. The two other newspapers to which the same Letters were syndicated were the New York *Sun* and the *Civil & Military Gazette* in Lahore. This is a significant detail because, for whatever reason, it was not *The Times* but the *Sun* and the *Civil & Military Gazette* which printed, as a feature of the main prose Letters, various pieces of original verse which Kipling had embodied in them. These were 'Buddha at Kamakura', 'For hope of gain', 'The stumbling-block', 'When Earth's last picture is painted' and the thirteen opening lines of 'The Rhyme of the Three Sealers'.

Phase 3: the book version

For some reason consistent with Kipling's tendency to relegate his travel writing, however well executed, to a lower category of work than his short stories and verse, these Letters of 1892 were not re-published till 1920. They then appeared in a volume entitled *Letters of Travel: 1892–1913*, containing three sets of articles written for newspapers or magazines. Two of these three sets belong to a later period than that which we are considering: 'Letters to the Family' (though we have cause to mention it in section (C) below) and 'Egypt of the Magicians'. The set with which we are here concerned is entitled 'From Tideway to Tideway'.

A comparison of the text of this, as it appeared in *The Times*, with the text as it was eventually re-published in *Letters of Travel*, has enabled us to correct a few slips (one or two of which very materially affect the sense of a phrase or sentence) and to make a few adjustments to punctuation. These are small but beneficial changes, which more exacting editing in 1920, and in later editions with their small textual variants, could have rendered unnecessary.

What is much more important, we have restored four of the five poems (two of which, being uncollected, were in effect unknown) to the positions where they appeared in the New York *Sun* and/or the *Civil & Military Gazette* – leaving only the fragment of 'The Three Sealers' for the separate and expanded treatment which that poem has proved to deserve.

(C) OTHER TEXTS

So much for the Letters of 1889 and 1892. They are not the whole story, and this book presents some other items by Kipling of miscellaneous origin.

In our Part One (1889) we have included a short story, 'Griffiths the Safe Man'. This was first written in one of the black notebooks, was sent to India and, in common with other such sketches that emanated from Kipling's journey, was published in July 1889 by the *Civil & Military Gazette* and re-published later that year in one of a series of small volumes, now very rare, entitled *Turnovers*, which were collations of newspaper stories mainly but not exclusively by Kipling. Years later, in 1909, 'Griffiths the Safe Man' was published in the USA as an item in Kipling's *Abaft the Funnel*, and we have used that text, with trifling amendments derived from the later Burwash Edition.

In Part Two (1892) we have included the following four pieces:–

(a) a speech delivered by Kipling at the Tokyo Club, as reported in the *Japan Weekly Mail* of 14 May 1892;
(b) an extract from *Something of Myself*, Kipling's posthumous autobiography first published in 1937;
(c) a minor poem, 'To the Dancers', previously unpublished, from the *Kipling Papers* in the Library of Sussex University;
(d) a major poem, 'The Rhyme of the Three Sealers', for which we have used the text in the Definitive Edition (1940) of *Kipling's Verse*.

Kipling would seem to have begun the poem in Japan, or on his way back to Vermont from Japan, and to have completed it later.

Finally, in our Appendix 1, the item requiring textual comment is a newspaper article entitled 'Labour', from which we quote at some length. As explained in that Appendix, 'Labour' was part of the 'Letters to the Family' series of 1908, re-published in 1920 in *Letters of Travel*. We have used the text from that book.

(D) LETTRES DU JAPON

When *From Sea to Sea* was published, less than a seventh of it related to Japan, but it could be seen that that small proportion had its own unity. If this was considered jointly with the Japanese Letters of 1892 there was plainly scope for a book – as it might be *Kipling's Japan* – which could logically have been compiled in 1899 or earlier, had Kipling wished. He evidently did not so wish, yet he curiously raised no objection to the 1889 Letters from Japan being produced on their own, not in English but in translation.

They were rendered into French by Louis Fabulet and Arthur Austin-Jackson in about 1904, the year of the outbreak of the Russo-Japanese War. The translation was published in France as *Lettres du Japon*, and ran through several impressions, and a moderately expensive limited and illustrated edition of 1925. Fabulet was confident that although Japan had evolved 'with giant strides' since 1889, this introduction to the country by 'one of the most powerful thinkers of our day' would find an interested public in France:

> *Malgré les progrès qu'a pu faire depuis quinze ans un peuple qui marche à pas de géant, j'ai cru qu'il serait d'un haut intérêt pour le public français, à l'heure où le monde a les yeux fixés sur ce peuple, d'apprendre à le connaître par un des plus puissants penseurs de notre époque, et surtout par un homme qui soumet son enthousiasme et son art au souci de l'exactitude et de l'impartialité.*

This French translation was not unique. *From Sea to Sea* was translated into several languages, and the Japan-related part may be read on its own in Polish under the title *Listy z Japonii*, as translated by Maryan Poloński in Warsaw in 1904. However, though they are a comment on Kipling's high reputation in the period running up to his being awarded the Nobel Prize for Literature in 1907, these renderings were very far from being comprehensive. They neither went behind the book text in *From Sea to Sea* to draw on the fuller newspaper version, nor included what he had written about Japan on his second visit in 1892.

(E) LETTERS FROM JAPAN

The only attempt to present in English a somewhat broader selection of Kipling on Japan was excessively unambitious. This was *Letters from Japan by Rudyard Kipling*, published in Tokyo in 1962 by Kenkyusha in its Pocket English Series. It is a modest paperback, edited by Donald Richie and Yoshimori Harashima, with an introduction in English and notes partly in Japanese. The introduction extends fulsome praise to Kipling for his 'enchanting, funny, pertinent, perspicacious, and devastatingly honest letters which give us the best view of Meiji-period Japan to be had in any language'. However, after this, the actual texts (out of *From Sea to Sea* and *Letters of Travel*) are so drastically abbreviated, and the annotation is so perfunctory, that the overall effect, for anyone aware of the great wealth of material that could have been used, is one of disappointment. The book makes no acknowledgment of copyright, and was therefore presumably unauthorised. The expiry of the Kipling copyright at the end of 1986 has now of course removed the barriers that formerly inhibited the reproduction of Kipling's published texts.

A Note on the Notes

Let there be no doubt. Kipling can still be read and enjoyed without the help of glossary or notes. Which being so, it behoves us to explain why we have thought fit to produce a volume of Kipling so densely annotated.

It is a truism, a commonplace of comment by the critics, that Kipling can profitably be read on more than one level. His writing is layered, packed, emphatically mannered, full of slight hints and unexplained allusions. For most of his works, with most of his readers, this quality demands no panoply of annotation: that would be burdensome. The beguiling pace and rhythm of his verse, the compacted tension of his prose, exert their spell unaided. The evocation of India in *Kim*, of an English school in *Stalky & Co.*, of the Newfoundland fisheries in *Captains Courageous*, is effective even when esoteric details are but dimly understood. The same applies to the short stories: some of the best known are, in their subtler implications, the most opaque.

When Kipling is set for study as 'English Literature' – a prospect that he viewed with some distaste – there is a strong case for notes. Obscurities call for elucidation, and even the reluctant student may find comprehension an aid to enjoyment. However, for *Kipling's Japan* we had no classroom in mind, but a wider and maturer audience. Why then were we at pains to interlard Kipling's vigorous reporting with slice upon slice of factual commentary?

Our answer is that Kipling the travel-reporter and Kipling the story-teller – though the *personae* overlap – wrote differently. His journalism is distinct from his more literary work, and after the lapse of a hundred years may demand more of today's reader than it is reasonable to expect. That is not to say that the vitality of Kipling's writing on Japan has ebbed so far, with the changes and chances of time, that it can survive only with an artificial life-support of notes. On the contrary, marked as it is by acute observation, coloured by a discriminating use of language, variegated by the writer's amusement or indignation or delight, it remains decidedly readable, unedited.

However, though it can still give pleasure taken neat, something of its original fresh aroma has been lost. In it, Kipling touched glancingly and esoterically upon so much. In 1889 and 1892 he could be confident that most of his allusions – political, topical, literary – would touch a responsive chord among the better-informed readers of the *Pioneer* and *The Times*. Today, though the narrative maintains its pace, the allusions have, for the most part, no such relevance.

To pursue the analogy of neat liquor, there are hardened imbibers who will yet take a drink of water after each tot of spirit. It provides a brake, a check on excess, a moment of blander reflection. Rather in that sense, after each rich instalment of Kipling, wherein he makes few enough concessions to the uninformed of his day and none to ours, we have interspersed in more prosaic terms our retrospective commentary. Kipling, it must be repeated, was writing ephemerally, so he thought, for the newspaper of a day. He did not expect to be re-read on the morrow, much less to be comprehensible in all his nuances to generations yet unborn. We, by contrast, have accommodated our explanations to the imagined needs of readers from different nationalities and backgrounds, with some interest in Kipling or Japan or both, but with very varying levels of understanding of the manifold issues upon which Kipling touched.

We hope that with the prompting we supply, these issues will come alive again. From the flatness of the print a third dimension, a perspective on the past, once so live and now so dead, can be recovered. The added depth and detail that Kipling's reporting then assumes repays the trouble. The theme itself is sufficiently significant: Kipling was a literary phenomenon, and Japan, now an economic superpower, continues still on her ascendant graph. The impact of so extraordinary a country upon so talented a commentator is of no mean interest; but, a century having gone by, an *apparatus criticus* of notes will be useful to most readers, for a fuller appraisal.

★ ★ ★

Be that as it may, as editors we did sometimes wonder what Kipling himself would have made of our efforts. In particular we feared he would have resented the occasional personal intrusiveness of our Notes. One day at an early stage in our work we were discussing just this, sitting after lunch over port and coffee at the long table of the Beefsteak Club. Here we should explain that the Beefsteak is a long-established dining club, which Kipling joined in his later years and particularly enjoyed. In *Something of Myself* he wrote of it with

27

affection; anecdotes about him are still recounted there; his portrait is on the wall. All of which perhaps put us off guard: we were less astonished than we ought to have been, at what happened next.

We would soon be the last at the table. The others were rising to leave. One of them, whom we had not noticed before, approached us with a smile, and leaned against the back of a chair. We recognised him at once. There was no mistaking this short, trim, elderly man, the heavy moustache and eyebrows, the bright eyes behind gold-rimmed glasses. No introductions seemed necessary, and anyway the tradition of the Beefsteak is rather against them.

'I couldn't help hearing something of what you young fellows were saying,' he began. 'Why the deuce must you stick scholarly notes on to a very young man's newspaper-work? You'll infallibly get it wrong. Old Japan has changed, even more than India.'

We explained, as well as we could.

'Well, don't expect me to be grateful. A damn liberty if you ask me – though I admit you could hardly have asked me. Look here, I don't mind your translating my Hindustani; I hardly mind your proving how wrong I was over Japan (though I ask you, was I so wrong?); but I resent your prying into my life and thinking you understand *me*!'

The words were gruff, but the manner was kindly. As tactfully as possible, we put to him the case for doing what we were doing, and doing it well. What he had written was durable, but some of it now stood in need of editing, precisely because the world had changed.

With a shrug he gave way. 'Whatever you do, don't clutter the bottom of the page with too many footnotes. I hate 'em. They proliferate like bacilli, a disease of the academic mind – like vanity. And they will put off the young – if the young still read me.'

We too were against footnotes, we assured him. But we had to assemble our material somehow. It would probably end up in large slices, in between his Letters. Assuming a confidence that we hardly felt, we told him our contribution would not be merely parasitic, but really would enhance his own.

'I have to admire your cheek. I'll even give you a tip. Do you know where the germ of my *Three Sealers* came from? No? Look through the *Weekly Mails* of the spring of – was it '92? You will notice something. I fear you'll also find the report of a speech I gave to some fellows at a Club, but I doubt that's worth putting in.'

He turned to go. 'One last thing. Would you intend to say in your book that we – met and had this talk? Against the traditions of this Club but – well, the circumstances *are* a little unusual.'

'We haven't had time to think.'

'Take a word of advice from an old hand. No one will believe you anyway, so write it as fiction, not as a matter of fact.'

So we did.

Part One: 1889

Bound for Japan, 1889

Kipling wrote in 1889 thirteen 'Letters' relating to Japan, that is, thirteen reports for the *Pioneer* in Allahabad, written between 15 April when he arrived at Nagasaki from Hong Kong and 28 May when he reached San Francisco at the end of a seventeen-day Pacific crossing from Yokohama. These Letters form the bulk of Part One of this book and, being derived from the original newspaper texts, are much fuller than the heavily edited versions which Kipling himself re-published ten years later, together with other of his journalistic articles, in *From Sea to Sea & Other Sketches*.

They can very well be read as the writer's self-standing commentary on a visit to Japan, which is how we present them. The fact that they were only a part of a long series – being preceded by ten Letters covering the earlier stages of his travels in March and April 1889, from Calcutta via Rangoon, Moulmein, Penang, Singapore, Hong Kong and Canton, and being followed by fifteen more describing his subsequent wanderings in North America – does not impair their unity.

In those previous letters, and likewise in the later ones, Japan is barely mentioned; nor was there much reason that it should be. However, there is one interesting reference – particularly having regard to Japan's eventual ascendancy in the production of photographic equipment – which occurs incidentally in the account of the visit to Hong Kong. For Kipling's travelling companion, Professor Hill, a keen photographer, it was a revelation to hear how technically advanced the Japanese capability in that field had already become.

'They make plates – instantaneous plates – in Tokyo, I'm told. What d'you think of that?' he said. 'Why, in India, the Survey Department are the only people who make their own plates. Instantaneous plates in Tokyo; think of it!'

I had owed the Professor one for a long time. 'After all,' I replied, 'it strikes me that we have made the mistake of thinking too much of India. We thought we were civilised, for instance. Let us take a lower place ...'

Sensitised plates were still in standard use in the cameras of the day. Portable roll film had only begun to be seriously marketed in 1888. (The term 'instantaneous' is of course relative: the sensitivity of the best plates in 1889 would not have been much better than a tenth of a second response at f.11 in moderate daylight conditions.)

How much Kipling knew about Japan before going there is matter for conjecture. Probably little. The freshness of its impact on him is a striking feature in his reporting. A superficial interest in Japanese art was by then usual among cultivated people in the west, and Kipling had clearly noted (as the first sentence of Letter One reveals) some recent ironic comments on the subject by Oscar Wilde; but his general knowledge of the country cannot have been great, though with characteristic energy and curiosity he did much to remedy this during his intensely active four weeks there.

His itinerary in Japan was probably not planned in detail beforehand. The Letters suggest that it was arranged according to whim, no doubt in agreement with the other two-thirds of the party, Professor and Mrs Hill. Incidentally, from a brief allusion in an unpublished letter to Mrs Hill which he had written in India in February 1889, it appears that Kipling at that time contemplated climbing Mt Fuji. If so, the idea was never fulfilled.

However, a mass of vivid experiences in Japan awaited him as his ship from Hong Kong, a sail-assisted steamer of the Peninsular and Oriental line, began to approach Nagasaki on 14 April. For the edification of his readers in India he brought his final letter about Hong Kong and Canton to an end in the following terms:

We do not laugh any more on the P. and O. s.s. *Ancona* on the way to Japan. We are deathly sick, because there is a cross-sea beneath us and a wet sail above. The sail is to steady the ship who refuses to be steadied. She is full of Globe-trotters who also refuse to be steadied. A Globe-trotter is extreme cosmopolitan. He will be sick anywhere.

1889: Letter One

OF JAPAN AT TEN HOURS' SIGHT, CONTAINING A COMPLETE ACCOUNT
OF THE MANNERS AND CUSTOMS OF ITS PEOPLE, A HISTORY OF ITS
CONSTITUTION, PRODUCTS, ART, AND CIVILISATION,[1] AND OMIT-
TING A TIFFIN IN A TEA-HOUSE WITH O-TOYO.[2]

> Thou canst not wave thy staff in air
> Or dip thy paddle in the lake,
> But it carves the brow of beauty there,
> And ripples in rhyme the oar forsake.[3]

Mister Oscar Wilde of the *Nineteenth Century*[4] is a long-toothed liar!
He wrote an article some short time back on the 'decay of lying'.
Among other things he, with his tongue in his brazen cheek, averred
that there was no such a place as Japan – that it had been created by
fans and picture-books just as he himself had been created by pottery
and fragments of coloured cloth. Never believe anything that Mister
Oscar Wilde tells you.

This morning, after the sorrows of the rolling night, my cabin
port-hole showed me two great grey rocks studded and streaked
with green and crowned by two stunted blue-black pines. Below the
rocks a boat, that might have been carved sandalwood for colour and
delicacy, was shaking out an ivory-white frilled sail to the wind of
the morning. An indigo-blue boy with an old ivory face and a
musical voice was hauling on a rope. Rock and tree and boat made a
panel from a Japanese screen, and I saw that the land was not a lie.
This good brown earth of ours has many pleasures to offer her
children, but there be few in her gift comparable to the joy of
touching a new country, a completely strange race, and manners
contrary. Though libraries may have been written aforetime, each
new beholder is to himself another Cortez, 'silent upon a peak in
Darien'.[5] And I was in Japan – the Japan of cabinets and joinery,
gracious folk and fair manners. Japan, whence the camphor and the
lacquer and the sharkskin swords come; among – what was it the
books said? – a nation of artists. To be sure, we should only stop at

35

Nagasaki[6] for twelve hours ere going on to Kobe, but in twelve hours one can pack away a very fair collection of new experiences.

An execrable man met me on the deck, with a pale-blue pamphlet fifty pages thick. 'Have you,' said he, 'seen the Constitution of Japan? The Emperor made it himself only the other day. It is on entirely European lines.'

I took the pamphlet and found a complete paper Constitution stamped with the Imperial Chrysanthemum[7] – an excellent little scheme of representation, reforms, payment of members, budget estimates, and legislation. It is a terrible thing to study at close quarters, because it is so pitifully English.

'Is the public mind agitated over these, these – these skittles?' I enquired. 'Do they talk of local self-government and proportionate minorities? Do they hold meetings and print reports in newspapers? If they do I will go back to my own place.'

And the man said:– 'You do not seem to be interested in Japanese progress.'

I made answer:– 'I come from India, let me get into a boat.'

There was a yellow-shot greenness upon the hills round Nagasaki different, so my willing mind was disposed to believe, from the green of other lands. It was the green of a Japanese screen, and the pines were screen pines. The city itself hardly showed from the crowded harbour. It lay low among the hills, and its business face – a grimy bund[9] – was sloppy and deserted. Business, I was rejoiced to learn, was at a low ebb in Nagasaki. The Japanese should have no concern with business, as you shall hear. Close to one of the still wharves lay a ship of the Bad People; *videlicet* a Russian steamer down from Vladivostok.[10] Her decks were cumbered with raffle of all kinds; her rigging was as frowsy and draggled as the hair of a lodging-house slavey, and her sides were filthy.

'That,' said a man of my people, 'is a very fair specimen of a Russian. You should see their men-of-war; they are just as filthy. Some of 'em come into Nagasaki to clean.'

It was a small piece of information and perhaps untrue, but it put the roof to my good humour as I stepped on to the bund and was told in faultless English by a young gentleman, with a plated chrysanthemum in his forage cap and badly-fitting German uniform on his limbs, that he did not understand my language. He was a Japanese customs official. Had our stay been longer, I would have wept over him because he was a hybrid – partly French, partly German, and partly American – a tribute to civilisation. All the Japanese officials from police upwards seem to be clad in Europe clothes, and never do those clothes fit.[11] I think the Mikado[12] made them at the same time as the Constitution. They will come right in time.

When the *'rickshaw*,[13] drawn by a beautiful apple-cheeked young man with a Basque face,[14] shot me into *The Mikado*, First Act,[15] I did not stop and shout with delight, because the dignity of India was in my keeping. I lay back on the velvet cushions and grinned luxuriously at Pitti-Sing, with her sash and three giant hair-pins in her hair – 'blue-black, lustrous, thick as horse hair' – and three-inch clogs on her feet. She laughed – even as did the Burmese girl in the old Pagoda at Moulmein.[16] And her laugh, the laugh of a lady, was my welcome to Japan. Can the people help laughing? I think not. You see they have such thousands of children in their streets that the elders must perforce be young lest the babes should grieve. Nagasaki is inhabited entirely by children. The grown-ups exist on sufferance. A four-foot child walks with a three-foot child, who is holding the hand of a two-foot child, who carries on her back a one-foot child, who – but you will not believe me if I say that the scale runs down to six-inch little Japanese dolls such as they used to sell in the Burlington Arcade.[17] These dolls wriggle and laugh. They are tied up in a blue bed-gown which is tied by a sash, which again ties up the bed-gown of the carrier. Thus if you untie that sash, baby and but little bigger brother are at once perfectly naked. I saw a mother do this, and it was for all the world like the peeling of hard-boiled eggs.

If you look for extravagance of colour, for flaming shop-fronts and glaring lanterns, you shall find none of these things in the narrow stone-paved streets of Nagasaki. But if you desire details of house construction, glimpses of perfect cleanliness, rare taste, and perfect subordination of the thing made to the needs of the maker, you shall find all you seek and more. All the roofs are dull lead colour, being shingled or tiled, and all the house-fronts are of the colour of the wood God made.

There is neither smoke nor haze, and in the clear light of a clouded sky I could see down the narrowest alleyway as I could see into the interior of a cabinet.

The books have long ago told you how a Japanese house is constructed, chiefly of sliding screens and paper partitions, and everybody knows the story of the burglar of Tokyo who burgled with a pair of scissors for jimmy and centre-bit[18] and stole the Consul's trousers. But all the telling in print will never make you understand the exquisite finish of a tenement that you could kick in with your foot and pound to match-wood with your fists. Behold a

From Sea to Sea

XI

Of Japan at ten hours' sight, containing a complete account of the manners and customs of its people, a history of its constitution products, art and civilization ~~against you~~ ~~men~~ and omitting a ~~breakfast~~ tiffin in a tea-house with O-Toyo⊙

sm
type

Thou canst not wave thy staff in air
Or dip thy paddle in the lake,
But it carves the brow of beauty there
And ripples in rhyme the oar forsake

Mister Oscar Wilde of the Nineteenth Century is a long-toothed liar! He wrote an article some short time back on the "decay of lying". Among other things he, with his tongue in his brazen cheek, averred that there was no such a place as Japan — that it had been created by fans and picture-books just as he himself had been created by pottery and fragments of coloured cloth⊙ Never believe anything that Mister Oscar Wilde tells you⊙ This morning after the sorrows of the rolling night my cabin port-hole showed me two great grey rocks studded and streaked with green and crowned by two stunted blue-black pines⊙ Below the rocks a boat that might have been carved sandalwood for colour and delicacy was shaking out an ivory white ~~frilled~~ sail to the hand of the morning ⊙ an indigo-blue boy with an old ivory face and a ~~musical~~ ~~toy~~ voice was hauling on a rope. ~~It was~~ Rock and tree and boat made a panel from a Japanese screen, and I saw that the land was not a lie⊙ This good brown earth of ours has many pleasures to offer her children but there be few in her gift comparable to the joy of touching a new country — a completely strange race and manners to ~~contrary~~ Though libraries may have been written ~~or~~ aforetime, ~~each~~ ⊙ each new beholder is to himself Columbus, "silent upon ~~the~~ a peak of Darien⊙ And I was in Japan — the Japan of cabinets and joinery, gracious folk and fair manners - Japan whence the camphor and the lacquer and the sharkskin swords come — among the ~~people who are~~ — what was it the books said? — a nation of artists⊙ To be sure we should only stop at ~~the~~ Nagasaki for twelve hours ere going on to Kobe; but in twelve hours one can ~~begin~~ ~~to~~ pack away a very fair collection of new experiences⊙ ~~Then~~ An execrable man met me on the deck with a pale blue pamphlet fifty pages thick⊙ "Have you" said he "seen the constitution of Japan? The Emperor made it himself only the other day It is on entirely European lines"⊙

IN HANDWRITTEN DRAFT

A page of Kipling's handwritten draft for the eleventh Letter overall – but the first from Japan – in the series published in 1889–90 by the *Pioneer* at Allahabad under the title 'From Sea to Sea' (see page 18). This has been copied, and reduced, from one of the original notebooks in which carbons of many of Kipling's drafts for that series can be found. It is published by permission of the Huntington Library, San Marino, California.

FROM SEA TO SEA.

XI.—Of Japan at ten hours' sight, containing a complete account of the manners
and customs of its people. A History of its
Constitution, Products, Art and Civilisation,
and omitting a Tiffin in a Tea-house with
O-Toyo.

"Thou canst not wave thy staff in air
  Or dip thy paddle in the lake,
But it carves the brow of beauty there,
  And ripples in rhyme the oar forsake."

This morning, after the sorrows of the rolling night, my cabin port-hole showed me two
great grey rocks studded and streaked with
green and crowned by two stunted blue-black
pines. Below the rocks a boat that might have
been carved sandalwood for colour and delicacy
was shaking out an ivory-white frilled sail to the
wind of the morning. An indigo-blue boy with
an old ivory face and a musical voice was hauling on a rope. Rock and tree and boat made a
panel from a Japanese screen, and I saw that
the land was not a lie. This " good brown earth"
of ours has many pleasures to offer her children,
but there be few in her gift comparable to the
joy of touching a new country, a completely
strange race and manners contrary. Though
libraries may have been written aforetime, each
new beholder is to himself another Cortez, " silent
upon a peak in Darien." And I was in Japan—
the Japan of cabinets and joinery, gracious folk
and fair manners. Japan whence the camphor
and the lacquer and the sharkskin swords come :
among what was it the books said ?—a nation
of artists. To be sure we should only stop at
Nagasaki for twelve hours ere going on to Kobe,
but in twelve hours one can pack away a very
fair collection of new experiences.

An execrable man met me on the deck with a
pale-blue pamphlet fifty pages thick. " Have
you," said he, " seen the Constitution of Japan ?
The Emperor made it himself only the other
day. It is on entirely European lines."

I took the pamphlet and found a complete paper
Constitution stamped with the Imperial Chrysanthemum—an excellent little scheme of representation, reforms, payment of members, budget
estimates, and legislation. It is a terrible thing to
study at close quarters, because it is so pitifully
English.

" Is the public mind agitated over these,
these—these skittles ?" I enquired. " Do they
talk of local self-government and proportionate
minorities ? Do they hold meetings and print
reports in newspapers ? If they do I will go
back to my own place."

And the man said :—" You do not seem to be
interested in Japanese progress."

I made answer :—" I come from India. Let
me get into a boat."

There was a yellow-shot greenness upon the hills
round Nagasaki different, so my willing mind
was disposed to believe, from the green of other
lands. It was the green of a Japanese screen and
the pines were screen-pines. The city itself hardly showed from the crowded harbour. It lay low
among the hills and its business face—a grimy
bund—was sloppy and deserted. Business I was
rejoiced to learn was at a low ebb in Nagasaki.
The Japanese have no concern with business, as
you shall hear. Close to one of the still wharves
lay a ship of the Bad People, videlicet a Russian
steamer down from Vladivostock. Her decks
were cumbered with raffle of all kinds ; her rigging was as frowsy and draggled as the hair of a
lodging-house " slavey," and her sides were filthy.
" That," said a man of my people, " is a very
fair specimen of a Russian. You should see their
men-of-war : they are just as filthy. Some of em'
come into Nagasaki to clean."

It was a small piece of information and perhaps untrue, but it put the roof to my good
humour as I stepped on to the bund and was
informed in faultless English by a young gentleman, with a plated chrysanthemum in his
forage cap and badly fitting German uniform
on his limbs, that he did not understand my
language. He was a Japanese customs official.
Had our stay been longer I would have wept
over him because he was a hybrid—partly French,
partly German and partly American—a tribute to civilisation. All the Japanese officials from
police upwards seem to be clad in Belatee clothes
and never do those clothes fit. I think the Mikado
made them at the same time as the Constitution.
They will come right in time.

When the 'rickshaw, drawn by a beautiful
apple-cheeked young man with a Basque face,
shot me into the Mikado, first act, I did not stop
and shout with delight because the dignity of
India was in my keeping. I lay back on the
velvet cushion and grinned luxuriously at Pitti-
sing with her sash and three giant hair-pins in
her hair—" blue-black, lustrous, thick as horse
hair"—and three-inch clogs on her feet. She
laughed—even as did the Burmese girls
in the old Pagoda at Moulmein. And her
laugh, the laugh of a lady, was my welcome
to Japan. Can the people help laughing ? I
think not. You see they have such thousands of
children in their streets that the elders must perforce be young lest the babes should grieve. Nagasaki is inhabited entirely by children. The
grown-ups only exist on sufferance. A four-
foot child walks with a three-foot child who is
holding the hand of a two-foot child who carries

IN NEWSPAPER FORM

On reaching Allahabad, Kipling's handwritten version was edited – rather imperfectly, see
pages 19–20 – for the *Pioneer* and its weekly *Pioneer Mail*. The extract above, photocopied by
the British Library, shows how a passage in the *Pioneer Mail* of 4 August 1889 differed from
Kipling's draft. The omission of the Oscar Wilde reference is only one among several
amendments.

XI

OF JAPAN AT TEN HOURS' SIGHT, CONTAINING A COMPLETE
ACCOUNT OF THE MANNERS AND CUSTOMS OF ITS PEOPLE, A
HISTORY OF ITS CONSTITUTION, PRODUCTS, ART, AND CIVILI-
SATION, AND OMITTING A TIFFIN IN A TEA-HOUSE WITH O-TOYO

Thou canst not wave thy staff in air,
Or dip thy paddle in the lake,
But it carves the bow of beauty there,
And the ripples in rhymes the oar forsake.

THIS MORNING, after the sorrows of the rolling night, my cabin
port-hole showed me two great grey rocks studded and streaked
with green and crowned by two stunted blue-black pines.
Below the rocks a boat, that might have been carved sandalwood for colour and delicacy, was shaking out an ivory-white
frilled sail to the wind of the morning. An indigo-blue boy with
an old ivory face hauled on a rope. Rock and tree and boat
made a panel from a Japanese screen, and I saw that the land
was not a lie. This 'good brown earth' of ours has many
pleasures to offer her children, but there be few in her gift
comparable to the joy of touching a new country, a completely
strange race, and manners contrary. Though libraries may have
been written aforetime, each new beholder is to himself another Cortez. And I was in Japan—the Japan of cabinets and
joinery, gracious folk and fair manners. Japan, whence the
camphor and the lacquer and the shark-skin swords come;
among—what was it the books said?—a nation of artists. To be
sure, we should only stop at Nagasaki for twelve hours ere

IN BOOK FORM

In 1899 the newspaper version on the preceding page was transmuted, with heavy
editing characterised by scores of major deletions, into book form for *From Sea to Sea*.
(Later editions of that book produced a further crop of minor emendations.) Here is the
same passage, as published in America in 1941 in the posthumous Burwash Edition.

going on to Kobé, but in twelve hours one can pack away a very fair collection of new experiences.

An execrable man met me on the deck, with a pale-blue pamphlet fifty pages thick. 'Have you,' said he, 'seen the Constitution of Japan? The Emperor made it himself only the other day. It is on entirely European lines.'

I took the pamphlet and found a complete paper Constitution stamped with the Imperial Chrysanthemum—an excellent little scheme of representation, reforms, payment of members, budget estimates, and legislation. It is a terrible thing to study at close quarters, because it is so pitifully English.

There was a yellow-shot greenness upon the hills round Nagasaki, different, so my willing mind was disposed to believe, from the green of other lands. It was the green of a Japanese screen, and the pines were screen pines. The city itself hardly showed from the crowded harbour. It lay low among the hills, and its business face—a grimy bund—was sloppy and deserted. Business, I was rejoiced to learn, was at a low ebb in Nagasaki. The Japanese should have no concern with business. Close to one of the still wharves lay a ship of the Bad People; a Russian steamer down from Vladivostok. Her decks were cumbered with raffle of all kinds; her rigging was as frowzy and draggled as the hair of a lodging-house slavey, and her sides were filthy.

'That,' said a man of my people, 'is a very fair specimen of a Russian. You should see their men-of-war; they are just as filthy. Some of 'em come into Nagasaki to clean.'

It was a small piece of information and perhaps untrue, but it put the roof to my good humour as I stepped on to the bund and was told in faultless English by a young gentleman, with a plated chrysanthemum in his forage-cap and badly-fitting German uniform on his limbs, that he did not

Continued from opposite. The passage chosen shows a typical instance of the development of the text from its original handwritten draft, but it is very far from being one of the most extensively altered sections. However, it is worth comparing it closely with the preceding versions and with our reassembled text on pages 35–6. Oscar Wilde and Columbus have disappeared, and so has a good deal of sprightly comment.

bunnia's (grain–dealer's) shop. He sells rice and chillies and dried fish and wooden scoops made of bamboo. The front of his shop is very solid. It is made of half-inch battens nailed side by side. Not one of the battens is broken; and each one is foursquare perfectly. Feeling ashamed of himself for this surly barring up of his house, he fills one-half the frontage with oiled paper stretched upon quarter-inch framing four inches square. Not a single square of oiled paper has a hole in it, and not one of the squares, which in more uncivilised countries would hold a pane of glass if strong enough, is out of line. Let me put it plainly. You would not keep hens behind˜ such a protection. And the *bunnia*, clothed in a blue dressing-gown, with thick white stockings on his feet, sits behind, not among his wares, on a pale gold-coloured mat of soft rice straw bound with black list at the edges. This mat is two inches thick, three feet wide and six long. You might, if you were a sufficient pig, eat your dinner off any portion of it. The *bunnia* lies with one wadded blue arm around a big brazier of hammered brass on which is faintly delineated in incised lines a very terrible dragon. The brazier is full of charcoal ash, but there is no ash on the mat. By the *bunnia's* side is a pouch of green leather tied with a red silk cord, that is his tobacco pouch holding tobacco cut fine as cotton. He fills a long black-and-red lacquered pipe with it, lights it at the charcoal in the brazier, takes two whiffs, and the pipe is empty. Still there is no speck on the mat. Behind the *bunnia* is a shadow-screen of bead and bamboo. This veils a room floored with pale gold and roofed with panels of grained cedar. There is nothing in the room save a blood-red blanket laid out as smoothly as a sheet of paper. Beyond the room is a passage of polished wood, so polished that it gives back the reflections of the white paper wall. At the end of the passage and clearly visible to this unique *bunnia* is a dwarfed pine two feet high in a green glazed pot, and by its side is a branch of azalea, blood-red as the blanket, set in a pale-grey crackle pot. The *bunnia* has put it there for his own pleasure, for the delight of his eyes, because he loves it. The white man has nothing whatever to do with his tastes, and he keeps his house specklessly pure because he likes cleanliness and knows it is artistic. What shall we say to such a *bunnia*?

His brother in Northern India may live behind a front of time-blackened open-work wood, but ... I do not think he would grow anything save *tulsi* – the sacred herb of the Hindus – in a pot, and that only to please the Gods and his womenfolk.

Let us not compare the two men, but go on through Nagasaki.

Except for the horrible policemen who insist on being continental, the people – the common people, that is – do not run after unseemly costumes of the West. The young men wear round felt hats, occasionally coats and trousers, and semi-occasionally boots. All these are vile. In the more metropolitan towns men say Western dress is rather the rule than the exception. If this be so, I am disposed to conclude that the sins of their forefathers in making enterprising Jesuit missionaries into beefsteak[19] have been visited on the Japanese in the shape of a partial obscuration of their artistic instincts. Yet the punishment seems rather too heavy for the offence.

A guide who called himself Y-Tokai,[20] and to whom I commend you, for he speaks but little and knows the town, insisted on taking me to a place called Deshima, which was once an island but is now a suburb connected by many bridges with the main town. It did not amuse, but he repeated something about the Dutch and the Japanese so many times that I was forced to feign interest. A complication not unattended with bloodshed had cropped up between the two peoples, and this island, Deshima, was the spot where the wicked Dutch were segregated. This the guide told me and, when I was panting with excitement, added, 'Three hundred years ago.'[21]

None the less there is a pottery at Deshima which would delight the hearts of every house-keeper in India. The prices unfortunately are almost as magnificent as the porcelain. We of the outer world do not see the best that the Japanese cup-and-platter artists can produce. One cannot judge offhand from a single roomful of designs: but it seemed that the Japanese patterns held more reserve and propriety than the Chinese, *exempli gratia*, in the matter of devils. The Chinese painter put his soul into elaborating as coldly grim and malignant a monster as he could. The Japanese stopped short of the last stroke that should complete the horror, and in its stead put some humorous or purely absurd touch, and the devil on the jar became at once a sympathetic and valued friend – ugly it is true, but intensely human.

Unless patterns and biscuits lie, a good deal of French pottery finds its way here for final decoration. Go to the Deshima pottery and try to restrain yourself from making purchases if you can. Buying things is the curse of travel. You do not want them twenty minutes after they are yours, and you do not know what to do with them when you next pack your trunks. Remember that anything the wide world produces may be bought at a price in London and hold your hand from carved ivories, chrysanthemum lacquer, bronze inlays, and the swords of the *samurai*. I did not.

Then I fell admiring the joinery of the houses and the filling of the water-pipes, the bloom on the people's cheeks, the three-cornered smiles of the fat babes, and the surpassing 'otherness' of everything round me. It is so strange to be in a clean land once more, and stranger to walk among dolls' houses. Japan is a soothing place for a small man. Nobody comes to tower over him, and he looks down upon all the women, as is right and proper. A dealer in curiosities bent himself double on his own doormat, and I passed in, feeling for the first time that I was a barbarian, and no true *sahib*. The slush of the streets was thick on my boots, and he, the immaculate owner, asked me to walk across a polished floor and white mats to an inner chamber. He brought me a foot-mat, which only made matters worse, for a pretty girl giggled round the corner as I toiled at it. Japanese shopkeepers ought not to be so clean. 'Tis unnatural and I protest that you pay for it in the bill. I went into a boarded passage about two feet wide, found a gem of a garden of dwarfed trees, in the space of half a tennis-court, whacked my head on a fragile lintel, and arrived at a four-walled daintiness where I involuntarily lowered my voice. Do you recollect Mrs Molesworth's *Cuckoo Clock*, and the big cabinet that Griselda entered with the cuckoo?[22] I was not Griselda, but my low-voiced friend, in his long, soft wraps, was the cuckoo, and the room was the cabinet. Again I tried to console myself with the thought that I could kick the place to pieces; but this only made me feel large and coarse and dirty, – a most unfavourable mood for bargaining. The cuckoo-man caused pale tea to be brought, – just such tea as you read of in books of travel, – and the tea completed my embarrassment. What I wanted to say was, 'Look here, you person. You're much too clean and refined for this life here below, and your house is unfit for a man to live in until he has been taught a lot of things which I have never learned. Consequently I hate you because I feel myself your inferior, and you despise me and my boots because you know me for a savage. Let me go, or I'll pull your house of cedar-wood over your ears.' What I really said was, 'Oh, ah yes. Awf'ly pretty. Awful queer way of doing business. How much this *netsuke*?'

I was relieved when the cuckoo-man proved to be a horrid extortioner who lowered his prices like a *kabari*;[23] but I was hot and uncomfortable till I got outside, and was a bog-trotting Briton once more. You have never blundered into the inside of a three-hundred-dollar cabinet, therefore you will not understand me.

We came to the foot of a hill, as it might have been the hill on which the Shway Dagon stands,[24] and up that hill ran a mighty flight of grey, weather-darkened steps, spanned here and there by mono-lithic *torii*. Every one knows what a *torii* is.[25] They have them in

Southern India. A great King makes a note of the place where he intends to build a huge arch, but being a King, does so in stone, not ink – sketches in the air two beams and a cross-bar, forty or sixty feet high, and twenty or thirty wide. In Southern India the cross-bar is humped in the middle. In the Further East it flares up at the ends. This description is hardly according to the books, but if a man begins by consulting books in a new country he is lost. Over the steps hung heavy blue-green or green-black pines, old, gnarled, and bossed. The foliage of the hillside was a lighter green, but the pines set the keynote of colour, and the blue dresses of the few folk on the steps answered it. There was no sunshine in the air, but I vow that sunshine would have spoilt all. We clomb for five minutes, – I and the Professor and the camera, – and then we turned and saw the roofs of Nagasaki lying at our feet – a sea of lead and dull brown, with here and there a smudge of creamy pink to mark the bloom of the cherry trees. The hills round the town were speckled with the resting-places of the dead, with clumps of pine and feathery bamboo.

'What a country!' said the Professor, unstrapping his camera. 'And have you noticed, wherever we go there's always some man who knows how to carry my kit? The *gharri* driver at Moulmein handed me the stops; the fellow at Penang knew all about it, too; and the 'rickshaw coolie has seen a camera before. Curious, isn't it?'

'Professor,' said I, 'it's due to the extraordinary fact that we are not the only people in the world. I began to realise it at Hong Kong. It's getting plainer now. I shouldn't be surprised if we turned out to be ordinary human beings, after all.'

Then I drank in Japan with my eyes and sniffed the ever-present scent of camphor-wood – cleanest and most housewifely of smells – and whacked a big time-worn lantern with the flat of my hand to assure myself that I was really in Japan, and thought longingly of the real Japanese tiffin that awaited me in the tea-house down the hill.

We entered a courtyard where an evil-looking bronze horse stared at two stone lions, and a company of children babbled among themselves. There is a legend connected with the bronze horse, which may be found in the guide-books. But the real true story of the creature is, that he was made long ago out of a fossil ivory of Siberia by a Japanese Prometheus, and got life and many foals, whose descendants closely resemble their father. Long years have almost eliminated the ivory in the blood, but it crops out in creamy mane and tail; and the pot-belly and marvellous feet of the bronze horse may be found to this day among the pack-ponies of Nagasaki, who carry pack-saddles adorned with velvet and red cloth, who wear

41

grass shoes on their hind feet, and who are made like to horses in a pantomime.

We could not go beyond this courtyard because a label said, 'No admittance,' and thus all we saw of the temple was rich-brown high roofs of blackened thatch, breaking back and back in wave and undulation till they were lost in the foliage. The Japanese play with thatch as men play with modelling clay; but how their light underpinnings can carry the weight of the roof is a mystery to the lay eye.

We went down the steps to tiffin, and a half-formed resolve was shaping itself in my heart the while. Burma was a very nice place, but they eat *gnapi*[26] there, and there were smells, and after all, the girls weren't so pretty as some others –

'You must take off your boots,' said Y-Tokai.

I assure you there is no dignity in sitting down on the steps of a tea-house and struggling with muddy boots. And it is impossible to be polite in your stockinged feet when the floor under you is as smooth as glass and a pretty girl wants to know where you would like tiffin. Take at least one pair of beautiful socks with you when you come this way. Get them made of embroidered *sambhur* skin,[27] of silk if you like, but do not stand as I did in cheap striped brown things with a darn at the heel, and try to talk to a tea-girl.

They led us – three of them, and all fresh and pretty – into a room furnished with a golden-brown bearskin. The *tokonoma*,[28] recess aforementioned, held one scroll-picture of bats wheeling in the twilight, a bamboo flower-holder, and yellow flowers. The ceiling was of panelled wood, with the exception of one strip at the side nearest the window, and this was made of plaited shavings of cedar-wood, marked off from the rest of the ceiling by a wine-brown bamboo so polished that it might have been lacquered. A touch of the hand sent one side of the room flying back, and we entered a really large room with another *tokonoma* framed on one side by eight or ten feet of an unknown wood bearing the same grain as a 'Penang Lawyer,'[29] and above by a stick of unbarked tree set there purely because it was curiously mottled. In this second *tokonoma* was a pearl-grey vase, and that was all. Two sides of the room were of oiled paper, and the joints of the beams were covered by the brazen images of crabs, half life-size. Save for the sill of the *tokonoma*, which was black lacquer, every inch of wood in the place was natural grain without flaw. A lumber-closet, clean and empty, opened from one corner by a door made of one sheet of some dark-grained wood, and the floor of course was of white straw mats. Outside lay the garden, fringed with a hedge of dwarf-pines and adorned with a tiny pond, water-smoothed stones sunk in the soil, and a blossoming cherry tree.

They left us alone in this paradise of cleanliness and beauty, and being only a shameless Englishman without his boots – a white man is always degraded when he goes barefoot – I wandered round the wall, trying all the screens. It was only when I stopped to examine the sunk catch of a screen that I saw it was a plaque of inlay work representing two white cranes feeding on fish. The whole was about three inches square and in the ordinary course of events would never be looked at. The screens hid a cupboard in which all the lamps and candlesticks and pillows and sleeping-bags of the household seemed to be stored. An Oriental nation that can fill a cupboard tidily is a nation to bow down to. Upstairs I went by a staircase of grained wood and lacquer into rooms of rarest device with circular windows that opened on nothing, and so were filled with bamboo tracery for the delight of the eye. The passages floored with dark wood shone like ice, and I was ashamed.

'Professor,' said I, 'they don't spit; they don't eat like pigs; they can't quarrel, and a drunken man would reel straight through every partition in the house and roll down the hill into Nagasaki. They can't have any children.' Here I stopped. Downstairs was full of babies!

'I give it up,' I said; and the maidens came in with tea in blue china and cake[30] in a red lacquered bowl – such cake as one gets at one or two houses in Simla. We sprawled ungracefully on red rugs over the mats, and they gave us chopsticks to separate the cake with. It was a long task and very cumbersome. Then we waited afresh and tried to fit ourselves into graceful postures.

'Is that all?' growled the Professor. 'I'm hungry, and cake and tea oughtn't to come till four o'clock.' Here he took a wedge of cake furtively with his hands.

They returned – five of them this time – with black lacquer stands a foot square and four inches high. Those were our tables. They bore a red lacquered bowlful of fish boiled in brine, and sea-anemones. At least they were not mushrooms. A paper napkin tied with gold thread enclosed our chopsticks; and in a little flat saucer lay a smoked crayfish, a slice of a compromise that looked like Yorkshire pudding and tasted like sweet omelette, and a twisted fragment of some translucent thing that had once been alive but was now pickled. They went away, but not empty handed, for thou, oh, O-Toyo, didst take away my heart – same which I gave to the Burmese girl in the Shway Dagon pagoda![31]

The Professor opened his eyes a little, but said no word. The chopsticks demanded all his attention, and the return of the girls took up the rest. O-Toyo, ebon-haired, rosy-cheeked, and made through-out of delicate porcelain, laughed at me because I devoured all the mustard-sauce[32] that had been served with my raw fish, and wept copiously till she gave me *sake* from a lordly bottle about four inches high. If you took some very thin hock, and tried to mull it and forgot all about the brew till it was half cold, you would get *sake*. I had mine in a saucer so tiny that I was bold to have it filled eight or ten times and loved O-Toyo none the less at the end. But to return to the tiffin.

After raw fish and mustard-sauce came some other sort of fish cooked with pickled radishes, and very slippery on the chopsticks. The girls knelt in a semicircle and shrieked with delight at the Professor's clumsiness, for indeed it was not I that nearly upset the dinner table in a vain attempt to recline gracefully. After the bamboo-shoots came a basin of white beans in sweet sauce – very tasty indeed. Try to convey beans to your mouth with a pair of wooden knitting-needles and see what happens. Some chicken cunningly boiled with turnips, and a bowlful of snow-white boneless fish and a pile of rice, concluded the meal. I have forgotten one or two of the courses, but when O-Toyo handed me the tiny lacquered Japanese pipe full of hay-like tobacco, I counted nine dishes in the lacquer stand – each dish representing a course. Then O-Toyo and I smoked by alternate pipefuls. Three whiffs exhausted the bowl, which was knocked out into a bamboo *pikdan*[33] and refilled from a cunning little lacquer box. The stiff joints of the barbarians had by this time necessitated a padding of pillows on the floor – blue and white pillows of the softest.

My very respectable friends at all the clubs and messes, have you ever after a good tiffin lolled on cushions and smoked, with one pretty girl to fill your pipe and four to admire you in an unknown tongue? You do not know what life is. I looked round me at that faultless room, at the dwarf pines and creamy cherry blossoms without, at O-Toyo bubbling with laughter because I blew smoke through my nose, and at the ring of *Mikado* maidens over against the golden-brown bearskin rug. Here was colour, form, food, comfort, and beauty enough for half a year's contemplation. I would not be a Burman any more.[34] I would be a Japanese – always with O-Toyo of course – in a cabinet-work house on a camphor-scented hillside.

'Heigho!' said the Professor. 'There are worse places than this to live and die in. D'you know our steamer goes at four? Let's ask for the bill and get away.'

We got: but I have left my heart with O-Toyo under the pines. Perhaps I shall get it back at Kobe.

1889: LETTER ONE
COMMENTARY

1. This first letter from Japan was the eleventh in the series that Kipling sent back to India in 1889 from various points on his homeward journey to England. It was published by the *Pioneer*, Allahabad, on 30 July 1889. Most but not all of these texts, heavily edited, were re-published in *From Sea to Sea* in 1899. For fuller details on all these Letters see the Note on the Texts on page 17.
2. Since this Letter does *not* omit the tiffin with O-Toyo, the word 'not' may have been mistakenly left out before 'omitting'. Kipling's hand-written text, now in the Huntington Library, likewise has no 'not'. *Tiffin*, a word of uncertain origin, was in common English use in India, meaning 'lunch'.
3. These lyrical lines, selected by Kipling to set off his delighted first impressions of the beauty of Japan, are from a poem called 'Woodnotes II' by Ralph Waldo Emerson (1803–82). The fourth line should correctly read, 'And the ripples in rhymes the oar forsake.'
4. This reference is to an article called 'The Decay of Lying', by Oscar Wilde (1854–1900). It had appeared in England in the January 1889 issue of a magazine, *The Nineteenth Century*, and it is noteworthy that Kipling, who had sailed eastward from India in March 1889, had seen it. It was re-published in 1891, with some revisions, in Wilde's book *Intentions*. 'The Decay of Lying' is an ingenious and provocative essay in literary and artistic criticism, set in dialogue form. On Japan, one of the speakers says:

> I know that you are fond of Japanese things. Now, do you really imagine that the Japanese people, as they are presented to us in art, have any existence? If you do, you have never understood Japanese art at all. The Japanese people are the deliberate self-conscious creation of certain individual artists. If you set a picture by Hokusai, or Hokkei, or any of the great native painters, beside a real Japanese

gentleman or lady, you will see that there is not the slightest resemblance between them. The actual people who live in Japan are not unlike the general run of English people; that is to say, they are extremely commonplace, and have nothing curious or extraordinary about them. In fact, the whole of Japan is a pure invention. There is no such country, there are no such people. One of our most charming painters went recently to the Land of the Chrysanthemum in the foolish hope of seeing the Japanese. All he saw, all he had the chance of painting, were a few lanterns and some fans. He was quite unable to discover the inhabitants, as his delightful exhibition at Messrs. Dowdeswell's Gallery showed only too well. He did not know that the Japanese people are, as I have said, simply a mode of style, an exquisite fancy of art. And so, if you desire to see a Japanese effect, you will not behave like a tourist and go to Tokyo. On the contrary, you will stay at home and steep yourself in the work of certain Japanese artists, and then when you have absorbed the spirit of their style, and caught their imaginative manner of vision, you will go some afternoon and sit in the Park or stroll down Piccadilly, and if you cannot see an absolutely Japanese effect there, you will not see it anywhere.

Wilde's reputation was approaching its height at this time: his downfall followed a famous court case in 1895. For whatever reason, the *Pioneer* edited out this opening passage, and began the despatch with the words 'This morning . . .'. When Kipling revised these newspaper despatches of 1889 for publication in book form in 1899, he did not resuscitate this lost reference to Wilde, which has remained virtually unknown, but he left in, a few lines later, the remark that 'the land was not a lie', which can now be seen to make more sense.

5. This reference is to the last four lines of a sonnet, 'On first looking into Chapman's Homer', by John Keats (1795–1821):

> Or like stout Cortez when with eagle eyes
>   He star'd at the Pacific – and all his men
> Look'd at each other with a wild surmise –
>   Silent, upon a peak in Darien.

It is well known that Keats was mistaken: it was not Cortez who was the first Spaniard to see the Pacific, but Balboa.

6. Nagasaki was one of the Treaty Ports. It had first developed in the late sixteenth century as a Christian centre. However, after the proscription of Christianity and the expulsion of all foreigners except for a few Dutch merchants, it became Japan's only window to the west, through the tiny nearby island of Deshima. Here the small colony of Dutch merchants were held in virtual captivity, apart from occasional missions

to the capital, Edo (now Tokyo), to pay tribute to the military ruler, the Shogun.

The first British treaty with Japan was concluded at Nagasaki by Admiral Sir James Stirling in October 1854. During the final years of the Shogunate (up to 1868), Nagasaki was an important trading centre for the sale of ships and arms to the outer fiefs which led the struggle against the Tokugawa Shoguns. It was also a centre of the tea trade.

In subsequent years Nagasaki declined as a centre of trade, but ship-building and other heavy industry developed in the neighbourhood: it was also important in the development of the Kyushu coal mines. Until the Second World War it was a favourite holiday resort for members of the merchant communities in Shanghai wishing to escape from the damp heat of the Shanghai summer.

7. The *mon*, or heraldic symbol, of the Imperial Family in Japan was the sixteen-petalled chrysanthemum, the *Kiku no Go-Mon*.

8. The Japanese constitution of February 1889 – the so-called Meiji Constitution – was, in its origin and its contents, much more German than English.

9. *Bund* was a term of Persian origin, common in India. It meant any artificial embankment such as a dam, dyke or causeway. It was also applied by the British to ports in China (but not Hong Kong or Macao), and meant the embanked quay along the shore.

10. To the British in India, Russian expansionism in Central Asia seemed a direct threat: it was the key element in the 'Great Game' on the North-West Frontier, and was a feature in Kipling's *Kim* (1901). In Japan, too, suspicion of Russian designs in the far east grew as the century approached its end. Russo-Japanese rivalry eventually led to the war of 1904–5, in which the Japanese fleet under Admiral Togo destroyed the Russian fleet in the Battle of the Japan Sea (Tsushima).

11. A feature of late nineteenth-century Japan was the attempt to adopt western clothing to show that the country was, by western standards, 'civilized'. The importance of a style of clothing as a symbol may now seem exaggerated; however, given the dominance of Europe at that time, and Victorian attitudes to nudity and communal bathing as shown in visitors' accounts of life in Japan, the effort to adapt to western dress was not illogical.

12. *Mikado*, literally 'Noble Gate', was a title for the Emperor much used by foreigners in the nineteenth century. The Japanese generally use the term *Tenno* ('Son of Heaven') or *Heika* ('His Majesty').

13. The Japanese word from which *rickshaw* or ('*rickshaw*) is derived is *jinrikisha*, literally 'man-power-vehicle'. This conveyance first became popular in the early 1870s, and the word came into English in the 1880s. A nineteenth-century English scholar of Japan, Basil Hall Chamberlain, in *Things Japanese*, first published in 1890, says:

47

The origin of the Jinrikisha is, to use a grandiloquent phrase, shrouded in obscurity. One native account attributes the spark of invention to a paralytic old gentleman of Kyoto, who, some time before 1868, finding his palanquin uncomfortable, took a little cart instead ... The usual foreign version is that an American named Goble, half cobbler and half missionary, was the person to suggest this idea of a modified perambulator about the year 1867 ...

14. The Basques, inhabiting parts of north-east Spain and south-west France, are a people whose origins are unknown. They speak a non-Aryan language, and are racially distinct from their neighbours, but exactly what Kipling meant by a Basque face is open to question.
15. *The Mikado, or The Town of Titipu*, the famous comic opera by Gilbert and Sullivan, was first produced in 1885 in London. During its original run of nearly two years the Japanese ambassador tried to have it suppressed, on the grounds that it ridiculed the Emperor; these objections were again voiced when a revival was projected in 1907. However, its popularity quickly went round the world. When it was produced in India, by the Amateur Dramatic Club in Simla in 1886, it is highly likely that Kipling saw it, and it is possible that he acted in it. Pitti-Sing was an endearing character in the opera, one of the 'three little maids from school'.
16. Earlier in this voyage, Kipling had been on a ship which put in briefly at Moulmein in Burma. Ashore, he visited a temple which he described in some detail without naming it. However,

I should better remember what that pagoda was like had I not fallen deeply and irrevocably in love with a Burmese girl at the foot of the first flight of steps. Only the fact of the steamer starting next noon prevented me from staying at Moulmein for ever ...

A year later, in June 1890, living in London, he wrote one of the most famous of all his poems, 'Mandalay', of which the opening lines are:

By the old Moulmein Pagoda, lookin' lazy at the sea,
There's a Burma girl a-settin', and I know she thinks o' me ...

17. A shopping arcade, running into Piccadilly, London.
18. A jimmy or jemmy is a tool such as a burglar might use: a bar with a chisel edge at one end. A centre-bit is a tool for boring holes in wood.
19. During the persecution of the Christians in Japan in the first half of the seventeenth century, 'enterprising' Jesuit missionaries from Portugal attempted to infiltrate the country. If caught they were liable to be subjected to various tortures.
20. *Y-Tokai* is not a normal Japanese name, and it is difficult to guess what

the real name was. *Tokai* could be as in *Tokaido*, the eastern sea road, but this would not be a usual name for a person.

21. Deshima: see Note 6 above.

22. *The Cuckoo Clock* was a novel published in 1877 by Mary Louisa Molesworth (1839–1921), an author best known for this and other childrens' books. Griselda was the central character, who was enabled to become small enough to enter a Japanese cabinet in the drawing room, and, guided by the cuckoo from the clock, found herself beyond it in the Land of the Nodding Mandarins.

23. A *kabari*: in India, a second-hand furniture dealer.

24. The Shway Dagon, more usually Shwe Dagon, in Rangoon, is among the most venerated places of worship in south-east Asia, attracting countless pilgrims. Its particular sanctity is that it is the only temple known to Buddhists as containing actual relics of Gautama and of the three Buddhas who preceded him in this world. It stands on a mound some 170 feet high. Kipling had visited it a few weeks earlier, in March 1889, on the first stage of his journey from India.

25. A *torii* is a gateway to a Shinto shrine, formed by two upright and two horizontal beams, of wood or stone. The derivation of the word is obscure, but the two characters used to write it are *tori* (a bird) and *i* (from *iru*, to dwell or to be).

26. By *gnapi* (otherwise *ngapi,* or *napi*) Kipling meant a well-known Burmese delicacy, of dried, decomposed and pungently smelling fish. Visiting Burma he had written, 'everybody who has been within downwind range of Rangoon knows what *napi* means, and those who do not will not understand'. The Venetian traveller Gasparo Balbi said of this delicacy, 'I would rather smell a dead dog, to say nothing of eating it' (*Viaggio dell' Indie Orientali*, 1590). However it is greatly esteemed by millions, and closely resembles the *belachan* of Malaya and the *trasi* of Java.

27. The *sambhur* (a word derived through Hindustani from the Sanskrit) is the largest of the Indian forest deer. According to *Hobson-Jobson* by Yule and Burnell, 'the word is often applied to the soft leather, somewhat resembling chamois leather, prepared from the hide'.

28. A *tokonoma* is a recess in a Japanese room constituting its focal point and usually containing a hanging scroll picture and a flower arrangement.

29. A 'Penang lawyer' was a walking-stick, or bludgeon. According to the *Shorter Oxford English Dictionary*, it was 'made from the stem of a dwarf palm having prickly stalks, and much used in settling disputes at Penang'. According to Partridge's *Dictionary of Slang and Unconventional English* (5th edition), the term was colloquial from about 1860, and may have derived as a corruption from Penang *liyar*, a wild Areca palm.

30. Probably *kasutera*, a sponge cake popular in Nagasaki since the time of the Portuguese missionaries in the sixteenth and seventeenth centuries. The Japanese name is derived from the Spanish *Castilla*, the ancient kingdom of Castile in Spain.

31. See Note 16 above. Kipling probably meant not the Shwe Dagon in Rangoon but the 'Old Pagoda' in Moulmein. However, the confusion may be explained by the fact that, as he described fully in an earlier despatch to his newspaper, he did meet a Burmese girl – a young woman with a baby – on the Shwe Dagon steps: it was an amusing and rather touching encounter.

32. This 'mustard sauce' was *wasabi*, Japanese horseradish mixed with soy sauce.

33. *Pikdan*, a Hindi term, means 'spittoon' (*pik* being strictly the expectorated juice of chewed betel).

34. This is a clear reference to something he had written from Rangoon, where he had been much struck in March 1889, on his only visit, by the style and the glamour of Burma:

> When I die I will be a Burman, with twenty yards of real King's silk, that has been made in Mandalay, about my body . . . and I will always walk about with a pretty almond–coloured girl . . .

'O-TOYO, EBON-HAIRED, ROSY-CHEEKED' (p. 44)

'O-Toyo, aux cheveux d'ébène, aux joues de rose, et tout entière faite de délicate porcelaine ...' The picture is from *Lettres du Japon* (see p. 24), an authorized French translation of some of the 1889 Letters, in an attractive limited edition published in 1925, strikingly illustrated by H. Tirman and G. Braun.

'BY WAY OF THE INLAND SEA' (p.51)

Another illustration from *Lettres du Japon*. In the words of L. Fabulet's and A. Austin-Jackson's translation: '*Nous – le steamer de la P. and O. [la compagnie de paquebots Peninsular and Oriental] – allons à Kobé par la mer Intérieure . . . un lac colossal, semé, aussi loin que le regard s'étende, d'îles de toutes dimensions . . .*'

1889: Letter Two

A FURTHER CONSIDERATION OF JAPAN. THE INLAND SEA, THE TEMP-
ERATURE OF ALLAHABAD, AND GOOD COOKERY. THE MYSTERY OF
PASSPORTS AND CONSULATES, AND CERTAIN OTHER MATTERS.

'Rome! Rome! Wasn't that the place where I got the good cigars?'
– *Memoirs of a Traveller*.[1]

Alas for the incompleteness of the written word! There was so much
more that I meant to tell you about Nagasaki and the funeral
procession that I found in her streets. You ought to have read about
the wailing women in white who followed the dead man shut up in a
wooden sedan-chair that rocked on the shoulders of the bearers,
while the bronze-hued Buddhist priest tramped on ahead, and the
little boys ran alongside.

I had prepared in my mind moral reflections, purviews of political
situations, and a complete essay on the future of Japan. Now I have
forgotten everything except O-Toyo in the tea-house.

From Nagasaki we – the P. and O. Steamer – are going to Kobe by
way of the Inland Sea. That is to say, we have for the last twenty
hours been steaming through a huge lake, studded as far as the eye
can reach with islands of every size, from four miles long and two
wide to little cocked-hat hummocks no bigger than a decent hayrick.
Messrs. Cook and Son charge about one hundred rupees extra for the
run through this part of the world, but they do not know how to
farm the beauties of nature. Under any skies the islands – purple,
amber, grey, green, and black – are worth five times the money
asked. I have been sitting for the last half-hour among a knot of
whooping tourists, wondering how I could give you a notion of
them. The tourists, of course, are indescribable. They say, 'Oh my!'
at thirty-second intervals, and at the end of five minutes 'call one to
another: 'Sa-ay, don't you think it's vurry much the same all along?'
Then they play cricket with a broomstick till an unusually fair
prospect makes them stop and shout 'Oh my!' again. If there were a
few more oaks and pines on the islands, the run would be three

51

hundred miles of Naini Tal lake. But we are not near Naini Tal;[2] for as the big ship drives down the alleys of water, I can see the heads of the breakers flying ten feet up the side of the echoing cliffs, albeit the sea is dead-still.

Now we have come to a stretch so densely populated with islands that all looks solid ground. We are running through broken water thrown up by the race of the tide round an outlying reef, and apparently are going to hit an acre of solid rock. Somebody on the bridge saves us, and we head out for another island, and so on, and so on, till the eye wearies of watching the nose of the ship swinging right and left, and the finite human soul, which, after all, cannot repeat 'Oh my!' through a chilly evening, goes below. When you come to Japan – it can be done comfortably in three months, or even ten weeks – sail through this marvellous sea, and see how quickly wonder sinks to interest, and interest to apathy. We brought oysters with us from Nagasaki. I am much more interested in their appearance at dinner to-night than in the shag-backed starfish of an islet that has just slidden by like a ghost upon the silver-grey waters, awakening under the touch of the ripe moon. Yes, it is a sea of mystery and romance, and the white sails of the junks are silver in the moonlight. But if the steward curries those oysters instead of serving them on the shell, all the veiled beauties of cliff and water-carven rock will not console me. Today being the seventeenth of April, I am sitting in an ulster under a thick rug, with fingers so cold I can barely hold the pen. This emboldens me to ask how your thermantidotes are working. A mixture of steatite and kerosene is very good for creaking cranks, I believe, and if the coolie falls asleep, and you wake up in Hades, try not to lose your temper.[3] I go to my oysters!

Two days later. This comes from Kobe (thirty hours from Nagasaki), the European portion of which is a raw American town.[4]. We walked down the wide, naked streets between houses of 'sham-damn' stucco, with Corinthian pillars of wood, wooden verandahs and *piazzas*, all stony grey beneath stony grey skies, and keeping guard over raw green saplings miscalled shade trees. I fainted in the Professor's arms. He has travelled a good deal. 'This place is all right,' said he. 'It is Portland, Maine, but it is a little bit too far west. Remarkable like Portland, Maine. You must go there.' In truth, Kobe is hideously American in externals. Even I, who have only seen pictures of America, recognised it at once. Like Nagasaki, it lives among hills, but the hills are all scalped, and the general impression is of out-of-the-wayness. Yet, ere I go further, let me sing the praises of the excellent M. Bégueux, proprietor of the Oriental Hotel,[5] upon whom be peace. His is a house where you can dine. He does not merely feed you. His coffee is the coffee of the beautiful France. For tea he gives you Peliti cakes (but better)[6] and the *vin ordinaire* which is *compris*, is good. Excellent Monsieur and Madame Bégueux! If the *Pioneer* were a medium for puffs, I would write a leading article upon your potato salad, your beefsteaks, your fried fish, and your staff of highly trained Japanese servants in blue tights, who looked like so many small Hamlets without the velvet cloak, and who obeyed the unspoken wish. No, it should be a poem – a ballad of good living. I have eaten curries of the rarest at the Oriental at Penang, the turtle steaks of Raffles's at Singapore still live in my regretful memory, and they gave me chicken liver and sucking-pig in the Victoria at Hong Kong which I will always extol.[7] But the Oriental at Kobe was better than all three. Remember this, and so shall you who come after slide round a quarter of the world upon a sleek and contented stomach.

It is not a little thing to enjoy once more spring mattresses, gas, electric bells and hot and cold water taps. We in India are cheated out of our birthright in all these things.

The Professor is a curious man. He notices the straws which show which way the wind blows. 'See that fork?' said he at breakfast. 'That's American. We're getting near now.'

'What's the matter with the fork?' It was an ordinary plated weapon.

'English fork, prongs larger than the spaces. 'Merican fork, spaces larger than the prongs. Ugh!' said the Professor, sententiously. A gipsy who picks up the twisted cross that marks which way his tribe have gone could not have spoken more to the point. Wisdom of the Professor's kind is worth having.

We are going from Kobe to Yokohama by various roads. This necessitates a passport,[8] because we travel in the interior and do not run round the coast on ship-board. We take a railroad, which may or may not be complete as to the middle, and we branch off from that railroad, complete or not, as the notion may prompt. This will be an affair of some twenty days, and ought to include forty or fifty miles by *'rickshaw*, a voyage on a lake, and, I believe, bedbugs. The Professor has a map with which he wrestles daily, and he knows all about the impending journey. *Nota bene*. – When you come to Japan stop at Hong Kong and send on a letter to the 'Envoy Extraordinary and Minister Plenipotentiary at Tokyo,' if you want to travel in the interior of this Fairyland. Indicate your route as roughly as ever you choose, but for your own comfort give the two extreme towns you intend to touch. Throw in any details about your age, profession, colour of hair, and the like that may occur to you, and ask to have a passport sent to the British Consulate at Kobe to meet you. Allow the man with a long title a week's time to prepare the passport, and you will find it at your service when you land. Only write distinctly, to save your vanity. My papers allow me to travel for three months over the whole of the island on condition that I do not scribble on temple walls, refrain from driving without lamps and never 'attend a fire on horseback' – I would much sooner attend Divine Service that way, but I am proud to think I belong to a nation of such desperate horsemen. The entire document is addressed to a Mister Kyshrig – 'Radjerd Kyshrig.' Wherefore, I say again, write your name distinctly.

The walk to the Consulate exhausted the European portion of Kobe, and the Professor and I went away to the Japanese town in 'rickshaws. The one man in the shafts was a curiosity. He began running on level ground as swiftly as though he was a whole team of *paharis*.[9] This vexed me and I gave him a half-mile on the flat, down the street. He stopped full of running. Then I ran him back again and finished with an ascent. He ran up that and said there was a curio-shop at five minutes' distance. He was clad in a blue jerkin, knee breeches and blue gaiters, and his number was painted on his back. Whence he drew his powers of endurance I cannot tell, but he ran eternally for ten cents an hour while I studied Japan.

As in Nagasaki, the town was full of babies, and as in Nagasaki, every one smiled except the Chinamen. I do not like Chinamen. They stand high above the crowd and they swagger, unconsciously parting the crowd before them as an Englishman parts the crowd in a native city. There was something in their faces which I could not understand, though it was familiar enough.

'The Chinaman's a native, 'Fessor,' I said. 'That's the look on a native's face, but the Japanese isn't a native, and he isn't a *sahib* either. What is it?' The Professor considered the surging street for a while.

'The Chinaman's an old man when he's young, just as a native is; but the Japanese is a child all his life. Think how grown-up people look upon children. That's the look that's puzzling you.'

I dare not say that the Professor is right, but to my eyes it seemed he spoke sooth. As the knowledge of good and evil sets its mark upon the face of a grown man of our people, so something I did not understand had marked the faces of the Chinamen. They had no kinship with the crowd beyond that which a man has to children.

'They are the superior race,' said the Professor, ethnologically.

'They can't be. They don't know how to enjoy life,' I answered immorally. 'And anyway, their art isn't human.'

'What does it matter?' said the Professor. 'Here's a shop full of the wrecks of old Japan. Let's go in and look.' We went in, but I want somebody to solve the Chinese question for me. It's too large to handle alone.

We entered the curio-shop aforementioned, with our hats in our hands, through a small avenue of carved stone lanterns and wooden sculptures of devils unspeakably hideous, to be received by a smiling image who had grown grey among *netsuke*[10] and lacquer. He showed us the banners and insignia of Daimyo long since dead, while our jaws drooped in ignorant wonder. He showed us a sacred turtle of mammoth size, carven in wood down to minutest detail. Through room after room he led us, the light fading as we went, till we reached a tiny garden and a woodwork cloister that ran round it. Suits of old-time armour made faces at us in the gloom, ancient swords clicked at our feet, quaint tobacco pouches as old as the swords swayed to and fro from some invisible support, and the eyes of a score of battered Buddhas, red dragons, Jain *tirthankars*,[11] and Burmese *beloos*[12] glared at us from over the fence of tattered gold brocade robes of state. The joy of possession lives in the eye. The old man showed us his treasures, from crystal spheres mounted in sea-worn wood to cabinet on cabinet full of ivory and wood carvings, and we were as rich as though we owned all that lay before us. The Professor raves about the cabinets in old gold and ivory studded with jade, lazuli, agate, mother-o'-pearl and cornelian, but to me more desirable than any wonder of five-stoned design are the buttons and *netsuke* that lie on cotton wool and can be taken out and played with. Unfortunately the merest scratch of Japanese character is the only clue to the artist's name, so I am unable to say who conceived, and in creamy ivory executed, the old man horribly embarrassed by a cuttle-fish; the priest who made the soldier pick up a deer for him and laughed to think that the brisket would be his and the burden his companion's; or the dry, lean snake coiled in derision on a jawless skull mottled with the memories of corruption; or the Rabelaisian badger who stood on his head and made you blush though he was not half an inch long; or the little fat boy pounding his smaller brother; or the rabbit that had just made a joke; or – but there were scores of these notes, born of every mood of mirth, scorn and experience that sways the heart of man; and by this hand that has held half a dozen of them in its palm I winked at the shade of the dead carver! He had gone to his rest, but he had worked out in ivory three or four impressions that I had been hunting after in cold print.

The Englishman is a wonderful animal. He buys a dozen of these things and puts them on the top of an overcrowded cabinet, where they show like blobs of ivory, and forgets them in a week. The Japanese hides them in a beautiful brocaded bag or a quiet lacquer box till three congenial friends come to tea. Then he takes them out slowly, and they are looked over with appreciation amid quiet chuckles to the deliberative clink of cups, and put back again till the mood for inspection returns. That is the way to enjoy what we call curios. Every man with money is a collector in Japan, but you shall find no crowds of 'things' outside the best shops.

We stayed long in the half-light of that quaint place, and when we went away we grieved afresh that such a people should have a 'constitution' or should dress every tenth young man in European clothes, put a white ironclad in Kobe harbour, and send a dozen myopic lieutenants in baggy uniforms about the streets.

'It would pay us,' said the Professor, his head in a clog-shop, 'it would pay us to establish an international suzerainty over Japan to take away any fear of invasion or annexation, and pay the country as much as ever it chose, on condition that it simply sat still and went on making beautiful things while our men learned. It would pay us to put the whole Empire in a glass case and mark it, *Hors Concours*, Exhibit A.'[13]

'H'mm,' said I. 'Who's us?'

'Oh, we generally – the *sahib-log*[14] all the world over. Our workmen – a few of them – can do as good work in certain lines, but you don't find whole towns full of clean, capable, dainty, designful people in Europe.'

Wherefore – 'Let's go to Tokyo and speak to the Emperor about it,' I said.

'Let's go to a Japanese theatre first,' said the Professor. 'It's too early in the tour to start serious politics.'

1889: LETTER TWO
COMMENTARY

1. The quotation is a joke derived from *Punch*. It appealed to Kipling, who returned to it in 1914 in a speech on 'Aspects of Travel' before the Royal Geographical Society. Speaking of 'those disappointing men who, after months of experience, can communicate no more than a hazy recollection' of places they have visited, he continued, '*Punch* has described this type in the man who said: "Rome – Rome. Wasn't that the place where I bought the shocking bad cigars?"'

2. Naini Tal, a hill station in what is now Uttar Pradesh, India, was in Kipling's day the summer residence of the Governor of the United Provinces and his staff. It is a place of great scenic beauty, but its famous lake is only a mile long and 400 yards wide.

3. The point of these remarks is that by mid-April Kipling's readers in the Indian lowlands would be experiencing very hot weather. A thermanti-dote was a device for cooling the air in a house. It consisted of a rotating fan, surrounded by wet 'tatties' (a wrapping or lining of grass or reed matting), fitted into a window in such a way as to propel cool air into a room. It was turned with a handle, by a coolie; its mechanism might need lubrication to make it quieter; steatite is a soft soapstone.

4. Before it was opened to foreign traders on 1 January 1868, Kobe had been no more than a small fishing village. Thereafter, it became the main port for foreign trade in the Kansai, the western part of the main island Honshu. Among all the Treaty Ports of Japan, Kobe was second only to Yokohama in importance and the size of its foreign community.

5. The Oriental Hotel still exists in Kobe, but its old buildings that Kipling knew have long since been replaced.

6. Peliti's was Peliti's Grand Hotel in Simla. It was best known for its high-class café, which was a notable social rendezvous often mentioned in Kipling's early writing. The name came from Signor (later Chevalier) Peliti, an Italian whom Lord Lytton as Viceroy had brought to India as his confectioner, and who later went into business with the hotel in Simla and a restaurant of the same name in Calcutta.

7. On his way to Japan Kipling had visited the well-known Eastern & Oriental Hotel in Penang, and the Raffles in Singapore, though it is not clear from his newspaper despatches whether he actually stayed in either. However, he did stay at the Victoria (now defunct) in Hong Kong, and praised its service and quality: the tariff including meals was three dollars a day.

8. A national of one of the Treaty powers wishing to travel outside the immediate vicinity of the Treaty Ports had to apply through his consular or diplomatic officials for a passport. This would specify the places to which he was permitted to travel. *Murray's Handbook* (1894

edition) recommended the applicant to state that the journey would be 'for the benefit of my health', or 'for scientific purposes'. It also stated that 'British subjects are mulcted by their Consuls in the sum of $2 per passport, while Americans obtain theirs for a few cents'.

9. *Pahari* was a general term in northern India for a hillman.

10. *Netsuke* are carved toggles, used with Japanese medicine cases called *inro*.

11. The *Tirthankars* of the Jains (an important sect of dissenters from Hinduism) were the twenty-three saints, mythical or historical, who were revered as having attained the condition of *nirvana*, and had become *Jinas* (leaders or conquerors), whence the name 'Jain'.

12. *Beloos*: a *beloo* here means a giant or ogre, from the Burmese.

13. *Hors concours* means 'not subject to competition'. During his visit Kipling repeatedly expressed regret that the Japanese, with their superlative artistic ability, should be distracted from it by material considerations of international ambition and industrial development.

14. Though the word *sahib*, originally deriving from an Arabic word meaning 'companion', had come to have various nuances in India both as a noun and as a title, it basically meant 'gentleman' or 'master'. During the period of British rule in India it came to be applied to Europeans generally. *Sahib-log*, meaning '*sahib*-folk' in that sense, is a facetious form.

1889: Letter Three

THE JAPANESE THEATRE AND THE STORY OF THE THUNDER CAT.
TREATING ALSO OF THE QUIET PLACES AND THE DEAD MAN IN THE
STREET.

In my last letter I said that the Professor had suggested our going to a Japanese theatre; and to a Japanese theatre we went, through the mud and much rain. It was somewhere in the slums beyond the railway bridge and a level crossing, and it blazed with gaudy pictures externally. Internally it was nearly dark, for the deep blue of the audience's dress soaked up the scanty light of the kerosene lamps. There was no standing room anywhere except next to the Japanese policeman, who in the cause of morals and the Lord Chamberlain[1] had a corner in the gallery and three chairs all to himself. He was quite four feet eight inches high, and Napoleon at St. Helena could not have folded his arms more dramatically. After some grunting – I fear we were upsetting the principles of the Constitution – he consented to give us one chair, receiving in return a Burma cheroot which I have every reason to believe blew his little head off. A pit containing fifty rows of fifty people and a bonding-layer of babies, with a gallery which might have held twelve hundred, made up the house. It took me some time to understand that the entire theatre was as delicate a piece of cabinet work as any of the houses; roof, floor, beams, props, verandahs and partitions were of naked wood, and every other person in the house was smoking a tiny pipe and knocking out the ashes every two minutes. Then I wished to fly; death by the *auto-da-fé* not being anywhere paid for in the tour; but there was no escape by the one little low door where pickled fish was being sold between the acts.

'Yes, it's not exactly a safe-looking place,' said the Professor, as the matches winked and sputtered all round and below. 'But if that curtain catches that naked light on the stage, or you see this match-wood gallery begin to blaze, I'll kick out the back of the refreshment-buffet, and we can walk away.'

With this cold comfort the drama began. The green curtain

59

dropped from above and was whisked away, and three gentlemen and a lady opened the ball by a dialogue conducted in tones between a 'burble' and a falsetto whisper. If you wish to know their costumes, look at the nearest Japanese fan. Real Japanese of course are like men and women, but stage Japanese in their stiff brocades are line for line as Japanese are drawn. When the four sat down, a little boy ran among them and settled their draperies, pulling out a sash bow here, displaying a skirt-fold there and putting a cushion where it was needed. The costumes were as gorgeous as the plot was incomprehensible. But we will call the play '*The Thunder Cat, or Harlequin Bag o' Bones and the Amazing Old Woman, or The Mammoth Radish, or The Superfluous Badger and the Swinging Lights*'[2]

A two-sworded man in the black and gold brocade rose up and imitated the gait of an obscure actor called Henry Irving,[3] whereat, not knowing that he was serious, I cackled aloud till the Japanese policeman looked at me austerely. Then the two-sworded man wooed the Japanese-fan lady, the rest of the characters commenting on his proceedings like a Greek chorus till something – perhaps a misplaced accent – provoked trouble, and the two-sworded man and a vermilion splendour enjoyed a Vincent Crummles fight[4] to the music of all the orchestra – one guitar and something that clicked – not castanets.[5] The small boy removed their weapons when the men had sufficiently warred, and, conceiving that the piece wanted light, fetched a ten-foot bamboo with a naked candle at the end, and held this implement about a foot from the face of the two-sworded man, following his every movement[6] with the anxious eye of a child intrusted with a typewriter. Then the Japanese-fan girl consented to the wooing of the two-sworded man, and with a scream of eldritch laughter turned into a hideous old woman – a boy took off her hair, but she did the making-up herself. At this terrible moment a gilded Thunder Cat, which is a cat issuing from a cloud, ran on wires from the flies to the centre of the gallery, and a boy with a badger's tail mocked at the two-sworded man. Then I knew that the two-sworded man had offended a Cat and a Badger, and would have a very bad time of it, for these two animals and the Fox are to this day black sorcerers. Fearful things followed, and the scenery was changed once every five minutes. The prettiest effect was secured by a double row of candles hung on strings behind a green gauze far up the stage and set swinging with opposite motions. This, besides giving a fine idea of uncanniness, made one member of the audience sea-sick.

But the two-sworded man was far more miserable than I. The bad

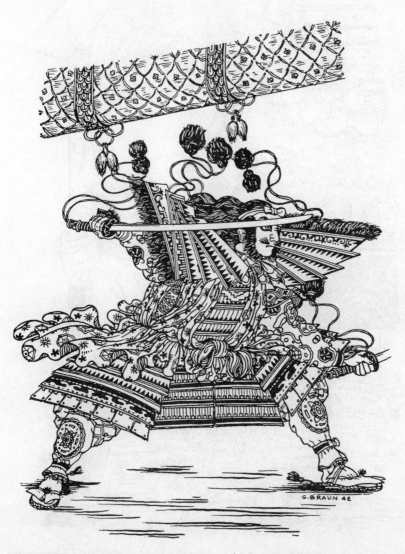

THE 'TWO-SWORDED MAN' IN 'THE THUNDER CAT' (p. 60)

An illustration from *Lettres du Japon*. Here, in fantastic dress and with extravagant posture, *'un homme à deux sabres, sous le brocart noir et or, se leva et imita la démarche d'un acteur obscur appelé Henry Irving'*. However, having 'offended a Cat and a Badger', the *samurai* was in for trouble – *'il en aurait de l'ennui'* – as was vividly demonstrated on the stage.

RINGING THE GREAT BELL (pp. 86–7)

An illustration from *Lettres du Japon*. The astonishing deep note of '*la grosse cloche de Kioto*', with its '*murmure zézayant*' which he at first mistook for the precursor of '*un tremblement de terre*', had woken Kipling at his hotel. Here, later, identifiable by his pipe as the Professor is by his camera, he watches it being rung.

Thunder Cat cast such spells upon him that I gave up trying to find out what he was. He was a fat-faced low comedian King of the Rats, assisted by other rats, and he ate a magic radish with side-splitting pantomine till he became a man once more. Then all his bones were taken away, – still by the Thunder Cat, – and he fell into a horrid heap, illuminated by the small boy with the candle – and would not recover himself till somebody spoke to a magic parrot, and a huge hairy villain and several coolies had walked over him. Then he was a girl, but, hiding behind a parasol, resumed his shape, with much surprise and feminine bewilderment, and then the curtain came down and the audience ran about the stage and circulated generally. One small boy took it into his head that he could turn head-over-heels from the Prompt side across. With great gravity, before the unregarding house, he set to work, but rolled over sideways with a flourish of chubby legs. Nobody cared, and the polite people in the gallery could not understand why the Professor and I were helpless with laughter when the child, with a clog for a sword, imitated the strut of the two-sworded man. The actors changed in public, and any one who liked might help shift scenes. Why should not a baby enjoy himself if he liked?

A little later we left. The Thunder Cat was still working her wicked will on the two-sworded man, but all would be set right next day. There was a good deal to be done, but Justice was at the end of it. The man who sold pickled fish and tickets said so.

'Good school for a young actor,' said the Professor. 'He'd see what unpruned eccentricities naturally develop into. There's every trick and mannerism of the English stage in that place, magnified thirty diameters, but perfectly recognisable. What colour and what dresses though! I didn't think people could look so like their pictures. How do you intend to describe it?'

'The Japanese comic opera of the future has yet to be written,' I responded grandiloquently. 'Yet to be written in spite of *The Mikado*. The badger has not yet appeared on an English stage, and the artistic mask as an accessory to the legitimate drama has never been utilised. Just imagine *The Thunder Cat* as a title for a serio-comic opera? Begin with a domestic cat possessed of magic powers, living in the house of a London tea-merchant who kicks her. Consider – '

'The lateness of the hour,' was the icy answer. 'Tomorrow we will go and write operas in the temple close to this place.'

*   *   *

61

Tomorrow brought fine drizzling rain. The sun, by the way, has been hidden now for more than three weeks. They took us to what must be the chief temple of Kobe and gave it a name which I do not remember.[7] It is an exasperating thing to stand at the altars of a faith that you know nothing about. There be rites and ceremonies of the Hindu creed that all have read of and must have witnessed, but in what manner do they pray here who look to Buddha, and what worship is paid at the Shinto shrines? The books say one thing; the eyes, another.

The temple would seem to be also a monastery and a place of great peace disturbed only by the babble of scores of little children. It stood back from the road behind a sturdy wall, an irregular mass of steep-pitched roofs bound fantastically at the crown, copper-green where the thatch had ripened under the touch of time, and dull grey-black where the tiles ran. Under the eaves some man who believed in his God, and so could do good work, had carved his heart into wood till it blossomed and broke into waves or curled with the ripple of live flames. Somewhere on the outskirts of Lahore city stands a mazy gathering of tombs and cloister walks called Chajju Bhagat's Chubara, built no one knows when and decaying no one cares how soon.[8] Though this temple was large and spotlessly clean within and without, the silence and rest of the place were those of the courtyards in the far-off Punjab. The priests had made many gardens in corners of the wall – gardens perhaps forty feet long by twenty wide, and each, though different from its neighbour, containing a little pond with goldfish, a stone lantern or two, hummocks of rock, flat stones carved with inscriptions, and a cherry or peach tree one mass of blossom.

Stone-paved paths ran across the courtyard and connected building with building. In an inner enclosure, where lay the prettiest garden of all, was a golden tablet ten or twelve feet high, against which stood in high relief of hammered bronze the figure of a goddess in flowing robes. The space between the paved paths here was strewn with snowy-white pebbles, and in white pebbles on red they had written on the ground the two words, 'How happy.' There was no offence in them. You might take them as you pleased – for the sigh of contentment or the question of despair.

The temple itself, reached by a wooden bridge, was nearly dark, but there was light enough to show a hundred subdued splendours of brown and gold, of silk and faithfully painted screen. If you have once seen a Buddhist altar where the Master of the Law sits among golden bells, ancient bronzes, flowers in vases, and banners of tapestry, you will begin to understand why the Roman Catholic Church once prospered so mightily in this country, and will prosper in all lands where it finds an elaborate ritual already existing. Since the beginning of the world, and as a pale and ineffectual return to the compliment paid him in the first chapter of Genesis, man has done his best to make God after his own image. An art-loving folk will have a God who is to be propitiated with pretty things as surely as a race bred among rocks and moors and driving clouds will enshrine their deity in the storm and make him the austere recipient of the sacrifice of the rebellious human spirit. Do you remember the story of the Bad People of Iquique?[9] The man who told me that yarn told me another – of the Good People of Somewhere Else. They also were simple South Americans with nothing to wear, and had been conducting a service of their own in honour of their God before a black-jowled Jesuit father. At a critical moment some one forgot the ritual, or a monkey invaded the sanctity of that forest shrine and stole the priest's only garment. Anyhow, an absurdity happened, and the Good People burst into shouts of laughter and broke off to play for a while.

'But what will your God say?' asked the Jesuit, scandalised at the levity.

'Oh! he knows everything. He knows that we forget, and can't attend, and do it all wrong, but he is very wise and very strong,' was the reply.

'Well, that doesn't excuse you.'

'Of course it does. He just lies back and laughs,' said the Good People of Somewhere Else, and fell to pelting each other with blossoms.

I forget what is the precise bearing of this anecdote. But to return to the temple. Hidden away behind a mass of variegated gorgeousness was a row of very familiar figures with gold crowns on their heads. One does not expect to meet Krishna the *makan chor* and Kali the husband-beater[10] so far east as Japan.

'What are these?'

'They are other Gods,' said a young priest, who giggled deprecatingly at his own creed every time he was questioned about it. 'They are very old. They came from India in the past. I think they are Indian Gods, but I do not know why they are here.'

I hate a man who is ashamed of his faith. There was a story connected with those Gods, and the priest would not tell it to me. So I sniffed at him scornfully, and went my way. It led me from the temple straight into the monastery, which was all made of delicate screens, polished floors, and brown wood ceilings. Except for my tread on the boards there was no sound in the place till I heard some one breathing heavily behind a screen. The priest slid back what had appeared to me a dead wall, and we found a very old priest half-asleep over his charcoal handwarmer. This was the picture. The priest in olive-green, his bald head, pure silver, bowed down before a sliding screen of white oiled paper which let in dull silver light. To his right a battered black lacquer stand containing the Indian ink and brushes with which he feigned to work. To the right of these, again, a pale yellow bamboo table holding a vase of olive-green crackle, and a sprig of almost black pine. There were no blossoms in this place. The priest was too old. Behind the sombre picture stood a gorgeous little Buddhist shrine, – gold and vermilion, and the things that look like golden *peepul* leaves[11] over the head of Buddha tinkled mournfully from time to time.

'He makes a fresh picture for the little screen here every day,' said the young priest, pointing first to his senior, and then to a blank little tablet on the wall. The old man laughed pitifully, rubbed his head, and handed me his picture for the day. It represented a flood over rocky ground; two men in a boat were helping two others on a tree half-submerged by the water. Even I could tell that the power had gone from him. He must have drawn well in his manhood, for one figure in the boat had action and purpose as it leaned over the gunwale; but the rest was blurred, and the lines had wandered astray as the poor old hand had quavered across the paper. I had no time to wish the artist a pleasant old age, and an easy death in the great peace that surrounded him, before the young man drew me away to the back of the shrine, and showed me a second smaller altar facing shelves on shelves of little gold and lacquer tablets covered with Japanese characters.

'These are memorial tablets of the dead,' he giggled. 'Once and again the priest he comes to pray here – for those who are dead, you understand?'

'Perfectly. They call 'em masses where I come from. I want to go away and think about things. You shouldn't laugh, though, when you show off your creed.'

'Ha, ha!' said the young priest, and I ran away down the dark polished passages with the faded screens on either hand, and got into the main courtyard facing the street, while the Professor was trying to catch temple fronts with his camera.

A procession came by of Japanese dressed in the English fashion more or less than pure Japanese, four abreast tramping through the sloshy mud. They did not laugh, which was strange, till I saw and heard a company of women in white walking in front of a little wooden palanquin carried on the shoulders of four bearers and suspiciously light. They sang a song, half under their breaths – a wailing, moaning song that I had only heard once before, from the lips of a native far away in the north of India, who had been clawed past hope of cure by a bear, and was singing his own death-song as his friends bore him along.

'Have makee die,' said my *'rickshaw* coolie. 'Few-yu-ne-ral.'

I was aware of the fact. Men, women, and little children poured along the streets, and when the death-song died down, helped it forward. The half-mourners wore only pieces of white cloth about their shoulders. The immediate relatives of the dead were in white from head to foot. 'Aho! Ahaa! Aho!' they wailed very softly, for fear of breaking the cadence of the falling rain, and they disappeared. All except one old woman, who could not keep pace with the procession, and so came along alone, crooning softly to herself. 'Aho! Ahaa! Aho!' she whispered.

The little children in the courtyard were clustered round the Professor's camera. But one child had a very bad skin disease on his innocent head, – so bad that none of the others would play with him, – and he stood in a corner and sobbed and sobbed as though his heart would break. Poor little Gehazi![12]

They give you a perfect potato salad and fowl *à la Marengo* at the Oriental. I went back to that. It was better than temples and funerals.

1889: LETTER THREE
COMMENTARY

1. A reference to the function of 'Licenser of Plays' exercised in England at that time by the head of the Royal Household, the Lord Chamberlain. Under legislation of 1737, redefined in 1843 and thereafter in force despite many protests for more than another century, the text of all plays had to be submitted to the Lord Chamberlain before performance. In the interests of 'preservation of good manners, decorum or the public peace' he could withhold a licence. This power of censorship was particularly resented by authors and playwrights.

2. It was a *Kabuki* theatre that Kipling visited. *Kabuki* is a form of drama which had been popular since the seventeenth century. Like the classical *No* theatre, it probably originated in the medieval *sarugaku* (literally 'monkey music'), a combination of dance and mime. It developed in parallel with the *joruri* or puppet drama: some of the stylized poses and gestures of *Kabuki* were derived from the way puppets were manipulated: indeed the best and most popular *Kabuki* plays were first written for puppet performances. Such plays included a great deal of recitative, sung by special performers with accompaniment. All *Kabuki* actors were men: female parts were played by specialists, the *onnagata*, and in classical *Kabuki* this is still the case. The titles Kipling gave to the play he saw were not entirely ridiculous: many *Kabuki* titles sound absurd when translated literally. '*Kanadehon Chushingura*', the title of a famous play about forty-seven *ronin*, or masterless *samurai* struggling to avenge their late master, means literally 'The Alphabetical List of the Treasury of Loyal Servants'.

3. An ironic allusion to the most famous British actor of the day, Henry Irving (1838–1905), who in 1895 was knighted, the first actor so honoured. Irving was best known for his performance of Shakespearean parts. His style was an original and intellectual one, but very heavily mannered.

4. Vincent Crummles was a character in Charles Dickens's novel *Nicholas Nickleby*. He was the actor-manager of a company of strolling players, whose hammed performances are vividly described in the story. Kipling would have had in mind a farcically over-acted sword-fight between two sailors in Chapter 22, with an accompanying illustration by 'Phiz'.

5. By 'guitar' Kipling meant the three-stringed *samisen*. By 'something that clicked' he meant the *hyoshigi*, blocks of wood clapped together to mark the end of a scene, or a highlight in the plot, when the *Kabuki* actor adopted a frozen posture.

6. The device of a candle at the end of a stick, held near an actor's face to illuminate his expression, was common in the days before modern stage lighting.

7. This temple in Kobe may have been the Sumadera, also known as Fukushoji. It was said to date from 886 AD and was famous for its cherry trees. Its chief object of worship is a bronze image of Kannon, possibly the bronze figure mentioned by Kipling. Kannon, or Kwannon or in Chinese Kuan-Yin, was a Bodhisattva who, although in India he would invariably have been a male deity, in China and Japan was usually depicted in female form.

8. A *chubara* was a sort of summerhouse in a garden. Chajju Bhagat's Chubara was on the south side of the Lahore city wall, near the Veterinary School. Kipling had described it in detail in 1887, in 'Hunting a Miracle', part of the 'Smith Administration' newspaper

series much later republished in *From Sea to Sea*. The place had made a deep impression on Kipling, with its atmosphere of profound peace.

9. Iquique is a seaport, ceded by Peru to Chile in 1883 after the bitterly fought War of the Pacific. The 'story of the Bad People' had been recounted in an earlier letter in this series, written at sea before calling at Penang. It was an amusing anecdote of how some primitive South American Indians had gone to Iquique to lay grievances before the governor, and had horrified the polite society of the city by their unashamed nakedness. It may have been apocryphal, but in Iquique clothes are certainly not needed as a protection against the wet: the rainfall, year after year, is nil.

10. These were familiar gods of the Hindu pantheon. Krishna was a deified hero, represented as the courageous but crafty incarnation of Vishnu. (*Makan Chor* means literally 'Butter Thief': Vishnu was one of the three gods of the major triad, the others being Brahma and Shiva.) Kali was a goddess, shown in various forms, often as an ogress maltreating her husband Shiva.

11. The *peepul* or *pipal*, *Ficus religiosa*, was the characteristic fig tree of India.

12. A reference to *II Kings*, 5, 27, in the Old Testament. Elisha's servant Gehazi was punished for deceit by being turned into 'a leper as white as snow'.

1889: Letter Four

EXPLAINS IN WHAT MANNER I WAS TAKEN TO VENICE IN THE RAIN, AND CLIMBED INTO A DEVIL FORT, A TIN-POT EXHIBITION, AND A BATH. OF THE MAIDEN AND THE BOLTLESS DOOR, THE CULTI-VATOR AND HIS FIELDS, AND THE MANUFACTURE OF ETHNOLOGICAL THEORIES AT RAILROAD SPEED. ENDS WITH A PLACE CALLED KYOTO.

'There's a deal o' fine confused feedin' about sheep's head.'
                                              – *Christopher North*.[1]

'Come along to Osaka,' said the Professor.

'Why? I'm quite comfy here, and we shall have lobster cutlets for tiffin; and, anyhow, it is raining heavily, and we shall get wet.'

'Come along to Osaka,' said the Professor. 'Trains run every two hours and the town is full of manufactures – chimneys and so on, y'know.'

Sorely against my will – for it was in my mind to fudge 'Japan' from a guide-book while I enjoyed the cookery of the Oriental at Kobe – I was dragged into a *'rickshaw* and the rain, and conveyed to a railway station constructed chiefly of elaborately grained wood. Even the Japanese cannot make their railway stations lovely, though they do their best. Their system of baggage-booking is borrowed from the Americans; their narrow-gauge lines, locos, and rolling-stock are English;[2] their passenger-traffic is regulated with the precision of the Gaul,[3] and the uniforms of their officials come from the nearest ragbag. The passengers themselves were altogether delightful. A large number of them were modified Europeans, and resembled nothing more than Tenniel's picture of the White Rabbit on the first page of *Alice in Wonderland*.[4] They were arrayed in neat little tweed suits with fawn-coloured overcoats, and they carried ladies' reticules of black leather and nickel platings. They rejoiced in paper and celluloid stuck-up collars which must have been quite thirteen inches round the neck, and their boots were number fours. On their hands – their wee-wee hands – they wore white cotton gloves, and they smoked cigarettes from fairy little cigarette cases. That was Young Japan – the Japan of the present day.

'Wah, wah, God is great,' said the Professor. 'But it isn't in human nature for a man who sprawls about on soft mats by instinct to wear Europe clothes as though they belonged to him. If you notice, the last thing that they take to is a pair of shoes. A man with shoes can't enter a Japanese house.'

I knew the Professor had picked the last sentence out of a guide-book. 'Don't they look just the least little bit in the world like Babus?'[5] I murmured. 'Not in their art of course, but in their hankering after our way of dressing.'

'The Babu has no arts and no manufactured products except himself,' said the Professor epigrammatically. 'If you think you can understand Japan from watching it at a railway station you are much mistaken.'

A lapis-lazuli coloured locomotive which, by accident, had a mixed train attached to it happened to loaf up to the platform just then, and we entered a first-class English compartment. There was no stupid double roof, window shade, or abortive thermantidote. It was a London and South-Western carriage.[6] Whereat, feeling home-sick, I mourned for my lost fatherland. Osaka[7] is about eighteen miles from Kobe, and stands at the head of the bay of Osaka. The train is allowed, when it is good, to go as fast as fifteen miles an hour and to play at the stations all along the line. That is to say the entire system could have been linked to the North-Western. But whether Colonel Conway-Gordon[8] would have approved of fragrant cherry-blossom trees at all the stations I greatly doubt. He would have admired the permanent-way and the embankments immensely. You must know that the line runs between the hills and the shore, and the drainage-fall is a great deal steeper than anything we have between Saharunpur and Umballa.[9] The rivers and the hill torrents come down straight from the hills on raised beds of their own formation, which beds again have to be bunded and spanned with girder bridges or – here, perhaps, I may be wrong – tunnelled. At any rate we went under three bridges of pine and bamboo, and if they did not hide an irrigation cut at the least I am a Japanese.

Lucky was the contractor who made the line. He must have received sanction for unlimited bridges and culverts.[10]

The stations are black-tiled, red-walled, and concrete-floored, and all the plant from signal levers to goods-truck is English. The official colour of the bridges is a yellow-brown most like unto a faded chrysanthemum. The uniform of the ticket-collectors is a peaked forage cap with gold lines, black frock-coat with brass buttons, very long in the skirt, trousers with black mohair braid, and buttoned kid boots. You cannot be rude to a man in such raiment.

But the countryside was the thing that made us open our eyes. It is not for me to say that the Japanese cultivator works his fields with a comb and tooth-pick. A mere layman has no right to opinions. You know how the cultivation runs round Patna, or in the first circle of the vegetable gardens near a big city, or in the hill-terraces of Kulu.[11] Imagine a land of rich black soil, very heavily manured, and worked by the spade and hoe almost exclusively, and if you split your field (of vision) into half-acre plots, you will get a notion of the raw material the cultivator works on. But all I can write will give you no notion of the wantonness of neatness visible in the fields; of the elaborate system of irrigation, and the mathematical precision of the planting. There was no mixing of crops, no waste of boundary in footpath, and no difference of value in the land. *Id est* the water was everywhere within ten feet of the surface, as the well-sweeps attested. On the slopes of the foothills each drop between the levels was neatly revetted with unmortared stones, and the edges of the water-cuts were faced in like manner. The young rice was transplanted very much as draughts are laid on the board; the tea might have been cropped garden box; and between the lines of the mustard the water lay in the drills as in a wooden trough, while the purple of the beans ran up to the mustard and stopped as though cut with a rule.

'I knew they had cabinet-makers to make their houses, but I didn't know they had 'em to construct their fields,' said the Professor.

'Oh these are the vegetable gardens that supply Kyoto,' I said at a venture.

That was not true. We ran into the district and the aspect of the country was still unchanged. On the seaboard we saw an almost continuous line of towns variegated with factory chimneys; inland, the crazy-quilt of green, dark-green and gold; and shutting out the view, fir-clad hills where other villages hid themselves. Even in the rain the view was lovely, and exactly as Japanese pictures had led me to hope for. Only one drawback occurred to the Professor and myself at the same time. Crops don't grow to the full limit of the seed on heavily worked ground cut up by *rajbahars*[12] and dotted with villages, without compensating disadvantages.

'Cholera?' said I, watching a stretch of well-sweeps.

'Cholera,' said the Professor. 'Must be, y'know. It's all sewage irrigation.'[13]

I felt that I was friends with the cultivators at once. These broad-hatted, blue-clad gentlemen who tilled their fields by hand – except when they borrowed the village buffalo to drive the share through the rice-slough – knew what the Scourge meant.

'How much do you think the Government takes in revenue from vegetable gardens of that kind?' I demanded.

'Bosh,' said he quietly, 'you aren't going to describe the land-tenure of Japan. Look at the yellow of the mustard!'[14]

It lay in sheets round the line. It ran up the hills to the dark pines. It rioted over the brown sandbars of the swollen rivers, and faded away by mile after mile to the shores of the leaden sea. The high-peaked houses of brown thatch stood knee-deep in it, and it surged up to the factory chimneys of Osaka when an hour's gentle exercise brought us to that place.

'Great place, Osaka,' said the guide. 'All sorts of manufactures there.' Did I tell you that we had invested in a guide at Kobe? You must also get one. It is humiliating, but it is indispensable when you journey beyond the limit of the treaty ports. The guide, who demands one dollar a day and seventy-five cents for food, knows exactly what is to be seen, knows the hotels and the prices of everything, and sees you through in a whole-souled manner which may or may not cover desire for *dasturi*.[15] Under any circumstances, 'tis more economical to take a guide, for none of the railway officials except the booking-clerk speak a word of English, and though smiles are vastly pleasant they will not guide you to a bed or supper. Take a guide and be not astonished if he dresses in European clothing and prefers to be addressed as Mister Such-an-one. He is very polite and not obtrusive.

Osaka is a town of between two hundred and fifty and three hundred thousand folk, built into and over and among one thousand eight hundred and ninety-four canals, rivers, dams, and water-cuts. The first computation is in the guide-books. The latter I made all by myself on the way from the station to the hotel, but I fancy the real number is four thousand and fifty-two; however if you doubt me you can go there yourself and count. What the multitudinous chimneys mean I cannot tell. They have something to do with rice polishing and cotton; but it is not good that the Japanese should indulge in trade, and I will not call Osaka a 'great commercial *entrepôt*'. 'People who live in paper houses should never sell goods,' as the proverb says.

Because of his many wants there is but one hotel for the Englishman in Osaka, and they call it Juter's.[16] Here the views of our civilisation and a counterfeit collide and the result is awful. The building is altogether Japanese; wood and tile and sliding screen from top to bottom; but the fitments are mixed. My room, for instance, held a *tokonoma*, made of the polished black stem of a palm and

71

delicate woodwork, framing a scroll picture representing in cool greys and whites storks in every attitude. There was also a fair screen fit for a lady's drawing-room. But on the floor over the white mats was stretched a Brussels carpet that made the indignant toes tingle. From the back verandah one overhung the river which ran straight as an arrow between two lines of ghâts[17] and houses. They have cabinet-makers in Japan to fit the rivers to the towns. From my verandah I could see three bridges – one a hideous lattice-girder arrangement – and part of a fourth. We were on an island and possessed a water-gate if we wanted to take a boat. That was a sight to be seen. The frail wood framing gave you a notion that you were stepping on a raft which would presently break up and drop you into a five-knot current.

Apropos of water, be pleased to listen to a Shocking Story.[18] It is written in all the books that the Japanese though cleanly are somewhat casual in their customs. They are supposed to bathe frequently with nothing on and together. This notion my experience of the country, gathered in the seclusion of the Oriental at Kobe, made me scoff at. I demanded a tub at Juter's. The infinitesimal man led me down verandahs and upstairs till he got me into a beautiful bath-house full of hot and cold water and fitted with cabinet-work, somewhere in a lonely out-gallery. There was naturally no bolt to the door any more than there would be a bolt to a dining-room. Had I been sheltered by the walls of a big Europe bath, I should not have cared, but I was preparing to wash when a pretty maiden opened the door, and indicated that she would tub in the deep, sunken Japanese bath at my side. When one is clad only in one's virtue and a pair of spectacles it is difficult to preserve sufficient dignity to shut the door in the face of a girl. She gathered that I was not happy, and withdrew giggling, while I fled into the hot water and thanked heaven, blushing profusely the while, that I had been brought up in a society which unfits a man to bathe *à deux*. Even an experience of the Paddington Swimming Baths would have helped me; but coming straight from India, Lady Godiva[19] was a ballet-girl in sentiment compared to this Actæon.[20]

To return to less important affairs. It rained monsoonishly, and the oppressively energetic Professor discovered a castle which he needs must see. 'It's Osaka Castle,' he said, 'and it has been fought over for hundreds of years.[21] Come along.'

'I've seen castles in India. Raighur, Jodhpur[22] – all sorts of places. Let's have some more boiled salmon. It's good in this station.'

'Pig,' said the Professor.

We threaded our way over the four thousand and fifty-two canals, etc., where the little children played with the swiftly running water, and never a mother said 'don't,' till our *'rickshaws* stopped outside a fort ditch thirty feet deep, and faced with gigantic granite slabs. On the far side uprose the walls of a fort. But such a fort! Fifty feet was the height of the wall, and never a pinch of mortar in the whole. Nor was the face perpendicular, but curved like the ram of a man-of-war from the bow to where it cut the water. They know the curve in China, and I have seen French artists introduce it into books describing a devil-besieged city of Tartary. Possibly everybody else knows it too, but that is not my affair; life as I have said being altogether new to me. The stone was granite, and the men of old time had used it like mud. The dressed blocks that made the profile of the angles were from twenty feet long, ten or twelve feet high, and as many in thickness. I paced several blocks in the main gate-way wall which were ten yards long, and fourteen or fifteen feet high. There was no attempt at binding, but there was no fault in the jointing.

'And the little Japanese built this!' I cried, awestricken at the quarries that rose round me.

'Cyclopean masonry,' grunted the Professor, punching with a stick a monolith of seventeen feet cube. 'Not only did they build it, but they took it. Look at this. Fire!'

The stones had been split and bronzed in places, and the cleavage was the cleavage of fire. Evil must it have been for the armies that led the assault on these monstrous walls. Castles in India I know, and the forts of great Emperors I had seen, but neither Akbar in the north, nor Scindia in the south,[23] had built after this fashion – without ornament, without colour, but with a single eye to savage strength and the utmost purity of line. Perhaps the fort would have looked less forbidding under sunlight. The grey, rain-laden atmosphere through which I saw it suited its spirit. Even when we came upon the barracks of the garrison, the commandant's very dainty house, a peach-garden, and two deer were foreign to the place. They should have peopled it with giants from the mountains, or the struggling phantoms that Doré[24] used to draw, instead of – Gurkhas! On second thoughts I withdraw the remark in deference to the little gentlemen with the big knives. A Japanese infantryman is not a Gurkha, though he might be mistaken for one as long as he stood still. The sentry at the quarter-guard belonged, I fancy, to the 4th Regiment. His uniform was black or blue, with red facings, and shoulder-straps carrying the number of the regiment in cloth. He was doing his sentry-go in full field-order. The rain necessitated an overcoat, but why he should have carried knapsack, blanket, boots, *and* binoculars I could not fathom. The knapsack was of cowskin with the hair on, the boots were strapped soles, cut on each side, while a heavy country blanket was rolled U-shape over the head of the knapsack, fitting close to the back. In the place usually occupied by the mess-tin was a black leather case shaped like a field-glass. This must be a mistake of mine, but I can only record as I see. The rifle was a side-bolt weapon of some kind,[25] and the bayonet an uncommonly good sword one, locked to the muzzle, English fashion. Both weapons were much too big for the man. The ammunition-pouches, as far as I could see under the greatcoat, ran on the belt in front, and were double-strapped down. This again must be an error. White spatter-dashes – very dirty – and peaked cap completed the outfit. I surveyed the man with interest, and would have made further examination of him but for fear of the big bayonet. His arms were well kept, – not speckless by any means, – but his uniform would have made an English colonel swear. There was no portion of his body except the neck that it pretended to fit. I peeped into the Quarter-Guard at Osaka fort and withdrew oppressed by laughter. Fans and dainty tea-sets do not go with one's notions of a barrack. Later on I saw a few of the men loafing through Osaka on pass. They carried swagger sticks in their hands. These sticks should have been laid about their stooping shoulders: they waddled and rolled and slouched and skipped about the gutters, and waved their white cotton gloves around like babies, while their garments hung in folds upon them. The Japanese makes a trim little blue-jacket, but he does not understand soldiering. One drunken defaulter of certain far-away regiments that I could name would not only have cleared out that Quarter-Guard, but brought away all its fittings except the rifle-racks.[26] Yet the little men, who were always gentle, and never got drunk, were mounting guard over a pile that, with a blue fire on the bastions, might have served for the guard-gates of Hell.

I climbed to the top of the fort and was rewarded by a view of thirty miles of country, chiefly pale yellow mustard and blue-green pine, and the sight of the very large city of Osaka fading away into mist. The guide took most pleasure in the factory chimneys. 'There is an exposition here – an exposition of industrialities. Come and see,' said he. He took us down from that high place and showed us the glory of the land in the shape of corkscrews, tin mugs, egg-whisks, dippers, silks, buttons, and all the trumpery that can be stitched on a card and sold for five-pence three farthings. The

Japanese unfortunately make all these things for themselves, and are proud of it. They have nothing to learn from the West as far as finish is concerned, and by intuition know how to showcase and mount wares tastefully. The exposition was in four large sheds running round a central building which held only screens, pottery, and cabinetware loaned for the occasion. I rejoiced to see that the common people did not care for the penknives, and the pencils, and the mock jewellery. They left those sheds alone and discussed the screens: first taking off their clogs that the inlaid floor of the room might not suffer. Of all the gracious things I beheld, two only remain in my memory, – one a screen in grey representing the heads of six devils instinct with malice and hate; the other, a bold sketch in monochrome of an old wood-cutter wrestling with the down-bent branch of a tree. Two hundred years have passed since the artist dropped his pencil, but you may almost hear the tough wood jar under the stroke of the chopper as the old man puts his back into the task and draws in the labouring breath between his clenched teeth. There is a picture by Legros of a beggar dying in a ditch, which might have been suggested by that screen.[27]

Next morning, after a night's rain which sent the river racing under the frail balconies at eight miles an hour, the sun broke through the clouds. Is this a little matter to you who can count upon him daily? I had not seen him since March, and was beginning to feel anxious on your account. Then the land of peach blossom spread its draggled wings abroad and rejoiced. All the pretty maidens put on their loveliest crêpe sashes, – fawn colour, pink, blue, orange, and lilac, – all the little children picked up a baby each, and went out to be happy. In a temple garden full of blossom I performed the miracle of Deucalion[28] with two cents' worth of sweets. The babies swarmed on the instant, till, for fear of raising all the mothers too, I forbore to give them any more sweets. They smiled and nodded prettily, and trotted after me, forty strong, the big ones helping the little, and the little ones skipping in the puddles as is the custom of babydom all the world over. A Japanese child never cries, never scuffles, never fights, and never makes mud-pies, except when it lives on the banks of a canal. Yet, lest it should spread its sash-bow and become a bald-headed angel, ere its time, Providence has decreed that it should never, never blow its little nose. Notwithstanding the defect, I love it.

There was no business in Osaka that day because of the sunshine and the budding of the trees. Everybody went to a tea-house with his friends. I went also, but first ran along a boulevard by the side of the river, pretending to look at the Mint.[29] This was only a common place of solid granite where they turn out dollars and rubbish of that kind. All along the boulevard the cherry, peach, and plum trees, pink, white, and red, touched branches and made a belt of velvety soft colour as far as the eye could reach. Weeping willows were the normal ornaments of the waterside, this revel of bloom being only part of the prodigality of Spring. The Mint may make a hundred thousand dollars a day, but all the silver in its keeping will not bring again the three weeks of the peach blossom which, even beyond the chrysanthemum, is the crown and glory of Japan. For some act of surpassing merit performed in a past life I have been enabled to hit those three weeks in the middle. Come at this season of the year if you can. It is worth the heat of Singapore, the chill of the China seas and the thermometer at 40° in the morning at Kobe.

'This is the Japanese festival of the cherry blossom,' said the guide. 'All the people will be festive. They will pray too and go to the tea-gardens.'

Now you might wall an Englishman about with cherry trees in bloom from head to heel, and after the first day he would begin to complain of the smell. As you know, the Japanese arrange a good many of their festivals in honour of flowers, and this is surely commendable, for blossoms are the most tolerant of gods.

The tea-house system of the Japanese filled me with pleasure at a pleasure that I could not fully comprehend. It pays a company in Osaka to build on the outskirts of the town a nine-storied pagoda of wood and iron, to lay out elaborate gardens round it, and to hang the whole with strings of blood-red lanterns, because the Japanese will come wherever there is a good view to sit on a mat and discuss tea and sweetmeats and *sake*. This Eiffel Tower is, to tell the truth, anything but pretty, yet the surroundings redeem it. Although it was not quite completed, the lower stories were full of tea-stalls and tea-drinkers. The men and women were obviously admiring the view. It is an astounding thing to see an Oriental so engaged; it is as though he had stolen something from a *sahib*. Once in India I heard about a man who was discovered looking at a sunset and making remarks about it which showed appreciation. But he was a Raja and, for aught we know, might have been playing up to his Political Agent.

From Osaka – canal-cut, muddy, and fascinating Osaka – the Professor, Mister Yamaguchi, – the guide, – and I took train to Kyoto, an hour from Osaka. On the road I saw four buffaloes at as many rice-ploughs – which was noticeable as well as wasteful. A buffalo at rest must cover the half of a Japanese field; but perhaps they are kept on the mountain-ledges and only pulled down when wanted. The Professor says that what I call buffalo is really bullock. The worst of travelling with an accurate man is his accuracy. We argued about the Japanese in the train, about his present and his future, and the manner in which he has ranged himself on the side of the grosser nations of the earth.

'Did it hurt his feelings very much to wear our clothes? Didn't he rebel when he put on a pair of trousers for the first time? Won't he grow sensible some day and drop foreign habits?' These were a few of the questions I put to the landscape and the Professor.

'He was a baby,' said the latter, 'a big baby. I think his sense of humour was at the bottom of the change, but he didn't know that a nation which once wears trousers never takes 'em off. You see "enlightened" Japan is only one-and-twenty years old, and people are not very wise at one-and-twenty.[30] Read Reed's *Japan*[31] and learn how the change came about. There was a Mikado and a Shogun who was Sir Frederick Roberts, but he tried to be the Viceroy and —'[32]

'Bother the Shogun! I've seen something like the Babu class, and something like the farmer class. What I want to see is the Rajput class[33] – the man who used to wear the thousands and thousands of swords in the curio-shops. Those swords were as much made for use as a Rajputana sabre. Where are the men who used 'em? Show me a *samurai*.'

The Professor answered not a word, but scrutinised heads on the wayside platforms. 'There doesn't seem to be a distinct fighting face among 'em, but I take it that the high-arched forehead, club nose, and eyes close together – the Spanish type – are from Rajput stock, while the German-faced Japanese is the *Khattri* – the lower class.'[34]

Thus we babbled of the natures and dispositions of men we knew nothing about till we had decided (1) that the painful politeness of the Japanese nation rose from the habit, dropped only twenty years ago, of extended and emphatic sword-wearing, even as the Rajput is the pink of courtesy because his friend is armed; (2) that this politeness will disappear in another generation, or will at least be seriously impaired; (3) that the cultured Japanese of the English pattern will corrupt and defile the tastes of his neighbours till (4) Japan altogether ceases to exist as a separate nation and becomes a button-hook manufacturing appanage of America; (5) that these things being so, and sure to happen in two or three hundred years, the Professor and I were lucky to reach Japan betimes; and (6) it was foolish to form theories about the country until we had seen a little of it.

So we came to the very great city of Kyoto in regal sunshine, tempered by a breeze that drove the cherry blossoms in drifts about the streets. One Japanese town, in the southern provinces at least, is very like another to look at – a grey-black sea of house roofs, speckled with the white walls of the fire-proof godowns where merchants and rich men keep their chief treasures. The general level is broken by the temple roofs, which are turned up at the edges, and remotely resemble so many terai-hats.[35] Kyoto fills a plain almost entirely surrounded by wooded hills, very familiar in their aspect to those who have seen the Siwaliks.[36] Once upon a time it was the capital of Japan, and to-day it numbers two hundred and fifty thousand people. It is laid out like an American town. All the streets run at right angles to each other.[37] That, by the way, is exactly what the Professor and I are doing. We are elaborating the Theory of the Japanese People, and we can't agree.

1889: LETTER FOUR
COMMENTARY

1. Kipling incorrectly but not unreasonably ascribes this quotation to 'Christopher North', which was the pen-name of the Scottish writer John Wilson (1785–1854), wit, eccentric, friend of Wordsworth and Coleridge, prolific contributor to *Blackwood's Magazine*. In fact, it comes from *Horae Subsecivae* ('Leisure Hours'), a miscellany by the Scottish essayist John Brown (1810–82), in a passage where a Scotsman is extolling sheep's head to an Englishman: 'Dish or no dish . . . there's a deal of fine confused feedin' about it.'

2. Whatever Kipling may have meant by American-style baggage-booking (a point on which Professor Hill or his American wife is likely to have enlightened him), the first Japanese railways, such as the line from Yokohama to Tokyo completed in 1872, were influenced by the British. The first lines were built under the direction of British engineers and the first trains were driven by British engine-drivers. The line from Kobe to Osaka was completed in November 1873, and the Osaka-Kyoto extension was opened in February 1877.

3. The 'Gaul', rightly or wrongly credited with making the trains in his own country run on time, is the Frenchman.

4. A reference to the famous drawing of a sprucely dressed rabbit,

anxiously consulting his watch for fear of being late, drawn by the illustrator Sir John Tenniel (1820-1914) for *Alice's Adventures in Wonderland* (1865) by 'Lewis Carroll' (C. L. Dodgson, 1832–98).

5. 'Babu' was originally a title of respect in India, but in the nineteenth century it came to be used by the British in an ironic or disparaging sense, particularly to describe an Indian clerk or petty official and his veneer of English culture.

6. The London & South Western, running out of Waterloo, was one of the many old railway companies of England. Kipling would have remembered the line from his childhood years at Southsea, 1871–7, with journeys to London. With the mergers brought about by the Railways Act, 1921, the L. & S.W.R. became part of the Southern Railway. The comment about a double roof, etc., is a reference to the railways of India.

7. Osaka was also one of the Treaty Ports, but British subjects did not have the right of permanent residence there as they did at Kobe, where anyhow the foreign trading community generally preferred to be, since access to Osaka harbour was restricted by sandbanks. They could reside in Osaka 'for the purposes of trade only', hiring houses in a designated area. During the Tokugawa era Osaka had been one of the main trading centres of Japan. After the Meiji Restoration it developed as one of Japan's main industrial cities, with many cotton mills. The first modern Japanese mint was established there.

8. The North Western was one of the railway companies of India, one with which Kipling was very familiar. The reference to slow speeds is typical: European travellers on Indian trains were often exasperated by their slowness. Colonel Conway-Gordon was the Director-General of Railways at Lahore. Kipling had mentioned him once before, in an article in the *Civil & Military Gazette* on 18 May 1887 describing the opening of a new railway bridge.

9. Saharunpur (now Saharanpur) and Umballa (now Ambala) are towns in, respectively, Uttar Pradesh and Haryana, in Northern India.

10. E. G. Holtham, a British railway engineer employed in Japan from 1873 to 1881, author of *Eight Years in Japan* published in London in 1883, had noted with amusement on his first visit to the Kobe-Osaka line that

> it appeared that the only known way of passing a stream of water eighteen inches wide under the line, was to build a couple of walls that would have served for the abutments of a fifty-foot bridge, a foot and a half apart, and span the yawning gulf between them by means of beams sixteen inches square, of expensive timber, of sufficient length to have about a dozen feet at each end buried in the embankment behind the masonry. The walls were of finely carved granite and must have cost a mint of money, but a structure of this description was to be found nearly every hundred yards.

11. Patna: a city of Bihar, India, on the Ganges. Kulu: a hill town in Himachal Pradesh, India, north of Simla.
12. *Rajbahars:* a rajbahar (or *rajbaha*) in India was a principal channel in a system of irrigation.
13. Cholera was endemic in nineteenth-century Japan, as it was in India.
14. What Kipling thought was mustard was probably rape.
15. *Dasturi* (from *dastur*, meaning 'custom') is defined in *Hobson-Jobson* as the 'commission or percentage on the money passing in any cash transaction which, with or without acknowledgment or permission, sticks to the fingers of the agent of payment. Such "customary" appropriations are, we believe, very nearly as common in England as in India . . .'.
16. The hotel was in fact called Jutei's not Juter's.
17. A *ghat* is a landing-place on a river bank or a flight of steps leading to it.
18. Victorian prudery (which it is clear from this and other passages that Kipling regretted and did not wholly share) was much shocked by the apparently casual attitude of the Japanese towards nudity. As a result of Victorian strictures the Japanese authorities insisted, for instance, that *jinrikisha* coolies should be 'decently' covered, and forbade mixed bathing in public baths – though in many cases the separation amounted to no more than a piece of rope across the bath!

    Kipling's wry account of this bathroom incident in Osaka finds an echo in a letter he wrote in 1908, advising Lord Milner on how to guard his privacy in Canadian hotels:

    > '. . . disconnect your bedroom telephone . . . Otherwise you will continue to enjoy the horrors of publicity in your bath and in your bed. Allah knows I have long since ceased to be a virgin, but I cannot help blushing when I am rung-up by women – with nothing on but spectacles and a bath-towel. Moreover I find it interferes with the peristaltic process, and Canada is a constipating land.'

19. Lady Godiva was the wife of Leofric, Earl of Mercia, in the eleventh century. According to the legend, when she pleaded with her husband to remit heavy taxation imposed on the citizens of Coventry, he agreed, subject to her riding through the town naked. This, after asking the townsfolk to stay indoors and shutter their windows, she did, making also such use as she could of her long hair.
20. Actaeon, in Greek legend, was a huntsman who, having the misfortune to come across the goddess Artemis bathing naked in a forest pool, was punished by being turned into a stag, whereupon his own hounds tore him to pieces.
21. Osaka Castle was originally built in 1586 by the famous military ruler Toyotomi Hideyoshi (1536–98). In 1615 it was almost completely destroyed after a siege by the Tokugawa forces opposed to Hideyoshi's son, Toyotomi Hideyori, but was later reconstructed by the Tokugawa.

In the civil war of 1868 it was destroyed again by fire. It was finally reconstructed in concrete in 1931.

22. Raighur: probably Raigarh in Madhya Pradesh. Jodhpur: in Rajasthan.

23. Akbar: this was Jelal-ed-din Mohammed, 'Akbar the Great' (1542–1605), the most impressive of the Mogul emperors of India. Scindia or Sindhia: this was the family name of the Maratha rulers of Gwalior (itself noted for its great fortress), who fought against both the Moguls and the British in the seventeenth and eighteenth centuries.

24. Gustave Doré (1833–83), a French painter and book illustrator. The reference is almost certainly to Doré's well-known illustrations to Dante's *Divina Commedia*, with which Kipling was familiar.

25. This was a rifle of Japanese manufacture, the 8 mm Murata of 1887, with an under-barrel tube magazine. From comments made later, in Tokyo, it is clear that Kipling thought it inadequate as a modern weapon: he was probably influenced by the recent issue to the British Army of the Lee-Metford rifle with its clip-fed magazine. In 1897 a new and improved Japanese rifle, modelled on the Mauser, was introduced.

26. An obvious reference to Kipling's close links with army units in India, which had inspired his short stories about the 'Soldiers Three'.

27. This was Alphonse Legros (1837–1911), an artist of French birth who had become a British citizen and was at this time Slade Professor in London. It has been suggested that Kipling had in mind Legros's picture entitled *'Le Bûcheron'* ('The Woodcutter').

28. In Greek myth, Deucalion was a son of Prometheus. When Zeus flooded the earth he and his wife Pyrrha took refuge in an ark. After disembarking on Mount Parnassus in Greece, they followed the instructions of an oracle and threw behind them stones, which thereupon turned into Greeks. This was the 'miracle' to which Kipling and his sweets provided a parallel.

29. In 1868, after the Meiji Restoration, the new government, through a well-known British merchant at Nagasaki, Thomas Glover, bought the old British Mint at Hong Kong. The machinery was sent to Osaka and set up in late 1868 but was destroyed by fire next year. New machinery was then imported from Britain and installed in 1870. Its first director was Major William Kinder, the former head of the Hong Kong Mint: he served in Osaka till 1875.

30. A reference to the Meiji restoration of 1868, twenty-one years earlier.

31. A reference to *Japan: Its History, Traditions and Religions*, including the *Narrative of a Visit in 1879*, by Sir Edward Reed (1830–1906). Reed was a Fellow of the Royal Society, an authority on ship design, and a Member of Parliament for many years. His two-volume book on Japan, published in 1880, can be found on the shelves of Kipling's study at Bateman's, his Sussex home.

32. This is an attempt, on the part of 'the Professor', to explain in a few words, and in contemporary Indian terms, the intricate political events in Japan in 1866–8. The famous soldier Sir Frederick (later Lord)

Roberts (1832–1914) was at this time Commander-in-Chief in India: if he had 'tried to be the Viceroy' of India, some sort of parallel might have been drawn with the avowed aim of supporters of the last of the Tokugawa Shoguns, who did not regard themselves as disloyal to the Imperial throne but as attempting to rescue it from undesirable political influences. But the analogy is not worth pursuing.

33. The Rajputs were a great Hindu class, virtually a race, for whom the profession of arms was traditionally hereditary. Their main home area was in the north-west of India, in Rajputana. They claimed to be the true *Kshatriyas*, i.e. the Warriors, the second of the four fundamental caste divisions of Hindu society, but these identifications are intricate and disputable. The significance and implications of being a Rajput varied confusingly as between different parts of India, and the caste factor was sometimes surprisingly unimportant, as with many Dogra Rajputs in the hills, who had long pedigrees but were prepared to ignore caste rules.

34. Khattri: this usage by Kipling is debatable and probably mistaken. *Khattri* is a Hindi word, derived from the Sanskrit *Kshatriya* (see Note 33). It means the military caste, but was often applied to members of the merchant class. It cannot logically be used as a synonym for a 'lower class'. Few Europeans ever clearly understood Hindu distinctions of caste, class and profession. As Philip Mason in his history of the Indian Army writes, 'nothing in the Indian social and religious system is simple'. He has also commented to us that in the Punjab, with which Kipling was familiar, *Khattri* could be used of Sikhs who had given up the principles of caste and were not of the land-owning class.

35. A *terai* hat is a wide-brimmed felt hat, often with a double crown. It derived its name from being worn by travellers in the Terai or Tarai, a belt of sub-tropical jungly land south of Darjeeling, India.

36. The *Siwaliks* was the name given to the long ranges of hills running parallel with, and subsidiary to, the Himalayas in north-central India and Nepal.

37. Kyoto was in fact built on a grid system on the model of the capital of the T'ang dynasty in China at Chang An.

1889: Letter Five

SHOWS HOW I FOUND MUSSOORIE IN PAHARTIBUS.[1] KYOTO, AND
HOW I FELL IN LOVE WITH THE CHIEF BELLE[2] THERE AFTER I HAD
CONFERRED WITH CERTAIN CHINA MERCHANTS WHO TRAFFICKED IN
TEA. SHOWS FURTHER HOW, IN A GREAT TEMPLE, I BROKE THE
TENTH COMMANDMENT IN FIFTY-THREE PLACES AND BOWED DOWN
BEFORE KANO[3] AND A CARPENTER. TAKES ME TO ARASHIYAMA[4]
BY WAY OF THE FIELDS, WITH A DISSERTATION ON MANURE AND
LANDSCAPES.

> Could I but write the things I see,
> My world would haste to gaze with me.
> But since the traitor Pen hath failed
> To paint earth's loveliness unveiled,
> I can but pray my folk who read –
> For lavish Will take starveling Deed.[5]

There has occurred a mistake somewhere, for we have stumbled into
the Charleville at Mussoorie and are consorting with sixty of the
sahib-log in the quaintest hotel that ever you saw.[6] It stands on the
hillside overlooking the whole town of Kyoto, and its garden is
veritable Japanese. Fantastically trimmed tea trees, junipers, dwarfed
pine, and cherry are mixed up with ponds of gold-fish, stone
lanterns, quaint rock-work, and velvety turf all at an angle of thirty-
five degrees. Behind us the pines, red and black, cover the hill and
run down in a long spur to the town. But an auctioneer's catalogue
cannot describe the charms of the place or deal justly with the tea-
garden full of cherry trees that lies a hundred yards below the hotel.
We were solemnly assured that hardly any one came to Kyoto. That
is why we meet every soul in the ship that had brought us to
Nagasaki and an ex-Commissioner of the Dacca Division[7]; and that
is why our ears are constantly assailed with the clamour of people
who are discussing places which must be 'done.' An Englishman is a
very horrible person when he is on the war-path; so is an American,
a Frenchman, or a German.

I had been watching the afternoon sunlight upon the trees and the town, the shift and play of colour in the crowded street of the cherry, and crooning to myself because the sky was blue and I was alive beneath it with a pair of eyes in my head.

Entered the Professor fresh from a ten-mile expedition in a *'rickshaw*. Two coolies by the way will run you twenty miles for one dollar and thirty cents the pair.

'The Doon has grown a great deal,' said the Professor wiping his forehead. 'It's climbed nearly to the top of the Siwaliks, but I recognized it all the same. I went through the Mohun Pass straight to Rajpur – first-class tea-house at Rajpur – then I went to Mussoorie and beyond to the Kamti Falls. Coming back I stopped at Jerrapani for beer but they hadn't any, so I took *sake*.[8]

'How much *sake*?' I demanded, for the Professor had started on his new geography without warning.

'Only four cents worth – enough to treat all the *'rickshaw* coolies and myself. But it's really true about the Doon. Take a *'rickshaw* and look.'

'What was the place called?'

'Takao. It's one of the places that must be done,' said the Professor.[9]

'Then I won't do it. I'll look it up in the guide-book and pretend that I have been. Was anyone ever killed or cremated at Takao?'

The guide-books gave me no information, and I have been compelled to use the Professor's account. By all means go to Takao if you cannot send a friend there to tell you about it.

I preferred to go to the tea-garden and lie upon a mat studying Japanese, which would be a fine language but for its many giggles. You ask her about the political aspirations of the country and she giggles. You ask her what her name is and she giggles. You ask her to give you a kiss and she giggles worse than ever. But she is always nice, and if she does charge you treble rates for the pleasure of drinking very vile tea, you must remember that the cherry trees are in bloom so very short a time, and that she has to pay for the ground on which they stand all the year round.

Immediately the sun went down behind the hills the air became bitterly cold, but the people in crêpe sashes and silk coats never ceased their sober frolicking. There was to be a great service in honour of the cherry blossom the next day at the chief temple of Kyoto, and they were getting ready for it. As the light died in a wash of crimson, the last thing I saw was a frieze of three little Japanese babies with fuzzy top-knots and huge sashes trying to hang head downwards from a bamboo rail. They did it, and the closing eye of day regarded them solemnly as it shut. The effect in *silhouette* was pyramidal, immense!

A company of China tea-merchants were gathered in the smoking-room after dinner, and by consequence talked their own 'shop', which was interesting. Their language is not our language, for they know nothing of the tea-gardens, of drying and withering and rolling, of the assistant who breaks his collar-bone in the middle of the busiest season, or of the sickness that smites the coolie-lines at about the same time. They are happy men who get their tea by the break of a thousand chests[10] from the interior of the country and play with it upon the London markets. None the less they have a very wholesome respect for Indian tea, which they cordially detest.[11] Here is the sort of argument that a Foochow man, himself a very heavy buyer, flung at me across the table.

'You may talk about your Indian teas, – Assam and Kangra,[12] or whatever you call them, – but I tell *you* that if ever they get a strong hold in England, the doctors will be down on them, Sir. They'll be medically forbidden. See if they aren't. They shatter your nerves to pieces. Unfit for human consumption – that's what they are. Though I don't deny they *are* selling at Home. They don't keep though. After three months, the musters that I've seen in London turn to hay.'

'I think you are wrong there,' said a Hankow man. 'My experience is that the Indian teas keep better than ours by a long way. But' – turning to me – 'if we could only get the China Government to take off the duties, we could smash Indian tea and every one connected with it. We could lay down tea in Mincing Lane[13] at threepence a pound. No, we do not adulterate our teas. That's one of *your* tricks in India. We get it as pure as yours – every chest in the break equal to sample.'

'You can trust your native buyers then?' I interrupted, for the discussion seemed to be growing unpleasantly warm, and after all, now that I had once 'drawn' the Chinaman, it was not my business to talk about what I didn't understand.

'Trust 'em? Of course we can,' cut in the Foochow merchant. 'There are no tea-gardens in China as you understand them. The peasantry cultivate the tea, and the buyers buy from them for cash each season. You can give a Chinaman a hundred thousand dollars and tell him to turn it into tea of your particular chop – up to sample. Of course the man may be a thorough-paced rogue in many ways, but he knows better than to play the fool with an English house. Back comes your tea – a thousand half-chests, we'll say. You open perhaps five, and the balance go Home untried. But they are all equal to sample. That's business, that is. The Chinaman's a born merchant and full of backbone. I like him for business purposes. The Jap's no use. He isn't man enough to handle a hundred thousand dollars. Very possibly he'd run off with it – or try to.'

'The Jap has no business savvy. God knows I hate the Chinaman,' said a bass voice behind the tobacco smoke, 'but you can do business with him. The Jap's a little huckster who can't see beyond his nose.'

They called for drinks and told tales, these merchants of China, – tales of money and bales and boxes, – but through all their stories there was an implied leaning upon native help which, even allowing for the peculiarities of China, was rather startling. 'The comprador did this: Ho Wang did that: a syndicate of Peking bankers did the other thing' – and so on. I wondered whether a certain lordly indifference as to details had anything to do with eccentricities in the China tea-breaks and fluctuations of quality which do occur in spite of all the men said to the contrary. Again, the merchants spoke of China as a place where fortunes are made – a land only waiting to be opened up to pay a hundredfold. They told me of the Home Government helping private trade, in kind and unobtrusive ways, to get a firmer hold on the Public Works Department contracts that are now flying abroad. This was pleasant hearing. But the strangest thing of all was the tone of hope and almost contentment that pervaded their speech. They were well-to-do men making money, and they liked their lives. You know how, when two or three are gathered together in our own barren pauper land, they groan in chorus and are disconsolate. The civilian, the military man, and the merchant, they are all alike with us. The one overworked and broken by Exchange,[13a] the second a highly organised beggar with no hopes, and the third a nobody in particular, always at loggerheads with what he considers an academical Government. I knew in a way that we were a grim and miserable community in India, but I did not know the measure of our fall till I heard men talking about fortunes, success, money, and the pleasure, good living, and frequent trips to England that money brings. Their friends did not seem to die with unnatural swiftness, and their wealth enabled them to endure the calamity of Exchange with calm. Yes, we of India are a wretched folk.

Very early in the dawn, before the nesting sparrows were awake, there was a sound in the air which frightened me out of my virtuous sleep. It was a lisping mutter – very deep and entirely strange. 'That's an earthquake, and the hillside is beginning to slide,' quoth I, taking measures of defence. The sound repeated itself again and again, till I argued, that if it were the precursor of an earthquake, the affair had stuck half-way. At breakfast men said: 'That was the great bell of Kyoto[14] just next door to the hotel a little way up the hillside. As a bell, y'know, it's rather a failure from an English point of view. They don't ring it properly, and the volume of sound is comparatively insignificant.'

'So I fancied when I first heard it,' I said casually, and went out up the hill under sunshine that filled the heart, and trees that filled the eye with joy. You know the unadulterated pleasure of that first clear morning in the Hills when a month's solid idleness lies before the loafer, and the scent of the deodars mixes with the scent of the meditative cigar. That was my portion when I stepped through the violet-studded long grass into forgotten little Japanese cemeteries – all broken pillars and lichened tablets – till I found, under a cut in the hillside, the big bell of Kyoto – twenty feet of green bronze hung inside a fantastically roofed shed of wooden beams. A beam, by the way, *is* a beam in Japan; anything under a foot thick is a stick. These beams were the best parts of big trees, clamped with bronze and iron to withstand the pull of the bell. A knuckle rapped lightly on the lip of the latter – it was not more than five feet from the ground – made the great monster breathe heavily, and the blow of a stick started a hundred shrill-voiced echoes round the darkness of its dome. At one side, guyed by half a dozen small hawsers, hung a battering-ram, a twelve-foot spar bound with iron, its nose pointing full-butt at a chrysanthemum in high relief on the belly of the bell. Then by special favour of Providence, which always looks after a loafer, they began to sound sixty strokes. Half a dozen men swung the ram back and forth with shoutings and outcries, till it had gathered sufficient way, and the loosened ropes let it hurl itself against the chrysanthemum. The boom of the smitten bronze was swallowed up by the earth below and the hillside behind, so that its volume was not proportionate to the size of the bell, exactly as the men had said. An English hanger would have made thrice as much of it. But then he would have lost the crawling jar that ran through rock-stone and pine for twenty yards round, that beat through the body of the listener and died away under his feet like the shock of a distant blasting. I endured twenty strokes and removed myself, not in the least ashamed of mistaking the sound for an earthquake. Many times since I have heard the bell speak when I was far off. It says *B-r-r-r* very deep down in its throat, but when you have once caught the noise you will never forget it. And so much for the big bell of Kyoto.

From its house a staircase of cut stone takes you down to a

maidan[15] and the temple of Chion-in, where I arrived on Easter Sunday just before service,[16] and in time to see the procession of the Cherry Blossom. They had a special service at a place called St. Peter's at Rome about the same time, but the priests of Buddha excelled the priests of the Pope. Thus it happened. The main front of the temple was three hundred feet long, a hundred feet deep, and sixty feet high. One roof covered it all, and saving for the tiles there was no stone in the structure; nothing but wood three hundred years old, as hard as iron. The pillars that upheld the roof were three feet, four feet, and five feet in diameter, and guiltless of any paint. They showed the natural grain of the wood till they were lost in the rich brown darkness far overhead. The cross-beams were of grained wood of great richness; cedar-wood and camphor-wood and the hearts of gigantic pine had been put under requisition for the great work. One carpenter – they call him only a carpenter – had designed the whole, and his name is remembered to this day. A half of the temple was railed off for the congregation by a two-foot railing, over which silks of ancient device had been thrown. Within the railing were all the religious fittings, but these I cannot describe. All I remember was row upon row of little lacquered stands each holding a rolled volume of sacred writings; an altar as tall as a cathedral organ where gold strove with colour, colour with lacquer, and lacquer with inlay; and candles such as Holy Mother Church uses only on her greatest days shed a yellow light that softened all. Bronze incense-burners in the likeness of dragons and devils fumed under the shadow of silken banners, behind which, wood tracery, as delicate as frost on a window-pane, climbed to the ridge-pole. Only there was no visible roof to this temple. The light faded away under the monstrous beams, and we might have been in a cave a hundred fathoms below the earth but for the sunshine and blue sky at the portals, where the little children squabbled and shouted.

On my word, I tried to note down soberly what lay before me, but the eye tired, and the pencil ran off into fragmentary ejaculations. But what would you have done if you had seen what I saw when I went round the temple verandah to what we must call a vestry at the back? It was a big building connected with the main one by a wooden bridge of deepest time-worn brown. Down the bridge ran a line of saffron-coloured matting, and down the matting, very slowly and solemnly, as befitted their high office, filed three-and-fifty priests, each one clad in at least four garments of brocade, crêpe, and silk. There were silks that do not see the light of the markets, and brocades that only temple wardrobes know.

Even to a mere male mind they were marvellous beyond description because they were so utterly different from anything before
seen. Their effect upon the otherwise well-conducted lady among
the onlookers was startling. 'Oh! Stop them, stop them,' she
murmured as the high priest in purple velvet and brocaded stole
rustled past her, 'stop them and – and kill them.' Then plaintively:-
'You know one of those dresses would make me happy for life, and
here are more than I can count: isn't it wicked?' I could not answer
her soberly, for in my mind too were wicked thoughts of looting and
a rush by the next train to the sea.

There was nothing in the passport against stealing sea-green
watered silk with golden dragons; or terra-cotta crêpe with
ivory-white chrysanthemums clustering upon it; or black-barred silk
shot with yellow flames; or lapis-lazuli silk and silver fishes; or
avanturine silk with plaques of grey-green let in; or cloth of gold
over dragon's blood; or saffron and brown silk stiff as a board with
embroidery. Mercifully the last priest and the last little acolyte went
by ere crime had overcome me, and we returned to the temple now
filled with gorgeous robes. The little lacquer stands were the priests'
book-racks. Some lay down among them, while others moved very
softly about the golden altars and the incense-burners; and the high
priest disposed himself, with his back to the congregation, in a
golden chair through which his robe winked like the shards of a
tiger-beetle.

Write it down to my credit that I was only calm with the calmness
of despair. I knew the thing was beyond my pen. But the Professor's
camera was just outside the temple ready to be unpacked, and neither
prayers nor pice[17] availed to get it inside. Wherefore the Professor went dancing-mad with suppressed photography, and so
missed the solemn calm of the opening service when the books
were unrolled, and the priests began chanting Pali texts[18] in
honour of the Apostle of Unworldliness, who had written that they
were not to wear gold or mixed colours, or touch the precious
metals. But for a few unimportant accessories in the way of half-seen
images of great men – but these could have been called saints – the
scene before me might have been unrolled in a Roman Catholic
cathedral, say the rich one at Arundel.[19] The same thought was in
other minds, for in a pause of the slow chant a voice behind me
whispered:–

To hear the blessed mutter of the mass
And see God made and eaten all day long.[20]

It was a man from Hong Kong, very angry that he too had not been permitted to photograph an interior. He called all this splendour of ritual and paraphernalia just 'an interior,' and revenged himself by spitting Browning at it.

The chant quickened as the service drew to an end, and the candles burned low. I had been meditating much fine writing and many hot pressed reflections on the vanity of things earthly, together with a complete inventory of all the temple fittings and a history of Buddha, when I found myself humming in time with the ever-quickening drone of the priests the burden of a classic song. Perhaps you know it –

'Hya! Hya! Hya! Twist their tails and go!' There was no mistake about the thing and I burst out laughing to the scandal of the pious English. The Japanese did not care.

'What's the trouble?' said the Professor.

'Listen to 'em – "And that's the way we sing all day, when hunting the buffalo." It may be Pali that they are reading but they are singing 'The Byle Battery'[21] or may I live and die in India.'

We went away to other parts of the temple pursued by the chorus of the devout till we were out of earshot in a paradise of screens. Two or three hundred years ago there lived a painterman of the name of Kano. Him the temple of Chion-in brought to beautify the walls of the rooms.[22] Since a wall is a screen, and a screen is a wall, Kano, R.A., had rather a large job. But he was helped by pupils and imitators, and in the end left a few hundred screens which are all finished pictures. As you already know, the interior of a temple is very simple in its arrangements. The priests live on white mats, in little rooms, with brown ceilings, that can at pleasure be thrown into one large room. This also was the arrangement at Chion-in, though the rooms were comparatively large and gave on to sumptuous verandahs and passages. Since the Emperor occasionally visited the place, there was a room set apart for him of more than ordinary splendour. Twisted silk tassels of intricate design served in lieu of catches to pull back the sliding screens, and the woodwork was lacquered. These be only feeble words, but it is not in my grip to express the restfulness of it all, or the power that knew how to secure the desired effect with a turn of the wrist. The great Kano drew numbed pheasants huddled together on the snow-covered bough of a pine; or a peacock in his pride spreading his tail to delight his womenfolk; or a riot of chrysanthemums poured out of a vase; or the figures of toilworn countryfolk coming home from market; or a hunting scene at the foot of Fujiyama. The equally great carpenter who built the temple framed each picture with absolute precision under a ceiling that was a miracle of device, and Time, the greatest artist of the three, touched the gold so that it became amber, and the woodwork so that it grew dark honey-colour, and the shining surface of the lacquer so that it became deep and rich and semi-transparent. As in one room, so in all the others. Sometimes we slid back the screens and discovered a tiny bald-pated acolyte praying over an incense-burner, and sometimes a lean priest eating his rice; but generally the rooms were empty, swept and garnished.

Minor artists had worked with Kano the magnificent. These had been allowed to lay brush upon panels of wood in the outer verandahs, and very faithfully had they toiled. It was not till the guide called my attention to them that I discovered scores of sketches in monochrome low down on the verandah doors. An iris broken by the fall of a branch torn off by a surly ape; a bamboo spray bowed before the wind that was ruffling a lake; a warrior of the past ambushing his enemy in a thicket, hand on sword, and mouth gathered into puckers of intensest concentration, were among the many notes that met my eye. How long, think you, would a sepia-drawing stand without defacement in the midst of our civilisation were it put on the bottom panel of a door, or the scantling of a kitchen passage? Yet in this gentle country a man may stoop down and write his name in the very dust, certain that, if the writing be craftily done, his children's children will reverently let it stand.

'Of course there are no such temples made nowadays,' I said, when we regained the sunshine, and the Professor was trying to find out how panel pictures and paper screens combined so well with the dark dignity of massive woodwork.

'They are building a temple on the other side of the city,' said Mister Yamaguchi. 'Come along, and see the hair-ropes which hang there.'

We came flying in our *'rickshaws* across the very large town of Kyoto, till we saw netted in a hundred cobwebs of scaffolding a temple even larger than the great Chion-in.[23]

'That was burned down long ago, – the old temple that was here, you know. Then the people made a penny subscription from all parts of Japan, and those who could not send money sent their hair to be made into rope. They have been ten years building this new temple. It is all wood,' said the guide.

The place was alive with men who were putting the finishing touches to the great tiled roof and laying down the floors. Wooden pillars as gigantic, carving as wantonly elaborate, eaves as intricate in their mouldings, and joinery as perfect as anything in the Chion-in temple met me at every turn. But the fresh-cut wood was creamy white and lemon where, in the older building, it had been iron-hard and brown. Only the raw ends of the joists were stopped with white lacquer to prevent the incursions of insects, and the deeper tracery was protected against birds by fine wire netting. Everything else was wood – wood down to the massive clamped and bolted beams of the foundation which I investigated through gaps in the flooring. After that the hair ropes – ten inch hawsers with human hair wove into the strands – were uninteresting. I wanted to sit down and see that temple filled up – it will be finished in another five years or so – but the guide bore me away.

Verily Japan is a great people. Her masons play with stone, her carpenters with wood, her smiths with iron, and her artists with life, death, and all the eye can take in. Mercifully she has been denied the last touch of firmness in her character which would enable her to play with the whole round world. We possess that – we, the nation of the glass flower-shade, the pink worsted mat, the red and green china puppy dog, and the poisonous Brussels carpet. It is our compensation . . .

'Temples!' said a man from Calcutta, some hours later, as I raved about what I had seen. 'Temples! I'm sick of temples. If I've seen one, I've seen fifty thousand of 'em – all exactly alike. But I tell you what is exciting. Go down the rapids at Arashiyama, – eight miles from here. It's better fun than any temple with a fat-faced Buddha in the middle.'

There are Englishmen who in another world will cavil at the smoothness of the Glassy Sea[24] and demand excitement at the door of St. Peter.

But I took my friend's advice, and the Professor his camera, and together upon a lovely morning we went into the district. Have I by the way managed to convey the impression that April is fine in Japan? Then I apologise. It is generally rainy, and the rain is cold; but the sunshine when it comes is worth it all. We shouted with joy of living when our fiery, untamed 'rickshaws bounded from stone to stone of the vilely paved streets of the suburbs and brought us into what ought to have been vegetable gardens but were called fields. The face of the flat lands was cut up in every direction by bunds, and all the roads seem to run on top of them.

'Never,' said the Professor, driving his stick into the black soil, 'never have I imagined irrigation so perfectly controlled as this is. Look at the *rajbahars* faced with stone and fitted with sluices; look at the water-wheels and, – phew! but they manure their fields too well.'

The first circle of fields round any town is always pretty rank, but this superfluity of scent continued throughout the country. Saving a few parts near Dacca and Patna, the face of the land was more thickly populated than Bengal and was worked five times better. There was no single patch untilled, and no cultivation that was not up to the full limit of the soil's productiveness. Onions, barley, in little ridges between the ridges of tea, beans, rice, and a half a dozen other things that we did not know the names of, crowded the eye already wearied with the glare of the golden mustard. Manure is a good thing, but manual labour is better. We saw both even to excess. When a Japanese *ryot*[25] has done everything to his field that he can possibly think of, he weeds the barley stalk by stalk with his finger and thumb. This is true. I saw a man doing it.

When you have taken in the nature of the country and its value per square yard, you understand why there are so few cattle abroad. We met a few strings of country carts bringing in *sake* in great white tubs bound with green withies. A cartload of *sake* smells like a spilt glass of sherry.

'How the dickens do they manage the carts?' said the Professor as his *'rickshaw* drew aside on the edge of a twenty-foot bund to let half-a-dozen pass. The bullocks were big black beasts very deep in the shoulder, and built about the head exactly like a bison according to the picture books. A bison with his mane off, *bien entendu*. They rolled red eyes at us under the shag of their foreheads as they hauled each one a two-wheeled beer-cart not more than three feet six in width and any length you please. The traces were ten or twelve feet long and the beasts pulled partly from an absurd little yoke not a foot long, made of a crooked stick, and partly from a pack-saddle closely resembling an *ekka*[26] pony's fitment, tightly fixed with rope behind the withers. The advantage of this shape of cart I understood later when I saw a man bring one down a steep hill. He used the tail-end as a skid and so avoided killing my precious self. But for the life of me I could not see why a bullock should pull half-a-dozen yards away from the cart – especially when he was walking on a narrow road with a steep drop on either side, and more especially when he was not being coerced in any way. I have seen no goad nor have I heard an angry word among the bullock drivers of the country since I have been in it. One could not be half a day in Bombay without noticing some brutality that would make one kick the man. And an Indian *byle wallah*[27] can sit on the pole; he has not to keep the balance of a long-tailed cart with his hands and attend to a bullock at the same time.

This is a digression. We headed through the marvellous country straight across the plain on which Kyoto stands, till we reached the range of hills on the far side and found ourselves mixed up with half a mile of lumber-yard.

'Bless de Lord, *now* I know where their timber comes from,' said the Professor piously. The matter had lain on his mind for a week or more. Cultivation and water-cuts were gone, and our tireless *jhampanis*[28] were running by the side of a broad, shallow river, choked with logs of every size. I am prepared to believe anything of the Japanese, but I do not see why Nature, which they say is the same pitiless Power all the world over, should send them their logs unsplintered by rocks, neatly barked, and with a slot neatly cut at the end of each pole for the reception of a rope. The Professor says that they make this last convenience with their own hands. I have seen timber fly down the Ravi[29] in spate, and it was hooked out as ragged as a tooth-brush. This material comes down clean. Consequently the slot is another miracle.

'When the day is fine,' said the guide softly, 'all the people of Kyoto come to Arashiyama to have picnics.'

'But they are always having picnics in the cherry-tree gardens. They picnic in the tea-houses. They – they –'

'Yes, when it is a fine day, they always go somewhere and picnic.'

'But why? Man isn't made to picnic.'

'But why? Because it is a fine day. Englishmen say that the money of the Japanese comes from heaven, because they always do nothing – so you think. But look now, here is a pretty place.'

The river charged down a turn in the pine-grown hills, and broke in silver upon the timber and the remains of a light bridge washed away some days before. On our side, and arranged so as to face the fairest view of the young maples, stood a row of tea-houses and booths built over the stream. The sunlight that could not soften the gloom of the pines dwelt tenderly among the green of the maples, and touched the reaches below where the cherry blossom broke in pink foam against the black-roofed houses of a village across the water.

There I stopped.

'OUR TIRELESS *JHAMPANIS*' (p. 94)

With more artistic licence than fidelity, Kipling is depicted in this illustration from *Lettres du Japon*. He and the Professor, conveyed by *'nos pousse-pousse infatigables'*, are wending through the hills beside the log-choked river, towards Arashiyama where, at blossom-time, the citizens of Kyoto *'sont toujours en pique-niques dans les jardins de cerisiers'*.

'JAPANESE MAIDS OF FOURTEEN OR FIFTEEN' (p. 134)

As they bathe and frolic in the hot springs at Miyanoshita, *'De jeunes Japonaises de quatorze ou quinze ans ne sont pas des plus désagréables à contempler'*. However this illustration from *Lettres du Japon* (1925) would hardly have found favour in 1889, though Kipling noted that the girls – in contrast to contemporary European, or Indian, inhibitions – were no whit disconcerted at being seen.

1889: LETTER FIVE
COMMENTARY

1. Mussoorie (strictly, in origin, Mansuri) was a hill station in what is now Uttar Pradesh, India: see also Note 8 below. In Kipling's day Mussoorie probably already had the reputation it certainly had soon after, of being the focus of a holiday life that was rather too 'fast' to be respectable. It came to be commonly said, in jest, that anyone who took his own wife to a Mussoorie hotel was charged corkage. As for *in pahartibus*, this is a pun on the word *pahari*, a hillman: Kipling is echoing ecclesiastical usage, whereby *in partibus* (with the word *infidelium* understood) meant abroad in a non-Christian country.

2. A punning reference to the great bell at the Chion-in temple.

3. Kano (after the artist Kano Masanobu, 1434–1530) was the name of a school of painting which developed in Japan in the sixteenth century, influenced by the painters of China's Ming dynasty. Instead of the subtle lines of the *sumi-e* (black and white) painters of the school of Sesshu they used gorgeous colours and bold decorative motifs. Painters of the Kano school adopted the surname Kano: among the most important were Eitoku (1543–90), Motonobu (1476–1559), Naonobu (1607–50), Mitsunobu (1597–1623), Sanraku (1559–1635) and Tanyu (1602–74).

4. Arashiyama (which Kipling misspelt as 'Arashima') remains a popular picnic spot for the inhabitants of Kyoto. It lies on the Katsura river just where the river emerges from a picturesque gorge. *Murray's Handbook for Japan* (1894 edition) notes that 'The place boasts some good tea-houses, especially the Nakamura-ya and Hototogisu'.

5. Kipling has been assumed to be the author of these lines.

6. This was Yaami's Hotel, as is apparent from Letter Six. It was in Maruyama, Kyoto, and with seventy-five rooms was one of the principal hotels used by foreign travellers in late nineteenth-century Japan. In style it was part-Japanese, part-European. It no longer exists. The Charleville was a Mussoorie hotel.

7. Dacca, or Dhaka, was a major city and administrative division in Eastern Bengal, and is now the capital of Bangladesh.

8. In India, a *doon* or *dun* was a valley, or more accurately a plateau among hills. The best-known, to which the Professor is referring as 'the Doon', was Dehra Dun, which, being a railhead town at an altitude of 2250 ft, with a healthy district adjoining, was half-way to being a hill station. The approach by road to Mussoorie, at 6750 ft, began at Dehra Dun and ascended by way of Rajpur (3000 ft) and Jharipani (5000 ft). The Professor, in comparing the scenery around Kyoto to that around Mussoorie in the Siwalik Hills, was making an illustration that would be instantly recognizable by many readers of the *Pioneer*.

9. Takao was celebrated for its maples. *Murray's Handbook for Japan* (1894 edition) noted that there was a tea-house at the top of the hill, 'with a delightful prospect, offering an excellent spot for a picnic'.
10. A chest of tea weighed 84 pounds: a break was a bulk consignment.
11. The trade rivalry between China and Indian teas was very keen. The Indian tea-trade was relatively recent, dating only from the 1830s, and the Ceylon trade began forty years later than that. Suggestions by the China merchants that tea from India and Ceylon was bad for health were commonplace.
12. Assam: north-east India, centre of tea industry. Kangra: in the Punjab.
13. Mincing Lane in the City of London was the focus of the tea-trade, where the annual auctions took place on arrival of the sea-borne tea.
13a. A reference to the chronic fall in the value of the rupee (from 2 shillings in 1873 to 1 shilling 4 pence by 1890). It caused hardship to expatriates in India (e.g. remitting funds to Britain for education). Not till 1893, when the rate reached 1 shilling 2 pence, were expatriate officials granted an exchange compensation allowance.
14. The 'great bell of Kyoto' was the bell of the Chion-in temple. It is hung in its own pavilion on high ground near the temple. It was cast in 1633 and is the largest bell of its kind in Japan, 5.4 metres high, 2.7 in diameter, and weighing 74 tons.
15. The term *maidan* was very common in India, meaning a planned space of open ground, or a *piazza*, in a town.
16. The Chion-in temple is one of the largest and most famous in Kyoto, and its grounds are extensive. The main hall and adjacent buildings were constructed between 1633 and 1639. The O-Hojo and Ko-Hojo (large and small reception rooms) lie behind the main hall, forming part of what was a palace used by high-ranking visitors. Its sliding screens are decorated by gorgeous paintings by artists of the Kano school, most notably Naonobu, Naomasa, Eitoku and Tanyu. The temple was used by the British Legation in March 1868 when Sir Harry Parkes, the British Minister, made his first visit to Kyoto to pay his respects to the young Emperor Mutsuhito. 1868 was the year of the end of the Tokugawa shogunate and the so-called Imperial restoration: it was a time of turmoil, and anti-foreign feelings were strong. On his way to the Palace, Parkes and his party were attacked by masterless *samurai* (called *ronin*); seven members of the escort were wounded and Sir Harry narrowly escaped assassination. The call was postponed, and the Chion-in temple became an improvised hospital for the wounded.
17. *Pice* is here used colloquially to mean 'money'. Strictly, under the system of currency prevailing in Kipling's day, a pice (from the Hindi *paisa*) was a small copper coin amounting to one quarter of an anna, and therefore one sixty-fourth of a rupee.
18. Many of the sacred texts of Buddhism are in Pali, a dead Indian language of great antiquity.
19. At Arundel, in Sussex, the castle and the Catholic cathedral of St Philip

Neri are among the landmarks that dominate the town. The castle is the seat of the Dukes of Norfolk, who have traditionally been Catholic. The 15th Duke built the cathedral in 1868–69.

20. The quotation comes from a passage in 'The Bishop Orders his Tomb at Saint Praxed's Church', by Robert Browning (1812–89):

> And then how shall I lie through centuries,
> And hear the blessed mutter of the mass,
> And see God made and eaten all day long,
> And feel the steady candle-flame, and taste
> Good strong thick stupefying incense-smoke!

21. We have not traced this song, which readers with Indian Army connections are likely to have known. A *byle* was an ox or bullock. A Byle Battery was a battery of artillery hauled by bullocks, as used by the Indian Army into this century. In the story 'Her Majesty's Servants' (*The Jungle Book*) Kipling describes 'the great sulky white bullocks that drag the heavy siege-guns when the elephants won't go any nearer to the firing'.

22. The reference is to the O-Hojo and Ko-Hojo (See Note 16 above).

23. Kipling is referring to the Higashi Honganji, which had been destroyed by fire in 1864 and was being rebuilt. It is one of the largest temples in Japan, its main building being 210 feet long, 170 broad and 120 high. *Murray's Handbook* (1894 edition) recorded that 'the rebuilding of this grand temple has been a strictly popular enterprise'.

24. A reference to lines from a hymn by Bishop Heber (1783–1826):

> Holy, Holy, Holy! All the Saints adore Thee,
> Casting down their golden crowns around the glassy sea.

The image is derived from *Revelation*, 4, 6–10.

25. A *ryot* (from the Urdu, *raiyat*) was an Indian peasant or cultivator – in essence a 'subject', who paid taxes. The term was used all over India.

26. An *ekka* pony was the pony that pulled a springless one-horse conveyance, widely used in India. It was called an *ekka* by derivation from the Hindi *ek*, 'one'. It might be compared to a small pony-trap with a canopy but no seats.

27. A *byle wallah* would be the man in charge of the *byle* or bullock. The word *wallah*, which long ago entered the English language from India, is a distortion of a Hindi verbal affix, *-wala*, which by transference came to be commonly attached to a noun to convey relationship or custody.

28. For comment on *jhampanis* see Letter 9 of 1889, Note 9.

29. The Ravi is a major river of the Punjab. It flowed by Lahore and was familiar to Kipling.

1889: Letter Six

THE PARTY IN THE PARLOUR WHO PLAYED GAMES. A COMPLETE
HISTORY OF ALL MODERN JAPANESE ART; A SURVEY OF THE PAST,
AND A PROPHECY OF THE FUTURE, ARRANGED AND COMPOSED IN
THE KYOTO FACTORIES.

'Oh, brave new world that has such creatures in it,
How beautiful mankind is!'[1]

And so I lay at Arashiyama which is near Kyoto, in a yellow straw
tea-house overlooking the beautiful river of which I have written,
my mouth full of fried mountain trout and my soul soaking in a great
calm.

How I got to the tea-house I cannot tell. Perhaps a pretty girl
waved a bough of cherry-blossom at me, and I followed the
invitation. I know that I sprawled upon the mats and watched the
clouds scudding across the hills and the logs flying down the rapids,
and smelt the smell of the raw peeled timber, and listened to the
grunts of the boatmen as they wrestled with that and the rush of the
river, and was altogether happier than it is lawful for a struggling
mortal to be.

The lady of the tea-house insisted upon screening us off from the
other pleasure-parties who were tiffining in the same verandah, and
we were left alone with the trout. She brought beautiful blue screens
with storks on them and slid them into grooves. I stood it as long as I
could. There were peals of laughter in the next compartment, the
pattering of soft feet, the clinking of little dishes, and at the chinks of
the screens the twinkle of diamond eyes. A whole family had come
in from Kyoto for the day's pleasuring. Mamma looked after
grandmamma, and the young aunt looked after a guitar,[2] and the
two girls of fourteen and fifteen looked after a merry little tomboy of
eight, who, when she thought of it, looked after the baby who had
the air of looking after the whole party. The tea girls flitted in and
out and attended to the wants of all. Grandmamma was dressed in
dark blue, mamma in blue and grey, the girls had gorgeous dresses

98

of lilac, fawn, and primrose crêpe with silk sashes, the colour of apple-blossom and the inside of a newly-cut melon; the tomboy was in old gold and russet brown; but the baby tumbled his fat little body across the floor among the dishes in the colours of the Japanese rainbow, which owns no crude tints. They were all pretty, all except grandmamma, who was merely good-humoured and very bald, and when they had finished their dainty dinner, and the brown lacquer stands, the blue and white crockery, and the jade-green drinking cups had been taken away, the aunt played a little piece on the *samisen*, and the girls played blindman's-buff all round the tiny room.

Flesh and blood could not have stayed on the other side of the screens. I wanted to play too, but I was too big and too rough, and so could only sit in the verandah, watching these dainty bits of Dresden[3] at their game. They shrieked and giggled and chattered and sat down on the floor with the innocent abandon of maidenhood, and broke off to pet the baby when he showed signs of being overlooked as babies will. They played puss-in-the-corner, their feet tied with blue and white handkerchiefs because the room did not allow unfettered freedom of limb, and when they could play no more for laughing, they fanned themselves as they lay propped up against the blue screens, – each girl a picture no painter could reproduce, – and I shrieked with the best of them till I rolled off the verandah and nearly dropped into the laughing street. Was I a fool? Then I fooled in good company; for an austere man from India – a person who puts his faith in race-horses and believes nothing except the Civil Code – was also at Arashiyama that day among some sweetmeat sellers' stalls on the bank of the river. I met him flushed and excited.

''Had a lively time,' he panted, with a hundred children at his heels. 'There's a sort of roulette-table here where you can gamble for half-pice cakes. I bought the owner's stock-in-trade for three dollars and ran the Monte Carlo[4] for the benefit of the kids – about five thousand of 'em. Never had such fun in my life. It beats the Simla[5] lotteries hollow. They were perfectly orderly till they had cleared the tables of everything except a big sugar tortoise. Then they rushed the bank, and I ran away.'

And he was a hard man who had not played with anything so innocent as sweetmeats for many years!

But to return. When we were all weak with laughing, and the Professor's camera was mixed up in a tangle of laughing maidens to the confusion of his pictures, we too ran away from the tea-house and wandered down the river bank till we found a boat of sewn planks which poled us across the swollen river, and landed us on a little rocky path overhanging the water where the iris and the violet ran riot together and jubilant waterfalls raced through the undergrowth of pine and maple. We were at the foot of the Arashiyama rapids, and all the pretty girls of Kyoto were with us looking at the view. Upstream a lonely black pine stood out from all its fellows to peer up the bend where the racing water ran deep in oily swirls. Downstream the river threshed across the rocks and troubled the fields of fresh logs on its bosom, while men in blue drove silver-white boats gunwale-deep into the foam of its onset and hooked the logs away. Underfoot the rich earth of the hillside sent up the breath of the turn of the year to the maples that had already caught the message from the fire-winds of April. Oh! it was good to be alive, to trample the lush stalks of the iris, to drag down the cherry-bloom spray in a wash of dew across the face, and to gather the violets for the mere pleasure of heaving them into the torrent and reaching out for fairer flowers.

'What a nuisance it is to be a slave to the camera!' said the Professor, upon whom the dumb influences of the season were working though he knew it not.

'What a nuisance it is to be a slave to the pen,' I answered, for the spring had come to the land. I had hated the spring for seven years because to me it meant discomfort.[6] 'Let us go straight Home and see the flowers come out in the Parks.'

'Let us enjoy what lies to our hand, you Philistine.' And we did till a cloud darkened and a wind ruffled the river-reaches, and we returned to our '*rickshaws* sighing with contentment.

'How many people do you suppose the land supports to the square mile?' said the Professor, at a turn in the homeward road. He had been reading statistics.

'Nine hundred,' I said at a venture. 'It's thicker set with humans than Sarun or Behar.[7] Say one thousand.'

'Two thousand two hundred and fifty odd. It *is* thicker set than Behar. Can you believe it?'

'Looking at the landscape I can, but I don't suppose many Collectors in India will believe it. S'pose I write fifteen hundred?'

'They'll say you exaggerate just the same. Better stick to the true total. Two thousand two hundred and fifty-six to the square mile, and not a sign of poverty in the houses. How do they do it?'

I should like to know the answer to that question. Japan of my limited view is inhabited almost entirely by little children whose duty is to prevent their elders from becoming too frivolous. The babies do a little work occasionally, but their parents interfere by petting them. At Yami's hotel[8] the attendance is in the hands of ten-year-olds because everybody else has gone out picnicking among the cherry-trees. The little imps find time to do a man's work and to scuffle on the staircase between whiles. My special servitor, called 'The Bishop' on account of the gravity of his appearance, his blue apron, and gaiters, is the liveliest of the lot, but even his energy cannot account for the Professor's statistics of population. . . .

I have seen one sort of work among the Japanese, but it was not the kind that makes crops. It was purely artistic. A ward of the city of Kyoto is devoted to manufactures. A manufacturer in this part of the world does not hang out a sign. He may be known in Paris and New York: that is the concern of the two cities. The Englishman who wishes to find his establishment in Kyoto has to hunt for him up and down slums with the aid of a guide. I have seen three manu-factories. The first was of porcelain-ware, the second of *cloisonnée*, and the third of lacquer, inlay, and bronzes. The first was behind black wooden palings, and for external appearance might just as well have been a tripe-shop. Inside sat the manager opposite a tiny garden, four feet square, in which a papery-looking palm grew out of a coarse stoneware pot and overshadowed a dwarfed pine. The rest of the room was filled with pottery waiting to be packed – modern Satsuma[9] for the most part, the sort of thing you buy at a Mussoorie auction, or even nearer to Allahabad.[10]

'This made send Europe – India – America,' said the manager calmly. 'You come to see?'

He took us along a verandah of polished wood to the kilns, to the clay vats, and the yards where the tiny 'saggers' were awaiting their complement of pottery. There are differences many and technical between Japanese and Burslem pottery[11] in the making, but these are of no consequence. In the moulding house, where they were making the bodies of Satsuma vases, the wheels, all worked by hand, ran true as a hair. The potter sat on a clean mat with his tea-things at his side. When he had turned out a vase-body he saw that it was good, nodded appreciatively to himself, and poured out some tea ere starting the next one. The potters lived close to the kilns and had nothing pretty to look at. It was different in the painting rooms which were reached by way of one or two Japanese gardens full of quaint flowers and the sound of the spring breezes. Here in a cabinet-like house sat the men, women, and boys who painted the designs on the vases after the first firing. That all their arrangements were scrupulously neat is only saying that they were Japanese; that their surroundings were fair and proper is only saying that they were artists. A sprig of a cherry-blossom stood out defiantly against the black of the garden paling; a gnarled pine cut the blue of the sky with its spiky splinters as it lifted itself above the paling, and in a little pond the iris and the horsetail nodded to the wind. The workers when at fault had only to lift their eyes, and Nature herself would graciously supply the missing link of a design. Somewhere in dirty England men dream of craftsmen working under conditions which shall help and not stifle the half-formed thought.[12] They even form guilds and write semi-rhythmical prayers to Time and Chance and all the other Gods that they worship, to bring about the desired end. Would they have their dream realised, let them see how they make pottery in Japan, each man sitting on a snowy mat with loveliness of line and colour within arm's length of him, while with downcast eyes he – splashes in the conventional diaper of a Satsuma vase as fast as he can! The Barbarians want Satsuma and they shall have it, if it has to be made in Kyoto one piece per twenty minutes. So much for the baser forms of the craft.

I saw others as good and as true as the eye could wish in grey, blue, violet, imitation Imari, royal Kaga and half a dozen other varieties of the worked clay which ignorance debars me from naming.[13]

The badness of the bad things I could describe at length: of the good I only know that they were desirable. With smiles and blandishments I besought an aged man who controlled the fat little boys and the pleasant-faced women to show me his pattern-book.

'No patterns. These come out of my head,' he grunted.

Now he lied, for the branch of cherry blossom he had just put on the side of a peach-bloom vase was borrowed from the garden without.

'Providence has given 'em neat hands, pleasant places to sit in and all their patterns growing and blowing. Instead of which they squat upon the floor making ormolu[14] Satsuma for cheap shops at home. I suppose it pays 'em,' said the Professor, as we left the calm of that place in search of *cloisonnée*.

The owner of the second establishment lived in a blackwood cabinet – it was profanation to call it a house – alone with a bronze of priceless workmanship, a set of blackwood furniture, and all the medals that his work had won for him in England, France, Germany, and America. He was a very quiet and cat-like man, and spoke almost in a whisper. Would we be pleased to inspect the manufactory? He led us through a garden – it was nothing in his eyes, but we stopped to admire long. Stone lanterns, green with moss, peeped through clumps of papery bamboos where bronze storks were pretending to feed. A dwarfed pine, its foliage trimmed to dish-like plaques, threw its arms far across a fairy pond where the fat, lazy carp grubbed and rooted, and a couple of eared grebes squawked at us from the protection of the – water-butt. So perfect was the silence of the place that we heard the cherry-blossoms falling into the water and the lisping of the fish against the stones. We were in the very heart of the Willow-Pattern Plate[15] and loath to move for fear of breaking it. The Japanese are born bower-birds.[16] They collect water-worn stones, quaintly-shaped rocks, and veined pebbles for the ornamentation of their homes. When they shift house they lift the garden away with them – pine trees and all – and the incoming tenant has a free hand.

Half a dozen steps took us over the path of mossy stones to a house where the whole manufactory was at work. One room held the enamel powders all neatly arranged in jars of scrupulous cleanliness, a few blank copper vases ready to be operated on, an invisible bird who whistled and whooped in his cage somewhere near the ceiling, and a case of gaily painted butterflies ready for reference when patterns were wanted. In the next room sat the manufactory – three men, five women, and two boys – all as silent as sleep. It is one thing to read of *cloisonnée* making, but quite another to watch it being made. I began to understand the cost of the ware when I saw a man working out a pattern of sprigs and butterflies on a plate about ten inches in diameter. With finest silver ribbon wire, set on edge, less than the sixteenth of an inch high, he followed the curves of the drawing at his side, pinching the wire into tendrils and the serrated outlines of leaves with infinite patience. A rough touch on the raw copper-plate would have sent the pattern flying into a thousand disconnected threads. When all was put down on the copper, the plate would be warmed just sufficiently to allow the wires to stick firmly to the copper, the pattern then showing in raised lines. Followed the colouring, which was done by little boys in spectacles. With a pair of tiniest steel chopsticks they filled from bowls at their side each compartment of the pattern with its proper hue of paste. There is not much room allowed for error in filling the spots on a butterfly's wing with avanturine[17] enamel when the said wings are less than an inch across. I watched the delicate play of wrist and hand till I was wearied, and the manager showed me his patterns – terrible dragons, clustered chrysanthemums, butterflies, and diapers as fine as frost on a window-pane – all drawn in unerring line. 'Those things are our subjects. I compile from them, and when I want some new colours I go and look at those dead butterflies,' said he. After the enamel has been filled in, the pot or plate goes to be fired, and the enamel bubbles all over the boundary lines of wires, and the whole comes from the furnace looking like delicate majolica.[18] It may take a month to put a pattern on the plate in outline, another month to fill in the enamel, but the real expenditure of time does not commence till the polishing. A man sits down with the rough article, all his tea-things, a tub of water, a flannel, and two or three saucers full of assorted pebbles from the brook. He does not get a wheel with tripoli, or emery, or buff.[19] He sits down and rubs. He rubs for a month, three months, or a year. He rubs lovingly, with his soul in his finger-ends, and little by little the efflorescence of the fired enamel gives way, and he comes down to the lines of silver, and the pattern in all its glory is there waiting for him. I saw a man who had only been a month over the polishing of one little vase five inches high. He would go on for two months. When I am in America[20] he will be rubbing still, and the ruby-coloured dragon that romped on a field of lazuli, each tiny scale and whisker a separate compartment of enamel, will be growing more lovely.

'There is also cheap *cloisonnée* to be bought,' said the manager, with a smile. 'We cannot make that. The vase will be seventy dollars.'

I respected him for saying 'cannot' instead of 'do not.' There spoke the artist. When I besought him to tell me how buff, slate, grey and avanturine enamels were made he smiled.

'We do not tell these things,' he said, and then politely: 'But of course you can make these things in England in another way.'

'Oh yes, in another way. Tell him some lies about Jaipur enamel,[21] Professor, for the honour of India,' I said.

I understood from the Professor that his opinion of India generally, and Jaipur enamel in particular, had suffered a change for the worse. Then we cast ourselves upon the entire finished stock of the house – *videlicet,*[22] three pairs of vases. They were perfect in shape and in colour. The largest were a foot high, the next six inches, and the next about three.

'Five hundred dollars, seventy-five dollars, and thirty-five dollars a pair,' said the manager sweetly when we had returned to his little room and were examining the treasures with microscopical eye. 'An Austrian Prince told us, and there was a letter from the government at Tokyo saying this also, that we should make him a pair of vases to take with him. We could have made a vase in eight months. You have seen. What can we do to make things quick?'

We left because we did not happen to have six hundred and thirty dollars to spare. I am certain that if either of us had been rich there would have been bloodshed in that cloistered garden of the grebe, and the pine, and the fish. The manager smiled us out. He knew we were clumsy foreigners.

''Fessor,' I said, when we were out of temptation, 'let's start a mission and save Japan from herself. I'll run along the streets and knock off the policemen's forage caps, while you go and tear up the railway and pull down the telegraph poles. If they are left to themselves they will make *cloisonnée* by machinery in another twenty years and build black factories instead of gardens.'

Our last visit was paid to the largest establishment in Kyoto, where boys made gold inlay on iron, sitting in camphor-wood verandahs overlooking a garden lovelier than any that had gone before. They had been caught young, even as is the custom in India. A real grown-up man was employed on the horrible story, in iron, gold, and silver, of two priests who waked up a Rain-dragon and had to run for it, all round the edge of a big shield; but the liveliest worker of the batch was a small fat baby who had been given a tenpenny nail, a hammer, and a block of metal to play with, that he might soak in the art by which he would live, through the pores of his skin. He crowed and chuckled as he whacked. There are not many five-year-olds in England who could hammer anything without pulping their little pink fingers. The baby had learned how to hit straight. On the wall of the room hung a Japanese painting of the Apotheosis of Art. It represented with fidelity all the processes of pottery from the digging of the clay to the last firing. But all the pencilled scorn of the artist was reserved for the closing scene, where an Englishman, his arm round his wife's waist, was inspecting a shop full of curios. The Japanese are not impressed with the grace of our clothing or the beauty of our countenances.

Later we beheld the manufacture of gold lacquer which is laid on speck by speck from an agate palette fitted on the artist's thumb; and the carving of ivory, which is exciting until you begin to realise that the graver never slips.

'A lot of their art is purely mechanical,' said the Professor, when he was safe back in the hotel.

'So's a lot of ours – 'specially our pictures. Only we can't be spiritedly mechanical,' I answered. 'Fancy a people like the Japanese solemnly going in for a constitution! Observe. The only two nations with a constitution worth having are the English and the Americans. The English can only be artistic in spots and by way of crazes over glimpses at the art of other nations – Sicilian tapestries, Persian saddle-bags, Khoten carpets,[23] and the sweepings of pawnbrokers' shops. The Americans are artistic so long as a few of 'em can buy their Art to keep abreast of the times with. They try to be artistic *dekhne ke waste.*[24] Spain is artistic, but she is also disturbed at intervals; France is artistic, but she must have her revolution every twenty years for the sake of fresh material; Russia is artistic, but she occasionally wishes to kill her Czar, and has no sort of Belaitee Government;[25] Germany is not artistic, because she experienced religion; and Italy is artistic, because she did very badly. India ——'

'When you have finished your verdict on the world, perhaps you'll go to bed.'

'Consequently,' I continued, with scorn, 'I am of opinion that a constitution is the worst thing in the world for a people who are blessed with souls above the average. It makes them vote; it makes them talk about politics; it makes them edit newspapers and start factories. Now the first demand of the artistic temperament is mundane uncertainty. The second is ——'

'Sleep,' said the Professor, and left the room.

1889 : LETTER SIX
COMMENTARY

1. A misquotation, eventually corrected in later editions, from Shakespeare's *The Tempest*, Act 1, Scene 2, where Miranda says:

   > How beauteous mankind is! O brave new world
   > That has such people in't.

2. The 'guitar' would have been a *samisen,* mentioned below.
3. 'Dresden', so called after the German city where it was manufactured, signified a white porcelain of an elaborate and delicate kind.
4. Monte Carlo: the gambling resort in the Principality of Monaco.

5. Simla, to which Kipling frequently alluded in these Letters, was an important hill station in northern India, at an altitude of over 7000 feet. Since 1865 it had been the official summer capital of British India: the Viceroy and senior officials moved there each year. It is now the capital of the Indian state of Himachal Pradesh.

6. Kipling's seven years in India were 1882–9. He had found the hot weather, which started by April, very trying, and one reason for his leaving India when he did was medical advice that his health would suffer if he stayed for another hot season.

7. In British India, Behar (also Bahar, but now Bihar) was a Province of Bengal: it had two Divisions, Bhagalpur and Patna. When Kipling refers to 'Sarun or Behar' he means the district of Sarun (now Saran) in the Patna Division, and the town and district called Behar (now Bihar) in the same division. 'Collectors' were district administrative officers.

8. Actually Yaami's Hotel: see Letter Five of 1889, Note 6.

9. Satsuma ware was made in the province of Satsuma, the modern Kagoshima Prefecture in southern Kyushu. White Satsuma is usually highly decorated and has a crackled white glaze. It is not made in Kyoto. Kipling must have visited the Kiyomizu potteries where decorated pottery is made: this is sometimes loosely referred to as Satsuma ware.

10. Allahabad: the *Pioneer* newspaper, for which Kipling was writing, was published in that city – in what is now Uttar Pradesh, India.

11. Burslem in Staffordshire was a major centre of pottery manufacture, one of the famous 'five towns' of that industry. Josiah Wedgwood set up in business there in 1759. Kipling's father, John Lockwood Kipling, was employed in Burslem as a pottery decorator and designer in the 1860s, immediately before going to Bombay as principal of a school of art. Not far away is Lake Rudyard, where Rudyard Kipling's parents became engaged, and after which he was named.

12. This is certainly an allusion to William Morris (1834–96), designer, poet, celebrator of medieval artistic values, and committed socialist. He had been a friend and associate of Kipling's father and especially of his uncle, Edward Burne-Jones, and Rudyard Kipling as a schoolboy had known him. Though he would have admired Morris's artistry and craftsmanship, he deplored the political ideals which led Morris to be regarded, in his later years, as an advocate of revolution.

13. Imari wares were produced in northern Kyushu, in what is now Saga Prefecture, and had been exported to Europe during the Tokugawa period through the Dutch trading post in Deshima, Nagasaki. By 'royal Kaga' Kipling presumably meant Kutani wares made in Kanazawa, now in Ishikawa Prefecture.

14. Ormolu was originally real gold or gold-leaf, ground and prepared for gilding the surface of another metal; later it came to mean imitation gold made from an alloy of copper, zinc and tin.

15. The well-known blue 'willow pattern' design, in widespread use on domestic crockery, was of unmistakably oriental inspiration but of Shropshire manufacture. It was first produced by Thomas Turner in the late eighteenth century at his Salopian China Warehouse.

16. 'Bower-bird' was the name given in the mid-nineteenth century to several varieties of Australian starling which have a tendency to collect ornamental objects such as shells and feathers with which they adorn their 'bower', which they then use not as a nest but as a place of resort.

17. Avanturine, now generally spelt 'aventurine', is a brownish glass flecked with copper-coloured spangles. The process of manufacturing it was first discovered by chance at Murano, near Venice: hence the name *avventurino*, 'accidental'.

18. Majolica, or maiolica: originally a type of Italian pottery coated with an opaque white and metallic-coloured enamel; later, any kind of glazed Italian ware.

19. Tripoli is a 'rotten-stone', a decomposed siliceous limestone used as a polishing-powder. Emery is a coarse granular mineral, of the category known as corundum, used for polishing. Buff is a stout leather (originally buffalo-hide, hence the name), usually from ox-hide and of a dull yellow colour (whence the name 'buff' as a colour).

20. From Japan Kipling sailed to North America, and was there from late May till late September 1889.

21. Jaipur was the chief city of Rajputana (now Rajasthan, India). It has long been noted for its traditional manufactures, particularly enamel-work. In an earlier section of *From Sea to Sea* ('Letters of Marque') Kipling had described in detail a visit to Jeypore (as he there called it) in late 1887.

22. *Videlicet*, usually contracted to *viz*, is a Latin term which here means 'namely' or 'to wit'.

23. Khoten is more correctly Khotan, now called Hotan: it is in Sinkiang, China, and has been noted for its carpets, which belong to the category of 'Eastern Turkestan' carpets.

24. *dekhne ke waste*, meaning literally 'in relation to seeing', was a widely used Urdu phrase, which carried an implication of a certain insincerity or hypocrisy. It can here be translated as 'for appearances'.

25. Czars (Tsars) assassinated had included Paul I (1801) and Alexander II (1881). Ex-Tsar Nicholas II was murdered in 1918. As for a 'Belaitee Government', Kipling meant a western or European government: he did not include the imperial governments of Russia in this class. *Belaitee* is the adjective from the noun *Belait* (otherwise variously *Bilayut*, *Vilayat*, etc), a term of Arabic origin widely used in India to mean 'Europe'. Kipling is well known for sentiments expressed in 'The Man Who Was' (*Life's Handicap*), where he said that 'the Russian is a delightful person till he tucks in his shirt. As an Oriental he is charming. It is only when he insists upon being treated as the most easterly of western peoples instead of the most westerly of easterns that he becomes a racial anomaly extremely difficult to handle.'

'Griffiths the Safe Man'

As the title indicates, this story deals with the safeness of Griffiths the safe man, the secure person, the reliable individual, the sort of man you would bank with. I am proud to write about Griffiths, for I owe him a pleasant day. This story is dedicated to my friend Griffiths, the remarkably trustworthy mortal.

In the beginning there were points about Griffiths. He quoted proverbs. A man who quotes proverbs is confounded by proverbs. He is also confounded by his friends. But I never confounded Griffiths – not even in that supreme moment when the sweat stood on his brow in agony and his teeth were fixed like bayonets and he swore horribly. Even then, I say, I sat on my own trunk, the trunk that opened, and told Griffiths that I had always respected him, but never more than at the present moment. He was so safe, y'know.

Safeness is a matter of no importance to me. If my trunk won't lock when I jump on it thrice, I strap it up and go on to something else. If my carpet-bag is too full, I let the tails of shirts and the ends of ties bubble over, and go down the street with the affair. It all comes right in the end, and if it does not, what is a man that he should fight against Fate?

But Griffiths is not constructed in that manner. He says: 'Safe bind is safe find.'[1] That, rather, is what he used to say. He has seen reason to alter his views. Everything about Griffiths is safe – entirely safe. His trunk is locked by two hermetical gun-metal double-end Chubbs;[2] his bedding-roll opens to a letter-padlock capable of two million combinations; his hat-box has a lever patent safety on it; and the grief of his life is that he cannot lock up the ribs of his umbrella safely. If you could get at his soul you would find it ready strapped up and labelled for heaven. That is Griffiths.

When we went to Japan together, Griffiths kept all his money under lock and key. I carried mine in my coat-tail pocket. But all Griffiths' contraptions did not prevent him from spending exactly as much as I did. You see, when he had worried his way through the big strap, and the little strap, and the slide-valve, and the spring lock, and the key that turned twice and a quarter, he felt as though he had earned any money he found, whereas I could get masses of sinful wealth by merely pulling out my handkerchief – dollars and five dollars and ten dollars, all mixed up with the tobacco or flying down the road. They looked much too pretty to spend.

'Safe bind, safe find,' said Griffiths in the treaty ports of Japan.

He never really began to lock things up severely till we got our passports to travel up-country. He took charge of mine for me, on the ground that I was an imbecile. As you are asked for your passport at every other shop, all the hotels, most of the places of amusement, and on the top of each hill, I got to appreciate Griffiths' self-sacrifice. He would be biting a strap with his teeth or calculating the combinations of his padlocks among a ring of admiring Japanese while I went for a walk into the interior.

'Safe bind, safe find,' said Griffiths. That was true, because I was bound to find Griffiths somewhere near his beloved keys and straps. He never seemed to see that half the pleasure of his trip was being strapped and keyed out of him.

We never had any serious difficulty about the passports in the whole course of our wanderings. What I purpose to describe now is merely an incident of travel. It had no effect on myself, but it nearly broke Griffiths' heart.

We were travelling from Kyoto to Otsu along a very dusty road full of pretty girls. Every time I stopped to play with one of them Griffiths grew impatient. He had telegraphed for rooms at the only hotel in Otsu, and was afraid that there would be no accommodation. There were only three rooms in the hotel, and 'Safe bind, safe find,' said Griffiths. He was always telegraphing ahead for something.

Our hotel was three-quarters Japanese and one-quarter European. If you walked across it it shook, and if you laughed the roof fell off. Strange Japanese came in and dined with you, and Japanese maidens looked through the windows of the bathroom while you were bathing.

We had hardly put the luggage down before the proprietor asked for our passports. He asked me of all people in the world. 'I have the passports,' said Griffiths with pride. 'They are in the yellow-hide bag. Turn it very carefully on to the right side, my good man. You have no such locks in Japan, I'm quite certain.' Then he knelt down and brought out a bunch of keys as big as his fist. You must know that every Japanese carries a little *belaiti*-made handbag with nickel fastenings. They take an interest in handbags.

'Safe bind, safe—— D—n the key! What's wrong with it?' said Griffiths.

The hotel proprietor bowed and smiled very politely for at least five minutes, Griffiths crawling over and under and round and about his bag the while. 'It's a percussating compensator,' said he, half to himself. 'I've never known a percussating compensator do this before.' He was getting heated and red in the face.

'Key stuck, eh? I told you those fooling little spring locks are sure to go wrong sooner or later.'

'Fooling little devils. It's a percussating comp—— There goes the key. Now it won't move either way. I'll give you the passports tomorrow. Passport *kul–demang–mañana*³–catchee in a little time. Won't that do for you?'

Griffiths was getting really angry. The proprietor was more polite than ever. He bowed and left the room. 'That's a good little chap,' said Griffiths. 'Now we'll settle down and see what the mischief's wrong with this bag. You catch one end.'

'Not in the least,' I said. '"Safe bind, safe find." You did the binding. How can you expect me to do the finding? I'm an imbecile unfit to be trusted with a passport, and now I'm going for a walk.' The Japanese are really the politest nation in the world. When the hotel proprietor returned with a policeman he did not at once thrust the man on Griffiths' notice. He put him in the verandah and let him clank his sword gently once or twice.

'Little chap's brought a blacksmith,' said Griffiths, but when he saw the policeman his face became ugly. The policeman came into the room and tried to assist. Have you ever seen a four-foot policeman in white cotton gloves and a stand-up collar lunging at a percussating compensator lock with a five-foot sword? I enjoyed the sight for a few minutes before I went out to look at Otsu, which is a nice town. No one hindered me. Griffiths was so completely the head of the firm that had I set the town on fire he would have been held responsible.

I went to a temple, and a policeman said 'Passport.' I said, 'The other gentleman has got.' 'Where is other gentleman?' said the policeman, syllable by syllable, in the Ollendorffian style.⁴ 'In the hotel,' said I; and he waddled off to catch him. It seemed to me that I could do a great deal towards cheering Griffiths all alone in his bedroom with that wicked bad lock, the hotel proprietor, the policeman, the room-boy, and the girl who helped one to bathe. With this idea I stood in front of four policemen, and they all asked for my passport and were all sent to the hotel, syllable by syllable – I mean one by one.

Some soldiers of the 9th N. I. were strolling about the streets, and they were idle.[5] It is unwise to let a soldier be idle. He may get drunk. When the fourth policeman said: 'Where is other gentleman?' I said: 'In the hotel, and take soldiers – those soldiers.'

'How many soldiers?' said the policeman firmly.

'Take all soldiers,' I said. There were four files in the street just then. The policeman spoke to them, and they caught up their big sword-bayonets, nearly as long as themselves, and waddled after him.

I followed them, but first I bought some sweets and gave one to a child. That was enough. Long before I had reached the hotel I had a tail of fifty babies. These I seduced into the long passage that ran through the house, and then I slid the grating that answers to the big hall-door. That house was full – pit, boxes and galleries – for Griffiths had created an audience of his own, and I also had not been idle.

The four files of soldiers and the five policemen were marking time on the boards of Griffiths' room, while the landlord and the landlord's wife, and the two scullions, and the bath-girl, and the cook-boy, and the boy who spoke English, and the boy who didn't, and the boy who tried to, and the cook, filled all the space that wasn't devoted to babies asking the foreigner for more sweets.

Somewhere in the centre of the mess was Griffiths and a yellow-hide bag. I don't think he had looked up once since I left, for as he raised his eyes at my voice I heard him cry: 'Good heavens! are they going to train the guns of the city on me? What's the meaning of the regiment? I'm a British subject.'

'What are you looking for?' I asked.

'The passports – your passports – the double-dyed passports! Oh, give a man room to use his arms. Get me a hatchet.'

'The passports, the passports!' I said. 'Have you looked in your great-coat? It's on the bed, and there's a blue envelope in it that looks like a passport. You put it there before you left Kyoto.'

Griffiths looked. The landlord looked. The landlord took the passports and bowed. The five policemen bowed and went out one by one; the 9th N. I. formed fours and went out; the household bowed, and there was a long silence. Then the bath-girl began to giggle.

When Griffiths wanted to speak to me I was on the other side of the regiment of children in the passage, and he had time to reflect before he could work his way through them.

They formed his guard-of-honour when he took the bag to the locksmith.

I abode on the mountains of Otsu till dinner-time.

'GRIFFITHS THE SAFE MAN'
COMMENTARY

Kipling was a supreme artist of the short story. Before his first visit to Japan at the age of twenty-three he had already turned out a large number of excellent stories, including powerful pieces such as 'The Man Who Would Be King'. It is therefore disappointing to have to acknowledge that 'Griffiths the Safe Man' is a trivial production. Its author knew this, and made no attempt to collect or revive it after its initial newspaper appearance. Part of its interest, paradoxically, lies in its comparative obscurity, and the reason for that.

Otherwise, its interest is in the fact that it is the only story by Kipling set in Japan. This is surprising since he found much to fascinate him in that country, and in general he found wide inspiration for his stories in his travels. However, 'Griffiths the Safe Man' stands alone. He wrote it in April 1889, and, though the farcical events it describes may have been invented, it purports to be autobiographical, and it obviously fits into the account of his journey from Kyoto to Otsu given in Letter Seven of 1889 (incidentally the one whole Letter which was suppressed when the texts were edited into book form in 1899).

As to the identity of Griffiths, on all the circumstantial evidence he seems to be a caricature, however much distorted, of Kipling's travelling-companion Professor Hill. All the same, while there is no reason to suppose it was a depiction of anyone else, there is also no reason to suppose that Hill shared the preposterous qualities that Griffiths displays in the story.

The central incident – of passports mislaid and resultant fuss – is narrated in slapstick terms but does reflect the conditions of the period, when foreigners travelling inland from the Treaty Ports needed a specific travel document which might be checked by Japanese officialdom at any time. An almost contemporaneous record of travel in Japan, in *A Social Departure* by Sara Duncan (1890), includes a somewhat similar account of a pother over a passport in a hotel at Nikko. The landlord came to the bedroom and politely but persistently demanded to be shown something, but owing to language problems it was impossible to guess what. He was offered, in ludicrous succession, miscellaneous items of baggage and personal effects, but they did not satisfy him. Meanwhile 'most of the inhabitants of Nikko' seemed to be in the room watching events. At last he came upon a passport and the problem was solved.

'I have never before or since participated in such a scene of mutual felicitation as followed.'

In common with his other newspaper despatches, Kipling mailed the story back to India, and it was published in Lahore in the *Civil & Military Gazette* on 31 July 1889; and soon afterwards reprinted in a collation of that paper's miscellaneous articles entitled *Turnovers*. Twenty years then passed before it reappeared. In 1909 an American publisher, B. W. Dodge, brought together a number of Kipling's forgotten newspaper articles including this, in an unauthorized book entitled *Abaft the Funnel*. Kipling, angered as always by such conduct, thereupon allowed his own American publishers, Doubleday, to reprint the same collection under the same title in a more cheaply priced edition which undercut the Dodge edition. However, the book never attained wide popularity, and in Britain was excluded from the author's standard editions. 'Griffiths the Safe Man' therefore remains among the least known of Kipling's prose works.

NOTES

1. 'Safe bind, safe find' is a more or less proverbial phrase attributed to Thomas Tusser (1524–80).
2. The name of Chubb, the British lock and safe manufacturer, was already well known. Charles Chubb, founder of the firm, had patented patterns of locks as early as the 1820s. The classic 'Chubb-lock' operated with tumblers that set the bolt immovably if the lock were tampered with.
3. This phrase is suggestive of Griffiths's frustration at being unable to express himself in Japanese. *Kul* represents *kal*, Hindustani for 'tomorrow' (but also, confusingly, for 'yesterday'); *demang* is French (*demain*), and *mañana* of course Spanish. The following phrase is in pidgin English.
4. This is a reference to Dr Heinrich Godefroy Ollendorff, whose 'New Method of Learning to Read, Write and Speak a Language in Six Months' had been adapted to French, Italian and other languages, and enjoyed a wide vogue from the 1840s. A central feature of the system was a tendency to simple and repetitive questions and answers, e.g. 'Have you my sugar?' 'Yes, Sir, I have your sugar.'
5. The term 'N.I.' was intended for readers in India who would recognise it immediately as 'Native Infantry'. The British Indian Army had contained numerous units so designated. Incidentally, the term 'Native', meaning Indian as distinct from British soldiers, had been officially discouraged in the Indian Army from 1885, and the units of Native Infantry were later redesignated; but the expression continued in use for some years. When Kipling revised 'Griffiths the Safe Man' in the 1930s for the Burwash Edition, among various slight changes he dropped 'N.I.' and called the unit the '9th Infantry'.

1889: Letter Seven

THE NAUTCH[1] OF CHERRY-BLOSSOMS AND THE TRAFFIC OF THE
TOWN OF KYOTO. TAKES ME ACROSS A LAKE AND INTO A STREET
ROW. SHOWS THAT THE SOLDIER IS VERY MUCH ALIKE ALL THE
WORLD OVER, WHILE THE OFFICER DIFFERS. DRAWS A VEIL OVER A
WASH-TUB AND SOME GIRLS NEAR IT.

> 'But blind or lame or sick or sound,
> We follow that which flies before.
> We know the merry world is round
> And we may sail for evermore.'[2]

'What is the use of leaving Kyoto until our steamer is ready for us at
Yokohama?'

'In order that we may see Japan. If I hadn't been with you, you
would have stayed at Kobe and never moved another step.'

'Very good. I'll come, but I want to see a nautch first – the nautch
of the cherry-blossoms. It performs itself at the theatre hung with
red lanterns, and the price of stalls is ten cents.'

It was night – a clear starry spring night – in Kyoto as the
Professor and I wrangled. Somewhere in the luminous mist below
the hotel lay a great city laughing to itself. The night wind blew
unseen cherry-blossoms across our faces and brought to our nostrils
the spice of the pines. The spirit of the spring riding on the night
called all the people out of their houses. They had lighted blood-red
lanterns in the tea gardens and were feasting in simple fashion.
Across the dim bulk of the city ran a line of light – the lamps of the
main street in truth, but to the eye a pathway of silver climbing to
the stars that tipped the hilltops across the plain.

We pranced joyously down the slope through the mobs of women
and little children gambling for sweetmeats at the roadside stalls,
under the grey eaves of fantastic temples and down flights of steps till
we reached a wonderful Japanese theatre lighted by electric light,
whose roof was supported by a single massive beam sixty feet in
length and four in the square. The nautch of the cherry-blossoms is

115

performed in cherry-blossom time, and so great is the rush to see it
that the dance is limited to one hour per audience. Then it begins all
over again. Sixteen maidens attired in the stiffest of old time Japanese
dresses and holding fans of pink cherry-buds filed from the right
wing of the stage – the Japanese stage has two wings about six feet
broad running the whole length of the house. Other sixteen maidens
waving fans of white buds filed from the left wing, while a chorus of
twenty-two girls sitting on the right and left of the house supplied
the music. The movements of the girls were slower even than in the
'weaving' nautch in India. They twisted their garments into quaint
shapes; they moved hands and fans and feet in perfect but slowest
time; they stamped with a single foot these two and thirty, while the
chorus twangled their guitars and dolorously mewed through their
pretty little noses. It ought to have been monotonous, but it was
attractive and for an hour at least even charming. There was a dainty
dignity about the groups and posings and an unexpectedness in the
outcries of the orchestra that the Indian nautch does not give.

    And the next morning the Professor tore me away from this
delicate city, the dancing girls, my lounging in the cherry gardens
and rambles under the eaves of huge temples. Put me in a *'rickshaw*
and removed me to a place called Otsu,[3] which is at the head of a
great lake – Lake Biwa, seven miles away from Kyoto. The lake is
called *Biwa*, as we should say *Sitar Sagar*, because it is supposed to
resemble in outline a Japanese guitar[4] – one forty miles long by
eighteen wide. The winds [play] on this great instrument and their
music is sometimes death to the trading junks. Before we saw the
lake we had to pass through seven continuous miles of village street
in the face of the current of local trade that was pouring into Kyoto
city. A gap which might have been the Mohun Pass led us through
the circle of hills many times mentioned. Over the saddle of the gap
poured the traffic. Sturdy oxen had dragged up the logs of timber,
the drays of *sake*, the crates of baskets and all the hundred oddments
that minister to the needs of a large town, from the slope below, and
with lowered heads and rolling red eyes were shouldering back
again. We met the two-wheeled carts coming down and hardly
restrained from breaking away by the two men in charge. The tail of
each cart acted as a skid and was used as such once every minute,
while the white dust flew up from the flinty road under the impact.
There is a well-known artist wandering through Japan now.[5] Will
he, I wonder, ever see the last half-mile of the Otsu road into Kyoto,
and later on delight the good folk at home by a picture of it? The red
and brown and yellow logs ploughing up the metalling, the green

and white *sake* tubs jolting on the wains, and the carters hanging back on the drag-ropes with shouts as their charge threatened a cart in front, the countrywomen now bound with blue and white handkerchiefs also wrestling with their little barrows of onions or fish, the wild rush of the *'rickshaws* dodging in and out of the timber, and at the head of the gaps the sullen jowls of the released bullocks snorting at their fellows – a brush could paint these things: a pen fails.

In plain English the road was feeding the city on one side as fast as the rail could do so on the other, and the former was a trifle congested. On the slope of the hills beyond the gap we could see the raw red side of a cutting which brought the pipes of the new reservoir into Kyoto, and half-trodden and half-hidden among the trees the line of the railway. The countryside was alive with people – hardworking, fat, ugly little people, whose houses lined the road along which our *'rickshaws* crawled. When the houses thickened and spread out we knew that we had reached another city without having quitted the last one. Lake Biwa shone at our feet, and grey temples gleamed through the pines of the hill overlooking the town. They took us to a purely Japanese hotel which maintained three small bedrooms for the use of passing foreigners. The rooms overhung a tiny garden and a pond full of goldfish. Mine host laughed and said we were welcome. Two pretty girls laughed and a fat child laughed. There is a pleasure in coming to a Japanese hotel even though you are an Englishman encumbered with boxes and passports. A gentleman of the country has a much better time of it: he carries no luggage. Why should he? On arrival he is shown into a specklessly clean room. The tiny tea set is placed ready for him on the floor. In a corner lie pillow and wadded sleeping suit for the night. In ten minutes his dinner is served. After dinner he bathes long and heatedly. The hotel gives him a prettily-coloured dressing-gown in which he wanders about, talks to the world generally and smokes until it is time to go to bed. That is comfort. When a Japanese attempts European comforts he is so impressed with the rarity of his purchases, such as knives, forks, cruets and tablecloths, that he leaves them strictly alone, whereby they become very filthy. Also when a Japanese abandons the customs of his ancestors and eats with a knife and fork he is prone to eat like a pig. This is a pity because personally he is of exquisite cleanliness. If you go to a Japanese hotel which attempts a *belaiti* compromise, insist on being fed in the Japanese manner. At the worst they will give you flaky-white fish boiled over charcoal, snowy rice and soy, with bamboo-shoots and spongecakes to follow. Go further into the kitchen and watch the cooking of

117

your meal to know what real refinement means. The girls will not tie a dish-clout to your coat, but they will box your ears if you try to interrupt them.

The great bathing question cropped up at Otsu. Apparently Englishmen were scarce in these parts and nothing could satisfy the maidens of the establishment but to peep through the bath-room screens and observe how one of the race tubbed. Covert watching of this kind, especially when it is accompanied by much giggling, is not nice. Even Lord Chesterfield never laid down any rules for deportment in a bath. You see one cannot stand up to argue with the unseen gallery.[6]

Otsu, like all the other towns in Japan, holds temples – Buddhist and Shinto[7] – built on the highest available points of land. There is a view from the chief shrine across the lake and over the city. I took it on trust, for the rain came down and a white-haired Shinto priest to whom I had given two cents was lighting candles in front of his little shrine at a scandalous rate. Views become monotonous all too quickly, but men and women never. Shinto priests are very like Hindu ones. A present to their temple makes you a co-warden for the time being. The Professor ran a sweetmeat stall for the babies at the bottom of the flight of steps that led to the temples while I investigated the mysteries of the Shinto creed at the top, and between us we very nearly managed to miss the steamer that was to take us across the lake.

'Now for the view,' said the Professor. The rain shut down upon the word, the steamer butted stone breakwaters of the harbour, slid into deep water and launched upon a sea that might have been boundless for aught we could tell. Nature never gives you the same chance twice. We had missed the view. A fellow-passenger who had many times crossed the Atlantic and more often the lake told us thrilling tales of wreck and misadventure upon the sleeping waters.

'The wind comes through the gaps in the mountains and throws up as heavy a sea as I care to be in. Last year when I was crossing – it's a four hours' trip by rights – we spent nineteen hours fooling about between the shores. To be sure we picked up the crew of a junk that had turned bottom upwards. Biwa's a nasty dangerous little lake, and I shall be glad when the railway round it is opened: then we shall be able to go straight through from Kobe to Yokohama without changing.[8] The lake line ought to be finished in two months. Just at present Japan is a very funny little country to deal with. You turn your back on it for six months, and when you come back half a dozen new lines are through and running – running like steam. I am going to America for a few months. Three fresh lines will be open by the time I return. You are going to Yokohama by railway from the head of the lake? Ah, then, go by the Tokaido or sea road line.[9] You'll see the loveliest landscapes under heaven, and that's a fact. Did you notice that lump of dark cloud that slid by half a minute ago? That's a big island in the middle of the lake and the only place to run to in a storm. I've lain half a day under the lee of that island, the steamer not daring to put her nose outside.'

So much for talking to folk by the way. I should have passed Biwa as a peaceful little pond instead of presenting her to the public as a treacherous and very big Ullswater.[10] There was nothing to watch but rain above and the manners and customs of young Japan in the first-class saloon below. The steamer company generously supplied tea (how long, I wonder, could a fine bronze kettle, a dainty teapot and set of china be left untended in a penny steamer at home?) and a small boy to hand it to the company. Young Japan in spats, tweed trousers, black 'diagonal' coat, stand-up collar, fawn silk tie, dogskin gloves and patent leather boots drank the liquid ceremoniously. From a neat little black bag he drew a pair of chopsticks, two chip boxes containing rice-stewed mushrooms, a little fish, some sauce and bamboo-shoots, ate his tiffin with all imaginable propriety, read his vernacular newspaper for a space, and then slipped off his boots, coat, tie, collar and waistcoat and lay down on the seats to slumber, the nape of his neck supported in default of a Japanese pillow, by the neat little handbag. Old Japan at his side slept on a red lacquer pillow, and it was curious to note how in both men the national attitude of repose was exactly alike. Though you expel nature with a Constitution dated the 11th of February, nevertheless she will return when a man wants to go to sleep. Nagahama, at the wrong end of Biwa and a place where lake sailing schooners thrust their bowsprits across the track, was the beginning of the line to Yokohama. When you come to Japan take special care to come across Lake Biwa in a steamer, because you may be wrecked and compelled to cling to the bottom of the boat and go through other exciting experiences. A Japanese ought not to be trusted with either a steamer or a horse. He is too familiar towards the former and too polite towards the latter. A man on the boat – really Lake Biwa was very like the pond of salt water that Alice fell into, as regarded the variety of queer fish in it[11] – gave the Japanese this character. He owns a sailing schooner that went sealing somewhere about the inhospitable Kurile Islands.[12] All day long her boat's crew used to row in and out of the creeks and fiords hunting seal, knocking 'em on the head. 'At night,' to use my friend's words, 'the men 'ud come back as dead as the seals in the boats – Danes, Norwegians, Americans, British and the like, with their tongues a yard out of their mouths. All except the Japanese. You can't tire a Jap sailor who comes of the fisherman lot. But the Lord protect me from a Jap engineer. He'd rivet a boiler with bamboo spikes and then wonder why it blew out the inside of the boat. "It's machinery," says the Jap, "and the wheels are bound to go round if you pile on the coals." He piles on the coals and, Gad! the wheels do go round till something happens, and that's generally no little smash. I've seen the engines of a Jap boat playing Handel's oratorium[13] with all the stops out and the engineer shouting down the stokehole to know whether the firemen were dead or how. If it had been my ship I'd ha' towed him over the side for a spell.'

By all means travel on the steamer and do not attempt the railway run from Nagahama without a break, but stop for the night four hours from Biwa at Nagoya where you may either put up at the finest pukka Japanese hotel in all the island or at a house of entertainment where they really know how to attend to Europeans. If the Japanese hotel be full you will be turned away without scruple, because you are only a foreigner and your wants and desires must be subordinated to those of the people. I admire the Japanese for this independence. There is no trace of discourtesy in it. You are one of the *queue* and you must take your chance with the others.

Nagoya must be a very wicked town. In my walks abroad I saw a crying baby and a street row. Japan being governed by children, the former affair was as serious as the death of the Mikado. A fat young sinner aged about two, had got hold of his elder sister's guitar and was literally sweeping the floor with it. The girl was naturally angry and tapped the baby on the head with such force that the head actually bobbed forward perhaps an inch. Then the baby yelled, and the last I saw of him was his cuddlement in his sister's bosom, the rest of the family standing round to condole with him. The guitar, the cause of all the trouble, lay unheeded on the floor and the girl trod on it as she walked to and fro with the baby. The street row was really amusing. A police officer had occasion to gently rebuke a soldier of the line for a breach of municipal conservancy regulations. The soldier was thick-set, pig-jowled, and deep-chested. The constable was thin, spectacled, white gloved, and a literate. He struck attitudes, he waved his white gloves in the air, and the soldier cursed him fluently because the streets were full of lounging privates and it would never do to be put down by a policeman.

'Soldiers and policemen always fighting,' said my guide with a grin.

The policeman would fain have withdrawn from the argument. 'Then what did you say I did for?' said the soldier with an overshoulder glance for the approval of the rapidly gathering crowd. 'Go it, 'Enery: give the beggar what for,' shouted a fellow private in the background. "E ain't worth 'itting,' was the response. 'Hi! Yi! You're afraid yourself,' shouted the crowd. 'No I ain't,' said the soldier and backed the little man of peace into a corner where he hustled him. The policeman pushed him in return. 'You do that again and I'll knock your 'ed off,' said the soldier. 'Well you leave me alone then,' said the policeman. "Oo are you to tell me wot I'm to do and wot I ain't? Take an' go 'ome.' 'I shan't. 'Oo are you a shovin' of?'

I have reproduced the outlines of the dialogue in English owing to an imperfect knowledge of Japanese, but I'll swear to the general purport being here set down. Both men had their arms – sword-bayonet and sword. I hoped they would fight fair, or at the worst draw and show me whether they could use their weapons. They faced each other and wrangled. The soldiers in the street loafed in to the crowd. Another policeman ran to the police barracks a little way up the street. Out rushed a gentleman with curled mustachios at least an inch long and a portentous sword. Out rushed three or four more policemen. 'What! Ain't there goin' to be no fight?' said the little street boys and dispersed. Policeman and soldier marched off to the police barracks together. I stood in the street and grieved with the little street boys. Mark the sequel. That night at dinner (in a room of screens ornamented with drawings of cherry, chrysanthemum and hawthorn, fit for a duchess's drawing-room at home, but here only good enough for an inn) entered mine host rather unhappy. 'A police officer wants to see you and – you have shown your passport?'

'F. Kundoo, police officer,' as his card attested,[14] came in and proved to be the little man with the curled mustachios that I had seen running from the barracks.

'If he wants to know anything about that row,' whispered the Professor, 'remember you know nothing. You can't be detained as a witness.'

Quick as the passing of a cup of tea to F. Kundoo, Esquire, I had matured half a dozen lies but – alas! for the vanity of poor human nature – his first question nearly disarmed.

'Are you an officer – an English officer?' said F. Kundoo.

Joy! I have been mistaken for a missionary and a doctor, but for an officer never!

'No, he isn't,' said the Professor swiftly. He saw my preened vanity poising herself for flight into the aether of imagination.

'No I am not,' I said with (I hope it properly impressed F. Kundoo) the air of one who might have been a Field-Marshal had he not preferred to come to Japan and watch street-fights.

'Oh-ah-Kung! Good-a-bye,' said F. Kundoo and disappeared.

'Has he gone?' said a tea-girl round the corner.

'He came to get a *sahib's* testimony about a row. Such is the incorruptible purity of *sahib-log* when they travel that the nations of the earth hasten to secure their testimony in courts of law,' I said softly. 'Now I could have taken brevet-rank[15] as a major for the rest of the trip if you hadn't interrupted. A major of cavalry.'

'Hasn't it struck you that the Japanese officer, so far as we have seen him, is about as measly, untidy and unsoldierly a little creature as you could wish to see?' said the Professor.

'It has not,' I said very shortly indeed.

Mister Yamaguchi, the guide, strolled into the room attired in a blue dressing-gown. By day in English kit he was merely very ordinary. At night he blossomed into silks and became a Japanese gentleman.

'That police officer. O! He come see if you want sketch the fort here. Sometimes not allow officers make sketches. Sometimes, yes. Kundoo, he come I think see what you look like; just like calls on gentlemans.'

'He came to get the evidence of an honest and upright *sahib*. I shouldn't be surprised if that poor Tommy isn't languishing in jail now. He was in the wrong all through, but I'd give evidence in his favour all the same because he's a Tommy.[16] Ah! the Japanese know when they have to deal with a race above prejudice. What a little beast the bobby was.'

That night I dreamed I was an officer until a tea-girl came and took away my uniform and made me wash myself in a lake full of boiling water, with no place to rest on except the bottom of a derelict junk manned entirely by a crew of F. Kundoos singing 'Good-a-bye'.

1889: LETTER SEVEN
COMMENTARY

1. *Nautch* was a word of Indian origin, but in common European use and misuse all over India, often signifying any sort of dance. Strictly, as here, it meant a formal display of dancing by women.
2. These are the last four lines of *The Voyage*, a highly romantic poem by Tennyson, published in 1864. It describes in fanciful and evocative terms an unending dream-voyage by ship around the world: 'that which flies before' is the mysterious quest, a shadowy figure symbolizing Romance.
3. Otsu (which Kipling erroneously called 'Otza') is in Shiga Prefecture at the southern tip of Lake Biwa. It has some important temples and shrines.
4. The *biwa* (as distinct from the *samisen* which was mentioned before) is the Japanese lute or mandolin: the outline of Lake Biwa was thought to resemble the shape of that instrument. *Sitar Sagar*: this would be Hindi for 'Sitar Lake' – the *sitar* being a well known Indian stringed instrument.
5. The 'well-known artist' would have been Mr (later Sir) Alfred East (1849–1913), later a President of the Royal Society of British Artists, who was in Japan from March to September 1889, on a visit sponsored by the Fine Art Society, and was painting assiduously throughout. He became an honorary member of the Meiji Bijutsu Kai. As to the reference a few lines later to the brush as against the pen, Kipling reverted strongly to this theme three years later. See Letter Four of 1892.
6. The reference is to the fourth Earl of Chesterfield (1694–1773) whose famous *Letters* of advice to his much loved illegitimate son Philip Stanhope (1732–68), published in 1774 when both were dead, contained a code of urbane manners catering for almost every social eventuality a gentleman of the day could expect to meet.
7. In Japan, Buddhist places of worship are normally called temples: Shinto places of worship are usually termed shrines.
8. At the time of this journey in 1889, the railway line along the south-eastern shore of the lake had not been completed. Kipling had therefore to take a boat from Otsu to Nagahama at the north-eastern end of the lake, to connect with the next stretch of line.
9. The *Tokaido* was a road route skirting the eastern coast up to Tokyo. Basil Hall Chamberlain in *Things Japanese* has this to say about that railway route:

> Japan is not naturally suited to railway construction: the country is too mountainous; the streams – mere beds of sand today – are tomorrow, after a heavy rain, wild surging rivers that sweep away

bridges and embankments. For these reasons, the idea of carrying the Tokyo–Kyoto railway along the Nakasendo, or backbone of the country, which would have been far better in time of war, as being removed from the possibility of an attack from the sea-side, fell through, the engineering difficulties proving insuperable. The only alternative was to follow the Tokaido, the great highway of Eastern Japan, which skirts the coast along the narrow strip of flat country intervening between the foot of the hills and the Pacific Ocean. This work was completed, and the thousandth mile of railway opened, in the summer of 1889.

10. Ullswater is the lake in northern England where Wordsworth saw the 'host of golden daffodils' that he made famous in verse. Though the second largest of English lakes, it is only nine miles long, less than a quarter the length of Lake Biwa.

11. The reference is to chapters 2 and 3 of *Alice's Adventures in Wonderland*, and the pool of tears in which various animals were swimming. 'They were indeed a queer-looking party that assembled on the bank.'

12. The Kuriles are a chain of islands extending north-east of Japan. They were formerly administered by Japan, but were transferred to the USSR in 1945.

13. 'Handel's oratorium': George Frederick Handel (1685–1759) wrote fifteen oratorios.

14. Kundoo is not a Japanese name. Kudo (with a long 'o') was probably the modern romanization of this police officer's name.

15. Brevet-rank denoted a system of promotion whereby an officer might be appointed to a higher rank, not substantively, without the salary, until such time as a vacancy should arise in the establishment of that rank.

16. Though still unknown in Britain at this time, Kipling had already made a name in India with short stories about the British private soldier (the notional 'Thomas Atkins'), and on his return to London he attained even greater publicity with verses on soldier themes. (See also Letter One of 1892, Note 7.) A 'bobby' is an English policeman. The name comes from Sir Robert Peel who established London's Metropolitan Police in 1829.

1889: Letter Eight

OF THE NATURE OF THE TOKAIDO AND JAPANESE RAILWAY CON-
STRUCTION. ONE TRAVELLER EXPLAINS THE LIFE OF THE *SAHIB-LOG*,
AND ANOTHER THE ORIGIN OF DICE. SHOWS HOW THE PROFESSOR
AND I WENT TO WASH, BUT REMAINED TO STARE. OF THE BABIES IN
THE BATH-TUB AND THE MAN IN D.T.

> When I went to Hell I spoke to the man on the road.
> *– Old Saw.*

You know the story of the miner who borrowed a dictionary and
returned it with the remark that the stories, though interesting in the
main, were considerably disconnected and too various. I have the
same complaint to make against Japanese scenery – twelve hours of it
by train from Nagoya to Yokohama. About seven hundred years
ago the king of those days built a sea-road which he called the
Tokaido (or else all the sea-coast was called the Tokaido, but it's of
no importance), which road endures to the present.[1] Later on, when
the English engineer appeared, he followed the Grand Trunk more
or less closely, and the result has been a railway that any nation
might take off their hat to. The last section of the through line from
Kyoto to Yokohama was only opened five days before the Professor
and I honoured it with an unofficial inspection. It grieved me that Sir
Guilford Molesworth[2] – not absolutely unknown in India – had gone
round from Kobe to Yokohama by sea, and so was saved from a few
hundred professional questions that I was dying to ask him.

The accommodation of all kinds is arranged for the benefit of the
Japanese; and this is distressing to the foreigner, who expects in a
carriage remotely resembling E.I.R.[3] rolling-stock the conveniences
of that pea-green and very dusty old line. But it suits the Japanese
admirably: they hop out at every other station – *pro re nata*[4] – and
occasionally get left behind. Two days ago they managed to kill a
Government official of high standing between a footboard and a
platform, and to-day the Japanese papers are seriously discussing the
advantages of lavatories. Far be it from me to interfere with the

125

arrangements of an artistic empire; but for a twelve hours' run there might at least *be* arrangements.

I got hold of a copy of the *Maru-Maru Chimbun*,[5] a sort of *Punch* with litho-cartoons explained by letter-press in English, and, between the pauses of my grief at not being able to understand the meaning of the allusions to the politics of the day, was admiring the drawings and the lampoons. I was reading about an elephant who 'resolved to commit at his own will but could not get back again' when the Professor began to grunt admiringly at the scenery. You can reach Yokohama by two roads – the Tokaido or the Nakasendo,[6] – and are rather looked down upon if you choose the former. The latter is supposed to be more mountainous and you *dak*[7] it in 'rickshaws. As the Tokaido is chiefly mountain I am content. So was the Professor.

We had left the close-packed cultivation at the foot of the hills and were running along the shores of a great lake,[8] all steel-blue from one end to the other, except where it was dotted with little islands. Then the lake turned into an arm of the sea, and we ran across it on a cut-stone causeway, and the profligacy of the pines ceased, as the trees had to come down from clothing dank hills, and fight with bowed head, outstretched arms, and firmly planted feet, against the sands of the Pacific, whose breakers were spouting and blowing not a quarter of a mile away from the causeway. The Japanese know all about forestry. They stake down wandering sand-torrents, which are still allowed to ruin our crops in the Hoshiarpur district,[9] and they plug a shifting sand-dune with wattle-dams and pine seedlings as cleverly as they would pin plank to plank. Were their forest officers trained at Nancy,[10] or are they local products? The stake-binding used to hold the sand is of French pattern, and the diagonal planting-out of the trees is also French.

Half a minute after the train dropped this desolate, hardly controlled beach it raced through four or five miles of the suburbs of Patna, but a clean and glorified Patna bowered in bamboo plantations.[11] Then it hit a tunnel and sailed forth into a section of the London, Chatham, and Dover, or whatever the line is that wants to make the Channel Tunnel.[12] At any rate, the embankment was on the beach, and the waves lapped the foot of it, and there was a wall of cut rock to landward. Then we disturbed many villages of fishermen, whose verandahs gave on to the track, and whose nets lay almost under our wheels. The railway was still a new thing in that particular part of the world, for mothers held up their babes to see it.

Anyone can keep pace with Indian scenery, arranged as it is in reaches of five hundred miles. This blending alternation of field, mountain, sea-beach, forest, bamboo grove, and rolling moor covered with azalea blossoms was too much for me, so I sought the society of a man who had lived in Japan for twenty years.

'Yes, Japan's an excellent country as regards climate. The Rains begin in May or latter April.[13] June, July and August are hot months. I've known the thermometer as high as 86° at night, but I'd defy the world to produce anything more perfect than the weather between September and May. When one gets seedy, one goes to the hot springs in the Hakone mountains close to Yokohama. There are heaps of places to recruit in, but we English are a healthy lot. Of course we don't have half as much fun as you do in India. We are a small community, and all our amusements are organised by ourselves for our own benefit – concerts, races, and amateur theatricals and the like. You have heaps of 'em in India, haven't you?'

'Oh, yes!' I said, 'we enjoy ourselves awfully, 'specially about this time of the year. I quite understand, though, that small communities dependent on themselves for enjoyment are apt to feel a little slow and isolated – almost bored, in fact.[14] But you were saying – ?'

'Well, living is not very dear, and house rent is. A hundred dollars a month gets you a decent house and you can get one for sixty. But house-property is down just now in Yokohama. Then your servants altogether may cost you about sixty or seventy dollars a month. A gardener gets ten dollars and a cook about eight a month. There is any amount of game and fish in the markets: the beef's good but we have no mutton. The races are on in Yokohama to-day and Monday. Are you going? No? You ought to go and see all the foreigners enjoying themselves.[15] But I suppose you've seen much better things in India, haven't you? You haven't anything better than old Fuji – Fujiyama[16] There he is now to the left of the line. What do you think of him?'

I turned and beheld Fujiyama across a sea of upward-sloping fields and woods. This is not quite strong enough. Let us be more precise. Fujiyama is the mountain which from time immemorial has appeared on the Japanese fan, is the heart of the country, the chosen home of legend, devil, goblin and sprite, and an extinct volcano to boot. It is about fourteen thousand feet high – not very much, according to our ideas. But fourteen thousand feet seen from seven thousand feet above the sea in the midst of sixteen-thousand-foot peaks, is quite another thing from the same height noted at sea-level in a comparatively flat country. The labouring eye crawls up every foot of the dead crater's smooth flank, and at the summit confesses

127

that it has seen nothing in all the Himalayas to match the monster. My view was graduated by three lines of clouds – the first where the green fields were drawn together at the base; the second where the green gave place to black rock streaked with the dirty snows of last winter; the third rested for a wreath on the white head. I was satisfied. Fujiyama was exactly as I had seen it on fans and lacquer boxes plus its own peculiar glory of colouring and outline, and I would not have sold my sight of it for the crest of Kinchinjunga[17] flushed with the morning. Fujiyama is the keynote of Japan. When you understand the one you are in a position to learn something about the other. I tried to get information from my fellow-traveller.

'Yes, the Japanese are building railways all over the island. What I mean to say is that the companies are started and financed by Japs, and they make 'em pay. I can't quite tell you where the money comes from, but it's all to be found in the country. Japan's neither rich nor poor, but just comfortable. I'm a merchant myself. Can't say that I altogether like the Jap way o' doing business. You can never be certain whether the little beggar means what he says. Give me a Chinaman to deal with. Other men have told you that, have they? You'll find that opinion at most of the treaty ports. But what I will say is, that the Japanese Government is about as enterprising a Government as you could wish, and a good one to have dealings with. When Japan has finished reconstructing herself on the new lines, she'll be quite a respectable little Power. See if she isn't. Now we are coming into the Hakone mountains. Watch the railway. It's rather a curiosity.'

We came into the Hakone mountains by way of some Irish scenery, a Scotch trout-stream, a Devonshire combe,[18] and an Indian river running masterless over half a mile of pebbles. This was only the prelude to a set of geological illustrations, including the terraces formed by ancient riverbeds, denudation, and half a dozen other 'ations that the Professor discoursed of learnedly. It was beautiful – wildly beautiful – till we came to a little Polau[19] driven through the mountains. First there was a tunnel, then a rock-cutting, then an embankment, then a bridge: one following the other as orderly as cards in a pack. In ten minutes the sequence was marred and we jumbled everything up together and whistled without ceasing for half an hour as we plunged from river to cliff, cliff to cascade, and cascade to terraced rice-field and water-mill. The line was very new indeed, so new that it seemed as if the engineer ought to be sitting somewhere on one of the bridges smiling at his work. He must have had good men to help him, and his assistants on the Hakone sections must have had lovely *shikar*.[20]

A great many of the cuttings were through rolled-out volcanic rock, and, by reason of their depth, at much too steep an angle to hold without help in so rainy a climate. Consequently the raw cut had been carefully turfed with sods, each sod pinned down by a dear little bamboo-pin. Where this was impossible the cut was corded by bamboo or grass ropes stretched diagonally across each other, and in their diamonds keeping safe tufts of bamboo. All the surface drains of the cuttings – and they were many – were laid in stone and the ballast was packed under the keys like counted shot in a cartridge case. Had these things occurred once or twice only as an evidence of what the Japanese could do, I should have smiled patronisingly; but when it came to miles and miles of sodded or corded cutting forty feet deep on the average I was angry. We do not do these things in India, even on the line to Rawalpindi,[21] and I do not believe, for all the Professor says, that continental lines are finished off with anything like the same neatness. But do you send home a professional by this road and let him write you his views of the Tokaido rail, and see if he does not speak well of it.

I was so busy telling the man from Yokohama lies about the height of the Himalayas that I did not watch things closely, till we got to Yokohama, at eight in the evening, and went to the Grand Hotel,[22] where all the clean and nicely dressed people who were just going in to dinner regarded us with scorn, and men, whom we had met on steamers aforetime, dived into photograph books and pretended not to see us. There's a deal of human nature in a man – got up for dinner – when a woman is watching him – and you look like a bricklayer – even in Yokohama.

The Grand is the Semi or Cottage Grand really, but you had better go there unless a friend tells you of a better. A long course of good luck has spoiled me for even average hotels. They are too fine and large at the Grand, and they don't always live up to their grandeur; unlimited electric bells, but no one in particular to answer 'em; printed menu, but the first comers eat all the nice things, and so forth. None the less there are points about the Grand not to be despised. It is modelled on the American fashion, and is but an open door through which you may catch the first gust from the Pacific slope. Officially, there are twice as many English as Americans in the port. Actually, you hear no languages but French, German, or American in the street. My experience is sadly limited, but the American I have heard up to the present, is a tongue as distinct from English as Patagonian. It differs in pitch, cadence, intonation, slang, reference, allusion and jest, and every third word has nothing whatever to do with England.

A gentleman from Boston was kind enough to tell me something about it. He defended the use of 'I guess' as a Shakespearian expression to be found in *Richard the Third*.[23] I have learned enough never to argue with a Bostonian.

'All right,' I said, 'I've never heard a real American say "I guess"; but what about the balance of your extraordinary tongue? Do you mean to say that it has anything in common with ours except the auxiliary verbs, the name of the Creator, and Damn? Listen to the men at the next table.'

'They are Westerners,' said the man from Boston, as who should say 'Observe this cassowary.'[24] 'They are Westerners, and if you want to make a Westerner mad tell him he is not like an Englishman. They think they are like the English. They are awfully thin-skinned in the West. Now in Boston it's different. *We* don't care what the English people think of us.'

The idea of the English people sitting down to think about Boston, while Boston on the other side of the water ostentatiously 'didn't care,' made me snigger. The man told me stories. He belonged to a Republic. That was why every man of his acquaintance belonged either 'to one of the first families in Boston' or else 'was of good Salem stock,[25] and his fathers had come over in the *Mayflower*.' I felt as though I were moving in the midst of a novel. Fancy having to explain to the casual stranger the blood and breeding of the hero of every anecdote. I wonder whether many people in Boston are like my friend with the Salem families. I am going there to see.

'There's no romance in America – it's all hard business facts,' said a man from the Pacific slope, after I had expressed my opinion about some rather curious murder cases which might have been called miscarriages of justice. Ten minutes later, I heard him say slowly, *apropos* of a game called 'Round the Horn' (This is a bad game. Don't play it with a stranger), 'Well, it's a good thing for this game that Omaha[26] came up. Dice were invented in Omaha, and the man who invented 'em he made a colossal fortune.'

I said nothing. I began to feel faint. The man must have noticed it. 'Six-and-twenty years ago, Omaha came up,' he repeated, looking me in the eye, 'and the number of dice that have been made in Omaha since that time in incalculable.'

I left the table while he was explaining the inwardness of some riots at Chicago which in his own speech were 'put through p.d.q.', *id est*, with great speed.

'There is no romance in America,' I moaned like a stricken ringdove, in the Professor's ear. 'Nothing but hard business facts, and the first families of Boston, Massachusetts, invented dice at Omaha when it first came up, twenty-six years ago, and that's the cold truth. What am I to do with a people like this?'

'Are you describing Japan or America? For goodness' sake, stick to one or the other,' said the Professor.

'It wasn't my fault. There's a bit of America in the bar-room, and on my word it's rather more interesting than Japan. Let's go across to 'Frisco and hear some more lies.'

'Let's go and look at photographs, and refrain from mixing our countries or our drinks.'

If you buy nothing else in Japan, and you will break yourself unless you begin as a pauper, you must buy photographs, and the best are to be found at the house of Farsari & Co.,[27] whose reputation extends from Saigon even to America. M. Farsari is a nice man, eccentric, and an artist, for which peculiarities he makes you pay, but his wares are worth the money. A coloured photograph ought to be an abomination. It generally is, but Farsari knows how to colour accurately and according to the scale of lights in this fantastic country. On the deck of the steamer I laughed at his red and blue hill-sides. In the hills I saw he had painted true. In his shop . . . but it's hardly worth mentioning. My friend the King of Italy was having an album of views made. I saw the book and ordered a better one. You needn't say anything about it, but if ever you happen to be turning over photos in the King's drawing room you may tell him this.

Seriously, spend as much money as you can afford on Farsari and let him choose illustrations of Japanese. Next door to his house stands the big, big curio-shop of Yokohama – Deakin's[28] – which is supposed to be good and convenient. All manner of lovely things are stored behind plate-glass windows, and if you have unlimited money you can enjoy yourself. But if you are wise do not bother your head about vanities of crockery and *cloisonnée*. There are only two kinds of both in Japan – the Arimas or what the seller has, and the Arimasen or what he has not.[29] Buy for colour and shape, for the lust of the eye and the delight of touch. There may be points about old Imari, Kaga, Kyoto, Satsuma with a golden small-pox upon it, lacquer of two hundred years polish, and *cloisonnée* of three, but you will not understand them. Get bits of things – go to the pawnshops, and wherever you find the European quarter of a town avoid it and go to the other side. Sometimes an eating house, a butcher's shop or a fishmonger's stall will sell you a plate from under the meat. Do not flatter yourself that you will ever make a bargain by this ransacking, but you will stumble on quaint things occasionally and more incidents than can be found in Deakin's shop.

But wherever you go in the Further East be humble to the white trader: Recollect that you are only a poor beast of a buyer with a few dirty dollars in your pockets, and you can't expect a man to demean himself by taking them. And observe humility not only in the shops, but elsewhere. I had something on my mind and was anxious in fact to know how I was to cross the Pacific to 'Frisco, and very foolishly went to an office where they might, under certain circumstances, be supposed to attend to these things. The steamers were full and I own I was anxious. But no anxiety troubled the sprightly soul who happened to be in the office-chair. 'There's heaps of time for finding out later on,' he said, 'and anyhow, I'm going to the races this afternoon. Come later on.' I put my head in the spittoon, and crawled out under the door.

When I am left behind by the steamer it will console me to know that that young man had a good time, and won heavily. Everybody keeps horses in Yokohama, and the horses are nice little fat little tubs, of the circus persuasion. I didn't go to the races, but a Calcutta man did, and returned saying that 'they ran 13.2 cart-horses,[30] and even time for a mile was four minutes and twenty-seven seconds.' Perhaps he had lost heavily, but I can vouch for the riding of the few gentlemen I saw outside the animals. It is very impartial and remarkably all round.

Just when the man from Boston was beginning to tell me some more stories about first families, the Professor developed an unholy taste for hot springs, and bore me off to a place called Miyanoshita to wash myself. 'We'll come back and look at Yokohama later on, but we must go to this because it's so beautiful.'

'I'm getting tired of scenery. It's all beautiful and it can't be described, but these men here tell you stories about America. Did you ever hear how the people of Carmel lynched Edward M. Petree for preaching the gospel without making a collection at the end of the service?[31] There's no romance in America – it's all hard business facts. Edward M. Petree was—'

'*Are* you going to see Japan or are you not?'

I went to see. First in a train for one hour in the company of a carriageful of howling Globe-trotters, then in a '*rickshaw* for four. You cannot appreciate scenery unless you sit in a '*rickshaw*. We struck after seven miles of modified flat – the flattery of Nature that lures you to her more rugged heart – a mountain river all black pools and boiling foam. Him we followed into the hills along a road cut into the crumbling volcanic rock and entirely unmetalled. It was as hard as the Simla cart-road, but those far hills behind Kalka have no such pine and maple, ash and willow.[32] It was a land of green-clothed cliff and silver waterfall, lovely beyond the defilement of the pen. At every turn in the road whence a view could be commanded, stood a little tea-house full of admiring Japanese. The Japanese dresses in blue because he knows that it contrasts well with the colour of the pines. When he dies he goes to a heaven of his own because the colouring of ours is too crude to suit him. I delivered this on the way to Miyanoshita.

We kept the valley of the glorified stream till the waters sank out of sight down the cliff-side and we could but hear them calling to one another through the tangle of the trees. Where the woodlands were loveliest, the gorge deepest, and the colours of the young hornbeam most tender, they had clapped down two vile hostelries of wood and glass, and a village that lived by selling turned wood and glass inlay things to the tourist.

But Providence is very just. When a man sins against colour it presently takes away his sense of form, as was pleasingly shown in the more expensive cabinets. Miyanoshita is a sort of second-hand Murree to the Pindi of Yokohama whence many people come in the summer.[33]

'I remember this place sixteen years ago before it was spoiled,' said a man at the hotel.[34] 'You took a coach of sorts from Yokohama to the foot of the hills and then got up here as you could. There were no ladies and no hotels then. You put up for a couple of months in a Jap tea-house, wore Japanese kit and splashed about in the hot springs all day long.'

Verily those must have been good times! Even the Japanese tea-girl, nicest of her sex, was nicer then.

Australians, Anglo-Indians, dwellers in London and the parts beyond the Channel were running up and down the slopes of the hotel garden, and by their strange dresses doing all they knew to deface the landscape. The Professor and I slid down the *khud* at the back and found ourselves back in Japan once more. Rough steps took us five or six hundred feet down through dense jungle to the bed of that stream we had followed all the day. The air vibrated with the rush of a hundred torrents, and whenever the eye could pierce the undergrowth it saw a headlong stream breaking itself on a boulder. We came face to face with one little river, six or eight feet broad and hung up by the tail to foam. It spat warm water at us, by which we knew that the hot springs were no invention of the guide book. Up

133

at the hotel we had left the grey chill of a November day and cold that numbed the fingers; down in the gorge we found the climate of Bengal with real steam thrown in. Green bamboo pipes led the hot water to a score of bathing-houses in whose verandahs Japanese in blue and white dressing-gowns lounged and smoked. From unseen thickets came the shouts of those who bathed and splashed water at one another, and – oh shame! round the corner strolled a venerable old lady chastely robed in nothing but a white bathing towel, and not too much of that. Then we went up the gorge, mopping our brows, and staring to the sky through arches of rampant foliage.

'Blue-green for young bamboo, indigo-blue for the pines, red for young maple leaves, sea-green and silver for the hornbeams,' murmured the Professor, taking an inventory of the glimpses. 'What a country! No wonder Farsari complains that people will not believe in his colouring. I wouldn't credit it unless I had seen the reality. How do you intend to describe that hillside?'

'For the tenth time, 'Fessor,' I made answer, 'I am not trying to describe things. Let us go and watch girls bathing and say nothing about it.'

Japanese maids of fourteen or fifteen are not altogether displeasing to behold. I have not seen more than twenty or thirty of them. Of these none were in the least disconcerted at the sight of the stranger. After all, 'twas but Brighton beach without the bathing-gowns. At the head of the gorge the heat became greater, and the hot water more abundant. The joints of the water-pipes on the ground gave off jets of steam; there was vapour rising from boulders on the river-bed, and the stab of a stick into the warm, moist soil was followed by a little pool of warm water. The existing supply was not enough for the inhabitants. They were mining for more in a casual and disconnected fashion. I tried to crawl down a shaft eighteen inches by two feet in the hillside, but the steam, which had no effect on the Japanese hide, drove me out. What happens, I wonder, when the pick strikes the liquid, and the miner has to run or be parboiled?

We scrambled up and down boulders, under and over wooden bridges, and through colonies of bath-houses till nightfall, the Professor making geological observations as profound as the gorge and bidding me note the evanescent colours of the dying day.

In the twilight, when we had reached upper earth once more and were passing through the one street of Miyanoshita, we saw two small fat cherubs about three years old taking their evening tub in a barrel sunk under the eaves of a shop. They feigned great fear, peeping at us behind outspread fingers, attempting futile dives, and trying to hide one behind the other in a hundred poses of spankable chubbiness, while their father urged them to splash us. It was the prettiest picture of the day, and one worth coming even to the sticky, paint-reeking hotel of Miyanoshita to see.

★   ★   ★

He was dressed in a black frock-coat, and at first I took him for a missionary as he mooned up and down the empty corridor.

'I have been under a ban for three days,' he whispered in a husky voice, 'through no fault of mine – no fault of mine. They told me to take the third watch, but they didn't give me a printed notification which I always require, and the manager of this place says that whisky would hurt me. Through no fault of mine, God knows, no fault of mine!'

I do not like being shut up in an echoing wooden hotel next door to a gentleman of the marine persuasion, who is just recovering from D.T.,[35] and who talks to himself all through the dark hours.

1889: LETTER EIGHT
COMMENTARY

1. For earlier references to the Tokaido (literally 'eastern sea road') see Letter Seven, Note 9. The road had fifty-three stages, the subject of a famous series of wood-block prints by Utagawa (Ando) Hiroshige (1797–1858). The Grand Trunk Road, with which Kipling, for the sake of his readers in India, suggests an analogy, was a major strategic highway in India before the days of railways. Actually, the original Tokaido railway line did not exactly follow the old Tokaido route. For instance, it did not go by Lake Hakone, where in Tokugawa days there had been a checkpoint on the road to prevent travellers from smuggling arms into Edo (Tokyo), but took a less precipitous route through the mountains via Gotemba between Hakone and Mt Fuji. Today the Tokaido railway line and the broad gauge Shinkansen line for the 'Bullet Train' pass under the Izu mountains by tunnel, between the hot spring resort of Atami and Mishima, whereas in Kipling's day there was no line to Atami or under the mountains.

2. Sir Guilford Molesworth (1828–1925) was a railway engineer of great distinction, with experience in Britain, Ceylon and India. From 1871 till 1889 when he retired he was consulting engineer to the government of India. He and Kipling were fellow-passengers on the *Ancona* to Kobe and the *City of Peking* to San Francisco.

3. The East Indian Railway Company operated one of India's major rail networks: it had existed in embryo as early as 1845, but its first short stretch of line out of Calcutta was not opened until 1854. In the previous year another company, the Great Indian Peninsula Railway, had opened its own first stretch out of Bombay, to a twenty-one-gun salute and the music of bands, inaugurating the first working railway in India.

4. In Latin *pro re nata* means 'in the circumstances', or 'things being what they are'. Kipling's implication here is 'for want of the "conveniences" referred to'. The reference that follows, to a fatal accident 'two days ago', is accurate (and incidentally enables us to date this journey of Kipling's at 29 April 1889). The accident was reported in some detail in the *Japan Weekly Mail* of 4 May. It had occurred on 27 April, and the man killed was a senior civil servant, formerly a naval officer, called Hida Hamagoro. He had been travelling south on the Tokyo–Kyoto line, and his death was directly attributable to the lack of lavatories on trains. At one station, Shizuoka, he had tried to use the station facilities, but they were too few for the crowd that needed them; at another, Fujieda, he alighted but the train moved on sooner than he had expected, and in attempting to re-enter it he fell between the platform and the train and was run over. The paper noted that the railway authorities evidently planned to 'run carriages with closets on all lines of any length': this, it felt, was an essential step, both 'in the cause of public decency' and to avoid further similar accidents.

5. The *Maru-Maru Chimbun* was a weekly comic magazine satirizing current events. At its peak, in 1879, it had been selling 15,000 copies, but it suffered a setback, and a year's closure, in 1880, when publication of a derogatory reference to the imperial family provoked a prosecution and the imprisonment of its editor-in-chief, Iwasaki Yoshimasa. Julia Meech-Pekarik has explained the origin of the title as follows:

> *Marumaru*, meaning 'circles,' derived from the little circles used by editors as a form of self-censorship in the galley proof stage (some books went into print with entire lines of little circles substituted for objectionable words), and *chimbun* was a pun on the word for newspaper, *shimbun*, implying 'strange writings'. (*The World of the Meiji Print*, Weatherhill, Tokyo & New York, 1987)

According to the same writer, the magazine's founder in 1877, and subsequent publisher, was Nomura Fumio, who had studied in

England in 1865–68 before returning to teach western studies in Hiroshima; he must have been inspired by the *Japan Punch*, a satirical journal for the foreign community which ran from 1862 to 1887, edited by Charles Wirgman, who had come to Yokohama in 1859 as correspondent for the *Illustrated London News* – and who is regarded today as 'the patron saint of the modern Japanese cartoon'.

6. For the *Nakasendo* (literally 'road through the middle of the mountains', also called the *Kiso-kaido* as it partly followed the line of the Kiso river) see an earlier mention in Letter Seven of 1889, Note 9. As an alternative route it became popular with Victorian travellers: they could both admire its scenery and enjoy the sensation of being off the beaten track.

7. To '*dak* it', a slang variant of to 'travel *dak*', was clear to Kipling's readers in India. The term *dak*, formerly spelt *dawk*, meant a post or stage or relay, hence travel by relays – in this case a relay system of rickshaws. (The familiar term '*dak* bungalow' meant the accommodation available for travellers at the staging posts.)

8. The 'great lake' was the Hamana lagoon. Murray's *Handbook for Travellers in Japan* (1894 edition) describes the railway as crossing the mouth of the lagoon on 'a long series of dykes and bridges, whence the roar of the breakers of the Pacific can be distinctly heard'.

9. Hoshiarpur: a town and district in the Punjab, India.

10. At Nancy, a city in France 175 miles east of Paris, there was a famous Institute of Forestry. It dated from 1824 and was among the oldest and most influential in the world. Some Indian Forestry Service officers in Kipling's day had received training there.

11. Kipling was fancying some resemblance between the city of Hamamatsu, through which the line passed, and Patna in Bihar, India.

12. By 1889 the concept of a tunnel under the English Channel, approximately between Dover and Calais, had been under practical consideration intermittently for some thirty years. (That is to ignore its genesis in a wild scheme proposed to Napoleon in 1802 by a Frenchman, Albert Mathieu.) Advancing technology made it increasingly feasible, and it reached the stage of an Anglo–French Convention being signed in 1875, but though a Channel Tunnel Company was formed, and preliminary tunnelling was done from both coasts, the scheme ran into military objections, political doubts and commercial obstruction, particularly on the British side. Kipling's doubt as to which railway company was involved is understandable: the violent rivalry of the London, Chatham & Dover and the South Eastern companies, consistent with their suicidal competition all over Kent, was a major factor in aborting the whole project, which has only recently been revived with any expectation of success. In the original (*Pioneer*) text Kipling called the railway the 'London, Brighton and South Coast'.

13. The rainy season in Japan normally begins in June and ends in late July.

14. Kipling's readers in India would have perceived the heavy irony of

these remarks, written as they were in April. They would also have read some of his most characteristic early prose and verse, which took as its theme the hardship of expatriates in lonely Indian outposts in an unhealthy climate.

15. The Yokohama races were very popular with the foreign community there, particularly the British. The first race meeting was organized in 1862; in 1866 a site for a course was secured and the Yokohama Race Club was formed. In the early days there were no professional jockeys: merchants and officials themselves rode in the races.

16. 'Fujiyama': in Japanese the correct term for Mount Fuji is 'Fuji-san': see the Notes on 'To the Dancers', page 242. The mountain is 3,776 metres (12,395 feet) high.

17. Kinchinjunga, variously spelt but now usually Kangchenjunga. It is a spectacular mountain, once believed to be the highest in the Himalayan range, on the Nepal/Sikkim border. Its altitude is 8,598 metres (28,225 feet).

18. A combe, or coomb, is a short valley or hollow on the flank of a hill.

19. Polau: this term has not been explained, and the paragraph of which it forms part was not included in *From Sea to Sea*. It may be a corruption, through misread handwriting, of the Hindi word *palan*, meaning a space of ground, possibly a corridor (though its standard meaning is space between occupied plots, reserved for future development, and this is hardly appropriate).

20. *Shikar*: a Hindi word of Persian derivation, meaning the sport of hunting or shooting. It was in common English use in India.

21. Rawalpindi: a city in what is now Pakistan, adjacent to the specially created capital, Islamabad. The 'line to Rawalpindi' was from Lahore.

22. At this time the Grand, at the west end of the Bund, was the principal hotel of Yokohama. According to an advertisement in the *Handbook for Travellers* (Chamberlain & Mason, 1894) it had 'upwards of 100 apartments, and [is] surrounded by fine Verandahs over 200 feet long, making an extensive promenade, [and it] affords its occupants a magnificent view of the Harbour and a cool and pleasant residence, even in the hottest days of the sultry season'. It also had 'fine Tennis Lawns and Walks', and its own steam launch.

23. 'I guess': Americans, finding themselves laughed at for over-use of this term in the sense of 'I suppose', were apt to be defensive about it. See, on a scholarly level, many references to the subject in H. L. Mencken's classic, *The American Language* (1919, abridged 1963), all hingeing on the comment that 'occasional English tolerance for things American was never extended to the American language'. As for 'I guess', though Shakespeare and others had used it, it had 'dropped out of use in England in the Eighteenth Century', and its survival in the USA was 'remarked by nearly all the early English travelers', e.g. H. B. Fearon who in *Sketches of America* illustrated its prevalence with dialogue:

138

> Q. What is your name?
> A. William Henry, *I guess.*
> Q. Is your wife alive?
> A. No, she is dead, *I guess.*

Though not essentially hostile to the USA (he married an American, counted Americans among his closest friends, and chose to live for four years in Vermont), Kipling remained critical and detached, and disliked what he regarded as American debasement of the language. Hence his reference to Patagonia (the bleak southernmost reaches of South America).

24. Cassowary: a large flightless bird of New Guinea and Australasia, related to the emu and ostrich. Hence, in this context, an exotic phenomenon. Here, and in his subsequent visit to the USA, Kipling had a journalist's quickness in detecting regional differences.
25. Salem: an Old Testament name for Jerusalem, given to an early English settlement in Massachusetts, north of Boston. Though Kipling said he was 'going there to see', he did not do so during his American tour of 1889.
26. Omaha: major city of Nebraska, USA. The reference to dice is of course nonsense, and to 'coming up' twenty-six years earlier is obscure: but the population of the city did increase almost tenfold in the 1860s.
27. A. Farsari & Co, at No 16, Bund, Yokohama, advertised that they had views of all the principal places of interest in Japan. They also did 'portraits in any of the latest styles and in Japanese costumes', and claimed that children were a 'speciality'.
28. Deakin Brothers and Company were opposite the Grand Hotel, and sold 'Japanese Works of Art'.
29. *Arimasu* means 'to be' or 'to have': *arimasen* is the negative.
30. '13.2 cart-horses': a sarcastic allusion to the lack of impressive horses in Japan. 13.2 hands would be a smaller size than polo ponies in India, which used to be about 14 hands, roughly 4 ft 8 inches at the shoulder. See also Letter Eleven, Note 16.
31. Carmel: there are various places of this name in the USA. The reference to 'Edward M. Petree' is presumably no more than a jocular indication that Kipling had been listening to further tall stories from Americans.
32. Simla was the summer capital of British India. Kalka is a town at the foot of the hills, on the approach to Simla from the plains. Until 1903, when the Kalka–Simla light railway was completed, travellers to Simla made the journey from the railhead at Kalka, a climb of some 5,000 feet in some fifty miles, by various kinds of horse-drawn conveyance.
33. Murree, now in Pakistan, was in the British India period the hill station most conveniently situated for Rawalpindi. It is at an altitude of 7,500 feet, 6,000 feet higher than Rawalpindi and thirty-seven miles away by road. The houses in Murree were built on a ridge, with magnificent views over forested hills.

34. Kipling probably stayed at the Fujiya Hotel: the other main hotel was the Naraya. The *Handbook for Travellers in Japan* (Chamberlain and Mason, 1894) described Miyanoshita as 'a pleasant resort for many reasons – the purity of the air, the excellence of the hotel accommodation, the numerous pretty walks both short and long, the plentiful supply of "chairs" and of specially large comfortable *kagos* for those who prefer to be carried, and the delicious hot baths, which, containing but faint traces of salt and soda, may be used without medical advice'.
35. The term DT (or by the 1880s more commonly 'the DTs') was in use from the second half of the nineteenth entury as an abbreviation for *delirium tremens*, a disordered mental and physical state resulting from chronic excess of alcohol.

1889: Letter Nine

CONCERNING A HOT-WATER TAP, AND SOME GENERAL CONVERSA-
TION. THE MAN WITH THE PICTURES AND THE WOMAN WITH THE
WASHING.

Always speak to the stranger. If he doesn't shoot, the chances are
he'll answer you. – *Western Proverb.*

It is a far cry from Miyanoshita to Michni[1] and Mandalay.[2] That
is why we have met men from both those stations, and have spent
a cheerful time talking about dacoits and the Black Mountain
Expedition. One of the advantages of foreign travel is that one takes
such a keen interest in, and hears so much about, Home. Three giddy
young gunners who are supposed to be seeing the scenery have just
spent an hour talking of exchange and promotion in the Royal
Regiment.[3] Truly, they change their trains, but not their train of
thought, who run across the sea.

'This is a most extraordinary place,' said the Professor, red as a
boiled lobster. 'You sit in your bath and turn on the hot or cold
spring, as you choose, and the temperature is phenomenal. Let's go
and see where it all comes from, and then let's go away.'

There is a place called the Burning Mountain[4] five miles in the
hills. There went we, through unbroken loveliness of bamboo-
copse, pine wood, villages of two houses, grass downs, and pine
wood again, while the river growled below, and polite villagers
rushed from their mats to proffer beer to the Briton. In the end we
found an impoverished and second-hand Hell, set out orderly on the
side of a raw and bleeding mountain. It looked as though a match-
factory had been whelmed by a landslip, and the trees had not found
time to cover the wreckage. Water, in which bad eggs had been
boiled, stood in blister-lipped pools, and puffs of thin white smoke
went up from the labouring under-earth. Despite the smell and the
sulphur incrustations on the black rocks, I was disappointed, till I felt
the heat of the ground, which was the heat of a boiler-sheathing.
They call the mountain extinct. If untold tons of viewless, pulsing

141

power, cased in a few feet of dirt, be the Japanese notion of extinction, glad I am that I have not been introduced to a lively volcano. Indeed, it was not an overweening notion of my own importance, but a tender regard for the fire-crust below, and a lively dread of starting the machinery by accident, that made me step so delicately, and urge return upon the Professor.

'Huh! It's only the boiler of your morning bath. All the sources of the springs are here,' said he.

'I don't care. Let 'em alone. Did you never hear of a boiler bursting? Don't prod about with your stick in that amateur way. You'll turn on the tap.'

When you have seen a burning mountain you begin to appreciate Japanese architecture. It is not solid. Every one is burned out once or twice and refers to the fact casually, as an index-date. Farsari has been burned out, Deakin has been burned out, three merchants that I talked to had all been burned out, and Naraya's hotel at Miyanoshita has been burned out twice.[5] A business isn't respectable until it has received its baptism of fire. But fire is of no importance. The one thing that inconveniences a Japanese is an earthquake. Consequently, he arranges his house so that it shall fall lightly as a bundle of broom upon his head. Still further safeguarding himself, he has no foundations, but the corner-posts rest on the crowns of round stones sunk in the earth. It is the next best thing to building a pukka house on round-shot in trenches.[6] The corner-posts take the wave of the shock, and, though the building may give way like an eel-trap, nothing very serious happens. This is what epicures of earthquakes aver. I wait for mine own experiences, but not near a suspected district such as the Burning Mountain.

It was only to escape from one terror to another that I fled Miyanoshita. A blue-breeched dwarf thrust me into a dwarf *'rickshaw* on spidery wheels, and down the rough road that we had taken four hours to climb ran me clamorously in half an hour. Take all the parapets off the Simla Road and leave it alone for ten years. Then run down the steepest four miles of any section, – not steeper than the drop to the old Gaiety Theatre,[7] – behind one man! You may occupy your time profitably as you bound from boulder to boulder to slough and rock-ridge to hole, in speculating on the chances of turning the next corner (*a*) with one wheel in the air, (*b*) without any wheels at all, or (*c*) by way of a drop down the *khud*[8] after having run over your *jhampani*.[9]

'We couldn't get six *paharis*[10] to take us in this style,' shouted the Professor as he spun by, his wheels kicking like a duck's foot, and the whole contraption an an angle of thirty. I am proud to think that not even sixty *paharis* would have gambolled with a *sahib* in that disgraceful manner. Nor would any tramway company in the Real East have run its cars to catch a train that used to start last year, but now – rest its soul – is as dead as Queen Anne.[11] This thing a queer little seven-mile tramway accomplished with much dignity. It owned a first-class car and a second-class car, – two horses to each, – and it ran them with a hundred yards interval – the one all but empty, and the other half full for the maintenance of dignity and economy of rolling-stock. When the very small driver could not control his horses, which happened on the average once every two minutes, he did not waste time by pulling them in. He screwed down the brake and laughed – possibly at the company who had paid for the very elaborate car. Yet he was an artistic driver. He wore no Philistine brass badge. Between the shoulders of his blue jerkin were done in white, three rail-heads in a circle, and on the skirts as many tram-wheels conventionalised. Only the Japanese know how to conventionalise a tram-wheel or make a key-pattern of rail-heads. Though we took twelve hours to cover the thirty miles that separated us from Yokohama, we admitted this much while we waited for our train in a village by the sea. [*Nota Bene*: A village of any size is about three miles long in the main street; then it changes its name and continues for another three miles as something else. Villages with a population of more than ten thousand souls take rank as towns.]

'And yet,' said a man at Yokohama that night, 'you have not seen the densest population. That's away in the western *kens* – districts, as you call them.[12] The folk are really crowded thereabouts, but, virtually, poverty does not exist in the country. You see, an agricultural labourer can maintain himself and his family, as far as rice goes, for four cents a day, and the price of fish is nominal. Rice now costs a hundred pounds to the dollar. What do you make it by Indian standards? From twenty to twenty-five seers the rupee.[13] Yes, that's about it. Well, he gets, perhaps, three dollars and a half a month. I can't explain why the wages are so much above the cost of living. The people spend a good deal in pleasuring. They must enjoy themselves. I don't think they save much. How do they invest their savings? In jewellery? No, not exactly; though you'll find that the women's hair-pins, which are about the only jewellery they wear, cost a good deal. Seven and eight dollars are paid for a good hair-pin, and, of course, jade may cost anything. What the women really lock their money up in is their *obis* – the things you call sashes. An *obi* is ten or twelve yards long, and I've known them sold wholesale for fifty dollars each. Every woman above the poorest class has at least one good dress of silk and an *obi*. Yes, all their savings go in dress, and a handsome dress is always worth having. The western *kens* are the richest taken all round. A skilled mechanic there gets a dollar or dollar and a half a day, and, as you know, lacquer-workers and inlayers – artists – get two. There's enough money in Japan for all current expenses. They won't borrow any for railroads. They raise it 'emselves. Most progressive people the Japanese are as regards railways. They make them very cheaply; much more cheaply than any European lines. I've some experience, and I take it that £3,600 a mile is the average cost of construction. Not on the Tokaido, of course – the line that you came up by.[14] That's a Government line, State-built, and a very expensive one. I'm speaking of the Japanese Railway Company from Tokyo to Shogawa with a mileage of three hundred, and the line from Kobe south, and the Kyushu line in the southern island. There are lots of little companies with a few score miles of line, but all the companies are extending.[15] The reason why the construction is so cheap is the nature of the land. There's no long haulage of rails, because you can nearly always find a creek running far up into the country, and dump out your rails within a few miles of the place where they are wanted. Then, again, all your timber lies to your hand, and your staff are Japs. There are a few European engineers, but they are quite the heads of the departments, and I believe if they were cleared out to-morrow, the Japs would go on building their lines. They know how to make 'em pay. One line started on a State guarantee of eight per cent. It hasn't called for the guarantee yet. It's making twelve per cent on its own hook. There's a very heavy freight-traffic in wood and provisions for the big towns, and there's a local traffic that you can have no idea of unless you've watched it. The people seem to move in twenty-mile circles for business or pleasure – 'specially pleasure. Oh, I tell you, Japan will be a gridiron of railways before long. In another month or two you'll be able to travel nearly seven hundred miles on and by the Tokaido line alone from one end to the other of the central islands. Getting from east to west is harder work. The backbone-hills of the country are just cruel, and it will be some time before the Japs run many lines across. But they'll do it, of course. Their country must go forward.

'If you want to know anything about their politics, I'm afraid I can't help you much. They are, so to speak, drunk with Western liquor, and are sucking it up by the hogshead. In a few years they will see how much of what we call civilisation they really want, and how much they can discard. 'Tisn't as if they had to learn the arts of life or how to make themselves comfortable. They knew all that long ago. When their railway system is completed, and they begin to understand their new Constitution, they will have learned as much as we can teach 'em. That's my opinion; but it needs time to understand this country. I've been a matter of eight or ten years in it, and my views aren't worth much. I've come to know some of the old families that used to be of the feudal nobility. They keep themselves to themselves and live very quietly. I don't think you'll find many of them in the official classes. Their one fault is that when they entertain they do so far beyond their means. They won't receive you informally and take you into their houses. They raise dancing-girls,[16] or take you to their club and have a big feed. They don't introduce you to their wives, and they haven't yet given up the rule of making the wife eat after the husband. Like the native of India you say? Well, I am very fond of the Jap; but I suppose he *is* a native any way you look at him. You wouldn't think that he is careless in his workmanship and dishonest. A Chinaman, on an average, is out and away a bigger rogue than a Jap; but he has sense enough to see that honesty is the best policy, and to act by that light. A Jap will be dishonest just to save himself trouble. He's like a child that way.'

How many times have I had to record such an opinion as the foregoing? Three or four times? Everywhere the foreigner says the same thing of the neat-handed, polite little people that live among flowers and babies, and smoke tobacco as mild as their own manners. I am sorry; but when you come to think of it, a race without a flaw would be perfect. And then all the other nations of the earth would rise up and hammer it to pieces. And then there would be no Japan.

'I'll give you a day to think over things generally,' said the Professor. 'After that we'll go to Nikko and Tokyo. Who has not seen Nikko does not know how to pronounce the word "beautiful"'[17]

It was altogether another word that I pronounced. I object to deliberately looking for loveliness. If it comes in the course of the day, well and good; if not, leave it alone. A kiss that involves strategy and forethought, for instance, never tastes half so well as one chance-caught on the staircase – the result of a happy inspiration or the unpremeditated turn of the head. When you come to Japan, as you will the next time you get three months' leave, do even as I have done. Secure a strong-minded friend to whom the *bandobast*[18] of travel is a pleasure. Let him arrange and think for you, and with him follow the fancy of the day, nothing doubting. But wherever you go cling to a guide – an English-speaking one, such as you catch in hotels. The Professor and I made our excursion to Miyanoshita without one on the grounds that Japanese was very like Hindustani if you spoke it quickly enough. We were repentant ere we had taken seats in the train and uncomfortable throughout, though it is not true that I was found at midnight clamouring for a *murgha-ka-dum*[19] in the belief that I should get a cocktail thereby.

Yokohama is not the proper place to arrange impressions in. The Pacific Ocean knocks at your door, asking to be looked at; the Japanese and American men-of-war demand serious attention through a telescope; and if you wander about the corridors of the Grand Hotel, you stop to play with Spanish Generals, all gold lace and spurs, or are captured by touts for curio-shops. It is not a nice experience to find a *sahib* in a Panama hat handing you the card of his firm for all the world like a Delhi silk-merchant. You are inclined to pity that man, until he sits down, gives you a cigar, and tells you all about his diseases, his past career in California, where he was always making money and always losing it, and his hopes for the future, in a language that he profoundly believes to be English. You see then that you are entering upon a new world. Talk to every one you meet, if they show the least disposition to talk to you, and you will gather, as I have done, a host of stories that will be of use to you hereafter. Unfortunately, they are not all fit for publication. When I tore myself away from the distractions of the outer world, and was just sitting down to write seriously on the Future of Japan, there entered a fascinating man, with heaps of money, who had collected Indian and Japanese curios all his life, and was now come to this country to get some old books which his collection lacked. Can you imagine a more pleasant life than his *dilettante* wanderings over the earth, with a lifetime's special knowledge to back each signature of his cheque-book?

In five minutes he had carried me far away from the clattering, fidgety folk around, to a quiet world where men meditated for three weeks over a bronze, and scoured all Japan for a sword-guard designed by a great artist and – were horribly cheated in the end.

'Who is the best artist in Japan now?' I asked.

'He died in Tokyo, last Friday, poor fellow, and there is no one to take his place. His name was K—,[20] and as a general rule he could never be persuaded to work unless he was drunk. He did his best pictures when he was drunk.'

'*Ému.*[21] Artists are never drunk.'

'Quite right. I'll show you a sword-guard that he designed. All the best artists out here do a lot of designing. K— used to fritter away his time on designs for old friends. Had he stuck to pictures he could have made twice as much. But he never turned out pot-boilers. When you go to Tokyo, make it your business to get two little books of his called *Drunken Sketches* – pictures that he did when he was – *ému*. There is enough dash and go in them to fill half a dozen studios. An English artist studied under him for some time. But K—'s touch was not communicable, though he might have taught his pupil something about technique. Have you ever come across one of K—'s crows? You could tell it anywhere. He could put all the wicked thoughts that ever came into the mind of a crow – and a crow is first cousin to the Devil – on a piece of paper six inches square, with a brush of Indian ink and two turns of his wrist. Look at the sword-guard I spoke of. How is that for feeling?'

On a circular piece of iron four inches in diameter and pierced by the hole for the tang of the blade, poor K—, who died last Friday, had sketched the figure of a coolie trying to fold up a cloth which was bellying to a merry breeze – not a cold wind, but a sportive summer gust. The coolie was enjoying the performance, and so was the cloth. It would all be folded up in another minute and the coolie would go on his way with a grin.

This thing had K— conceived, and the faithful workman executed, with the lightest touches of the graver, to the end that it might lie in a collector's cabinet in London.

'Wah! wah!' I said, and returned it reverently. 'It would kill a man who could do that to live after his touch had gone. Well for him he died – but I wish I had seen him. Show me some more.'

'I've got a painting by Hokusai[22] – the great artist who lived at the end of the last century and the beginning of this. Even *you* have heard of Hokusai, haven't you?'

'A little. I have heard it was impossible to get a genuine painting with his signature attached.'

'That's true; but I've shown this one to the Japanese Government expert in pictures – the man the Mikado consults in cases of doubt – to the first European authority on Japanese art, and of course I have my own opinion to back the signed guarantee of the seller. Look!'

He unrolled a silk-scroll of the kind that adorn the recesses of the guest-chamber, and showed me the figure of a girl in pale blue and grey crêpe, carrying in her arms a bundle of clothes that, as the tub behind her showed, had just been washed. A dark-blue handkerchief was thrown lightly over the left forearm, shoulder, and neck, ready

147

to tie up the clothes when the bundle should be put down. The flesh of the right arm showed through the thin drapery of the sleeve, and the sleeve pockets of thicker material were lined with red. The right hand merely steadied the bundle from above; the left gripped it firmly from below. Through the stiff blue-black hair showed the outline of the left ear.

That there was enormous elaboration in the picture, from the ornamentation of the hair-pins to the graining of the clogs, did not strike me till after the first five minutes, when I had sufficiently admired the certainty of touch.

'Recollect there is no room for error in painting on silk,' said the proud possessor. 'The line must stand under any circumstances. All that is possible before painting is a little dotting with charcoal, which is rubbed off with a feather-brush. Did he know anything about drapery or colour or the shape of a woman? Is there any one who could teach him more if he were alive to-day?'

I wondered how long the enthusiasm would last, could a word of mine prove conclusively that Hokusai was not the creator of that woman with the washing. Happy is the man who knows nothing but whether he is pleased or pained. I had seen real Japanese painting at last, and would admire it heart-free without a thought to sealed guarantees.

Then we went to Nikko.

1889: LETTER NINE
COMMENTARY

1. Michni, or Michni Kandao, is in the Khyber Pass, now in Pakistan, but in Kipling's day on the North-West Frontier of India. Hence, in the next sentence, the reference to the 'Black Mountain Expedition', the name given at the time to some punitive operations conducted in the Black Mountains north of Rawalpindi, by the Hazara Field Force of the British/Indian Army, after the murder of a British survey party in the area. This had been in late 1888 and was still recent news for Kipling's readers at 'Home', which here means India.
2. Mandalay: though Kipling later wrote a famous poem of this name, on

his visit to Burma in 1889 he did not go as far as Mandalay. It had been the capital of the independent Burmese kingdom until 1886 when this was annexed after the brief Third Burmese War of 1885. However, the aftermath of that war had been prolonged paramilitary operations, which were still not over by 1889, against armed gangs ranging from bandits (in most cases) to resistance fighters. The British called them all *dacoits*, a Hindi term long prevalent in Bengal to describe armed robbers: hence the reference in the next sentence.

3. This is a reference to the Artillery arm of the British Army. Its full title is 'Royal Regiment of Artillery'.

4. Kipling is referring to the area known as Owakidani ('Valley of the Greater Boiling'). Another name is Jigokudani ('Valley of Hell'): *ojigoku* was the 'big hell' and *kojigoku* the 'small hell'.

5. For Farsari and Deakin, see Letter Eight, Notes 27 and 28. For Naraya's Hotel (or the Naraya) see Letter Eight, Note 34.

6. *Pukka* was a word of Hindi origin very common in English: from an original meaning of 'ripe' or 'mature' or 'cooked', it had come to mean 'thorough' or 'proper'. It had a particular application to buildings, as in this reference, meaning those made of permanent materials such as bricks. As to 'round-shot' or cannon-balls, the concept of spherical projectiles was not unfamiliar in 1889, though elongated shells fired from rifled guns had by now superseded them.

7. The 'old' Gaiety Theatre in Simla was rather inconveniently placed, down the main steep slope from the central ridge of the town, close to the Lower Bazaar. The 'new' theatre of that name had been built in 1887, much higher, but the old premises continued in use. However, in May 1889, just after Kipling wrote this, and long before it appeared in print in the *Pioneer*, the old Gaiety was destroyed by fire.

8. The term *khud*, variously spelt and of debatable derivation, was in constant use in British Indian hill stations in the Himalayas, and meant a precipitous hillside or steep valley. See also page 133.

9. A *jhampani*, though in the present context a rickshaw man in Japan, was essentially in India one of a team of men who carried a *jhampan*. Both words were variously spelt, and their origin has been learnedly debated. One theory mentioned in *Hobson-Jobson* (Yule and Burnell) is that it may indicate that the *jhampan* was originated in Japan. Anyway, it was a kind of sedan chair at one time much used by European ladies at hill stations in northern India. It was carried by two pairs of men, each carrying on his shoulders a bar from which the shafts of the sedan chair were slung. Hence Kipling's surprise at the downhill speed attained by a single Japanese rickshaw man.

10. *Paharis*: hillmen, of northern India.

11. Queen Anne, who reigned from 1702–14, somehow gave rise after her death to the expression, 'Queen Anne's dead.' This was a sarcastic retort to anyone who gave stale information as if it were news.

12. The *Ken*, or Prefecture, replaced the *Kuni*, or Province, as the major administrative division of Japan after the Meiji Restoration of 1868.

13. A *seer* was an Indian unit of weight. However, its weight in practice varied greatly in different parts of the subcontinent, though British legislation in the nineteenth century did much to standardize it at about the equivalent of one kilogram.

14. For the Tokaido see Letter Eight, Note 1. When the 1889 *Pioneer* text was re-published in 1899 the figure of £3,600 was reduced to £2,000.

15. When Kipling arrived in Japan the Japanese railway network was being rapidly expanded. See earlier Notes, e.g. Letter Four, Notes 2 and 10, Letter Seven, Notes 8 and 9. When the 1889 text was re-published in 1899 the words 'from Tokyo to Shogawa' were omitted. Shogawa has not been identified with certainty.

16. By 'dancing-girls' Kipling's interlocutor meant *geisha*, who are professional entertainers (*not* prostitutes).

17. This is a reference to a Japanese proverb, a play on words to the effect that one cannot say '*kekko*' (meaning wonderful or magnificent) until one has seen *Nikko*.

18. The Hindi term *bandobast* (from the Persian, meaning literally a 'tying and binding') was in familiar English usage in the sense of 'discipline', 'system', 'arrangements'.

19. A *murgha-ka-dum* meant literally the tail (strictly *dhum*) of a cock (*murgha*).

20. This was Kawanabe Kyosai, famous for vigorous and humorous drawings and prints. He was born in 1831, and he died on Friday 26 April 1889. In due course, on 18 May, a long and laudatory article about him was published in the *Japan Weekly Mail*, from which his great stature as an artist clearly emerges, as do two of the points referred to by Kipling.

    First, the matter of his doing his best work when drunk. From the article it appeared that this was an overstatement, and that he did not usually drink till his work was done. But there was no denying that his imaginative powers could be splendidly stimulated by *sake*, and the artist himself 'recognised that under the influence of Bacchus some of his strangest fancies, freshest conceptions and boldest touches were inspired, and he humorously assumed on that account the name of Shojo, after the legendary Bacchus of Japan'.

    Second, his talent in the drawing of a crow. The article mentioned a famous occasion, at an art exhibition in 1877, when Kyosai had merely sent 'a bold and simple painting of a crow', which he priced at 100 yen. When the judges remonstrated, Kyosai replid that 'it was not the price of a *common crow*, but a small fraction of the price of the fifty years of study that had enabled him to dash off his picture in this manner'.

21. The French word *ému*, here ironically used as a euphemism for 'drunk', means 'moved' in the sense of 'affected' or 'touched'.

22. This was the famous painter and print artist Katsuchika Hokusai (1760–1849).

1889: Letter Ten

CURSES A NATION AND DESCRIBES A TEMPLE. THE LEGEND OF NIKKO
FORD AND THE STORY OF THE AVOIDANCE OF MISFORTUNE.

A rose-red city, half as old as Time.[1]

The journey to Nikko from Yokohama began with a difficulty as
regards the American Nation. I required something to read on the
way, for well I knew that unadulterated nature even in her sweetest
aspects becomes swiftly monotonous. There was a shop which
unhappily is not yet burned down. It sold every novel of any
pretensions that has been published within the last five and twenty
years at a uniform price of twenty cents, or something between six
and nine pence. In other words it was the receiving shop – the fence –
for property stolen by American thieves with printing machines
from English authors.

I had read a good deal and thought more about what is euphemisti-
cally called piracy of literature,[2] but I was not prepared for the black
record of crime put forward by a nest of filchers called the 'Seaside
Publishing Company',[3] and put into my hand by the obliging
shopman. 'I think you'll find everything you want there.'

O! did he? I should have been exacting had I not done so. Apart
from the mighty dead who are all the world's property, because they
still compete with the living author, I found the names of all the
lesser lights who twinkle from the tops of one, two or three columns
today. Besant, Braddon, Inglesant, Haggard, Stevenson, Hall Caine,
Anstey, 'Q', Farjeon, Ouida, Farrar, George Moore and others
whom the pen holds not in remembrance were all on the list, and
their works did follow their names orderly.[4]

The riot of rapine did not end there. The catalogue concluded with
a section headed 'Miscellaneous'. No attempt at organisation marked
this last 'round up' of little authors. They were packed into it hoof,
horn and hide like cattle. You would see how the head-thief who
regulated the lifting had marked the *Saturday*'s reviews[5] in red ink by
the batch, while his underlings did the mechanical work of stealing.

151

Not content with this the Library – forgive me for using that word – poured foul and fulsome praise on the larger authors – trotted them out before the American public – while it improved their spelling according to the notion prevalent in the School Boards of the States. When Thackeray is made to talk about 'travelers' and 'theaters' it is time for England to declare war. The crown and flower of these insults was a warning to the public not to buy books from firms other than the Seaside Library because the latter gave all the stories unabridged. The big thief was congratulating himself on the completeness of his fraud.

'Don't you want any of these publications?' said the shopman.

'These aren't publications, they are burglaries, what you call thefts: do you understand? Things that men in civilised countries get imprisoned for,' I responded.

'They've stopped the sale of them in Singapore and Hong Kong,' he answered, 'and I think they are going to stop the sale of them here. But everybody buys 'em. Aren't you going to have any?'

I was not going to assist the disgrace. I was going to express my opinions, but not in the shop. The loathsome library had been cribbing Anglo–Indian stories not altogether unknown to me.[6] It might have left our unhappy country alone. Then I cursed the Seaside Library and the United States that bred it very copiously ...[7]

'Yes, yes. I dare say we shall find the American Eagle as sick as the Jackdaw of Rheims[8] when he has digested that,' said the Professor soothingly as I puffed the tale of my wrongs into his ear on the Yokohama platform. 'But before you go on swearing in that libertine fashion just think how much better it would be for the English author if he published his book in the first instance at prices that defied competition.'

'There's no romance in America. It's all hard business facts.[9] You bet the animals would find out a new way of cheating. Take me away to commune with nature.'

Five hours in the train took us to the beginning of a *'rickshaw* journey of twenty-five miles. The guide unearthed an aged *dâk-ghari* on Japanese lines, and seduced us into it by promises of speed and comfort beyond anything that a *'rickshaw* could offer. Never go to Nikko in a *dâk-ghari*. The town of departure is full of pack-ponies who are not used to it, and every third animal tries to get a kick at his friends in the shafts. This renders progress sufficiently exciting till the bumpsomeness of the road quenches all emotions save one.

Nikko is reached through one avenue of *cryptomerias* – cypress-like trees eighty feet high, with red or dull silver trunks and hearse-plume foliage of darkest green.[10] When I say one avenue, I mean one continuous avenue twenty-five miles long, the trees so close to each other throughout that their roots interlace and form a wall of wood on either side of the sunken road. Where it was necessary to make a village along the line of march, – that is to say once every two or three miles, – a few of the giants had been wrenched out – as teeth are wrenched from a full-planted jaw – to make room for the houses. Then the trees closed up as before to mount guard over the road. The banks between which we drove were alight with azaleas, camellias, and violets. 'Glorious! Stupendous! Magnificent!' sang the Professor and I in chorus for the first five miles, in the intervals of the bumps. The avenue took not the least notice of our praise except by growing the trees even more closely together. 'Vistas of pillared shade' are very pleasant to read about,[11] but on a cold day the ungrateful heart of a man could cheerfully dispense with a mile or two of it if that would shorten the journey. We were blind to the beauty around; to the files of pack-ponies, with manes like hearth-brooms and the tempers of Eblis,[12] coquetting about the path; to the pilgrims with blue and white handkerchiefs on their heads, enviable silver-grey leggings on their feet, and Buddha-like babies on their backs; to the trim country drays pulled by miniature cart-horses bringing down copper from the mines and *sake* from the hills; to the colour and movement in the villages where all the little children shouted 'Ohio's!'[13] and all the old people laughed. We wanted Nikko and nothing but Nikko. The grey tree-trunks marched us solemnly along over that horrid bad road which had been mended with brushwood, and after five hours we got what we wanted in the shape of a long village at the foot of a hill, and capricious Nature, to reward us for our sore bones, laughed on the instant in floods of sunshine. And upon what a mad scene did the light fall! The *cryptomerias* rose in front of us a wall of green darkness, a tearing torrent ran deep-green over blue boulders, and between stream and trees was thrown a blood-red bridge – the sacred bridge of red lacquer that no foot save the Mikado's may press.[14]

Very cunning artists are the Japanese. Long ago a great-hearted king came to Nikko River and looked across at the trees, upstream at the torrent and the hills whence it came, and downstream at the softer outlines of the crops and spurs of wooded mountains. 'It needs only a dash of colour in the foreground to bring this all together,' said he, and he put a little child in a blue and white dressing-gown under the awful trees to judge the effect. Emboldened by his tenderness, an aged beggar ventured to ask for alms. Now it was the ancient privilege of the great to try the temper of their blades upon beggars and such cattle. Mechanically the king swept off the old man's head, for he did not wish to be disturbed. The blood spurted across the granite slabs of the river-ford in a sheet of purest vermilion. The king smiled. Chance had solved the problem for him. 'Build a bridge here,' he said to the court carpenter, 'of just such a colour as that stuff on the stones. Build also a bridge of grey stone close by, for I would not forget the wants of my people.' So he gave the little child across the stream a thousand pieces of gold and went his way. He had composed a landscape. As for the blood, they wiped it up and said no more about it; and that is the story of Nikko Bridge. You will not find it in the guide-books – which is the sign of its truth.

When a Japanese makes red lacquer to stand out in the open he coats it with common red paint for the sake of preservation. The lacquer is there just the same, only the finger of faith is needed to discover it. I rubbed foolishly, walked round a little, rubbed some more and dropped a futile lower jaw. Then I tried to scratch the lacquer with my finger nail, but it wouldn't scratch. The Professor was for photographing the wonder on the spot, but the guide dissuaded thus:- 'In a by and by seeing beauties much more than this by several times, keep your plate and everything for anything. Not now doing pictures, come and go about.'

Three fierce attacks on the poor man – and on my faith all I wanted was honest information – had weakened the mind of the guide. Moreover he had been possibly puzzled by a thing called a bedding-roll. (By the way, never abandon your bedding-roll in Japan. It is unsightly but very convenient.) 'Gentlemen come here bringing round box or square box, or hand-box or band-box', he piped confidentially to the Professor. 'That all right. Load he up all right, load he down too. But *this* gentleman that come with you has no box – neither round nor square-face. Sometimes both and then so fat in he side. No gentleman I know bring that sort of box – all cloth and soft.'[15] The Professor took him away up hill and soothed him.

I followed the voice of the river through a rickety toy-village, across some rough bottom-land, till, crossing a bridge, I found myself among lichened stones, scrub, and the blossoms of spring. A hillside, steep and wooded as the flanks of the red Aravallis,[16] rose on my left; on my right, the eye travelled from village to crop-land, crop to towering cypress, and rested at last on the cold blue of an austere hill-top encircled by streaks of yet unmelted snow. The Nikko hotel stood at the foot of this hill; and the time of the year was May. Then a sparrow came by with a piece of grass in her beak, for she was building her nest; and I knew that the spring was come to Nikko. One is so apt to forget the changes of the year over there with you in India.

Sitting in a solemn line on the banks of the river – it was a stream really, but it made so much noise that I gave it brevet rank – were fifty or sixty cross-legged images which the untrained eye put down immediately as so many small Buddhas.[17] They had all, even when the lichen had cloaked them with leprosy, the calm port and unwinking regard of the Lord of the World. They are not Buddhas really, but other things – presents from forgotten great men to dead-and-gone institutions, or else memorials of ancestors. The guide-book will tell you. They were a ghostly crew. As I examined them more closely I saw that each differed from the other. Many of them held in their joined arms a little store of river pebbles, evidently put there by the pious. When I inquired the meaning of the gift from a stranger who passed, he said: 'Those so distinguished are images of the God who Plays with Little Children up in the Sky.[18] He tells them stories and builds them houses of pebbles. The stones are put in his arms either that he may not forget to amuse the babies or to prevent his stock running low.'

I have no means of telling whether the stranger spoke the truth, but I prefer to believe that tale as gospel truth. Only the Japanese could invent the God who Plays with Little Children. Thereafter the images took a new aspect in my eyes and were no longer 'Graeco-Buddhist sculptures,' but personal friends. I added a great heap of pebbles to the stock of the cheeriest among them. His bosom was ornamented with small printed slips of prayers which gave him the appearance of a disreputable old parson with his bands in disorder. A little further up the bank of the river was a rough, solitary rock hewn into what men called a Shinto shrine. I knew better: the thing was Hindu, and I looked at the smooth stones on every side for the familiar dab of red paint. On a flat rock overhanging the water were carved certain characters in Sanskrit, remotely resembling those on a Tibetan prayer-wheel. Not comprehending these matters, and grateful that I had brought no guide-book with me, I clambered down to the lip of the river – now compressed into a raging torrent. Do you know the Strid near Bolton – that spot where the full force of the river is pent up in two yards' breadth?[19] The Nikko Strid is an improvement upon the Yorkshire one. The blue rocks are hollowed like soapstone by the rush of the water. They rise above head-level

and in spring are tufted with azalea blossom. The stranger of the
godlings came up behind me as I basked on a boulder. He pointed up
the little gorge of rocks, 'Now if I painted that as it stands, every
critic in the papers would say I was a liar.'

From our standpoint the mad stream came down directly from a
blue hill blotched with pink, through a sky-blue gorge also pink-
blotched. An obviously impossible pine mounted guard over the
water. I would give much to see an accurate representation of that
view. The stranger departed growling over some hidden grief –
connected with the Academy perhaps.[20]

Hounded on by the Professor, the guide sought me by the banks
of the river and bade me 'come and see temples.' Then I fairly and
squarely cursed all temples, being stretched at my ease on some
warm sand in the hollow of a rock, and ignorant as the grass-shod
cattle that tramped the further bank. 'Very fine temples,' said the
guide, 'you come and see. By and by temples be shut up because
priests make half an hour more time.' Nikko time is half an hour
ahead of the standard, because the priests of the temples have
discovered that travellers arriving at three p.m. try to do all the
temples before four – the official hour of closing. This defrauds the
church of her dues, so her servants put the clock on, and Nikko,
knowing naught of the value of time, is well content.

When I cursed the temples I did a foolish thing, and one for which
this poor pen can never make fitting reparation. We went up a hill by
way of a flight of grey stone slabs. The *cryptomerias* of the Nikko road
were as children to the giants that overshadowed us here. Between
their iron-grey boles were flashes of red – the blood-red of the
Mikado's bridge. That great king who killed the beggar at the ford
had been well pleased with the success of his experiment. Passing
under a mighty stone arch we came into a square of splendour alive
with the sound of hammers. Thirty or forty men were tapping the
pillars and steps of a cornelian shrine heavy with gold. 'That,' said
the guide impassively, 'is a godown.[21] They are renewing the
lacquer. First they extract it.'

Have you ever 'extracted' lacquer from wood? I smote the foot of
a pillar with force, and after half a dozen blows chipped off one small
fragment of the stuff, in texture like red horn. Betraying no surprise,
I demanded the name of a yet more magnificent shrine across the
courtyard. It was red-lacquered like the others, but above its main
door were carved in open work three apes – one with his hands to his
ears, another covering his mouth, and a third blinding his eyes.

'That place,' said the guide, 'used to be a stable when the Daimyo kept his horses there. The monkeys are the three who hear no wrong, say no wrong, and see no wrong.'[22]

'Of course,' I said. 'What a splendid device for a stable where the syces steal the grain!' I was angry because I had grovelled before a godown and a stable, though the round world cannot hold their equals.

We entered a temple, or a tomb, I do not know which, through a gateway of carven pillars. Eleven of them bore a running pattern of trefoil – the apex pointing earthward – the twelfth had its pattern reversed.

'Make 'em all the same – no good,' said the guide emphatically. 'Something sure to come bad by an' by. Make one different all right. Save him so. Nothing happen then.'

Unless I am mistaken, that voluntary breaking of the set was the one sacrifice that the designer had made to the great Gods above who are so jealous of the craft of men. For the rest he had done what he pleased – even as a God might have done – with the wood in its gleaming lacquer sheath, with enamel and inlay and carving and bronze, hammered work, and the work of the inspired chisel. When he went to his account he saved himself from the jealousy of his judges, by pointing to the trefoil pillars for proof that he was only a weak mortal and in no sense their equals. Men say that never man has given complete drawings, details, or descriptions of the temples of Nikko. Only a German would try, and he would fail in spirit. Only a Frenchman could succeed in spirit, but he would be inaccurate. I have a recollection of passing through a door with *cloisonnée* hinges, with a golden lintel and red lacquer jambs, with panels of tortoise-shell lacquer and clamps of bronze tracery. It opened into a half-lighted hall on whose blue ceiling a hundred golden dragons romped and spat fire in a hundred different attitudes. A priest moved about the gloom with noiseless feet, and showed me a pot-bellied lantern four feet high, that the Dutch traders of old time had sent as a present to the temple. There were posts of red lacquer dusted over with gold, to support the roof. On one post lay a rib of lacquer, six inches thick, that had been carved or punched over with high relief carvings and had set harder than crystal.

The temple steps were of black lacquer, and the frames of the sliding screens red. That money, lakhs and lakhs[23] of money, had been lavished on the wonder impressed me but little. I wished to know who were the men that, when the *cryptomerias* were saplings, had sat down and spent their lives on a niche or corner of the temple, and dying passed on the duty of adornment to their sons, though neither father nor child hoped to see the work completed. This question I asked the guide, who plunged me in a tangle of Daimyo and Shoguns, all manifestly extracted from a guide-book.

Shelving further demands he took me further up the hill by way of a stone staircase, the rails of which were made out of solid stone – four rails with top and bottom pieces being carved *en bloc*. At each story, and I counted four, we found a temple or a shrine for the accommodation of temple drums standing on a platform cut into the hillside and overshadowed by the funereal green of the *cryptomerias*. After a while the builder's idea entered into my soul.

He had said: 'Let us build blood-red chapels in a Cathedral.' So they planted the Cathedral three hundred years ago, knowing that tree-boles would make the pillars and the sky the roof.

Round each temple stood a small army of priceless bronze or stone lanterns, stamped, as was everything else, with the three leaves that make the Daimyo's crest.[24] The lanterns were dark green or lichened grey, and in no way lightened the gloom of the red. Down below, by the sacred bridge, I believed red was a joyous colour. Up the hillside under the trees and the shadow of the temple eaves I saw that it was the hue of sorrow. When the great king killed the beggar at the ford he did not laugh, as I have suggested. He was very sorry, and said: 'Art is Art, and worth any sacrifice. Take that corpse away and pray for the naked soul.' Once, in one of the temple courtyards, nature dared to rebel against the scheme of the hillside. Some forest tree, all unimpressed by the *cryptomerias*, had tossed a torrent of tenderest pink flowers down the face of a grey retaining wall that guarded a cutting. It was as if a child had laughed aloud at some magnificence it could not understand.

'You see that cat?' said the guide, pointing out a pot-bellied pussy painted above a door. 'That is the Sleeping Cat. The artist he paint it left-handed. We are proud of that cat.'

'And did they let him remain left-handed after he had painted that thing?'

'Oh yes. You see he was always left-handed.'[25]

The infinite tenderness of the Japanese towards their children extends, it would seem, even to artists. Every guide will take you to see the Sleeping Cat. Don't go. It is bad. Coming down the hill, I learned that all Nikko was two feet under snow in the winter, and while I was trying to imagine how fierce red, white, and black-green would look under the light of a winter sun I met the Professor murmuring expletives of admiration.

'What have you done? What have you seen?' said he.

'Nothing. I've accumulated a lot of impressions of no use to any one but the owner.'[26]

'Which means you are going to slop over for the benefit of the people in India,' said the Professor.

And the notion so disgusted me that I left Nikko that very afternoon, the guide clamouring that I had not seen half its glories. 'There is a lake,' he said; 'there are mountains. You must go see!'

'I will return to Tokyo and study the modern side of Japan. This place annoys me because I do not understand it.'

'Yet I am *the* good guide of Yokohama,' said the guide.

1889: LETTER TEN
COMMENTARY

1. The Reverend J. W. Burgon (1813–88), though the author of several books, is only remembered today on account of this single line from his poem 'Petra' (1845). Correctly, it reads, 'A rose-red city – "half as old as Time"!', the last five words being in fact a quotation from a poem by Samuel Rogers (1763–1855), a more prolific poet who on the death of Wordsworth in 1850 was offered, but declined, the Poet Laureateship.
2. Book piracy seriously embittered Kipling's view of the USA. During the next twenty years Kipling was among the most indignant and outspoken of British authors concerning this vexed subject, and more than once took legal proceedings though with limited success. The USA had not been a party to the 1886 Berne Convention on Copyright, and though piracy of foreign books by American publishers gradually diminished, grounds for complaint remained until the US Copyright Act of 1909.
3. The 'Seaside Publishing Company', which Kipling also called (below) the 'Seaside Library', was in fact a firm called George Munro, of New York, which published a series called the Seaside Library.
4. The list or prospectus which Kipling would have seen in the Yokohama bookshop has never been traced, but his account presents few difficulties with regard to the names he cites: the allusion to their appearance in articles of one, two or three columns reflects the widespread practice of serialization of stories in newspapers and magazines in both Britain and the USA. Details of the names are as follows:

Besant: Sir Walter Besant (1836–1901), novelist and founder of the Society of Authors, which was instrumental in the reform of copyright law. Kipling felt much beholden to Besant: in his autobiography he related how it had been one of Besant's novels which inspired him to come away in 1889 from the obscurity of Indian journalism and 'measure myself against the doorsills of London'.

Braddon: Mary Elizabeth Braddon (1837–1915), popular writer of some seventy lurid and melodramatic novels.

Inglesant: This was probably a slip of the pen. Kipling may either have had in mind J. H. Shorthouse (1834–1903), author of the best-selling novel *John Inglesant* (1881), or else the woman poet and novelist Jean Ingelow (1820–97), best remembered now for her poem, 'The High Tide on the Coast of Lincolnshire'.

Haggard: Sir Rider Haggard (1856–1925), who in the past four years had written three famous novels, *King Solomon's Mines*, *She* and *Allan Quatermain*. He later became a close friend of Kipling's.

Stevenson: Robert Louis Stevenson (1850–94), the famous and extremely popular novelist, poet and essayist, whom Kipling held in high respect.

Hall Caine: Sir Thomas Henry Hall Caine (1853–1931), a highly successful novelist, who made a fortune, especially from the dramatization of one novel, *The Deemster* (1887).

Anstey: 'F. Anstey' was the pseudonym of Thomas Anstey Guthrie (1856–1934), though the 'F' was originally due to a printer's misreading. By 1889 he was on the staff of *Punch*, and had already written the best remembered of his many novels of fantasy and humour, *Vice Versa*.

'Q': This was the pseudonym of Sir Arthur Quiller-Couch (1863–1944), now remembered as a distinguished critic and lecturer, but in 1889 coming to prominence for novels such as *Dead Man's Rock*.

Farjeon: This was Benjamin Leopold Farjeon (1838–1903), writer of many melodramatic novels, of which the best was *Devlin the Barber* (1888). He was the father of the well-known children's writer, Eleanor Farjeon.

Ouida: the pen-name of Marie Louise de la Ramée (1839–1908), writer of some forty-five highly romantic novels.

Farrar: The Very Reverend F. W. Farrar (1831–1903), eventually Dean of Canterbury. He was a theologian, but also wrote 'edifying' and extremely successful school stories, notably *Eric, or Little by Little* and *St Winifred's, or the World of School*. In 1898 he took grave offence when Kipling's *Stalky & Co.* permanently (and specifically) debunked his sanctimonious style of writing about school life.

George Moore: The Anglo-Irish novelist and playwright George Augustus Moore (1852–1933). By the 1880s his stylish and unorthodox novels were attracting attention: the most successful of them was *Esther Waters* (1894).

5. 'The *Saturday*' was possibly the American *Saturday Evening Post*, though in 1889, ten years before the great editorship of G. H. Lorimer, this was not the significant magazine it later became. Much more probably it was the influential British *Saturday Review*, which ran from 1855 to 1938.

6. This is an unmistakable reference to Kipling's own work, and helps to explain the intensity of his anger. The Seaside Library pirated eleven titles by Kipling between 1888 and 1899. Bibliographers, however, have been in some doubt, on account of the dubious issue dates of these cheap editions, as to which of his books he found on sale in Yokohama: it was probably *Wee Willie Winkie*. A different doubt is raised by a letter Mrs Hill wrote in Yokohama, dated Saturday 11 May 1889. In it she said:

> We are sailing today for America. When Ruddy went to the shop to buy books for our Pacific trip he found an American pirated edition of his own tales. He was so furious that he stalked out of the shop and bought us nothing, to our great dismay . . .

A reasonable inference from this is that Kipling's visit to the bookshop was on or just before the day of his sailing with the Hills from Yokohama; whereas the clear inference from Kipling's own account is that he was getting something to read in the train on the trip to Nikko, which was at least a few days earlier. He may, in writing up the episode in retrospect, have altered the order of events.

7. Kipling's lengthy and petulant 'curse' against America is omitted here: he suppressed it himself in *From Sea to Sea*, and its irrelevance to Japan removes any justification for resuscitating it in the present context.

8. 'The Jackdaw of Rheims' is a famous poem in *The Ingoldsby Legends* by R. H. Barham (1788–1845). The Cardinal Archbishop of Rheims loses his ring, and elaborately curses whoever has stolen it –

> Never was heard such a terrible curse!
> But . . . Nobody seem'd one penny the worse.

However, the tame jackdaw which has in fact stolen the ring is found to be in poor condition –

> His pinions droop'd – he could hardly stand, –
> His head was as bald as the palm of your hand;
> His eye so dim, so wasted each limb,
> That, heedless of grammar, they all cried, 'That's him!'

9. This echoes the words of 'the man from the Pacific slope' in Letter Eight – see pages 130 and 132.

10. *Cryptomeria japonica* is a coniferous tree of China and Japan. The avenue of huge cryptomerias leading to Nikko has survived only in parts.

11. This is a quotation from Milton's *Paradise Lost*, Book IX, lines 1105–7:

> The bended Twigs take root, and Daughters grow
> About the Mother Tree, a Pillard shade
> High overarch't, and echoing Walks between . . .

12. Eblis was a fallen angel, called Azazel before his fall, in Muslim demonology. It is recounted in the *Quran* that he disobeyed God's command to give respect to the newly created Adam, and was turned into an evil *jinn*, sometimes called Shaitan, father of devils.

13. *Ohio* is Kipling's way of writing *o-hayoo*. Its literal meaning is 'honorably early', and it is used to mean 'good morning'. The correct and full phrase is *o-hayoo gozaimasu*.

14. The 'blood-red bridge' is the *Mi Hashi*, spanning the Daiya-gawa, a stream about forty feet wide. It was first put up in 1638 (though it has since been rebuilt) for the exclusive use of the Shogun, military rulers of Japan in the Tokugawa period (1600–1868). Kipling has invented the story he tells about the bridge.

15. Now an obsolete item of luggage, the bedding-roll was a canvas cover or hold-all, with a carrying-handle, commonly used by travelling Europeans in India and elsewhere to convey bedding or other things.

16. The Aravalli hills are a range north-west of Udaipur in what is now Rajasthan, India.

17. The 'Buddhas' which Kipling saw are stone images of *Jizo-bosatsu* (or *Bodhisattva*) at Kanman (or Ganman) -ga-fuchi, near Nikko. The statues, dating from the mid-seventeenth century, originally numbered a hundred: they are sometimes called the 'ghostly statues' because when counted more than once the number of them seems to vary.

18. See Note 17. *Jizo* (in Sanskrit Khsitigarbha), who saves suffering beings in evil realms, was especially popular in Japan as the saviour of the souls of dead children. According to popular belief, children's souls go after death to the *Sai-no-kawara*, roughly corresponding to the Styx, the sinister river of ancient Greek mythology. Here a merciless she-devil, the hag *Shozuka-no-Baba*, first steals the children's clothes, then sets them the task of piling stones on the river bank, telling them that by building towers tall enough they will be able to reach Paradise. The task, however, is rendered indefinite because the hag and her company of devils scatter the stones as fast as they are piled. The situation is saved by the benign *Jizo*, who drives the demons away, comforts the children and hides them in his great sleeves. Hence a belief that every stone placed with a prayer in the lap of a statue of *Jizo* shortens the penance of some young soul, and each of the pitiful items of children's clothing hung on the images will clothe a child's soul.

19. The Strid (a name derived from an Early English word meaning 'turmoil') is near Bolton Abbey in Yorkshire, where the river Wharfe passes through a narrow cleft in limestone. Kipling would have seen it as a schoolboy visiting his paternal grandmother in Yorkshire.

20. This 'stranger', with his Royal Academy preoccupations, was evidently the artist to whom Kipling later alluded, in what was obviusly the same context of Nikko, in 'Half-a-Dozen Pictures' (Letter Four of 1892). It is possible that he was Alfred East, (see Letter Seven of 1889, Note 5).

21. A *godown* (from the Malay gudang) is a warehouse or store, a term in widespread use in the far east. The Toshogu Mausoleum complex contains three storehouses.

22. The stable at the Toshogu Mausoleum recently housed a white horse, a gift to the shrine from New Zealand: the horse was kept 'for the use of the god'.

23. The word *lakh*, in universal use in India, meant 100,000, whether in regard to people or things or, commonly as here, units of currency – rupees being probably in Kipling's mind.

24. The *mon* or crest of the Tokugawa dynasty consisted of three leaves of *asarum*, a plant related to hazelwort, in a circle (*mitsu-aoi*).

25. This 'sleeping cat', of which Kipling took an unenthusiastic view, is a standard tourist sight which Fodor's modern *Guide to Japan* simply says 'is easy to miss'. The left-handed sculptor was *Hidari* (i.e. 'Left') *Jingoro* (1594–1634), a legendary carver of architectural detail to whom many colourful myths attach.

26. It is characteristic of Kipling that, recognizing the splendours of Nikko as indescribable, he played them down in the concluding passages of this despatch. (In Letter Twelve, at page 184, he called Nikko 'fairest of all places under the sun'.) He may have been right to say that 'never man has given complete drawings, details or descriptions' of Nikko. Fodor's *Guide* notes that many visitors have been greatly impressed by the magnificence of the mausolea, while others have found them gaudy and vulgar.

1889: Letter Eleven

SHOWS HOW I GROSSLY LIBELLED THE JAPANESE ARMY, AND EDITED
A CIVIL AND MILITARY GAZETTE OF TOKYO, WHICH IS NOT IN THE
LEAST TRUSTWORTHY.

'And the Duke said, "Let there be cavalry," and there were
cavalry. And he said, "Let them be slow," and they were slow,
d—d slow, and the Japanese Imperial Horse called he them.'

I was wrong. I know it. I ought to have clamoured at the doors of the
Legation for a pass to see the Imperial Palace. I ought to have
investigated Tokyo and called upon some of the political leaders of
the Liberal and Radical parties. There are a hundred things which I
ought to have done, but somehow or other the bugles began to blare
through the chill of the morning, and I heard the tramp of armed
men under my window. The parade-ground was within a stone's
throw of the Tokyo hotel;[1] the Imperial troops were going on
parade. Would *you* have bothered your head about politics or
temples? I ran after them.

It is rather difficult to get accurate information about the Japanese
army. It seems to be in perpetual throes of reorganisation. At
present, so far as one can gather, it is about one hundred and seventy
thousand strong.[2] Everybody has to serve for three years,[3] but
payment of one hundred dollars will shorten the term of service by
one year. At least, this is what a man who had gone through the mill
told me. He capped his information with this verdict: 'English Army
no use. Only Navy any good. Have seen two hundred English
Army.[4] No use.' The idea of Japan standing up in its wool-boots and
passing criticism on us made me laugh in my informant's face. But
this is a digression.

On the parade-ground they had a company of foot and a wing of
what, for the sake of brevity, I will call cavalry under instruction.
The former were being put through some simple evolutions in close
order; the latter were variously and singularly employed. To the
former I took off the hat of respect; at the latter I am ashamed to say I

164

pointed the finger of derision.[5] But let me try to describe what I saw. The likeness of the Japanese infantryman to the Gurkha grows when you see him in bulk. Thanks to their wholesale system of conscription the quality of conscripts varies immensely. I have seen scores of persons with spectacles whom it were base flattery to call soldiers, and who I hope were in the medical or commissariat departments.[6] Again I have seen dozens of bull-necked, deep chested, flat-backed, thin-flanked little men who were as good as a Colonel Commanding could desire. There was a man of the 2nd Infantry whom I met at an up-country railway station. He carried just the proper amount of insolent swagger that a soldier should, refused to answer any questions of mine, and parted the crowd round him without ceremony.

A Gurkha of the Prince of Wales's Own[7] could not have been trimmer. In the crush of a ticket-collecting – we both got out together – I managed to run my hand over that small man's forearm and chest. They must have a very complete system of gymnastics in the Japanese army, and I would have given much to have stripped my friend and seen how he peeled. If the 2nd Infantry are equal to sample, they are good.

The men on parade at Tokyo belonged either to the 4th or the 9th, and turned out with their cowskin valises strapped, but I think not packed. Under full kit, such as I saw on the sentry at Osaka Castle,[8] they ought to be much too heavily burdened. Their officers were as miserable a set of men as Japan could furnish – spectacled, undersized even for Japan, hollow-backed and hump-shouldered. They squeaked their words of command and had to trot by the side of their men to keep up with them. The Japanese soldier has the long stride of the Gurkha, and he doubles[9] with the easy lope of the *'rickshaw* coolie. Throughout the three hours that I watched them they never changed formation but once, when they doubled in pairs across the *maidan*, their rifles at the carry.[10] Their step and intervals were as good as anything that our native regiments have to show, but they wheeled rather promiscuously, and were not checked for this by their officers. So far as my limited experience goes, their formation was not ours, but Continental.[11] Does a company in column move on a face of nine files, or how? The words of command were as beautifully unintelligible as anything our parade-grounds produce; and between them the officers of each half-company vehemently harangued their men, and shook their swords at 'em in distinctly unmilitary style. The precision of their movements was beyond praise. They enjoyed three hours of steady drill, and in the rare intervals when they stood easy to draw breath I looked for slackness all down the ranks, inasmuch as 'standing easy' is the crucial test of men after the first smartness of the morning has worn off. They stood 'easy', neither more nor less, but never a hand went to a shoe or stock or button while they were so standing. When they knelt, still in this queer column of company, I understood the mystery of the long sword-bayonet which had puzzled me sorely. I had expected to see the little fellows lifted into the air as the bayonet-sheath took ground; but they were not. They kicked it sideways as they dropped. All the same, the authorities tie men to the bayonets instead of bayonets to the men. When at the double there was no grabbing at the cartridge-pouch with one hand or steadying the bayonet with the other, as may be seen any day at running-firing on Indian ranges. They doubled cleanly – as our Gurkhas double.

It was an unchristian thought, but I would have given a good deal to see that company being blooded on an equal number of our native infantry – just to know how they would work. If they have pluck, and there is not much in their past record to show that they have not, they ought to be first-class enemies. Under British officers instead of the little anatomies at present provided,[12] and with a better rifle, they should be as good as any troops recruited east of Suez. I speak here only for the handy little men I saw. The worst of conscription is that it sweeps in such a mass of fourth and fifth-rate citizens who, though they may carry a gun, are likely, by their own excusable ineptitude, to do more harm to the morale and set-up of a regiment than execution in front of them. In their walks abroad the soldiery never dream of keeping step. They tie things to their side-arms, they carry bundles, they slouch, and dirty their uniforms so that all the world may say: 'Who's that civilian who has stolen a uniform?'.

And so much for a raw opinion on Japanese infantry. The cavalry were having a picnic on the other side of the parade-ground – circling right and left by sections, trying to do something with a troop, and so forth. I would fain believe that the gentlemen I saw were recruits. But they wore all their arms and their officers were just as clever as themselves. Half of them were in white fatigue-dress and flat cap — though no need to say whence those had been borrowed – and wore half-boots of brown leather with short hunting-spurs and black straps; no chains. They carried carbine and sword – the sword fixed to the man, and the carbine slung over the back with the pouch. No martingales,[13] but breastplates and crupper,[14] a huge, heavy saddle, with single hide-girth, over two *numdahs*,[15] completed the equipment which a thirteen-hand pony,[16] all mane and tail, was trying to get rid of. When you thrust a two-pound bit and bridoon[17] into a small pony's mouth, you hurt his feelings. When the riders wear, as did my friends, white worsted gloves, they cannot take a proper hold of the reins. When they ride with both hands, sitting well on the mount's neck, knuckles level with its ears and the stirrup leathers as short as they can be, the chances of the pony getting rid of the rider are manifestly increased. Never have I seen such a wild dream of equitation as the Tokyo parade-ground showed. Do you remember the picture in *Alice in Wonderland*, just before Alice found the Lion and the Unicorn; when she met the armed men coming through the woods?[18] I thought of that, and I thought of the White Knight in the same classic, and I laughed aloud. Here were a set of very fair ponies, sure-footed as goats, mostly entires,[19] and full of go. Under Japanese weights they would have made very thorough mounted infantry animals. And here was this blindly imitative nation trying to turn them into heavy cavalry. As long as the little beasts were gravely trotting in circles they did not mind their work. But when it came to slashing at the Turk's head[20] they objected very much indeed. I affiliated myself to a section who, armed with long wooden swords, were enjoying some Turk's-heading. Out started a pony at the gentlest of canters, while the rider bundled all the reins into one hand, and held his sword like a lance. Then the pony shied a little shy, shook his shaggy head, and began to passage round the Turk's head. There was no pressure of knee or rein to tell him what was wanted. The man on top began kicking with the spurs from shoulder to rump, and shaking up the ironmongery in the poor brute's mouth. The pony could neither rear, not kick, nor buck; but it shook itself free of the incubus who slid off, and patiently waited till it was remounted. Three times I saw this happen. The catastrophe didn't rise to the dignity of a fall. It was the blundering collapse of incompetence plus worsted gloves, two-handed riding, and a hay-stack of equipment. Very often the pony went at the post, and the man delivered a back-handed cut at the Turk's head which nearly brought him out of his world-too-wide saddle. Again and again this solemn performance was repeated. I can honestly say that the ponies are very willing to break rank and leave their companions, which is what an English troop-horse fails in; but I fancy this is more due to the urgent private affairs of the pony than any skill in training. The troops charged once or twice in a terrifying canter. When the men wished to stop they leaned back and tugged, and the pony put his head to the ground, and bored all he knew. They charged me, but I was merciful, and forebore to empty half the saddles, as I assuredly could have done by throwing up my arms and yelling 'Hi!' The saddest thing of all was the painful conscientiousness displayed by all the performers in the circus. They had to turn these rats into cavalry. They knew nothing about riding, and what they did know was wrong; but the rats must be made troop-horses. Why wouldn't the scheme work? There was a patient, pathetic wonder on the faces of the men that made me long to take one of them in my arms and try to explain things to him – bridles, for instance, and the futility of hanging on by the spurs. Just when the parade was over, and the troops were ambling off, Providence sent diagonally across the paradeeground, at a gallop, a big rawboned man on a lathy-red American horse wild with the intoxication of the keen morning air. The brute cracked his nostrils, and switched his flag[21] abroad, and romped across the plain, while his rider dropped one hand and sat still, swaying lightly from the hips. The two served to scale the surroundings. Some one really ought to tell the Mikado that *ekka* ponies were never intended for dragoons.

If the changes and chances of military service ever send you against Japanese troops, be tender with their cavalry. They mean no harm. Put some fusees down for the horses to step on, and send a fatigue-party out to pick up the remnants. But if you meet Japanese infantry, led by a Continental officer, commence firing early and often and at the longest ranges compatible with getting at them. They are bad little men who know too much.

Having thoroughly settled the military side of the nation exactly as my Japanese friend at the beginning of this letter settled us, – on the strength of two hundred men caught at random,[22] – I devoted myself to a consideration of Tokyo. The Professor had gone off to look at temples. I am wearied of temples. Their monotony of splendour makes my head ache. You also will weary of temples unless you are an artist, and then you will be disgusted with yourself. Some folk say that Tokyo covers an area equal to London. Some folk say that it is not more than ten miles long and eight miles broad. There are a good many ways of solving the question. I found a tea-garden situated on a green plateau far up a flight of steps, with pretty girls smiling on every step. From this elevation I looked forth over the city, and it stretched away from the sea, as far as the eye could reach – one grey expanse of packed house-roof, the perspective marked by number-less factory chimneys. Then I went several miles away and found a park, another eminence, and some more tea-girls prettier than the last; and, looking again, the city stretched out in a new direction as far as the eye could reach. Taking the scope of the eye on a clear day

1. KYOTO, APRIL 1889. This photograph (like nos. 2–4) was taken by Kipling's travelling-companion, Professor Hill. To judge from the handwritten caption in the Hills' photograph album – four lines of Tennyson's 'Palace of Art', beginning *I built my soul a lordly pleasure-house* – this building made a profound impression. It may have been part of the Yaami's Hotel complex.

2. NAGASAKI, 15 APRIL 1889. The setting of the 'evil-looking bronze horse' (page 40).

3. KOBE, APRIL 1889. A courtyard of what is described in the Hills' photograph album as 'the "How Happy" Temple, Hiogo' (page 62).

4. NIKKO, MAY 1889. Kipling at first resisted persuasion to 'come and see temples' (page 156), but on seeing them admitted he was wrong.

5. YAAMI'S HOTEL, KYOTO. From an engraving of 1887 or earlier. This was 'the quaintest hotel that ever you saw' (page 83).

6. THE 'BIG BELL OF KYOTO'. Its 'lisping mutter' was 'very deep and entirely strange' (pages 86–7).

7. GRAND HOTEL, YOKOHAMA, as it looked in Kipling's day – 'the Semi or Cottage Grand really, but you had better go there' (page 129).

8. LOBBY OF THE GRAND HOTEL. Here the 'nicely dressed people who were just going in to dinner regarded us with scorn' (page 129).

9. THE BUND, YOKOHAMA. The large building is the United Club, over-looking the sea. 'The population of the club changes with each steamer in harbour' (page 212).

10. A PIER (HATOBA) AT YOKOHAMA. The Bund commanded a view of 'a harbour full of steamers as a Piccadilly cab-rank of hansoms' (page 215).

11. BUDDHA AT KAMAKURA. Calling this great image 'beyond all hope of description', Kipling deplored the insensitivity of Christian viewers of the Buddha, and tasteless photographs of 'tourists standing on his thumbnail' (page 201).

12. SS *CITY OF PEKING*. The sail-assisted steamer by which Kipling crossed the Pacific in May 1889: 'for all practical purposes she is the United States' (page 190).

at eighteen miles, I make Tokyo thirty-six miles long by thirty-six miles broad exactly; and there may be some more which I missed.[23] The place roared with life through all its quarters. Double lines of trams ran down the main streets for mile on mile, rows of omnibuses stood at the principal railway station, and the 'Compagnie Générale des Omnibus de Tokio' paraded the streets with gold and vermilion cars. All the trams were full, all the private and public omnibuses were full, and the streets were full of '*rickshaws*. From the seashore to the shady green park, from the park to the dim distance, the land pullulated with people.

Here you saw how Western civilisation had eaten into them. Every tenth man was attired in Europe clothes from hat to boots. It is a queer race. It can parody every type of humanity to be met in a large English town. Fat and prosperous merchant with mutton-chop whiskers; mild-eyed, long-haired professor of science, his clothes baggy about him; schoolboy in Eton jacket, broadcloth trousers; young clerk, member of the Clapham Athletic Club, in tennis flannels; artisans in sorely worn tweeds; top-hatted lawyer with clean-shaven upper lip and black leather bag; sailor out of work; and counter-jumper; all these and many, many more you shall find in the streets of Tokyo in half an hour's walk. But when you come to speak to the imitation, behold it can only talk Japanese. You touch it, and it is not what you thought. I fluctuated down the streets addressing myself to the most English-looking folk I saw. They were polite with a graciousness that in no way accorded with their raiment, but they knew not a word of my tongue. One small boy in the uniform of the Naval College said suddenly: 'I spik Englees,' and collapsed. The rest of the people in our clothes poured their own vernacular upon my head. Yet the shop-signs were English, the tramway under my feet was English gauge, the commodities sold were English, and the notices on the streets were in English. It was like walking in a dream. I respected the Babu in that hour because he did not dress deceitfully in flannel or dittos,[24] and spoke our tongue none the less. But then, the Babu had an Educational Department behind him and more Englishmen about him than ever did the Japanese.

I reflected. Far away from Tokyo and off the line of the rail I had met men like these men in the streets. Perfectly dressed Englishmen to the outer eye, but dumb. The country must be full of their likes.

'Good gracious! Here is Japan going to run its own civilisation without learning a language in which you can say Damn satisfactorily. I must inquire into this.'

Chance had brought me opposite the office of a newspaper, and I ran in demanding an editor. He came – the Editor of the *Tokyo Public Opinion*, a young man in a black frock-coat. There are not many editors in other parts of the world who would offer you tea and a cigarette ere beginning a conversation. My friend had but little English. His paper, though the name was printed in English, was Japanese. But he knew his business. Almost before I had explained my errand, which was the pursuit of miscellaneous information, he began: 'You are English? How you think now the American Revision Treaty?'[25] Out came a note-book and I sweated cold. It was not in the bargain that he should interview *me*.

'There's a great deal,' I answered, remembering Sir Roger, of blessed memory,[26] – 'a great deal to be said on both sides. The American Revision Treaty – h'm – demands an enormous amount of matured consideration and may safely be referred –'

'But we of Japan are now civilised.' Have I told you that the construction of Japanese and Hindustani is very much the same, and a Japanese speaking or writing English glides into Babuese? Read some of their Anglo-vernacular papers if you doubt this.

Japan says that she is now civilised. That is the crux of the whole matter so far as I understand it. 'Let us have done with the idiotic system of treaty-ports and passports for the foreigner who steps beyond them,' says Japan in effect. 'Give us our place among the civilised nations of the earth, come among us, trade with us, hold land in our midst. Only be subject to our jurisdiction and submit to our – tariffs'. Now since one or two of the foreign nations have won special tariffs for their goods in the usual way, they are not over-anxious to become just ordinary folk. The effect of accepting Japan's views would be excellent for the individual who wanted to go up-country and make his money, but bad for the nation. For our nation in particular.

All the same I was not prepared to have my ignorance of a burning question put down in any note-book save my own. I Gladstoned[27] about the matter with the longest words I could. My friend recorded them much after the manner of Count Smorltork.[28] Then I attacked him on the subject of civilisation – speaking very slowly because he had a knack of running two words of mine together, and turning them into something new.

'You are right,' said he. 'We are becoming civilised. But not too quick, for that is bad. Now there are two parties in the State – the Liberal and the Radical: one Count he lead one, one Count lead the other.[29] The Radical say that we should swiftly become all English. The Liberal he says not so quick, because that nation which too swiftly adopt other people's customs he decay.[30] That question of civilisation and the American Revision Treaty he occupied our chief attentions. Now we are not so zealous to become civilised as we were two – three years gone. Not so quick – that is our watchword. Yes.'

If matured deliberation be the wholesale adoption of imperfectly understood arrangements, I should dearly like to see Japan in a hurry. We discussed comparative civilisations for a short time, and I protested feebly against the defilement of the streets of Tokyo by rows of houses built after glaring European models. 'Surely there is no need to discard your own architecture,' I said.

'Ha,' snorted the chief of the *Public Opinion*. 'You call it picturesque. I call it too. Wait till he light up – incendiate. A Japanese house then is only one fire-box. *That* is why we think good to build in European fashion. I tell you, and you must believe, that we take up no change without thinking upon it. Truth, indeed, it is not because we are curious children, wanting new things, as some people have said. We have done with that season of picking up things and throwing them down again. You see?'

'Where did you pick up your Constitution, then?'

I did not know what the question would bring forth, yet I ought to have been wise. The first question that a Japanese on the railway asks an Englishman is: 'Have you got the English translation of our Constitution?' All the bookstalls sell it in English and Japanese, and all the papers discuss it. This child is not yet three months old.[31]

'Our Constitution? – That was promised to us – promised twenty years ago. Fourteen years ago the provinces they have been allowed to elect their big men – their heads. Three years ago they have been allowed to have assemblies, and thus Civil Liberty was assured.'

I was baffled here for some time. In the end I thought I made out that the municipalities had been given certain control over police funds and the appointment of district officials. I may have been entirely wrong, but the editor bore me along on a torrent of words, his body rocking and his arms waving with the double agony of twisting a foreign tongue to his service and explaining the to-be-taken-seriouslyness of Japan. Whack came the little hand on the little table, and the little tea-cups jumped again.

'Truly, and indeed, this Constitution of ours has *not* come too soon. It proceeded step-by. You understand that? Now your Constitution, the Constitutions of the foreign nations, are all bloody – bloody Constitutions. Ours has come step-by. We did not fight as the barons fought with King John at Runnymede.'[32]

This was a quotation from a speech delivered at Otsu, a few days previously, by a member of the Government. I grinned at the brotherhood of editors all the world over. Up went the hand anew.

'We shall be happy with this Constitution and a people civilised among civilisations!'

'Of course. But what will you actually do with it? A Constitution is rather a monotonous thing to work after the fun of sending members to Parliament has died out. You have a Parliament, have you not?'

'Oh yes, *with* parties – Liberal and Radical.'

'Then they will both tell lies to you and to each other. Then they will pass bills, and spend their time fighting each other. Then all the foreign governments will discover that you have no fixed policy.'

'Ah, yes. But the Constitution.' The little hands were crossed in his lap. The cigarette hung limply from his mouth.

'No fixed policy. Then, when you have sufficiently disgusted the foreign Powers, they will wait until the Liberals and Radicals are fighting very hard about the character of some pirate who may be a member of Parliament, and then they will blow you out of the water.'

'You are not making fun? I do not quite understand' said he. 'Your Constitutions are all so bloody.'

'Yes. That is exactly what they are. You are very much in earnest about yours, are you not?'

'Oh yes, we all talk politics now.'

'And write politics, of course. By the way, under what – h'm, arrangements with the Government is a Japanese paper published? I mean, must you pay anything before starting a press?'

'Literary, scientific, and religious papers – no. Quite free. All purely political papers pay five hundred yen – give to the Government to keep, or else some man says he will pay.'

'You must give security, you mean?'

'I do not know, but sometimes the Government can keep the money. We are purely political.'

Then he asked questions about India, and appeared astonished to find that the natives there possessed considerable political power, and controlled Districts.

'But have you a Constitution in India?'

'I am afraid that we have not.'

'Ah!'

He crushed me there, and I left very humbly, but cheered by the promise that the *Tokyo Public Opinion* would contain an account of my words.[33] Mercifully, that respectable journal is printed in Japanese, so the hash will not be served up to a large table. I would give a good deal to discover what meaning he attached to my forecast of Constitutional government is Japan.

'We all talk politics now'. That was the sentence which remained to me. It was true talk. Men of the Educational Department in Tokyo told me that the students would 'talk politics' by the hour if you allowed them. At present they were talking in the abstract about their new plaything, the Constitution, with its Upper House and its Lower House, its committees, its questions of supply, its rules of procedure, and all the other skittles we have played with for six hundred years.

Japan is the second Oriental country which has made it impossible for a strong man to govern alone. This she has done of her own free will. India, on the other hand, has been forcibly ravished by the Secretary of State and the English M.P., aided by the telegraph.[34]

Japan is luckier than India.

1889 : LETTER ELEVEN
COMMENTARY

1. Kipling's hotel was probably the Imperial. However, it was not the well-known building erected later, which was designed by the famous American architect Frank Lloyd Wright and which survived both the earthquake of 1923 and the wartime bombing of Tokyo. (That in turn has since been replaced by a more modern but less distinguished structure.)
2. In the first edition (1890) of *Things Japanese*, Basil Hall Chamberlain said the Japanese Army numbered 196,620 men all told, according to the latest statistics published (which in this case related to December 1886). Within that total, 107,673 were the reserve and 32,717 the 'territorial army', while other figures were attributed to gendarmerie, military schools, etc., leaving an 'actual fighting strength of the army in ordinary times' of just under 50,000. The known fact that the army was being expanded was borne out by figures published by Captain G.J. Younghusband of the Queen's Own Corps of Guides, in *On Short Leave to Japan* (London, 1894), to the effect that the total was by then

228,848. This, after deducting 113,229 in the reserve, 53,137 in the territorial force, and figures for gendarmerie, etc., left a peacetime strength of 56,589.

3. In December 1872 a system of conscription had been announced: one result, as intended, was to deprive the *samurai* of their monopoly of the profession of arms and thereby to destroy the basis of their class. All Japanese males on reaching the age of twenty became liable to three years' military service. As to exemptions, Basil Hall Chamberlain in the 1902 edition of *Things Japanese* said that 'when the system was first introduced, numerous exceptions were allowed; but now the application of the law is stringent, no excuse othen than physical unfitness being entertained'.

4. In the troubled 1860s a British military contingent had been stationed in Japan to protect British interests. Apart from that, Kipling's informant might have seen British troops in Hong Kong or elsewhere abroad. As to the Royal Navy, it played a greatly respected role in the development and training of the Imperial Japanese Navy.

5. In the words of Basil Hall Chamberlain, 'The cavalry has always been the weakest branch of the Japanese army, owing to the absence of good horses' (*Things Japanese*, 1902 edition).

6. The fact that he was himself below average height, and handicappped by very poor sight, possibly increased Kipling's tendency, all his life, to take an idealized, or at least admiring, view of soldiers.

7. The Gurkha units in the British Indian Army eventually formed ten regiments of two battalions each. The 4th Regiment, formed at the time of the Mutiny of 1857, had the title of The Prince of Wales's Own.

8. See the account in Letter Four of 1889, pages 73–4.

9. To double, in military parlance, is to run at a disciplined pace, 'double time'. In the British Army, this meant a step of 33 inches maintained at a rate of 150 (later 165) per minute. Incidentally, this use of the verb, by Kipling in 1889, is of some interest as an early literary example of the term: in the *Shorter Oxford English Dictionary* the first recorded use is in 1890.

10. Actually the 'carry', with the rifle close against the shoulder and the muzzle upright, is probably *not* meant. Kipling is likely to have meant the 'trail', with the rifle held down at arm's length, parallel with the ground.

11. After the Meiji Restoration, the new Japanese conscript army was indeed organized with some assistance from Continental advisers, initially French, later some Italians, but primarily Germans.

12. As a race, the Japanese have greatly increased in physical height in the past century. In 1889 many Japanese soldiers were not much over 5 feet, and conscription standards permitted recruitment a little under that height. To European observers, this seemed very short indeed. By comparison, it is interesting to note (from A. R. Skelley, *The Victorian*

Army at Home) that in 1888 only 4 per cent of recruits to the British Army were below 5ft 3 inches, while 68 per cent were over 5ft 6 inches. (Incidentally, those figures represented a marked decline from the standards of twenty-five years previously, when recruits had been drawn from rural areas rather than industrial slums: the 1864 proportions, for instance, were 2½ per cent and 93 per cent.)

13. A martingale is a strap fastened at one end to the horse's nose band, at the other end to its girth, to prevent rearing, etc.

14. A crupper is a strap buckled to the back of the saddle and looped under the horse's tail.

15. A *numdah* (from the Persian *namad*, a carpet) was an Indian embroidered felt rug or saddlecloth.

16. A 'hand' is a four-inch measure used only for the height of horses. A thirteen-hand pony, i.e. one measuring 4ft 4ins at the shoulder, would be about three hands shorter than the desirable height for a cavalry horse.

17. A bridoon is the snaffle (curbless bit) and rein of a cavalry bridle.

18. The picture in question, by Tenniel, actually occurs not in *Alice in Wonderland* but in chapter 7 of *Through the Looking-Glass*; likewise, the picture of the White Knight in chapter 8. This slip was corrected, nearly fifty years later, in Kipling's Sussex edition.

19. An 'entire' is an uncastrated horse.

20. A Turk's Head was a kind of target set up for a mounted swordsman to strike at. In shape it somewhat resembled a long-handled broom known as a Turk's Head or Pope's Head.

21. 'Flag' is the term for the tail of certain breeds of dog, e.g. setters; it can also be used as here, more rarely, for a horse's tail.

22. See Note 4 above.

23. In this straight-faced computation of area, Kipling is quite clearly not serious. However, it was taken more than half-seriously, perhaps literally, by none other than Lafcadio Hearn, who was Professor of English Literature at Tokyo University a few years later, and who occupied a unique position as interpreter of Japanese culture to the West, and *vice versa*. Hearn called this whole passage 'the work of a practical man with a practical eye – interested in facts above all things ...anybody who reads that paragraph will have an idea of the size of Tokyo.'

24. 'Dittos' meant a suit of clothes made of the same cloth throughout.

25. Between 1854 and 1869 the USA and many European countries entered into treaty relations with Japan. There were three main diplomatic consequences, briefly: (a) opening of the Treaty Ports; (b) extraterritoriality, i.e. exemption of their nationals from Japanese court jurisdiction; (c) lowered duties on trade goods entering Japan. By the 1870s there was strong Japanese pressure for 'revision' of these treaties, including abrogation of the clauses that were offensive to Japanese

self-respect with their implication that Japan and her legal institutions were uncivilized. As early as 1876 the USA nearly, but not quite, arrived at a revision. Again, in 1889 several countries including the USA made substantial progress towards revision. Thereupon suddenly Japanese public opinion veered round, opposing aspects of revision as likely to expose Japan to foreign exploitation. During that year, the year of Kipling's first visit, the issue became highly inflammatory, provoking violent incidents culminating in October in a bomb attack on the Minister for Foreign Affairs.

26. Sir Roger de Coverley was a fictitious character. He had been portrayed at various times in the *Spectator* by Joseph Addison and Sir Richard Steele, as a type of English country gentleman of the reign of Queen Anne. The particular reference (20 July 1711) is: 'My friend Sir Roger ... told them, with the air of a man who would not give his judgements rashly, that much might be said on both sides.'

27. A reference to the long-winded oratory of W. E. Gladstone (1809–98), the English Liberal statesman and Prime Minister. Kipling strongly objected to Gladstone's policies, particularly in imperial affairs, and had already expressed this as a young journalist in India.

28. Count Smorltork was a character in Charles Dickens's *Pickwick Papers* (1837). He was 'the famous foreigner' at Mrs Leo Hunter's party in chapter 15, a 'well-whiskered individual in a foreign uniform' who was 'gathering materials for his great work on England' – and getting everything hopelessly wrong.

29. When Kipling came to Japan in 1889 the Liberal Party (*Jiyuto*) was headed by Count Taisuke Itagaki, and the Progressive Party (*Rikken Kaishinto*) by Count Shigenobu Okuma.

30. The Liberals advocated French-style radicalism, argued that sovereignty lay with the people, and called for universal suffrage. The Progressives advocated English-style gradualism. There is thus some confusion in Kipling's account.

31. On the 1889 Constitution, see Introduction 1, particularly page 5; also Letter One, Note 8 at page 47.

32. A reference to a major constitutional event in feudal England, the granting by King John in 1215 of Magna Carta, the charter recognizing the rights of barons, church and freemen.

33. Unfortunately, although there is every likelihood that this newspaper report, or something like it, was published as Kipling implied, we have failed to trace it, despite some painstaking research undertaken on our behalf by Professor Tetsuro Nakasuga who scanned lists and records both in the National Diet Library and at Tokyo University. The anglicized title *Tokyo Public Opinion* makes for uncertainty, but can probably be equated with the *Tokyo Koron*, some old issues of which were tracked down by the Professor in the Library of the Faculty of Law at the University. The *Tokyo Koron*, the direct successor of the

Koron Shaho, was a small newspaper apparently published daily (except on Monday and on the day following a national holiday) between 25 January 1889 and 23 November 1890. However, the issues for the most likely dates (between 7 and 11 May 1889) are missing. At that period, of course, there were many minor and ephemeral newspapers, and the issues known to have survived to the present day are, not surprisingly, patchy. Nevertheless, the possibility remains that some day someone will unearth the account, by the editor whom Kipling met, of what appears to have been a mutually disconcerting encounter.

34. This is a reflection of something which came over several times in Kipling's early prose and verse – his strong hostility to a type of Member of Parliament, usually a Liberal, who, though profoundly ignorant of the fundamental problems of India, tried with officious high-mindedness to interfere with the British administration of that country.

1889: Letter Twelve

SHOWS THE SIMILARITY BETWEEN THE BABU AND THE JAPANESE AND
THE WAY WE SETTLED THINGS. CONTAINS THE EARNEST OUTCRY OF
AN UNBELIEVER. THE EXPLANATION OF MR. SMITH OF CALIFORNIA
AND ELSEWHERE. TAKES ME ON BOARD SHIP AFTER DUE WARNING TO
THOSE WHO FOLLOW.

Very sadly did we leave it, but we gave our hearts in pledge
To the pine above the city, to the blossoms by the hedge,
To the cherry and the maple and the plum tree and the peach,
And the babies – Oh, the babies! – romping fatly under each.
Eastward ho! Across the water see the black bow drives and swings
From the Land of Little Children, where the Babies are the Kings.[1]

The Professor discovered me in meditation amid tea-girls at the back
of the Ueno Park[2] in the heart of Tokyo. My *'rickshaw* coolie sat by
my side drinking tea from daintiest china, and eating macaroons. I
thought of Sterne's donkey[3] and smiled vacuously into the blue
above the trees. The tea-girls giggled. One of them captured my
spectacles, perched them on her own snubby-chubby nose, and ran
about among her cackling fellows.

'"And lose your fingers in the tresses of The cypress–slender
minister of wine,"' quoted the Professor,[4] coming round a booth
suddenly. 'Why aren't you at the Mikado's garden-party?'

'Because he didn't invite me, and, anyhow, he wears Europe
clothes – so does the Empress – so do all the Court people. Let's sit
down and consider things. This people puzzles me. It has points in
common with the Babu.'

And I told my story of the interview with the Editor of the *Tokyo
Public Opinion*. The Professor had been making investigation into
the Educational Department. 'And further,' said he at the end of the
tale, 'the ambition of the educated student is to get a place
under Government. Therefore he comes to Tokyo: will accept any
situation at Tokyo that he may be near to his chance.'

'Whose son is that student?'

'Son of the peasant, yeoman-farmer, and shopkeeper, *ryot, tehsildar,* and *bunnia*.[5] While he waits he imbibes Republican leanings on account of the nearness of Japan to America. He talks and writes and debates, and is convinced he can manage the Empire better than the Mikado.'

'Does he go away and start newspapers to prove that?'

'He may; but it seems to be unwholesome work. A paper can be suspended without reason given under the present laws; and I'm told that one enterprising editor has just got three years' simple imprisonment for caricaturing the Mikado.'[6]

'Then there is yet hope for Japan. I can't quite understand how a people with a taste for fighting and quick artistic perceptions can care for the things that delight our friends in Bengal.'

'You make the mistake of looking on the Bengali as unique. So he is in his own peculiar style; but I take it that the drunkenness of Western wine affects all Oriental folk in much the same way. What misleads you is that very likeness. Followest thou? Because a Japanese struggles with problems beyond his grip in much the same phraseology as a Calcutta University student, and discusses Administration with a capital A, you lump Japanese and Chatterjee[7] together.'

'No, I don't. Chatterjee doesn't sink his money in railway companies, or sit down and provide for the proper sanitation of his own city, or of his own notion cultivate the graces of life, as the Japanese does. He is like the *Tokyo Public Opinion* – "purely political." He has no art whatever, he has no weapons, and there is no power of manual labour in him. Yet he is like the Japanese in the pathos of his politics. Have you ever studied Pathetic Politics? *Why* is he like the Japanese?'

'Both drunk, I suppose,' said the Professor. 'Get that girl to give back your gig-lamps,[8] and you will be able to see more clearly into the soul of the Far East.'

'The "Far East" hasn't got a soul. She swapped it for a Constitution on the Eleventh of February last. Can any Constitution make up for the wearing of Europe clothes? I saw a Japanese lady just now in full afternoon calling-kit. She looked atrocious. Have you seen the later Japanese art – the pictures on the fans and in the shop windows? They are faithful reproductions of the changed life – telegraph-poles down the streets; conventionalised tram-lines, top-hats, and carpet-bags in the hands of the men. The artists can make those things almost passable, but when it comes to conventionalising a Europe dress, the effect is horrible.'

179

'Japan wishes to take her place among civilised nations,' said the Professor.

'That's where the pathos comes in. It's enough to make you weep to watch this misdirected effort – this wallowing in unloveliness for the sake of recognition at the hands of men who paint their ceilings white, their grates black, their mantelpieces French grey, and their carriages yellow and red. The Mikado wears blue and gold and red, his guards wear orange breeches with a stone-blue stripe down them; the American missionary teaches the Japanese girl to wear bangs – "shingled bangs" – on her forehead, plait her hair into a pigtail, and to tie it up with magenta and cobalt ribbons. The German sells them the offensive chromos[9] of his own country and the labels of his beer-bottles. Allen and Ginter devastate Tokyo with their blood-red and grass-green tobacco-tins. And in the face of all these things the country wishes to progress toward civilisation! I have read the entire Constitution of Japan, and it is dearly bought at the price of one of the kaleidoscope omnibuses plying in the street there.'

'Are you going to inflict all that nonsense on them at home?' said the Professor.

'I am. For this reason. In the years to come, when Japan has sold her birthright for the privilege of being cheated on equal terms by her neighbours; when she has so heavily run into debt for her railways and public works that the financial assistance of England and annexation is her only help; when the Daimyo through poverty have sold the treasures of their houses to the curio-dealer, and the dealer has sold them to the English collector; when all the people wear slop-trousers and ready-made petticoats, and the Americans have established soap factories on the rivers and a boarding-house on the top of Fujiyama, some one will turn up the files of the *Pioneer*[10] and say: "This thing was prophesied." Then they will be sorry that they began tampering with the great sausage-machine of civilisation. What is put into the receiver must come out at the spout; but it must come out mincemeat. *Dixi!*[11] And now let us go to the tomb of the Forty-Seven *Ronins*.'[12]

'It has been said some time ago, and much better than you can say it,' said the Professor, *apropos* of nothing that I could see.

Distances are calculated by the hour in Tokyo. Forty minutes in a *'rickshaw*, running at full speed, will take you a little way into the city; two hours from the Ueno Park brings you to the tomb of the famous Forty-Seven, passing on the way the very splendid temples of Shiba,[13] which are all fully described in the guide-books. Lacquer, gold-inlaid bronze-work, and crystals carved with the words 'Om' and 'Shri' are fine things to behold, but they do not admit of very varied treatment in print.[14] In one tomb of one of the temples was a room of lacquer panels overlaid with gold-leaf. An animal of the name of V. Gay had seen fit to scratch his entirely uninteresting name on the gold. Posterity will take note that V. Gay never cut his finger-nails, and ought not to have been trusted with anything prettier than a hog-trough.

'It is the handwriting upon the wall,'[15] I said, when the commination service[16] was over. 'Presently there will be neither gold nor lacquer – nothing but the finger-marks of foreigners. Let us pray for the soul of V. Gay all the same. Perhaps he was a missionary.'[17]

★   ★   ★

The Japanese papers occasionally contain, sandwiched between notes of railway, mining, and tram concessions, announcements like the following: 'Dr. —— committed *hara-kiri* last night at his private residence in such and such a street. Family complications are assigned as the reason of the act.' Nor does *hara-kiri* merely mean suicide by any method. *Hara-kiri* is *hara-kiri*, and the private performance is even more ghastly than the official one. It is curious to think that any one of the dapper little men with top-hats and reticules who have a Constitution of their own, may, in time of mental stress, strip to the waist, shake their hair over their brows, and, after prayer, rip themselves open.[18] When you come to Japan, look at Farsari's[19] *hara-kiri* pictures and his photos of the last crucifixion (twenty years ago) in Japan. Then at Deakin's,[20] inquire for the modelled head of a gentleman who was not long ago executed in Tokyo. There is a grim fidelity in the latter work of art that will make you uncomfortable. The Japanese, in common with the rest of the East, have a strain of bloodthirstiness in their compositions. It is very carefully veiled now, but some of Hokusai's[21] pictures show it, and show that not long ago the people revelled in its outward expression. Yet they are tender to all children beyond the tenderness of the West, courteous to each other beyond the courtesy of the English, and polite to the foreigner alike in the big towns and in the Mofussil.[22] What they will be after their Constitution has been working for three generations the Providence that made them what they are alone knows!

All the world seems ready to proffer them advice. Colonel Olcott[23] is wandering up and down the country now, telling them that the Buddhist religion needs reformation, offering to reform it, and eating with ostentation rice-gruel which is served to him in cups by admiring handmaidens. A wanderer from Tokyo tells me that in the Chion-in, loveliest of all the temples, he saw only three days ago the Colonel mixed up with a procession of Buddhist priests, just such a procession as the one I tried vainly to describe, and 'tramping about as if the whole show belonged to him.' You cannot appreciate the solemnity of this until you have seen the Colonel and the Chion-in temple. The two are built on entirely different lines, and they don't seem to harmonise. It only needs now Madame Blavatsky,[24] cigarette in mouth, under the *cryptomerias* of Nikko,[25] and the return of Mr. Caine, M.P.[26], to preach the sin of drinking *sake*, and Mister Oscar Wilde to prove that Japan never existed,[27] and the menagerie would be full. America imports barbarians from the West, to meet kindred barbarians from the East, and the two breeds are 'elevating the country'.

Something should be done to America. That she steals from England is no great matter.[28] Badly brought up children frequently steal from their fathers, and America, alas! has been dragged up. But she should not infect other and happier lands with her own disease. There are many American missionaries in Japan, and some of them construct clapboard churches and chapels for whose ugliness no creed could compensate. They further instil into the Japanese mind wicked ideas of 'Progress,' and teach that it is well to go ahead of your neighbour, to improve your situation, and generally to thresh yourself to pieces in the battle of existence. They do not mean to do this; but their own restless energy enforces the lesson. The American is objectionable. And yet – this is written from Yokohama – how pleasant in every way is a nice American whose tongue is cleansed of 'right there,' 'all the time,' 'noos,' 'revoo,' 'raound,' and the Falling Cadence. I have met such an one even now – a Californian ripened in Spain, matured in England, polished in Paris, and yet always a Californian. His voice and manners were soft alike, temperate were his judgments and temperately expressed, wide was his range of experience, genuine his humour, and fresh from the mint of his mind his reflections. It was only at the end of the conversation that he startled me a little.

'I understand that you are going to stay some time in California. Do you mind my giving you a little advice? I am speaking now of towns that are still rather brusque in their manners. When a man offers you a drink accept at once, and then stand drinks all round. I don't say that the second part of the programme is as necessary as the first, but it puts you on a perfectly safe footing. Above all, remember that where you are going you must never carry anything.[29] The men you move among will do that for you. They have been accustomed to it. It is in some places, unluckily, a matter of life and death as well as daily practice to draw first. I have known really lamentable accidents occur from a man carrying a revolver when he did not know what to do with it. Do you understand anything about revolvers?'

'N-no,' I stammered, 'of course not.'

'Do you think of carrying one?'

'Of course not. I don't want to kill myself.'

'Then you are safe. But remember you will be moving among men who go heeled,[30] and you will hear a good deal of talk about the thing and a great many tall stories. You may listen to the yarns, but you must not conform to the custom however much you may feel tempted. You invite your own death if you lay your hand on a weapon you don't understand. No man flourishes a revolver in a bad place. It is produced for one specified purpose and produced before you can wink.'

'But surely if you draw first you have an advantage over the other man,' said I valorously.

'You think so? Let me show you. I have no use for any weapon, but I believe I have one about me somewhere. An ounce of demonstration is worth a ton of theory. Your pipe-case is on the table. My hands are on the table too. Use that pipe-case as a revolver and as quickly as you can.'

I used it in the approved style of the penny dreadful – pointed it with a stiff arm at my friend's head. Before I knew how it came about the pipe-case had quitted my hand, which was caught close to the funny-bone and tingled horribly. I heard four persuasive clicks under the table almost before I knew that my arm was useless. The gentleman from California had jerked out his pistol from its pocket and drawn the trigger four times, his hand resting on his hip while I was lifting my right arm.

'Now do you believe?' he said. 'Only an Englishman or an Eastern man fires from the shoulder in that melodramatic manner. I had you safe before your arm went out, merely because I happened to know the trick; and there are men out yonder who in a trouble could hold me as safe as I held you. They don't reach round for their revolver, as novelists say. It's here in front, close to the second right brace-button, and it is fired, without aim, at the other man's stomach. You will understand now why in the event of a dispute you should show very clearly that you are unarmed. You needn't hold up your hands ostentatiously; keep them out of your pockets, or somewhere where your friend can see them. No man will touch you then. Or if he does, he is pretty sure to be shot by the general sense of the room.'

'That must be a singular consolation to the corpse,' I said.

'I see I've misled you. Don't fancy that *any* part in America is as free-and-easy as my lecture shows. Only in a few really tough towns do you require *not* to own a revolver. Elsewhere you are all right. Most Americans of my acquaintance have got into the habit of carrying something; but it's only a habit. They'd never dream of using it unless they are hard pressed. It's the man who draws to enforce a proposition about canning peaches, orange-culture, or town lots or water-rights that's a nuisance.'

'Thank you,' I said faintly. 'I purpose to investigate these things later on. I'm much obliged to you for your advice.'

When he had departed it struck me that, in the language of the East, 'he might have been pulling my leg.'[31] But there remained no doubt whatsoever as to his skill with the weapon he excused so tenderly.

I put the case before the Professor. 'We will go to America before you forejudge it altogether,' said he. 'To America in an American ship will we go, and say good-bye to Japan.' That night we counted the gain of our sojourn in the Land of Little Children more closely than many men count their silver. Nagasaki with the grey temples, green hills, and all the wonder of a first-seen shore; the Inland Sea, a thirty-hour panorama of passing islets drawn in grey and buff and silver for our delight; Kobe, where we fed well and went to a theatre; Osaka of the canals and the peach blossom; Kyoto – happy, lazy, sumptuous Kyoto, and the blue rapids and innocent delights of Arashiyama; Otsu on the shoreless, rainy lake; Miyanoshita in the hills; Kamakura by the tumbling Pacific, where the great god Buddha sits and equably hears the centuries and the seas murmur in his ears;[32] Nikko, fairest of all places under the sun; Tokyo, the two-thirds civilised and altogether progressive warren of humanity; and composite Franco-American Yokohama; we renewed them all, sorting out and putting aside our special treasures of memory. If we stayed longer, we might be disillusioned, and yet – surely, that would be impossible.

'What sort of mental impression do you carry away?' said the Professor.

'A tea-girl in fawn-coloured crêpe under a cherry tree all blossom. Behind her, green pines, two babies, and a hog-backed bridge spanning a bottle-green river running over blue boulders. In the fore-ground a little policeman in badly-fitting Europe clothes drinking tea from blue and white china on a black lacquered stand. Fleecy white clouds above and a cold wind up the street,' I said, summarising hastily.

'Mine is a little different. A Japanese boy in a flat-headed German cap and baggy Eton jacket; a King taken out of a toyshop, a railway taken out of a toyshop, hundreds of little Noah's Ark trees and fields made of green-painted wood. The whole neatly packed in a camphor-wood box with an explanatory book called the Constitution – price twenty cents.'

'You looked on the darker side of things. But what's the good of writing impressions? Every man has to get his own at first hand in this marvellous place. Suppose I give an itinerary of what we saw?'

'You couldn't do it,' said the Professor blandly. 'I'm the man who struck out all the routes and made all the arrangements. Besides, by the time the next Anglo-Indian comes this way there will be a hundred more miles of railway and all the local arrangements will have changed. Write that a man should come to Japan without any plans. The guide-books will tell him a little, and the men he meets will tell him ten times more. Let him get first a good guide at Kobe, and the rest will come easily enough. An itinerary is only a fresh manifestation of that unbridled egoism which——'

'And the expenses?' I interrupted. 'What shall I say about the expenses? We have been rather more than two months out of India.'

'If you intend publishing a record of waste and profligacy tell them the truth.'

'I shall write that a man can do himself well from Calcutta to Yokohama, stopping at Rangoon, Moulmein, Penang, Singapore, Hong Kong, Canton, and taking a month in Japan, for about sixty pounds – rather less than more. But if he begins to buy curios, that man is lost. Five hundred rupees cover his month in Japan and allow him every luxury. Above all, he should bring with him thousands of cheroots – enough to serve him till he reaches 'Frisco. Singapore is the last place on the line where you can buy Burmas. Beyond that point wicked men sell Manila cigars with fancy names for ten, and Havanas for thirty-five, cents. No one inspects your boxes till you reach 'Frisco. Bring, therefore, at least one thousand cheroots.'

'Do you know, it seems to me you have a very queer sense of proportion?'

And that was the last word the Professor spoke on Japanese soil.

1889: LETTER TWELVE
COMMENTARY

1. These lines, unmistakably by Kipling, were not placed in any collections of his verse. They were presumably written after embarkation on about 11 May 1889 on the *City of Peking*, the American ship that took him 'eastward . . . across the water' from Yokohama to San Francisco. Note the 'black bows swinging' in Letter Thirteen, page 191
2. The Ueno Park in Tokyo covers a large area, in a north-easterly direction from the Imperial Palace. In Kipling's day it was high on the list of places for tourists to visit, for its temples, tombs and museum. Today it contains several of the city's leading museums and the principal zoo.
3. A reference to *Tristram Shandy* by Lawrence Sterne (1713–69). In Chapter 32 of 'volume 7' of that eccentrically structured novel, Sterne describes, with some effective pathos, an encounter at Lyons with an overloaded donkey. He enjoys with it a kind of conversation:

   > He was eating the stem of an artichoke . . . and, in the little peevish contentions of nature betwixt hunger and unsavouriness, had dropt it out of his mouth . . . God help thee, Jack! said I . . . thou hast not a friend, perhaps, in all this world, that will give thee a macaroon. – In saying this, I pull'd out a paper of 'em, which I had just purchased, and gave him one; and, at this moment that I am telling it, my heart smites me that there was more of pleasantry in the conceit of seeing *how* an ass would eat a macaroon – than of benevolence in giving him one . . .

4. A quotation from *The Rubaiyat of Omar Khayyam* by Edward Fitzgerald (1809–83). His free translation from the Persian was produced in several variations, but the Professor's quotation here, with its sly likening of a Japanese 'tea-girl' to the girl who serves the wine in the Persian poem, comes directly from verse 41 in the 4th edition of Fitzgerald:–

   > Perplext no more with Human or Divine,
   > Tomorrow's tangle to the winds resign,
   > And lose your fingers in the tresses of
   > The Cypress-slender Minister of Wine.

The cypress tree as a symbol of feminine beauty occurs constantly in Persian poetry. Another example from *The Rubaiyat*, which was only in the 2nd edition of Fitzgerald, is:–

   > Do you, within your little hour of Grace,
   > The Waving Cypress in your Arms enlace . . .

5. A *ryot* was a small farmer or cultivator in India; a *tehsildar* or *tahsildar* was a native tax collector or revenue officer; a *bunnia* was a small trader or merchant.

6. The Meiji authorities exercised tight censorship over what appeared in the Japanese press at this period.

7. Chatterjee: a well-known Indian family name, sometimes rather derisively used by the British in India as a label for people inclined to *chattering* or prolixity of speech. As it stands it is not a correct form, but an abbreviation of the full Bengali name Chattopadhyaya.

8. The term 'gig-lamps', meaning spectacles, had been introduced at Oxford in the 1840s, and had become general. Kipling as a schoolboy had been nicknamed *Gigger* because he wore spectacles.

9. *Chromo* was a colloquial abbreviation of chromolithograph, a coloured picture printed from stone. The term dated from the 1860s.

10. The *Pioneer* had been Kipling's newspaper in Allahabad, and these letters were written to be published in it.

11. *Dixi* is Latin for 'I have spoken'.

12. The tomb of the forty-seven *Ronin* is at Sengakuji temple, near Shinagawa in Tokyo. The *Ronin* (masterless *Samurai*) were vassals of Lord Asano Naganori who in 1701,for the crime of drawing his sword in the Shogun's palace when insulted by Lord Kira Yoshinaka, was ordered to commit suicide. His retainers determined to avenge him, eventually killed Kira, and were then in their turn ordered to commit suicide. They have come to be regarded as heroes who sacrificed their lives out of loyalty to their master. The play *Chushingura* is a dramatic account of the incident.

13. Shiba Park, with well-known temples and the tombs of Tokugawa Shoguns, featured on the list of favourite tourist sights. The main temple of Zojoji was almost entirely destroyed during the second World War: the present building, apart from the gateway, is a modern reconstruction.

14. *Om*, or *aum*, is an untranslatable word, representing the most important sacred sound in the Vedic and Hindu tradition and the focus for meditation in yoga. Its mystical significance has been the subject of much learned speculation. *Shri* (or *sri*), likewise of Sanskrit origin, means 'holy' – though in a non-religious context it also serves as an honorific title.

15. A reference to the 'writing on the wall' in the Bible (*Daniel*, chapter 5), which was a portent of impending disaster.

16. A reference to the Service of Commination in the *Book of Common Prayer*, a liturgical threatening of retribution against sinners.

17. Missionaries, like Liberal politicians, always tended to provoke Kipling's disparagement rather than admiration. He resented their cultural intrusion and assumption of superior enlightenment, and did not care for the notion that non-Christians were 'heathen'.

18. *Hara-kiri* historically had taken one of two forms – either officially ordered (as with the *Ronin*, Note 12 above) or privately decided. By the late nineteenth century the former practice had been abolished, but the latter was still not uncommon. The term *hara-kiri* was actually less used by the Japanese themselves than the synonymous but more elegant *seppuku*, but the meaning in both cases was 'belly-cutting': this, of course, was the way it was done (with or without an attendant friend whose function was to expedite the proceedings by decapitating the suicide as he disembowelled himself), though for women the equivalent mode was by cutting not the belly but the throat.

19. Farsari: see Letter Eight, Note 27, at page 139.

20. Deakin: see Letter Eight, Note 28, at page 139.

21. Hokusai: see Letter Nine, Note 22, at page 150.

22. The *Mofussil*. This term, derived from Hindi and originally from Arabic, was in very wide use among the British in India. It could be a noun or an adjective, and its precise meaning depended on the context, but in general it meant the rural areas, away from the administrative or urban centre, 'up-country'.

23. Colonel Henry Steel Olcott, born in New Jersey, USA, in 1832, died in India, where he had latterly lived, in 1907. After training as a lawyer he served in the American Civil War as the Union's Special Commissioner first for the War Department, then for the Navy. In 1875, together with Madame Blavatsky (see Note 24), he founded the Theosophical Society, a religious organization with its roots in mysticism, and remained its President till his death. At one time he was prominent in working for a conciliation of the Japanese and Ceylonese Buddhist sects. The reference to the Chion–in temple relates to Kipling's account of it in Letter Five, at pages 88–91.

24. Madame Helena Petrovna Hahn Blavatsky was born in Russia in 1831 and died in London in 1891. In between she had an active and highly controversial career, visiting Tibet in 1856, residing in New York in the 1870s where she was a founder of the Theosophical Society (see Note 23), and going to India in 1879 to establish with Colonel Olcott a headquarters of the movement in Madras. Here she attracted vast publicity, and thousands of devout followers, not least by her display of occult and spiritualistic phenomena, which strongly influenced the credulous. Kipling's father had known her fairly well in the 1880s, and had described her (as quoted much later by Kipling in *Something of Myself*) as 'one of the most interesting and unscrupulous impostors he had ever met. This, with his experience, was a high compliment.'

25. See Letter Ten, at pages 153–8; also Note 10 at page 162.

26. William Sproston Caine (1842-1903). He was an energetic Liberal MP, who had held ministerial office under Gladstone; he was a militant advocate of temperance and President of the British Temperance League; he had visited India extensively and was a leading exponent of

the principle of early self-government for India, and also Secretary of the Anglo-Indian Temperance Association. This added up to a worthy career, but not to the attributes which most commended themselves to Kipling. As for Kipling's reference to Caine returning to Japan to inveigh against the evils of *sake*, this is a well-based supposition. Caine had recently been round the world, and visited Japan en route, and described his experiences in a book entitled *A Trip Round the World in 1887–88*. At his hotel in Nikko he had noted that drinking water was 'placed in a Scotch whisky bottle, and a Bass's beer bottle, with the labels still attached, giving a festive and rakish, though thoroughly English, appearance to the meal, hardly acceptable, however, to good teetotallers like the whole of our party'. He also commented on *sake*, the effect of which, he thought, 'makes the drinker more supremely silly than any other known intoxicant'.

27. This reference to Oscar Wilde was deleted by Kipling when these newspaper Letters were edited into book form in 1889. There would have been two reasons: first, the fact that by then Wilde was living in destitution and disgrace in France, shortly before his death; second, the fact that the point about Japan never existing would have been meaningless to most readers. When Kipling wrote this letter Twelve in May 1889, out on the Pacific, he could not know that his Letter One, of a month earlier, would be edited in Allahabad in the way it was, for appearance in late July. This allusion to Wilde is explained by the opening passage of Letter One (shown as Kipling wrote it) and by Note 4 to that Letter (explaining how the references to Wilde were cut out by the *Pioneer*).

28. Kipling's petulant remark may be explained not so much by general considerations of the derivativeness of the culture of the United States as a new country, as by his particular fury, which took a very long time to die down, over the instances of book piracy described in Letter Ten, at page 151–2, and explained in Notes 2 to 7 of that Letter.

29. Carrying 'anything' here means carrying a gun.

30. In American slang dating from 1883 or earlier, 'heeled' meant 'provided, especially with a revolver' (*Shorter Oxford English Dictionary*).

31. Writing in 1889, Kipling put this phrase in inverted commas and found it necessary to explain that it was slang. It was indeed relatively new and had not yet entered standard English. In Partridge's *Dictionary of Slang and Unconventional English* (5th edition) its first recorded instance is given as 1888.

32. Kamakura: this reference makes it clear that Kipling visited the great Buddha, the Daibutsu, in 1889. His full account of the Daibutsu in prose, together with the famous verses he wrote as accompaniment, stemmed from his visit to Kamakura in 1892, and appear later in this volume, in Letter One of 1892, at pages 201–4.

1889: Letter Thirteen

(This Letter which, in common with Letter Twelve, Kipling wrote during
the voyage from Yokohama to San Francisco between 11 and 28 May 1889,
refers only marginally to Japan. It is much more concerned with a highly
entertaining account of shipboard life, with the violent weather that the ship
at one stage encountered, and with impressions of the country of destination. Its opening words are: 'This is America. They call her the *City of
Peking*, and she belongs to the Pacific Mail Company, but for all practical
purposes she is the United States.'

However, the Letter does contain three passages which justify extraction
below. Incidentally, editing the text in 1899 for *From Sea to Sea*, Kipling
deleted the sentence in the Second Excerpt, about the Yokohama – San
Francisco steamer route (4,750 miles) being the world's 'longest straight
run'. He probably remembered the greater length of the eastward traverse
from South Africa, experienced in 1891 and described in 'McAndrew's
Hymn'. Cape Town to Adelaide, for example, is 5,400 miles.)

First Excerpt: on Missionary Effort

The missionaries are perhaps the queerest portion of the cargo. Did
you ever hear an English minister sit down and lecture for half an
hour on the freight-traffic receipts and general working of, let us
say, the Midland? The Professor has been sitting at the feet of a
keen-eyed, close-bearded, swarthy man who expounded unto him
kindred mysteries with a fluency and precision that a city leader-
writer might have envied. 'Who's your financial friend with the
figures at his fingers' ends?' I asked. 'Missionary – Presbyterian
Mission to the Japanese,' said the Professor. I laid my hand upon my
mouth and was dumb.

The Americans have a large spiritual traffic with Japan. One of the
most pathetic things of the many that one finds in the religious
papers I noted a few days ago, when a record of missionary
enterprise rejoiced over the extension of church work in Japan. There
were, let us say, a hundred and fifty thousand converts in the island:
of these one hundred and eight thousand odd had been recruited by
the Church of Rome. On the next page of the same paper were some
casual remarks on the nature and tendencies of that Church. These
were not complimentary. . .

Second Excerpt: on the Yokohama
– San Francisco Passage

We have resigned ourselves to the infinite monotony of a twenty days' voyage. The Pacific Mail advertises falsely. Only under the most favourable circumstances of wind and steam can their under-engined boats cover the distance in fifteen days. Our *City of Peking*, for instance, had been jogging along at a gentle ten knots, a pace out of all proportion to her five thousand tons bulk. 'When we get a wind,' says the captain, 'we shall do better'. She is a four-master and can carry any amount of canvas. It is not safe to run steamers across this void under the poles of Atlantic liners. Unless you take a sailing-ship and beat from India to Australia this is about the longest straight run in the world. The monotony of the sea is paralysing. We have passed the wreck of a little sealing-schooner lying bottom up and covered with gulls. She weltered by in the chill dawn, unlovely as the corpse of a man, and the wild birds piped thinly at us as they steered her across the surges. The pulse of the Pacific is no little thing even in the quieter moods of the sea. It set our black bows swinging and nosing and ducking ere we were a day clear of Yokohama, and yet there was never swell nor crested wave in sight . . .

Third Excerpt: on Bureaucracy

And the conversation drifted naturally into the question of the government of men – English, Japanese (we have several travelled Japanese aboard), and Americans throwing the ball from one to another. We bore in mind the golden rule: 'Never agree with a man who abuses his own country,' and got on well enough.

'Japan,' said a little gentleman who was a rich man there, 'Japan is divided into two administrative sides. On the one the remains of a very strict and quite Oriental despotism; on the other a mass of – what do you call it? – red-tapeism which is not understood even by the officials who handle it. We copy the red tape, and when it is copied we believe that we administer. That is a vice of all Oriental nations. We are Orientals.'

'Oh no, say the most westerly of the westerns, reckoning from 'Frisco out,' purred an American soothingly.

The little man was pleased. 'Thanks. That is what we hope to believe, but up to the present it is not so. Look now. A farmer in my country holds a hillside cut into little terraces. Every year he must submit to his Government a statement of the size and revenue paid, not on the whole hillside, but on each terrace. The complete statement makes a pile of our thin paper three inches high, and is of no use when it is made except to keep in work thousands of officials to check the returns. Is that administration? By God! we call it so, but we multiply officials by the twenty, and *they* are not administration. What country is such a fool? Look at our Government offices eaten up with clerks and men with swords. Some day, I tell you, there will be a smash.'

This was new to me, but I might have guessed it. In every country where swords and uniforms accompany civil office there is a natural tendency towards an ill-considered increase of officialdom.

'You might pay India a visit some day,' I said. 'I fancy that you would find that our country shares your trouble.'

Thereupon a Japanese gentleman in the Educational Department began to cross-question me on the matters of his craft in India, and in a quarter of an hour got from me the very little that I knew about primary schools, higher education, and the value of an M.A. degree. He knew exactly what he wanted to ask, and only dropped me when the tooth of Desire had clean picked the bone of Ignorance ...

*　*　*

(After he had disembarked at San Francisco, Kipling travelled alone, at a leisurely pace and by various routes, across the continent to New York, whence he sailed for Liverpool on 25 September 1889. During his four months in North America – mainly in the United States but with excursions into Canada – he saw a great deal that was of interest, and sent off fifteen more of these letters, vividly and often pungently recording his experiences. But his mentions of Japan were now few and slight. He did, however, in one letter from San Francisco, refer again to the 'tea-girl' who had so caught his fancy on his very first day in Japan:– 'I am hopelessly in love with about eight American maidens – all perfectly delightful till the next one comes into the room. O-Toyo was a darling, but she lacked several things; conversation, for one. You cannot live on giggles. She shall remain unmoved at Nagasaki while I roast a battered heart before the shrine of a big Kentucky blonde. . . .'

So much for Kipling's Japan in 1889. When he came back, in 1892, it was no longer as the unknown journalist from India but – after an abrupt and dizzying emergence from obscurity, which has often been compared with the rise to fame of Dickens fifty years before – as a major writer whose name had suddenly become familiar throughout the English-speaking world.)

Part Two: 1892

1892: Letter One

THE EDGE OF THE EAST

The mist was clearing off Yokohama harbour and a hundred junks had their sails hoisted for the morning breeze, so that the veiled horizon was stippled with square blurs of silver. An English man-of-war showed blue-white on the haze, so new was the daylight, and all the water lay out as smooth as the inside of an oyster shell. Two children in blue and white, their tanned limbs pink in the fresh air, sculled a marvellous boat of lemon-hued wood, and that was our fairy craft to the shore across the stillness and the mother-o'-pearl levels.

There are ways and ways of entering Japan. The best is to descend upon it from America and the Pacific – from the barbarians and the deep sea.[1] Coming from the East, [2] the blaze of India and the insolent tropical vegetation of Singapore dull the eye to half-colours and little tones. It is at Bombay that the smell of All Asia boards the ship miles off shore, and holds the passenger's nose till he is clear of Asia again.

That is a violent, an aggressive smell, apt to prejudice the stranger, but kin none the less to the gentle and insinuating flavour that stole across the light airs of the daybreak when the fairy boat went to shore – a smell of very clean new wood; split bamboo, wood-smoke, damp earth, and the things that people who are not white people eat – a homelike and comforting smell. Then followed on shore the sound of an Eastern tongue, that is beautiful or not as you happen to know it. The Western races have many languages, but a crowd of Europeans heard through closed doors talk with the Western pitch and cadence. So it is with the East. A line of *jinrickshaw* coolies sat in the sun discoursing to each other, and it was as though they were welcoming a return in speech that the listener must know as well as English. They talked and they talked, but the ghosts of familiar words would not grow any clearer till presently the Smell came down the open streets again, saying that this was the East where nothing matters, and trifles old as the Tower of Babel mattered less

195

than nothing, and that there were old acquaintances waiting at every corner beyond the township. Great is the Smell of the East! Railways, telegraphs, docks, and gunboats cannot banish it, and it will endure till the railways are dead. He who has not smelt that smell has not lived.

Three years ago Yokohama was sufficiently Europeanised in its shops to suit the worst and wickedest taste. To-day it is still worse if you keep to the town limits. Ten steps beyond into the fields all the civilisation stops exactly as it does in another land a few thousand miles further West. The globe-trotting millionaires, anxious to spend money with a hose on whatever caught their libertine fancies, had explained to us aboard ship that they came to Japan in haste, advised by their guide-books to do so, lest the land should be suddenly civilised between steamer-sailing and steamer-sailing. When they touched land they ran away to the curio shops to buy things which are prepared for them – mauve and magenta and blue-vitriol things. By this time they have a *Murray*[3] under one arm and an electric-blue eagle with a copperas[4] beak and a yellow '*E pluribus unum*'[5] embroidered on apple-green silk, under the other.

We, being wise, sit in a garden that is not ours, but belongs to a gentleman in slate-coloured silk, who, solely for the sake of the picture, condescends to work as a gardener, in which employ he is sweeping delicately a welt of fallen cherry blossoms from under an azalea aching to burst into bloom. Steep stone steps, of the colour that nature ripens through long winters, lead up to this garden by way of clumps of bamboo grass. You see, the Smell was right when it talked of meeting old friends. Half-a-dozen blue-black pines are standing akimbo against a real sky – not a fog-blur nor a cloud-bank, nor a gray dish-clout wrapped round the sun – but a blue sky. A cherry tree on a slope below them throws up a wave of blossom that breaks all creamy white against their feet, and a clump of willows trail their palest green shoots in front of all. The sun sends for an ambassador through the azalea bushes a lordly swallow-tailed butterfly, and his squire, very like the flitting 'chalk-blue' of the English downs. The warmth of the East, that goes through, not over, the lazy body, is added to the light of the East – the splendid lavish light that clears but does not bewilder the eye. Then the new leaves of the spring wink like fat emeralds and the loaded branches of cherry-bloom grow transparent and glow as a hand glows held up against flame. Little warm sighs come up from the moist, warm earth, and the fallen petals stir on the ground, turn over, and go to sleep again. Outside, beyond the foliage, where the sunlight lies on the slate-coloured roofs, the ridged rice-fields beyond the roofs, and the hills beyond the rice-fields, is all Japan – only all Japan; and this that they call the old French Legation[6] is the Garden of Eden that most naturally dropped down here after the Fall. For some small hint of the beauties to be shown later there is the roof of a temple, ridged and fluted with dark tiles, flung out casually beyond the corner of the bluff on which the garden stands. Any other curve of the eaves would not have consorted with the sweep of the pine branches; therefore, this curve was made, and being made, was perfect. The congregation of the globe-trotters are in the hotel, scuffling for guides, in order that they may be shown the sights of Japan, which is all one sight. They must go to Tokyo, they must go to Nikko; they must surely see all that is to be seen, and then write home to their barbarian families that they are getting used to the sight of bare brown legs. Before this day is ended, they will all, thank goodness, have splitting headaches and burnt-out eyes. It is better to lie still and hear the grass grow – to soak in the heat and the smell and the sounds and the sights that come unasked.

Our garden overhangs the harbour, and by pushing aside one branch we look down upon a heavy-sterned fishing-boat, the straw-gold mats of the deck-house pushed back to show the perfect order and propriety of the housekeeping that is going forward. The father-fisher, sitting frog-fashion, is poking at a tiny box full of charcoal, and the light white ash is blown back into the face of a largish Japanese doll, price two shillings and threepence in Bayswater. The doll wakes, turns into a Japanese baby something more valuable than money could buy – a baby with a shaven head and aimless legs. It crawls to the thing in the polished brown box, is picked up just as it is ready to eat live coals, and is set down behind a thwart, where it drums upon a bucket, addressing the firebox from afar. Half-a-dozen cherry blossoms slide off a bough, and waver down to the water close to the Japanese doll, who in another minute will be overside in pursuit of these miracles. The father-fisher has it by the pink hind leg, and this time it is tucked away, all but the top-knot, out of sight among umber nets and sepia cordage. Being an Oriental it makes no protest, and the boat scuds out to join the little fleet in the offing.

Then two sailors of a man-of-war come along the sea face, lean over the canal below the garden, spit and roll away. The sailor in port is the only superior man.[7] To him all matters rare and curious are either 'them things' or 'them other things.' He does not hurry himself, he does not seek adjectives other than those which custom puts into his mouth for all occasions; but the beauty of life penetrates his being insensibly till he gets drunk, falls foul of the local policeman, smites him into the nearest canal, and disposes of the question of treaty revision with a hiccup. All the same, Jack says that he has a grievance against the policeman, who is paid a dollar for every strayed seaman he brings up to the Consular Courts[8] for overstaying his leave, and so forth. Jack says that the little fellows deliberately hinder him from getting back to his ship, and then with devilish art and craft of wrestling tricks – 'there are about a hundred of 'em, and they can throw you with every qualified one' – carry him to justice.[9] Now when Jack is softened with drink he does not tell lies. This is his grievance, and he says that them blanketed Consuls ought to know. 'They plays into each other's hands, and stops you at the Hatoba'[10] – the policemen do. The visitor who is neither a seaman nor drunk cannot swear to the truth of this, or indeed anything else. He moves not only among fascinating scenes and a lovely people but, as he is sure to find out before he has been a day ashore, between stormy questions. Three years ago there were no questions that were not going to be settled off-hand in a blaze of paper lanterns. The Constitution was new. It has a grey, pale cover with a chrysanthemum at the back, and a Japanese told me then, 'Now we have Constitution same as other countries, and *so* it is all right. Now we are quite civilised because of Constitution.'

[A perfectly irrelevant story comes to mind here. Do you know that in Madeira once they had a revolution which lasted just long enough for the national poet to compose a national anthem, and then was put down? All that is left of the revolt now is the song that you hear on the twangling *nachettes*, the baby-banjoes, of a moonlight night under the banana fronds at the back of Funchal. And the high-pitched nasal refrain of it is 'Consti-tuci-*oun!*'][11]

Since that auspicious date it seems that the questions have impertinently come up, and the first and the last of them is that of Treaty Revision. Says the Japanese Government, 'Only obey our laws, our new laws that we have so carefully compiled from all the wisdom of the West, and you shall go up country as you please and trade where you will, instead of living cooped up in concessions and being judged by Consuls. Treat us as you would treat France or Germany, and we will treat you as our own subjects.'

Here, as you know, the matter rests between the two thousand foreigners and the forty million Japanese – a God-send to all the editors of Tokyo and Yokohama, and the despair of the newly arrived in whose nose, remember, is the smell of the East, One and Indivisible, Immemorial, Eternal, and, above all, Instructive.

Indeed, it is only by walking out at least half a mile that you escape from the aggressive evidences of civilisation, and come out into the rice-fields at the back of the town. Here men with twists of blue and white cloth round their heads are working knee-deep in the thick black mud. The largest field may be something less than two tablecloths, while the smallest is, say, a speck of undercliff, on to which it were hard to back a 'rickshaw, wrested from the beach and growing its clumps of barley within spray-shot of the waves. The field paths are the trodden tops of the irrigating cuts, and the main roads as wide as two perambulators abreast. From the uplands – the beautiful uplands planted in exactly the proper places with pine and maple – the ground comes down in terraced pocket on pocket of rich earth to the levels again, and it would seem that every heavily-thatched farmhouse was chosen with special regard to the view. If you look closely when the people go to work you will see that a household spreads itself over plots, maybe, a quarter of a mile apart. A revenue map of a village shows that this scatteration is apparently designed, but the reason is not given. One thing at least is certain. The assessment of these patches can be no light piece of work – just the thing, in fact, that would give employment to a large number of small and variegated Government officials, any one of whom, assuming that he was of an Oriental cast of mind, might make the cultivator's life interesting. I remember now – a second-time-seen place brings back things that were altogether buried – seeing three years ago the pile of Government papers required in the case of one farm. They were many and systematic, but the interesting thing about them was the amount of work that they must have furnished to those who were neither cultivators nor Treasury officials.

If one knew Japanese, one could collogue with that gentleman in the straw hat and the blue loin-cloth who is chopping within a sixteenth of an inch of his naked toes with the father and mother of all weed-spuds. His version of local taxation might be inaccurate, but it would be sure to be picturesque. Failing his evidence, be pleased to accept two or three things that may or may not be facts of general application. They differ in a measure from statements in the books. The present land-tax is nominally $2\frac{1}{2}$ per cent, payable in cash on a three, or as some say a five, yearly settlement. But, according to certain officials, there has been no settlement since 1875. Land lying fallow for a season pays the same tax as land in cultivation, unless it is unproductive through flood or calamity (read earthquake here). The Government tax is calculated on the capital value of the land, taking a measure of about 11,000 square feet or a quarter of an acre as the unit.

Now, one of the ways of getting at the capital value of the land is to see what the railways have paid for it. The very best rice land, taking the Japanese dollar at three shillings, is about £65.10s. per acre. Unirrigated land for vegetable growing is something over £9.12s., and forest £2.11s. As these are railway rates, they may be fairly held to cover large areas. In private sales the prices may reasonably be higher.

It is to be remembered that some of the very best rice land will bear two crops of rice in the year. Most soil will bear two crops, the first being millet, rape, vegetables, and so on, sown on dry soil and ripening at the end of May. Then the ground is at once prepared for the wet crop, to be harvested in October or thereabouts. Land-tax is payable in two instalments. Rice land pays between the 1st of November and the middle of December and the 1st of January and the last of February. Other land pays between July and August and September and December. Let us see what the average yield is. The gentleman in the sun-hat and the loin-cloth would shriek at the figures, but they are approximately accurate. Rice naturally fluctuates a good deal, but it may be taken in the rough at five Japanese dollars (fifteen shillings) per *koku*[12] of 330 lbs. Wheat and maize of the first spring crop is worth about eleven shillings per *koku*. The first crop gives nearly $1\frac{3}{4}$ *koku* per *tan*[13] (the quarter-acre unit of measurement aforesaid), or eighteen shillings per quarter acre, or £3:12s. per acre. The rice crop at two *koku* or £1:10s. the quarter acre gives £6 an acre. Total £9:12s. This is not altogether bad if you reflect that the land in question is not the very best rice land, but ordinary No. 1, at £25:16s. per acre, capital value.

A son has the right to inherit his father's land on the father's assessment, so long as its term runs; or, when the term has expired, has a prior claim as against any one else. Part of the taxes, it is said, lies by in the local prefecture's office as a reserve fund against inundations. Yet, and this seems a little confusing, there are between five and seven other local, provincial, and municipal taxes which can reasonably be applied to the same ends. No one of these taxes exceeds a half of the land-tax, unless it be the local prefecture tax of $2\frac{1}{2}$ per cent.

In the old days the people were taxed, or perhaps squeezed would be the better word, to about one-half of the produce of the land. There are those who may say that the present system is not so advantageous as it looks. Beforetime, the farmers, it is true, paid heavily, but only on their nominal holdings. They could, and often did, hold more land than they were assessed on. Today a rigid bureaucracy surveys every foot of their farms, and upon every foot they have to pay. Somewhat similar complaints are made still by the simple peasantry of India, for if there is one thing that the Oriental detests more than another, it is the damnable Western vice of accuracy. That leads to doing things by rule. Still, by the look of those terraced fields, where the water is led so cunningly from level to level, the Japanese cultivator must enjoy at least one excitement. If the villages up the valley tamper with the water supply, there must surely be excitement down the valley – argument, protest, and the breaking of heads.

The days of romance, therefore, are not all dead.

*　　*　　*

This that follows happened on the coast twenty miles through the fields from Yokohama, at Kamakura, that is to say, where the great bronze Buddha sits facing the sea to hear the centuries go by.[14] He has been described again and again – his majesty, his aloofness, and every one of his dimensions, the smoky little shrine within him, and the plumed hill that makes the background to his throne. For that reason he remains, as he remained from the beginning, beyond all hope of description – as it might be, a visible god sitting in the garden of a world made new. They sell photographs of him with tourists standing on his thumbnail,[15] and, apparently, any brute of either gender can scrawl his or her ignoble name over the inside of the massive bronze plates that build him up. Think for a moment of the indignity and the insult! Imagine the ancient, orderly gardens with their clipped trees, shorn turf, and silent ponds smoking in the mist that the hot sun soaks up after rain, and the green-bronze image of the Teacher of the Law wavering there as if half seen through incense clouds. The earth is all one censer, and myriads of frogs are making the haze ring. It is too warm to do more than to sit on a stone and watch the eyes that, having seen all things, see no more – the down-dropped eyes, the forward droop of the head, and the colossal simplicity of the folds of the robe over arm and knee. Thus, and in no other fashion, did Buddha sit in the old days when Ananda asked questions[16] and the dreamer began to dream of the lives that lay behind him ere the lips moved, and as the Chronicles say: 'He told a tale.' This would be the way he began, for dreamers in the East tell something the same sort of tales to-day: 'Long ago when Devadatta was King of Benares,[17] there lived a virtuous elephant, a reprobate ox, and a King without understanding.' And the tale would end, after the moral had been drawn for Ananda's benefit: 'Now, the reprobate ox was such an one, and the King was such another, but the virtuous elephant was I myself, Ananda.' Thus, then, he told the tales in the bamboo grove, and the bamboo grove is there to-day. Little blue and grey and slate-robed figures pass under its shadow, buy two or three joss-sticks, disappear into the shrine, that is, the body of the god, come out smiling, and drift away through the shrubberies. A fat carp in a pond sucks at a fallen leaf with just the sound of a wicked little worldly little kiss. Then the earth steams, and steams in silence, and a gorgeous butterfly, full six inches from wing to wing, cuts through the steam in a zigzag of colour and flickers up to the forehead of the god. And Buddha said that a man must look on everything as illusion – even light and colour – the time-worn bronze of metal against blue-green of pine and pale emerald of bamboo – the lemon sash of the girl in the cinnamon dress, with coral pins in her hair, leaning against a block of weather-bleached stone – and, last, the spray of blood-red azalea that stands on the pale gold mats of the tea-house beneath the honey-coloured thatch. To overcome desire and covetousness of mere gold, which is often very vilely designed, that is conceivable; but why must a man give up the delight of the eye, colour that rejoices, light that cheers, and line that satisfies the innermost deeps of the heart? Ah, if the Bodhisat[18] had only seen his own image![19]

At the entrance to the gardens there is a quaint little printed appeal, half pathetic and half dignified, put forward by the priests of the place, for reverence and decent behaviour on the part of the visitors.[20] It might perhaps be done into rhyme, something after this style:–[21]

> O ye who tread the Narrow Way[22]
> By Tophet-flare[23] to Judgment Day,
> Be gentle when 'the heathen' pray
>   To Buddha at Kamakura!
>
> To Him the Way, the Law, apart
> Whom Maya held beneath her heart,
> Ananda's Lord, the Bodhisat,[24]
>   The Daibutz of Kamakura.
>
> For though He neither burns nor sees
> Nor hears ye thank your Deities
> Ye have not sinned with such as these,
>   His children at Kamakura,

Yet spare us still the Western joke
When joss-sticks turn to scented smoke
The little sins of little folk
    That worship at Kamakura –

The grey-robed, gay-sashed butterflies
That flit beneath the Master's eyes.
He is beyond the Mysteries
    But loves them at Kamakura.

And whoso will, from Pride released,
Contemning neither creed nor priest,
May feel the Soul of all the East
    About him at Kamakura.

Yea, every tale Ananda heard,
Of birth as fish or beast or bird,
While yet in lives the Master stirred,
    The warm wind brings Kamakura,

With voice of every soul that clung
To Life that strove from rung to rung
When Devadatta's rule was young,
    In worship at Kamakura.

Till drowsy eyelids seem to see
Far-flaming 'neath her golden *htee*[25]
The Shwe-Dagon[26] flare easterly
    From Burma to Kamakura,

And down the loaded air there comes
The thunder of Tibetan drums,
And droned *Om mane padme hum's*[27]
    A world's width from Kamakura.

Yet Brahmans rule Benares still,[28]
Buddh-Gaya's ruins pit the hill,[29]
And beef-fed zealots[30] threaten ill
    To Buddha and Kamakura.

A tourist-show, a legend told,
A rusting hulk of bronze and gold,

So much, and scarce so much, ye hold
The meaning of Kamakura?

But when the morning prayer is prayed,
Think, ere ye pass to strife and trade,
Is God in human image made
No nearer than Kamakura?

1892: LETTER ONE
COMMENTARY

1. After getting married in London on 18 January 1892, the Kiplings set out on a voyage intended to take them round the world. They sailed from Liverpool on 3 February, reached New York eight days later, and spent several weeks in the USA during which they bought the land for their future house in Vermont, before sailing from Vancouver to Yokohama. The *Japan Weekly Mail* of 23 April 1892, amid the many details of 'Latest Shipping', recorded the arrival on 20 April of 'Mr. and Mrs. Rudyard Kipling' among the passengers 'Per British steamer *Empress of India*, 3,003 [tons], [Captain] Marshall, R.N.R., [from] Vancouver, B.C., 6th April, Mails and General'. The ship departed next day for 'Hongkong viâ ports'.

2. For Kipling 'the East', as here, clearly meant India and his own route of 1889. This makes for logical confusion a little later in this Letter, both when the Japanese are referred to as 'Eastern' and when India is referred to as 'another land a few thousand miles further West'.

3. *Murray's Handbook for Travellers in Japan* (3rd edition, 1891) had been edited by Basil Hall Chamberlain and W. B. Mason.

4. Copperas, in English usage, tended to mean green vitriol or ferrous sulphate, which was used in dyeing.

5. 'Out of many, one', the motto of the United States of America.

6. In the early years after establishment of diplomatic relations, foreign legations had premises in both Yokohama and Edo (or Tokyo, as Edo became in 1868).

7. Kipling was by now famous for his stories and poems about the life of the British soldier, a subject no other man of letters had touched in a comparable way. By contrast, this passage provides an early example of his dawning interest in the British sailor, in those days still nicknamed

Jack Tar, about whom he would later write with similar vividness and commitment. (See also Letter Seven of 1889, Note 16.) The nickname in question (often abbreviated as 'Jack' or 'tar') meant a common sailor. It dated from 1781 or thereabouts, and arose from the canvas breeches often worn by sailors, tarred to keep out water.

8. Under the as-yet-unrevised 'unequal treaties' foreigners were subject to the jurisdiction of their home state; under the system of extra-territoriality justice was administered through consular courts.

9. This reference by Kipling to judo techniques was picked up in the *Transactions & Proceedings of the Japan Society*, volume 1 (1892). The Society, founded in London in January 1892, held its first meeting in April: after an inaugural address by its president (the Japanese minister, Viscount M. Kawase), there was a lecture on '*Ju-jitsu*: the ancient art of self-defence by sleight of body' by an authority on the subject, Mr. T. Shidachi. He coupled with it a practical demonstration in which, despite 'repeatedly throwing Mr. Goh [the Society's honorary secretary] over his head, apparently with the greatest ease', he did so 'with such dexterity that neither the Lecturer nor Mr. Goh showed the slightest disorder in their evening dress'. Mr. Shidachi described *Ju-do* as a development from *Ju-jitsu*, involving mental as well as physical training, and added that it was 'due to the study of *Ju-do* that the Japanese police, in spite of their small stature, are so skilful in seizing malefactors'. By the time this was printed, 'The Edge of the East' had appeared in *The Times* (2 July 1892), enabling a footnote to Mr. Shidachi's speech to cite Kipling's appreciation of the 'devilish art and craft of wrestling tricks'.

10. *Hatoba* is the Japanese for 'pier'. In the early days of the Yokohama settlement there were two *hatoba*, the English and the French.

11. Kipling had been to Madeira in August 1891 en route to Cape Town.

12. Though Kipling cites it as a weight, a *koku* is more properly defined as a measure, approximating to 40 gallons, or 5 bushels, or 10 cubic feet. In feudal times the wealth of the Daimyo was reckoned by the number of *koku* of rice their domains produced.

13. A *tan* was precisely 0.245 acres. Through various editions of Kipling the misprint *tau* has been perpetuated.

14. (See also Letter Twelve of 1889, Note 32.) The big Buddha at Kamakura, usually referred to as the Daibutsu (meaning 'big Buddha'), is one of the most impressive images in Japan, and dates from the thirteenth century. A preceding Daibutsu had been made of wood in 1243, but after its temple had been destroyed by a storm in 1248 the decision was made to cast a new Daibutsu in bronze. With great difficulty on account of its size (height 11.4 metres, circumference at the knees 29.4 metres, weight 93 tons) this was done by 1252. At first it was in a building, but this was damaged by storms in 1335 and 1368, and wrecked by a tidal wave in 1495. Since then, in the words of Michael Cooper (*Exploring Kamakura*,

Tokyo, 1979), it has remained 'seated calmly and serenely in the open'; in his view, which Kipling would have echoed but which would not have impressed some of the Christian missionaries of that time, 'the more you visit the Great Buddha, the more beautiful it appears, the more meaningful its message'. Kipling's tribute to the great power of the Daibutsu received unstinted praise from Lafcadio Hearn (in his posthumously published *Japanese Letters*, Constable, London, 1911, pages 27 and 110). Writing to Basil Hall Chamberlain in December 1892, he had said:

I hope Mason has preserved for you the pretty lines of Rudyard Kipling about the Daibutsu at Kamakura [in *The Times*, 2 July]. I enjoy him, – not the poetry of the effort, but the prose of it. It is delicious. Alas! I had written my commonplace stuff about the Daibutsu long ago ... Would I could atone for it now! But then Kipling is a giant in all things compared to me ... I despair when I read that man's work.

Writing again to Chamberlain in June 1893, he praised the 'true art' of

Kipling's little sketch of Kamakura ... perfectly controlled, subtle, didactic. But I wonder if the mass of his readers can feel the delicacy of him. I fear they mostly seek the story only.

15. The reference to missionaries in the preceding Note, and Kipling's mention of the thumbnail of the Daibutsu, call to mind a complacent passage in *Life and Adventures in Japan* by E. Warren Clark (American Tract Society, New York, 1878, page 20):

Dai-Butz is very imposing without, but he is entirely empty within; for you may go inside of him, by passing through a small door, and find his hollow form lined with shelves, on which small gilt images are ranged ... After studying the image as a work of art, I climbed up into his capacious lap, and sat upon one of his thumbs, which were placed together in a devout attitude. Here I began to sing the long-metre doxology, to the astonishment of the priest standing below, who could not understand the words, and wondered what the matter was! A year after this I sang the same hymn in Dai-Butz's lap, with half-a-dozen other people; and we told the priest we were praising the TRUE GOD, that the time was at hand when idolatry in Japan was going down, never to rise again ...

16. Ananda, a cousin of the Buddha, was one of the earliest converts to the new faith, and became a favourite disciple.

17. Benares, now Varanasi, is a very ancient city of north-eastern India, and a sacred place in the Hindu religion. However, it also has profound significance in the history of Buddhism, and was the centre of an area in which the Buddha preached for some forty years after his 'enlightenment', which may have been in the sixth century BC. Devadatta, King of Benares, was a cousin of the Buddha, but according to the legend hostile to him. The story goes that he tried to drive the Buddha away, or even to kill him by turning loose against him an elephant that had been primed to a state of rage by drugs. However the plan misfired, since the elephant instantly recognized the holiness of the Buddha, and declined to attack him.

18. The *Bodhisat* (for earlier mention of the variant *Bodhisattva* see Letter Ten of 1889, Note 17): this term can have different significances, either meaning a 'potential' Buddha or the Buddha himself during the period before his 'vocation' and 'enlightenment'. The word implies a being with divine attributes, who has earned the condition of Nirvana but has chosen to remain on the human plane in order to help others towards salvation. In its Sanskrit origin it means the 'essence (*sattva*) of enlightenment (*bodhi*)'.

19. This is the point at which the present Letter, 'The Edge of the East', was made to end when edited in 1920 as part of *Letters of Travel*. However, the paragraph that follows, and the concluding verses, were an integral part of the Letter when it appeared in *The Times* in 1892.

20. This notice was almost certainly the one recorded by Countess Iso Mutsu in *Kamakura: Fact and Legend* (Kamakura, 1918), as follows:

> *Stranger, whosoever thou art, and whatsoever be thy creed, when thou enterest this sanctuary remember thou treadest upon ground hallowed by the worship of ages. This is the temple of Buddha and the gate of the Eternal, and should therefore be entered with reverence.*

The identical text greets the visitor today, headed KOTOKU-IN MONASTERY, KAMAKURA, and ending BY ORDER OF THE PRIOR.

21. The poem that follows, written originally as a pendant to the newspaper article, and as an imaginative extension of the Prior's notice at the shrine, later became famous in its own right and was read with appreciation by many who barely knew where Kamakura was and were unaware that Kipling had ever been to Japan. Three of its verses were used as chapter headings in the novel *Kim* (1901), and the whole poem appeared in *The Five Nations* (1903), and thereafter in other collections of Kipling's poetry. However, it appears that Kipling was unsatisfied with the verses as they were first composed: at various times he made several changes in both the words and the punctuation, and he reduced the length from thirteen to twelve verses. Here we reproduce it with most of the later emendations but in its original length. Some of the

Kipling's Japan

references in the poem are esoteric and need explanation by the Notes and also by comparison with the preceding prose passage. One or two expressions remain obscure, e.g. the meaning of 'burns' in the third verse. Kipling had an almost infallible sense of rhythm. In the recurrent refrain produced by the last line of each verse, he has clearly taken into account the fact that *Kamakura*, in the Japanese, is not pronounced *Kámakúra* as Europeans tend to pronounce it, but with a much more even stress on each of its four syllables. When the name is read in that way, the rhythm, otherwise clumsy, falls precisely into place.

22. A reference to the Bible (*St Matthew*, 7, 14): 'Strait is the gate, and narrow is the way, which leadeth unto life, and few there be that find it.' The Narrow Way is contrasted with the 'Middle Way' of Buddhism: it is no coincidence that chapter 1 of *Kim*, in which the Lama first extols the Middle Way, is introduced by this verse, in which something of Kipling's lifelong abhorrence of Calvinistic Christianity comes across. It dated from the bigotry and intolerance to which he had been exposed in childhood under the tutelage of his Southsea guardian, Mrs. Holloway.

23. The Bible contains several sinister references to Tophet (e.g. II *Kings*, 23, 10). It was an area on the southern outskirts of Jerusalem (also called Gehenna): fires were always burning there since it was the place where refuse was disposed of. Its evil reputation came from a period when the Jews lapsed into idolatry and offered human sacrifices to Moloch there, notably children, who were burnt alive. The derivation of *Tophet* is either from a term meaning 'place to spit on', or from *tabret*, the name for the tambourines used to drown the cries of the children. It came to symbolize the place of torment in the after-life.

24. These first three lines of the second verse are also cited in the first chapter of *Kim*, where the Lama is made to utter them at a moment of deep religious feeling, as part of 'the wonderful Buddhist invocation'.

25. The *htee*, or *hti*, on a Burmese pagoda is the gilded umbrella-shaped topmost piece surmounting the dome.

26. The Shwe-Dagon pagoda in Rangoon is one of the most magnificent centres of worship in all the world. For Buddhists it has unique status by virtue of containing within its structure various relics both of the principal Buddha, Gautama, and of the three Buddhas believed to have existed before his time. Kipling had visited Rangoon, and admired the Shwe-Dagon, a few weeks before his first arrival in Japan. At that time the dome had been damaged, and the *htee* thrown down, by an earthquake, and repairs were being done. That *htee*, which had been placed on the top by King Mindon, was eventually destroyed in a further earthquake in 1930, and replaced by the present *htee*, inlaid with diamonds, in 1931.

27. *Om mane padme hum.* (For *Om*, see Letter Twelve of 1889, Note 14.) Among Tibetans and Tantric Buddhists this is a mystic formula of wide

208

application. It signifies the existence of the 'jewel' (individuality) at the heart of the 'lotus' (the universal being). These words are among the first taught to a child and the last uttered on the deathbed of the pious. As to Tantrism, Sir Charles Eliot in *Japanese Buddhism* defines it as a system of religious magic making use of spells and formulae in which the sound and the mystic symbolism are of more potency than any 'meaning' in the ordinary sense. Tibetan Buddhism is frequently called 'Tantric': in Japan it is the Shingon sect of Buddhism, founded by a famous priest Kobo Daishi, that may best be described as a form of Tantric Buddhism.

28. A reference to the fact that Buddhism failed to take any lasting hold in Benares. See Note 17 above.

29. Buddh Gaya is a very ancient centre of Buddhism, now largely in ruins. It is near Gaya, south of Patna in Bihar, India, and is a leading archaeological site among many in an area where, in the words of *Murray's Handbook*, 'the rocky hills abound in remains, sculptures, images and sites of the religion of Buddha, many diverted to Hindu worship'. The ancient Temple of Buddh Gaya is closely connected with events of the Buddha's lifetime, but now belongs to a Hindu monastery. Major restorations were done to it, by government initiative, in the 1880s. Nearby is the 'Bodhi tree', the famous *pipal* under which the Buddha received his enlightenment.

30. Christian missionaries (whose fondness for beef would be offensive both to Hindus, for whom the cow is sacred, and to Buddhists, for whom the taking of life is forbidden).

1892: Letter Two

OUR OVERSEAS MEN

> For hope of gain, or sake of peace,
>   Or greed of golden fee,
> You must not sell your galley slaves
>   That row you over the sea.
>
> For they come of your own blood,
>   By your own gods they swear,
> So you must not sell them overseas,
>   Because they rowed you there.
>
> KING EURIC.[1]

All things considered, there are only two kinds of men in the world –
those that stay at home and those that do not. The second are the
most interesting. Some day a man will bethink himself and write a
book about the breed, called 'The Book of the Overseas Club,' for it
is at the clubhouses all the way from Aden[2] to Yokohama that the life
of the Outside Men is best seen and their talk is best heard. A strong
family likeness runs through both buildings and members, and a
large and careless hospitality is the note. There is always the same
open-doored, high-ceiled house, with matting on the floors; the
same come and go of dark-skinned servants, and the same assembly
of men talking horse or business, in raiment that would fatally
scandalise a London committee, among files of newspapers from a
fortnight to five weeks old. The life of the Outside Men includes
plenty of sunshine, and as much air as may be stirring.

At the Cape,[3] where the Dutch housewives distil and sell the
very potent Vanderhum,[4] and the absurd home-made hansom cabs
waddle up and down the yellow dust of Adderley Street, are the
members of the big import and export firms, the shipping and
insurance offices, inventors of mines, and exploiters of new

territories, with now and then an officer strayed from India to buy mules for the Government, a Government House aide-de-camp, a sprinkling of the officers of the garrison, tanned skippers of the Union and Castle Lines, and naval men from the squadron at Simon's Town.[5] Here they talk of the sins of Cecil Rhodes,[6] the insolence of Natal,[7] the beauties or otherwise of the solid Boer vote, and the dates of the steamers. The *argot* is Dutch and Kaffir, and every one can hum the national anthem that begins 'Pack your kit and trek, Johnny Bowlegs.'[8]

In the stately Hong Kong[9] Clubhouse, which is to the further what the Bengal Club[10] is to the nearer East, you meet much the same gathering, *minus* the mining speculators and *plus* men whose talk is of tea, silk, shirtings,[11] and Shanghai ponies. The speech of the Outside Men at this point becomes fearfully mixed with pidgin-English and local Chinese terms, rounded with corrupt Portuguese. At Melbourne,[12] in a long verandah giving on a grass plot, where laughing-jackasses[13] laugh very horribly, sit wool-kings, premiers, and breeders of horses after their kind. The older men talk of the days of the Eureka Stockade[14] and the younger of 'shearing wars' in North Queensland, while the traveller moves timidly among them wondering what under the world every third word means.

At Wellington,[15] overlooking the harbour (all right-minded clubs should command the sea), another, and yet a like, sort of men speak of sheep, the rabbits, the land-courts, and the ancient heresies of Sir Julius Vogel;[16] and their more expressive sentences borrow from the Maori. And elsewhere, and elsewhere, and elsewhere among the Outside Men it is the same – the same mixture of every trade, calling, and profession under the sun; the same clash of conflicting interests touching the uttermost parts of the earth; the same intimate, and sometimes appalling, knowledge of your neighbour's business and shortcomings; the same large-palmed hospitality, and the same keen interest on the part of the younger men in the legs of a horse. Decidedly, it is at the Overseas Club all the world over that you get to know some little of the life of the community.

London is egoistical, and the world for her ends with the four-mile cab radius. There is no provincialism like the provincialism of London. That big slack-water coated with the drift and rubbish of a thousand men's thoughts esteems itself the open sea because the waves of all the oceans break on her borders. To those in her midst she is terribly imposing, but they forget that there is more than one kind of imposition. Look back upon her from ten thousand miles, when the mail is just in at the Overseas Club, and she is wondrous tiny. Nine-tenths of her news – so vital, so epoch-making over there – loses its significance, and the rest is as the scuffling of ghosts in a back attic.

Here in Yokohama the Overseas Club has two mails and four sets of papers – English, French, German, and American, as suits the variety of its constitution – and the verandah by the sea, where the big telescope stands, is a perpetual Pentecost.[17] The population of the club changes with each steamer in harbour, for the sea-captains swing in, are met with 'Hello! where did you come from?' and mix at the bar and billiard-tables for their appointed time and go to sea again. The white-painted warships supply their contingent of members also, and there are wonderful men, mines of most fascinating adventure, who have an interest in sealing-brigs that go to the Kurile Islands,[18] and somehow get into trouble with the Russian authorities.[19] Consuls and judges of the Consular Courts meet men over on leave from the China ports, or it may be Manila, and they all talk tea, silk, banking, and exchange with the fixed residents. Everything is always as bad as it can possibly be, and everybody is on the verge of ruin. That is why, when they have decided that life is no longer worth living, they go down to the skittle-alley – to commit suicide. From the outside, when a cool wind blows among the papers and there is a sound of smashing ice in an inner apartment, and every third man is talking about the approaching races, the life seems to be a desirable one.

'What more could a man need to make him happy?' says the passer-by. A perfect climate, a lovely country, plenty of pleasant society, and the politest people on earth to deal with. The resident smiles and invites the passer-by to stay through July and August. Further, he presses him to do business with the politest people on earth, and to continue so doing for a term of years. Thus the traveller perceives beyond doubt that the resident is prejudiced by the very fact of his residence, and gives it as his matured opinion that Japan is a faultless land, marred only by the presence of the foreign community. And yet, let us consider. It is the foreign community that has made it possible for the traveller to come and go from hotel to hotel, to get his passport for inland travel, to telegraph his safe arrival to anxious friends, and generally to enjoy himself much more than he would have been able to do in his own country. Government and gunboats may open a land, but it is the men of the Overseas Club that keep it open. Their reward (not alone in Japan) is the bland patronage or the scarcely-veiled contempt of those who profit by their labours. It is hopeless to explain to a traveller who has been 'ohayoed' into half-a-dozen shops and 'sayonaraed' out of half-a-dozen more[20] and politely cheated in each one, that the Japanese is an Oriental, and, therefore, embarrassingly economical of the truth.[21]

'That's his politeness,' says the traveller. 'He does not wish to hurt your feelings. Love him and treat him like a brother, and he'll change.'

To treat one of the most secretive of races on a brotherly basis is not very easy, and the natural politeness that enters into a signed and sealed contract and undulates out of it so soon as it does not sufficiently pay is more than embarrassing. It is almost annoying. The want of fixity or commercial honour may be due to some natural infirmity of the artistic temperament, or to the manner in which the climate has affected, and his ruler has ruled, the man himself for untold centuries.

Those who know the East know, where the system of 'squeeze,' which is commission, runs through every transaction of life, from the sale of a groom's place upward, where the woman walks behind the man in the streets, and where the peasant gives you for the distance to the next town as many or as few miles as he thinks you will like, that these things must be so. Those who do not know will not be persuaded till they have lived there. The Overseas Club puts up its collective nose scornfully when it hears of the New and Regenerate Japan sprung to life since the 'seventies. It grins, with shame be it written, at an Imperial Diet modelled on the German plan and a Code Napoléon *à la Japonaise*. It is so far behind the New Era as to doubt that an Oriental country, ridden by etiquette of the sternest, and social distinctions almost as hard as those of caste, can be turned out to Western gauge in the compass of a very young man's life. And it *must* be prejudiced, because it is daily and hourly in contact with the Japanese, except when it can do business with the Chinaman whom it prefers. Was there ever so disgraceful a Club!

Just at present, a crisis, full blown as a chrysanthemum, has developed in the Imperial Diet.[22] Both Houses accuse the Government of improper interference – this Japanese for 'plenty stick and some bank-note' – at the recent elections. They then did what was equivalent to passing a vote of censure on the Ministry and refusing to vote Government measures. So far the wildest advocate of representative government could have desired nothing better. Afterwards, things took a distinctly Oriental turn. The Ministry refused to resign, and the Mikado prorogued the Diet for a week to think things over. The Japanese papers are now at issue over the event. Some say that representative government implies party government,

and others swear at large. The Overseas Club says for the most part –
'Skittles!'

It is a picturesque situation – one that suggests romances and
extravaganzas. Thus, imagine a dreaming Court intrenched behind a
triple line of moats[23] where the lotus blooms in summer – a Court
whose outer fringe is aggressively European, but whose heart is
Japan of long ago, where a dreaming King sits among some wives or
other things,[24] amused from time to time with magic-lantern
shows[25] and performing fleas – a holy King whose sanctity is used to
conjure with, and who twice a year gives garden-parties[26] where
every one must come in top-hat and frock coat. Round this Court,
wavering between the splendours of the sleeping and the variety
shows of the Crystal Palace,[27] place in furious but carefully-veiled
antagonism the fragments of newly shattered castes, their natural
Oriental eccentricities overlaid with borrowed Western notions.
Imagine, now, a large and hungry bureaucracy,[28] French in its fretful
insistence on detail where detail is of no earthly moment, Oriental in
its stress on etiquette and punctilio, recruited from a military caste
accustomed for ages past to despise alike farmer and trader.[29]This
caste, we will suppose, is more or less imperfectly controlled by a
syndicate of three clans,[30] which supply their own nominees to
the Ministry. These are adroit, versatile, and unscrupulous men,
hampered by no Western prejudice in favour of carrying any plan to
its completion. Through and at the bidding of these men, the holy
Monarch acts; and the acts are wonderful. To criticise these acts
exists a wild-cat Press, liable to suppression at any moment, as
morbidly sensitive to outside criticism as the American, and almost
as childishly untruthful, fungoid in the swiftness of its growth, and
pitiable in its unseasoned rashness.[31] Backers of this press in its
wilder moments, lawless, ignorant, sensitive and vain, are the
student class, educated in the main at Government expense, and a
thorn in the side of the State. Judges without training handle laws
without precedents,[32] and new measures are passed and abandoned
with almost inconceivable levity. Out of the welter of classes and
interests that are not those of the common folk is evolved the thing
called Japanese policy; that has the proportion and perspective of a
Japanese picture.

Finality and stability are absent from its councils. To-day, for
reasons none can explain, it is pro-foreign to the verge of servility.[33]
Tomorrow, for reasons equally obscure, the pendulum swings back,
and – the students are heaving mud at the foreigners in the streets.
Vexatious, irresponsible, incoherent, and, above all, cheaply

mysterious, is the rule of the land – stultified by intrigue and counter-intrigue, chequered with futile reforms begun on European lines and light-heartedly thrown aside; studded, as a bower-bird's run is studded with shells and shining pebbles, with plagiarisms from half the world – an operetta of administration, wherein the shadow of the King among his wives, *samurai* policemen, doctors who have studied under Pasteur, kid-gloved cavalry officers from St. Cyr,[34] judges with University degrees, harlots with fiddles, newspaper correspondents, masters of the ancient ceremonies of the land, paid members of the Diet, secret societies that borrow the knife and the dynamite of the Irish, sons of dispossessed Daimyo returned from Europe and waiting for what may turn up, with ministers of the syndicate who have wrenched Japan from her repose of twenty years ago, circle, flicker, shift, and re-form, in bewildering rings, round the foreign resident. Is the extravaganza complete?

Somewhere in the background of the stage are the people of the land – of whom a very limited proportion enjoy the privileges of representative government. Whether in the past few years they have learned what the thing means, or, learning, have the least intention of making any use of it, is not clear. Meantime, the game of government goes forward as merrily as a game of puss-in-the-corner,[35] with the additional joy that not more than half-a-dozen men know who is controlling it or what in the wide world it intends to do. In Tokyo live the steadily-diminishing staff of Europeans employed by the Emperor as engineers, railway experts, professors in the colleges and so forth. Before many years they will all be dispensed with, and the country will set forth among the nations alone and on its own responsibility.

In fifty years then, from the time that the intrusive American first broke her peace,[36] Japan will experience her new birth and, reorganised from sandal to top-knot, play the *samisen* in the march of modern progress. This is the great advantage of being born into the New Era, when individual and community alike can get something for nothing – pay without work, education without effort, religion without thought, and free government without slow and bitter toil.[37]

The Overseas Club, as has been said, is behind the spirit of the age. It has to work for what it gets, and it does not always get what it works for. Nor can its members take ship and go home when they please. Imagine for a little, the contented frame of mind that is bred in a man by the perpetual contemplation of a harbour full of steamers as a Piccadilly cab-rank of hansoms. The weather is hot, we will suppose; something has gone wrong with his work that day, or his children are not looking so well as might be. Pretty tiled bungalows, bowered in roses and wistaria, do not console him, and the voices of the politest people on earth jar sorely. He knows every soul in the club, has thoroughly talked out every subject of interest, and would give half a year's – oh, five years' – pay for one lung-filling breath of air that has life in it, one sniff of the haying grass, or half a mile of muddy London street where the muffin bell[38] tinkles in the four o'clock fog. Then the big liner moves out across the staring blue of the bay. So-and-so and such-an-one, both his friends, are going home in her, and some one else goes next week by the French mail. He, and he alone, it seems to him, must stay on; and it is so maddeningly easy to go – for every one save himself. The boat's smoke dies out along the horizon, and he is left alone with the warm wind and the white dust on the Bund. Now Japan is a good place, a place that men swear by and live in for thirty years at a stretch. There are China ports a week's sail to the westward where life is really hard, and where the sight of the restless shipping hurts very much indeed.

Tourists and you who travel the world over, be very gentle to the men of the Overseas Clubs. Remember that, unlike yourselves, they have not come here for the good of their health, and that the return ticket in your wallet may possibly a little colour your views of their land. Perhaps it would not be altogether wise on the strength of much kindness from Japanese officials to recommend that these your countrymen be handed over[39] lock, stock, and barrel to a people that are beginning to experiment with fresh-drafted half-grafted codes which do not include juries, to a system that does not contemplate a free Press, to a suspicious absolutism from which there is no appeal. Truly, it might be interesting, but as truly it would begin in farce and end in tragedy, that would leave the politest people on earth in no case to play at civilised government for a long time to come. In his concession, where he is an apologetic and much sat-upon importation, the foreign resident does no harm. He does not always sue for money due to him on the part of a Japanese. Once outside those limits, free to move into the heart of the country, it would only be a question of time as to where and when the trouble would begin. And in the long run it would not be the foreign resident that would suffer. The imaginative eye can see the most unpleasant possibilities, from a general overrunning of Japan by the Chinaman,[40] who is far the most important foreign resident, to the shelling of Tokyo by a joyous and bounding Democracy, anxious to vindicate her national honour and to learn how her newly-made Navy works.

But there are scores of arguments that would confute and overwhelm this somewhat gloomy view. The statistics of Japan, for instance, are as beautiful and fit as neatly as the woodwork of her houses. By these it would be possible to prove anything; yet remember what the singer says:

> The stumbling-block of Western lore
> Is faith in old arithmetics –
> That two and two are always four
> And three and three make ever six,
> Whereas 'neath less exacting skies
> These numbers total otherwise.
>
> Equality of A to B
> Is interesting – Greenwich way;
> But does not for a moment pre-
> dicate the like 'twixt B and A.
> For East of Suez, be it said,
> B is the sum of XYZ.
>
> It may be heat or damp or dew
> That warps the numbers one to ten so,
> And twists the alphabet askew
> Disproving Euclid and Colenso;[41]
> Or else there must be people who
> Don't think as other people do.[42]

1892: LETTER TWO
COMMENTARY

1. Though this Letter, in common with others in Kipling's 1892 series from Japan, was published in *The Times*, the New York *Sun* and the *Civil & Military Gazette* in Lahore, this verse heading appeared only in the New York *Sun* (30 July 1892). It is unmistakably by him, but was

never collected among his verse. Its meaning is consistent with the theme of the whole Letter, being a tribute to the role of the expatriate Europeans abroad – visualized as centring on the Clubs, mainly in the then British Empire, which Kipling had seen – and a reminder that they are apt to be forgotten or belittled by their fellow-countrymen at home. As for 'King Euric', this was Euric or Evaric, the formidable and aggressive ruler of the Vizigoths, who came to power in the period 466 to 484 AD, conquering much of what is now France and Spain. He rose to quasi-imperial eminence, but to link his expansionism with galleys seems fanciful: Gibbon, in the sixth volume of his *Decline and Fall of the Roman Empire*, describes him as 'destitute of any naval force'.

2. Kipling had visited the United Services Club, Aden, on about 31 December 1891, on his way back to England after his brief and final visit to India earlier that month.

3. He had visited Cape Town in September 1891 on his way to New Zealand, before returning via India.

4. Van der Hum (a name of uncertain origin) is a tangerine-flavoured South African liqueur.

5. Simon's Town, or Simonstown, was the naval station just south of Cape Town.

6. Kipling had first briefly met Cecil Rhodes (1853–1902) in September 1891. Several years later the two became very close friends. 1891 had in many ways marked the highest point of Rhodes's remarkable career. He was Prime Minister of Cape Colony and was busily furthering his projects of expansion, in finance and politics, in railway building and the opening up of the territory that became Rhodesia.

7. There was frequent rivalry between Cape Colony and the other British colony in South Africa, Natal, commonly displayed in disputes over railway schemes or customs tariffs.

8. This, or a variant of it, is quoted in a short story by Kipling about the Boer War, 'The Way That He Took' (1900):

> Vat jou goet en trek, Ferriera,
> Vat jou goet en trek;
> Zwaar draa, alle en de ein kant,
> Jannie met de hoepel bein!
>
> (Pack your kit and trek, Ferriera,
> Pack your kit and trek;
> A long pull, all on one side,
> Johnnie with the lame leg!)

9. Kipling had been in Hong Kong shortly before his first visit to Japan in 1889.

10. The Bengal Club, Calcutta, was the best-known club in India.

11. Shirtings: stout cotton cloth suitable for shirts. (This word, as printed in *The Times*, is almost certainly correct: the variant *shortings*, as reprinted in *Letters of Travel*, seems meaningless.)
12. Kipling had twice visited Melbourne in November 1891.
13. Though a jackass is a male donkey, a Laughing Jackass is an Australian giant kingfisher (*Dacelo gigas*), so called from its cry.
14. Kipling is here referring to the battle which marked both the culmination and the suppression of the serious disturbances that took place in 1854 at the gold-mining town of Ballarat in Victoria, Australia. The method of licensing the miners, together with other more political grievances, provoked a local rebellion which was firmly put down. Some 500 insurgent miners, who had constructed the fortified 'Eureka Stockade', were eventually attacked by some 270 troops and police, who took the position at the point of the bayonet, killing about 30 miners in the battle.
15. Kipling had visited Wellington in October 1891.
16. Sir Julius Vogel (1835–99) was the British-born New Zealand journalist, politician and Prime Minister. As to his 'heresies', his ambitious expansionist policies for New Zealand, especially his schemes for financing swift development by extensive borrowing, were controversial. In 1889 he had written an imaginative and prophetic novel, *Anno Domini 2000, or Women's Destiny*.
17. Pentecost: the reference is to the speaking of foreign languages, derived from the second chapter of *Acts* in the Bible. On the Jewish festival of Pentecost an event occurred which is commemorated in the Christian festival of Whitsun, the seventh Sunday after Easter. The Apostles first heard 'a sound from heaven as of a rushing mighty wind', whereupon 'tongues like as of fire' came down on them, and they became endowed with linguistic ability, and 'began to speak with other tongues'.
18. The Kuriles are a group of some thirty islands in the North Pacific, between Kamchatka and Hokkaido. The Japanese took over the northern Kuriles from the Russians in 1875, waiving in return their claims to Sakhalin. In 1945 the whole chain of Japanese islands was occupied by the Russians. The Japanese now demand the return from the Russians of the most southerly islands, Kunashiri, Etorofu, Habomai and Shikotan, which they held in 1855 and do not regard as part of the Kuriles proper – to which they renounced any claim in the peace treaty with the Allied Powers (excluding the Soviet Union) which came into force in 1952. The main interest of the islands is fisheries, but they are also of strategic importance in relation to the Sea of Okhotsk. (See the map on page 266.)
19. 'Trouble with the Russian authorities': an incident of precisely this kind had occurred in the autumn of 1891 and was fully recounted in the *Japan Weekly Mail* in April and May 1892 while Kipling was there. A Captain James Curtis, the American master of the British sealing schooner

Mystery, was arrested by a Russian gunboat for poaching, and the crew were taken to Vladivostok. Kipling certainly saw this account: elements in it are reflected in his poem, 'The Rhyme of the Three Sealers'. (See pages 255–69.)

20. For the greeting *ohayo* see Letter Ten of 1889, Note 5. *Sayonara*, literally 'if this be so', is used for 'goodbye'.

21. 'Economical of the truth': this phrase, which attracted some publicity when it featured in the evidence given before an Australian court in a sensationalized case in 1986, was attributed by some learned commentators to Kipling, citing this reference. Others, however, found its origins earlier, e.g. in a concept of the Early Christian Fathers who used it in the favourable sense of adapting the truth to their hearers' minds. As such it was disparaged by Voltaire; in 1796 Burke used it to mean what the *Shorter Oxford Dictionary* called 'a (discreditable) reticence'.

22. The 'crisis' to which Kipling refers is of considerable interest – and incidentally enables us to date this letter in the third week of May 1892.

    As to the general political position in Japan in 1892, this is well summarized in Professor W. G. Beasley's *Modern History of Japan* (London, 1963): 'The elections of 1892 were notorious for the Government's attempt to use the police to dictate the voting, an attempt which left twenty-five dead and nearly 400 injured to mark the campaign. Nor did it in any way reduce the Diet's hostility to the men in office. The session, which started in May, was as stormy as ever and brought Matsukata's resignation, Ito following him as Premier in August.' Ito Hirobumi, later Prince Ito, was one of the outstanding leaders of the Meiji period and the main architect of the Meiji constitution.

    As to the more detailed position in May 1892, the *Japan Weekly Mail*, which Kipling may be confidently presumed to have read, wrote in a leader of 21 May that the crisis arose because politicians wanted the cabinet to 'hold office solely by the fiat of the majority in the House of Representatives'. This followed an outcry that had arisen over alleged official interference in the elections. The Opposition, in the first session of the House on 12 May, had attacked the Government 'by the indirect method of the Budget', by reducing supplies; but a compromise had been found. In the second session, 'instead of proposing a vote of no confidence', the Opposition had rejected 'every Bill proposed by the Government on the ground that the cabinet could not be trusted'; the session had been dissolved. In the third session, the Opposition had proposed an Address to the Throne by way of a 'sweeping impeachment of the Government. The greatest excitement prevailed.' The resolution on this having failed by 146 votes to 143, they had proposed another on 14 May, which amounted to accepting 'as proved the charges of official interference' in the elections, and this had been passed by 154 to 111. On 16 May the Emperor had ordered the prorogation of the Diet for seven days.

When the Diet was reconvened on 23 May, the House of Representatives and the House of Peers were soon locked in dispute over their respective powers in regard to the budget. The Privy Council, convened to adjudicate, determined that they had equal rights on budgetary matters, though the deliberations of the Lower House came first. In any case, when the special session first convened on 6 May ended on 14 June, a compromise was reached on the budget, but the Government had failed to make progress on the other bills it had wished to enact. It was against this background that Count Matsukata later resigned.

23. The Imperial Palace in Tokyo, having been the castle and residence of the Tokugawa Shogun, was surrounded by a series of moats.

24. The Empress Haruko was childless: the Crown Prince Yoshihito (the Taisho Emperor) was the son of a concubine.

25. An obvious reference to an event reported in the *Japan Weekly Mail* of 14 May 1892, under the heading 'Stereopticon Display at the Palace'. A Mr de Guerville, who represented an American newspaper syndicate and the Chicago World's Fair, and had been introduced to the Imperial Household by the US Chargé d'Affaires, showed the Emperor and Empress some 'striking views of the World's Fair, of Chicago, of New York, of Boston, of Philadelphia, of Washington, of Milwaukee, of St Paul, of San Francisco, of Del Monté, of San José, of Kern County, of the Yosemite Valley, of Yellowstone Park, of Niagara Falls, of New Orleans, and so forth, as well as of several European cities and places of historical interest. The views were accompanied by descriptions in French which were faithfully rendered into Japanese, and the lecture lasted two-and-a-half hours. Their Majesties, however, did not seem to find the interval at all too long, though two brief recesses had to be taken in order to change the gas of the apparatus.'

26. There is an earlier reference to a garden party in the opening passage of Letter Twelve of 1889, with the implication that Kipling might on that occasion have been invited to it, and with a disparaging reference to the fact that all present would wear 'Europe clothes'. Three years later, the *Japan Weekly Mail* of 23 April 1892 reported an Imperial Garden Party to be held that day at the Hama Detached Palace: correct formal western dress was *de rigueur* for all who attended.

27. The Crystal Palace was the building in which the Great Exhibition of 1851 was mounted in Hyde Park; it was later dismantled and re-erected in south-east London, where it was destroyed by fire in 1936. 'The sleeping' is obscure: possibly a corrupt misreading of *The Sleeping Beauty*.

28. The Japanese bureaucracy had been all-powerful until the establishment of the Diet under the 1889 Constitution: even thereafter it remained very strong, since the powers of the politicians were carefully circumscribed by the Constitution. As for emphasis on detail and etiquette, this reflected long-standing Japanese traditions.

29. The four recognized classes under the Tokugawa Shogunate had been *Shi – no – ko – sho*, i.e. *samurai*, farmer, artisan and merchant.

30. The 'three clans' to which Kipling refers did indeed dominate the governments of the early Meiji period. They were *Tozama Daimyo* (i.e. the Outer Daimyo) of *Satsuma* (Kagoshima Prefecture), *Choshu* (Yamaguchi Prefecture) and *Tosa* (Kochi Prefecture).
31. As to the 'wild-cat press', Japanese newspapers of small circulation and short life proliferated at this period. Managers, editors and their policies were regarded by the authorities as irresponsible: newspapers were frequently suppressed and their editors fined or imprisoned.
32. The Meiji Government struggled to produce criminal and civil codes on western lines which would satisfy the Treaty powers and induce them at last to accept treaty revision and an end to extra-territoriality. These codes, being new, were the more arbitrary for lacking 'precedent' – which was an essential feature of the British system, being the basis of Common Law and an important ingredient in the interpretation of Statute Law.
33. Since a primary objective of the Japanese Government at this time was the revision of the 'unequal treaties', they forced the adoption of western dress and customs, including such un-Japanese activities as ballroom dancing. However, anti-foreign feeling was never far beneath the surface, and the prevalence of *soshi* (bully-boy toughs) frequently embarrassed Japanese leaders striving to prove that their country was now a responsible power with a society civilized in the western manner. Throughout this cutting passage Kipling displays his irritation with the posturing of the leaders of Japan, and the inconsistency of their policies: he failed to appreciate the difficulties they faced, and the great success they had achieved in effecting a major social revolution.
34. St Cyr was a French military academy, founded by Napoleon in 1808 near Versailles.
35. 'Puss-in-the-Corner' was a traditional English children's game, already old when recorded by Joseph Strutt in *Sports and Pastimes of the People of England* (1801). One player stood in each corner of a room, and a fifth in the centre. When those in the corners changed positions, the one in the centre tried to reach a vacant corner first, whereupon the loser went to the centre. (It is also mentioned on page 99.)
36. A reference to Commodore Matthew Perry of the US Navy. Perry's arrival with warships in Edo Bay in July 1853, to press President Fillimore's demand for international relations with Japan, led to the US/Japanese treaty of March 1854 and was the first step in the opening up of the country to foreign penetration.
37. This ironic sentence is an early sample of a theme to which Kipling would often return – the essentially debasing effect on society of any system that permitted people to get something for nothing.
38. The muffin, a bread-like cake best eaten toasted and buttered, was sold in English towns by peripatetic muffin-men, who would advertise their presence by ringing a muffin-bell. The practice has ceased.

39. This is the theme of 'King Euric', at the head of this Letter.
40. Insofar as 'overrunning' implied military defeat, this is consistent with the view of most outside observers who predicted that in the event of war China would rout Japan. This expectation was proved false by the actual outcome of the Sino-Japanese war of 1894–5, when the Japanese heavily defeated the Chinese on land and sea in less than a year. In 1892, when Kipling was writing this, Japanese tensions over Korea were growing as the Chinese tried to link Korea commercially with China. As for the 'bounding Democracy' with a 'newly-made Navy', that was the USA, which was indeed committed to a programme of modern warship construction.
41. John William Colenso (1814–83), Bishop of Natal, had been a highly controversial churchman, at one time excommunicated and deposed by the Bishop of Cape Town for theological unorthodoxy, later reinstated by the courts. In this context, however, reference is to his mathematical prowess, which was impressive. His textbooks on arithmetic and algebra, if not destined to last as long as Euclid's on geometry, were widely used.
42. This poem, which has no title and was never collected among Kipling's verse, was not published by *The Times*, but did appear in the New York *Sun* and the *Civil & Military Gazette*. However, it remains virtually unknown since Kipling did not place it in *Letters of Travel*, where this Letter is made to end with the words, '... it is possible to prove anything'. The theme – that it is an erroneous assumption in the west that all peoples are basically alike – is characteristic of Kipling.

Kipling at the Tokyo Club

7 MAY 1892

(TRANSCRIPT FROM THE *JAPAN WEEKLY MAIL* OF SATURDAY 14 MAY 1892)

On Saturday evening the members of the Tokyo Club[1] entertained Mr. Rudyard Kipling at dinner. About fifty assembled to do honour to their distinguished guest, but owing to engagements connected with various entertainments given by or to the newly assembled Houses of the Diet, the Japanese members were unable to be present.

The chair was taken by the foreign Vice-President, Mr. H. W. Denison, and the vice-chair by Captain Ingles, R.N.[2] Dinner was served in the principal dining salon of the Rokumeikan;[3] the table was pleasingly decorated, the *menu* excellent, and the Band of the Imperial Guards played throughout the repast. After the Emperor's health had been drunk, Mr Denison rose and said:–

Gentlemen, – There is an old Spanish proverb to the effect that the Lord sends nuts to them that have no teeth. I am unable from personal experience to testify to the truth of the saying, but, reasoning from analogy, I should be disposed to believe in its absolute verity, since I know that speech is demanded from them that have no talent for the business.

Nevertheless, the wind is always given in measure to the close-shorn sheep, and if nuts are sent to the teethless, nut-crackers are not wanting; if speech is demanded of the speechless, some honourable means of escape for the unfortunates are provided. In this instance my theme is my salvation. An author who has no shop-worn editions or uncut volumes; whose goings and comings are of universal interest, and whose doings and sayings are in the mouths of all men; a writer who at this the end of the 19th century has proved beyond a peradventure that there is no
decline in Adam's line.[4]
Of such a person it is not difficult to speak. Show me the man who has not read 'Soldiers Three,' or 'The Incarnation of Krishna Mulvaney,' or 'The Drums of the Fore and Aft,'[5] and I will show you a man who is either rich in anticipated pleasure or is fully

equipped for jury service. It will indeed be a sorry day for the world at large

When the Rudyards cease from Kipling.[6]

Let us hope that our guest of this evening may be condemned to return late to Heaven, and that in the meantime he may be compelled to continue to fill the world with words that burn and numbers that ring. We are all familiar with the writings of Mr. Kipling, and to know them is to admire them. He has placed us under a double obligation by accepting our invitation for this evening, and in the name of the Tokyo Club I beg to thank him. In this far-away but albeit happy corner of the globe, where but faint and distant echoes reach us of that fierce and never-ending struggle that is the common heritage of our kith beyond ken, it is indeed an honour and a pleasure for us to welcome one who has been in the heat and forefront of that conflict in which the worthiest is the victor, who has, by sheer force of intellect, raised himself high above common humanity, and who is at the same time a jolly good fellow. Gentlemen, I give you the health of our guest, Mr. Rudyard Kipling. – [*Loud applause*]

Mr. Rudyard Kipling, who on rising to reply was greeted with an ovation, said:–

Gentlemen, – If you knew my private opinion of you all I feel sure that you would not applaud, because in this case I can truthfully use the well-worn lie of the after dinner speaker and say, in all sincerity, that I did not know a speech was expected of me tonight. I have to thank you, and I do thank you most heartily, for the kindness that has prompted you to bid me be your guest tonight and for the cordiality that you have just shown.

Mr. Denison has been good enough to say more about me than I am ever likely to live up to: but, so far as regards anything of good that I may have been permitted to do in my own business, you who have done work, as you all have done work, know as well as I do, how outside a man and beyond a man, and having nothing whatever to do with a man, a man's best work is.

I can make no claim to being identified with the world of strife and turmoil beyond these horizons, where men do all the wonderful things that you have just heard about. It is enough for me to belong to the outlying colonies of men whose life is severed from that of their fellows at home; the little isolated communities beyond the seas who are looked upon so curiously and sometimes so curiously misrepresented by wondering tourists. Therefore if you count me as an outsider it – it isn't quite kind of you. For I meet here, if not the very same men, at least the very same type of men as those among whom I have been bred and trained – the men of the Treaty Ports, Singapore, Burmah, and India, men afar and apart from the surroundings and supports of their own countries, but playing no small part in their countries' greatness; those who are the builders of trade, the makers of ways, and the teachers of all good influences; each upholding and advancing the honour and the dignity of his country whatever that country may be. And it is as such that I salute you.[7] – [*Prolonged applause*]

1. The Tokyo Club, established in 1884, was organized and operated on the lines of a typical London club, with membership restricted to men only. ('Supporting members' were elected from the Imperial Family; 'honorary members' from among prominent Japanese and foreigners; 'special members' from among foreign ambassadors, senior officials appointed by the Emperor, the Mayor of Tokyo, etc. The 'regular members' were gentlemen both Japanese and foreign.) The Tokyo Club remains a highly prestigious male club on traditional lines, for Japanese and foreigners.

2. Denison and Ingles were significant figures in the expatriate community in Japan.

   Henry Willard Denison, an American from Vermont, held a senior position as a legal adviser to the Japanese government. He had been employed by the State Department in consular appointments in Japan, but had resigned in 1878 to practise law in Yokohama, before entering Japanese service in 1880. As personal adviser to successive Japanese foreign ministers he played an important role in the matter of Treaty Revision, and also during the Sino-Japanese War of 1894–5, the Anglo-Japanese negotiations for the Alliance of 1902, and the Russo-Japanese War of 1904–5. On his death in 1914 he was given a state funeral.

   Captain John Ingles, R.N., served in Japan from 1887–93 as a British adviser to the Japanese Navy Ministry. He played a major role in the development of advanced training for naval officers at the *Kaigundaigakko* (Navy War College) at Tsukiji in Tokyo.

3. Until 1894 the Tokyo Club had its premises within the *Rokumeikan* (literally the 'Deer Cry Pavilion') in the area of what is now Hibiya Park. It was a western-style building erected to provide a location for social gatherings between Japanese and foreigners in surroundings to which foreigners would normally be accustomed, and it had been opened in 1883 by the Foreign Minister, Prince Inoue Kaoru. It was thus part of the

process of westernisation which the Meiji Government saw as an element in catching up with the west and achieving revision of the 'unequal treaties'.

4. This quotation comes from Kipling's poem 'Tomlinson'. The Devil, examining the newly-deceased Tomlinson, found his wretched sins insufficiently robust to qualify him for Hell, and exclaimed:

> *There's sore decline in Adam's line if this be spawn of earth.*

Denison was remarkably up to date, and expected his audience to be so. 'Tomlinson' had first appeared in the *National Observer*, in England, on 23 January 1892, and then been collected in *Barrack-Room Ballads* in London and New York in late March 1892, so, given the steamer schedules of the day, it was prompt for it to be quoted in Japan on 7 May.

5. *Soldiers Three*, a collection of seven short stories, had appeared in India in 1888 and in England in 1890, giving wide publicity to three fictional British privates, Mulvaney, Learoyd and Ortheris. 'The Incarnation of Krishna Mulvaney' is a story in *Life's Handicap* (1891). 'The Drums of the Fore and Aft' is a story in *Wee Willie Winkie & Other Stories* (India 1888, England 1890). Though Denison paid glowing tributes to Kipling's distinguished standing, it is worth remembering how narrowly based it still was: at that date four-fifths of his ultimate literary output, including most of the work for which he is best remembered today, was still unwritten. Nor could Denison, speaking in May 1892, have yet seen any of the 1892 Letters which Kipling was currently despatching from Japan – nor presumably the longer series of 1889 which at that stage were still confined to the files of the *Pioneer*.

6. This quotation comes from an agreeable piece of light verse by J. K. Stephen, which had been published in 1891 and had become famous. It was an attack on what Stephen considered to be the inflated reputations of Kipling and Rider Haggard, and the last four of its sixteen lines looked forward to a time

> When there stands a muzzled stripling,
> Mute, beside a muzzled bore:
> When the Rudyards cease from Kipling
> And the Haggards Ride no more.

7. This speech of Kipling's, short though it is, has considerable intrinsic interest on two grounds. First, it is virtually unknown, since it was never collected and it antedates by fifteen years the first of the speeches that Kipling did collect and publish eventually in *A Book of Words*. Second, early though it came in his career – he was still only twenty-six – it covers in a few words, lucidly and with conviction, a theme that would recur in his later prose and verse, namely the importance of honest and constructive work well done, abroad.

227

1892: Letter Three

SOME EARTHQUAKES

A Radical Member of Parliament at Tokyo has just got into trouble with his constituents, and they have sent him a priceless letter of reproof.[1] Among other things they point out that a politician should not be 'a waterweed which wobbles hither and thither according to the motion of the stream.' Nor should he 'like a ghost without legs drift along before the wind.' 'Your conduct,' they say, 'has been both of a waterweed and a ghost, and we purpose in a little time to give you proof of our true Japanese spirit.' That member will very likely be mobbed in his 'rickshaw and prodded to inconvenience with swordsticks; for the constituencies are most enlightened. But how in the world can a man under these skies behave except as a waterweed and a ghost? It is in the air – the wobble and the legless drift. An energetic tourist would have gone to Hakodate,[2] seen Ainos[3] at Sapporo,[4] ridden across the northern island under the gigantic thistles, caught salmon, looked in at Vladivostok, and done half a hundred things in the time that one lazy loafer has wasted watching the barley turn from green to gold, the azaleas blossom and burn out, and the spring give way to the warm rains of summer. Now the iris has taken up the blazonry of the year,[5] and the tide of tourists ebbs westward.

The permanent residents are beginning to talk of hill places to go to for the hot weather, and all the available houses in the resort are let. In a little while the men from China will be coming over for their holidays,[6] but just at present we are in the thick of the tea season,[7] and there is no time to waste on frivolities. 'Packing' is a valid excuse for anything, from forgetting a dinner to declining a tennis party, and the tempers of husbands are judged leniently. All along the sea face is an inspiring smell of the finest new-mown hay, and canals are full of boats loaded up with the boxes jostling down to the harbour. At the Club men say rude things about the arrivals of the mail. There never was a post-office yet that did not rejoice in knocking a man's Sabbath into flinders. A fair office day's work may begin at eight and end at six, or, if the mail comes in, at midnight. There is no overtime or eight-hours' baby-talk[8] in tea. Yonder are the ships; here is the

228

stuff, and behind all is the American market. The rest is your own affair.

The narrow streets are blocked with the wains bringing down, in boxes of every shape and size, the up-country rough leaf. Some one must take delivery of these things, find room for them in the packed warehouse, and sample them before they are blended and go to the firing.

More than half the elaborate processes are lost work so far as the quality of the stuff goes; but the markets insist on a good-looking leaf, with polish, face, and curl to it, and in this, as in other businesses, the call of the markets is the law. The factory floors are made slippery with the tread of bare-footed coolies, who shout as the tea whirls through its transformations. The over-note to the clamour – an uncanny thing too – is the soft rustle-down of the tea itself – stacked in heaps, carried in baskets, dumped through chutes, rising and falling in the long troughs where it is polished, and disappearing at last into the heart of the firing-machine – always this insistent whisper of moving dead leaves. Steam-sieves sift it into grades, with jarrings and thumpings that make the floor quiver, and the thunder of steam-gear is always at its heels; but it continues to mutter unabashed till it is riddled down into the big, foil-lined boxes and lies at peace.

A few days ago the industry suffered a check which, lasting not more than two minutes, lost several hundred pounds of hand-fired tea. It was something after this way. Into the stillness of a hot, stuffy morning came an unpleasant noise as of batteries of artillery charging up all the roads together, and at least one bewildered sleeper waking saw his empty boots where they 'sat and played toccatas stately at the clavicord.'[9] It was the washstand really but the effect was awful. Then a clock fell and a wall cracked, and heavy hands caught the house by the roof-pole and shook it furiously. To preserve an equal mind when things are hard[10] is good, but he who has not fumbled desperately at bolted jalousies that will not open while a whole room is being tossed in a blanket does not know how hard it is to find any sort of mind at all. The end of the terror was inadequate – a rush into the still, heavy outside air, only to find the servants in the garden giggling (the Japanese would giggle through the Day of Judgment) and to learn that the earthquake was over.[11]

Then came the news, swift borne from the business quarters below the hill, that the coolies of certain factories had fled shrieking at the first shock, and that all the tea in the pans was burned to a crisp. That, certainly, was some consolation for undignified panic;

and there remained the hope that a few tall chimneys up the line at Tokyo would have collapsed. They stood firm, however, and the local papers, used to this kind of thing, merely spoke of the shock as 'severe.' Earthquakes are demoralising; but they bring out all the weaknesses of human nature. First is downright dread; the stage of – 'only let me get into the open and I'll reform,' then the impulse to send news of the most terrible shock of modern times flying east and west among the cables. (Did not your own hair stand straight on end, and, therefore, must not everybody else's have done likewise?) Last, as fallen humanity picks itself together, comes the cry of the mean little soul: 'What! Was *that* all? I wasn't frightened from the beginning.'

It is wholesome and tonic to realise the powerlessness of man in the face of these little accidents. The heir of all the ages,[12] the annihilator of time and space, who politely doubts the existence of his Maker, hears the roof-beams crack and strain above him, and scuttles about like a rabbit in a stoppered warren. If the shock endure for twenty minutes, the annihilator of time and space must camp out under the blue and hunt for his dead beneath rubbish. Given a violent convulsion (only just such a slipping of strata as carelessly piled volumes will accomplish in a book-case) and behold, the heir of all the ages is stark, raving mad – a brute among the dishevelled hills. Set a hundred of the world's greatest spirits, men of fixed principles, high aims, resolute endeavour, enormous experience, and the modesty that these attributes bring – set them to live through such a catastrophe as that which wiped out Nagoya last October,[13] and at the end of three days there would remain few whose souls might be called their own.

So much for yesterday's shock. To-day there has come another; and a most comprehensive affair it is. It has broken nothing, unless maybe an old heart or two cracks later on; and the wise people in the settlement are saying that they predicted it from the first. None the less as an earthquake it deserves recording.[14]

It was a very rainy afternoon; all the streets were full of gruelly mud, and all the business men were at work in their offices when it began. A knot of Chinamen were studying a closed door from whose further side came a most unpleasant sound of bolting and locking up. The notice on the door was interesting. With deep regret did the manager of the New Oriental Banking Corporation, Limited (most decidedly limited), announce that on telegraphic orders from home he had suspended payment.[15] Said one Chinaman to another in pidgin-Japanese: 'It is shut,'[16] and went away. The noise of barring up continued, the rain fell, and the notice stared down the wet street. That was all. There must have been two or three men passing by to whom the announcement meant the loss of every penny of their savings – comforting knowledge to digest after tiffin. In London, of course, the failure would not mean so much; there are many banks in the City, and people would have had warning. Here banks are few, people are dependent on them, and this news came out of the sea unheralded, an evil born with all its teeth.

After the crash of a bursting shell every one who can picks himself up, brushes the dirt off his uniform, and tries to make a joke of it. Then some one whips a handkerchief round his hand – a splinter has torn it – and another finds warm streaks running down his forehead. Then a man, overlooked till now and past help, groans to the death. Everybody perceives with a start that this is no time for laughter, and the dead and wounded are attended to.

Even so at the Overseas Club when the men got out of office. The brokers had told them the news. In filed the English, and Americans, and Germans, and French, and 'Here's a pretty mess!' they said one and all. Many of them were hit, but, like good men, they did not say how severely.

'Ah!' said a little P. and O. official,[17] wagging his head sagaciously (he had lost a thousand dollars since noon), 'It's all right *now*. They're trying to make the best of it. In three or four days we shall hear more about it. I meant to draw my money just before I went down coast, but —' Curiously enough, it was the same story throughout the Club. Everybody had intended to withdraw, and nearly everybody had – not done so. The manager of a bank which had *not* failed was explaining how, in his opinion, the crash had come about. This was also very human. It helped none. Entered a lean American, throwing back his waterproof all dripping with the rain; his face was calm and peaceful. 'Boy, whisky and soda,' he said.

'How much haf you losd?' said a Teuton bluntly. 'Eight-fifty,' replied the son of George Washington sweetly. 'Don't see how that prevents me having a drink. My glass, Sirr.' He continued an interrupted whistling of 'I owe ten dollars to O'Grady' (which he very probably did), and his countenance departed not from its serenity. If there is anything that one loves an American for it is the way he stands certain kinds of punishment. An Englishman and a heavy loser was being chaffed by a Scotchman whose account at the Japan end of the line had been a trifle overdrawn. True, he would lose in England, but the thought of the few dollars saved here cheered him.

More men entered, sat down by tables, stood in groups, or remained apart by themselves, thinking with knit brows. One must think quickly when one's bills are falling due. The murmur of voices thickened, and there was no rumbling in the skittle-alley to interrupt it. Everybody knows everybody else at the Overseas Club, and everybody sympathises. A man passed stiffly and some one of a group turned to ask lightly, 'Hit, old man?' 'Like hell,' he said, and went on biting his unlit cigar. Another man was telling, slowly and somewhat bitterly, how he had expected one of his children to join him out here, and how the passage had been paid with a draft on the O.B.C. But now ...

There, ladies and gentlemen, is where it hurts, this little suspension out here. It destroys plans, pretty ones hoped for and prayed over, maybe for years; it knocks pleasant domestic arrangements galley-west over and above all the mere ruin that it causes. The curious thing in the talk was that there was no abuse of the bank. The men were in the Eastern trade themselves and they knew. It was the Yokohama manager and the clerks thrown out of employment (connection with a broken bank, by the way, goes far to ruin a young man's prospects) for whom they were sorry. 'We're doing ourselves well this year,' said a wit grimly. 'One free-shooting case, one thundering libel case, and a bank smash. Showing off pretty before the globe-trotters, aren't we?'

'Gad, think of the chaps at sea with letters of credit. Eh? They'll land and get the best rooms at the hotels and find they're penniless,' said another.

'Never mind the globe-trotters,' said a third. 'Look nearer home. This does for so-and-so, and so-and-so, and so-and-so, all old men; and every penny of theirs goes. Poor devils!'

'That reminds me of some one else,' said yet another voice. '*His* wife's at home, too. Whew!' and he whistled drearily. So did the tide of voices run on till men got to talking over the chances of a dividend. 'They went to the Bank of England,' drawled an American, 'and the Bank of England let them down. Said their securities weren't good enough.'

'Great Scott!' – a hand came down on a table to emphasise the remark – 'I sailed half way up the Mediterranean once with a Bank of England director; wish I'd tipped him over the rail and lowered him a boat on his own security – if it was good enough.'

'Baring's goes.[18] The O.B.C. don't,' replied the American, blowing smoke through his nose. 'This business looks de-ci-ded-ly prob-le-mat-i-cal. Wha-at?'

'Oh, they'll pay the depositors in full. Don't you fret,' said a man who had lost nothing and was anxious to console.

'I'm a shareholder,' said the American, and smoked on.

The rain continued to fall, and the umbrellas dripped in the racks, and the wet men came and went, circling round the central fact that it was a bad business, till the day, as was most fit, shut down in drizzling darkness. There was a refreshing sense of brotherhood in misfortunes in the little community that had just been electrocuted and did not want any more shocks. All the pain that in England would be taken home to be borne in silence and alone was here bulked, as it were, and faced in line of companies.[19] Surely the Christians of old must have fought much better when they met the lions by fifties at a time.

At last the men departed; the bachelors to cast up accounts by themselves (there should be some good ponies for sale shortly) and the married men to take counsel. May heaven help him whose wife does not stand by him now! But the women of the Overseas settlements are as thorough as the men. There will be tears for plans forgone, the changing of the little ones' schools and elder children's careers, unpleasant letters to be written home, and more unpleasant ones to be received from relatives who 'told you so from the first.' There will be pinchings too, and straits of which the outside world will know nothing, but the women will pull it through smiling.

Beautiful indeed are the operations of modern finance – especially when anything goes wrong with the machine. To-night there will be trouble in India among the Ceylon planters, the Calcutta jute- and the Bombay cotton-brokers, besides the little households of small banked savings. In Hong Kong, Singapore, and Shanghai there will be trouble too, and goodness only knows what wreck at Cheltenham, Bath, St. Leonard's, Torquay, and the other camps of the retired Army officers. They are lucky in England who know what happens when it happens, but here the people are at the wrong end of the cables, and the situation is not good. Only one thing seems certain. There is a notice on a shut door, in the wet, and by virtue of that notice all the money that was theirs yesterday is gone away, and it may never come back again. So all the work that won the money must be done over again; but some of the people are old, and more are tired, and all are disheartened. It is a very sorrowful little community that goes to bed to-night, and there must be as sad ones the world over. Let it be written, however, that of the sections under fire here (and some are cruelly hit) no man whined, or whimpered, or broke down. There was no chance of fighting. It was bitter defeat, but they took it standing.[20]

1892: LETTER THREE
COMMENTARY

1. The Radical MP was Yoshimizu Watanabe. According to the *Japan Weekly Mail* of 4 June 1892 he had been 'returned as a Radical, but after his election he began to act against the Radical interests, and was finally expelled from the Party. His constituents, hearing this, were much incensed . . . and presented the following document to him, demanding his resignation:–

Sir,
We, the undersigned, hereby beg to suggest your immediate resignation of your position as a member of the Diet. At the end of last year when the Diet was dissolved, we, knowing you were a member of the Jiyuto [Radical Party – literally liberal or free party] and believing your professions, abandoned our occupations, and, regardless of our private affairs, went about day and night, to canvass for you. Finally we succeeded in getting you elected to represent us in the House. Have you not violated your pledges to us? Have you not disobeyed the popular opinion of the country? Can you pretend that you have discharged your responsibilities as our representative? We desire to recall some facts to your mind . . . Why were you never present at the Jiyuto meetings? Why did you sell the Jiyuto? Why were you expelled from the party? Why did you cheat us all? . . . So numerous are your faults that we have no time to count them all . . . You may attempt to explain, thereby rebutting our charges. But we recommend you not to waste any idle words . . . For the sake of your own individual interests you have forgotten the welfare of the nation and of its people. You are veritably a pseudo-popular member! . . . You have been blinded by your own interests, and have entirely lost your moral sense. A true representative of the people is not like a river-weed, wobbling from side to side or up and down according to the motion of the stream; nor is he like a ghost without legs, wafted along by the wind. But as for you, your conduct is like that of a weed or a ghost! . . . If you will not take our advice, we shall adopt other

steps. Though we are but simple farmers in a remote country district, our zealous love for our Sovereign and our country is great. We shall soon give you evidence of our true Japanese spirit. Examine and re-examine yourself, and determine what you will do . . .'

2. Hakodate, in 'the northern island', Hokkaido, had been opened to foreign shipping in 1854, and was the only Treaty Port in Hokkaido, with a British consulate since 1859. Hakodate had been the last strong-hold of the Shogun's forces in the civil war of 1868–9. It did not become a major trading centre in the nineteenth century but was much used by whalers and sealers.

3. 'Ainos' is incorrect, and the term 'Aino' should never be used. Dr John Batchelor, in *The Ainu of Japan*, published in 1892, pointed out that '*Aino* means "mongrel" or "half-breed", and has reference to a degrading Japanese tradition, which describes the descent of the Ainu from a human being and a dog'. The Ainu were the original inhabitants of northern Japan, and were forced by Japanese pressure in medieval times to retreat to the island of Hokkaido (formerly known as Ezo, Yezo or Yesso). They were racially distinct from the Japanese, and were more hirsute, and were hence referred to as the 'hairy Ainu'. The first dictionary in their language was compiled by Batchelor, a British scholar and missionary. Few pure-bred Ainu now remain. Their primitive way of life put them at a disadvantage, and they succumbed both to Japanese colonization pressure and to the diseases which the Japanese brought with them.

4. Sapporo, which was founded in 1870, became the capital of Hokkaido in 1886 when the island's prefectures were amalgamated. It had previously been the headquarters of the *kaitakushi* or colonization bureau, which until it was abolished in 1880 expended large sums in attempting to develop the resources of Hokkaido.

5. This was written in June, a month when irises bloom in vast numbers in Japan. The 'lazy loafer' was of course Kipling, who was indeed uncharacteristically static, in and around Yokohama, during this second visit to Japan. The fact that his wife was pregnant may well have been a factor.

6. Expatriate merchants from Shanghai and other parts of China used to visit Japan for summer holidays at this period.

7. Tea had been a principal export of Japan since the 1860s: it was shipped from Nagasaki and Yokohama, mainly to North America. Japanese tea is green tea, needing to be dried, or 'fired', before being packed. During the season the smell of tea being fired permeated the settlements.

8. In Britain, and other European countries, political pressure for the limitation of working hours was frequently expressed in the second half of the nineteenth century in terms of an 'eight-hour day'.

9. Quoted from the sixth stanza of Robert Browning's 'A Toccata of Galuppi's':

Well, and it was graceful of them – they'd break talk off and afford
– She, to bite her mask's black velvet – he, to finger on his sword,
While you sat and played Toccatas, stately at the clavichord?

10. If Browning was a favourite author of Kipling's, so, quite as emphatically, was Horace. Here there is a clear reference to *Odes*, II, iii:

> *Aequam memento rebus in arduis*
> *Servare mentem . . .*

literally, 'Remember to preserve an equal mind in hard matters'.

11. This was the 'violent earthquake' reported in the *Japan Weekly Mail* of 11 June 1892 as having been 'felt in the capital on Friday morning [i.e. on 3 June] at 7h. 9m. 57s. The duration was 7 minutes and 30 seconds, the direction being from E.S.W. to W.N.W. ... The shock was commenced with up and down movements, and then followed by horizontal motions ... Walls were cracked and slight damage caused to houses in various parts of Tokyo.' The incident made enough impression on Kipling to be recorded vividly (together with the other 'earthquake', namely the bank failure) in his autobiography, *Something of Myself.* See the excerpt that follows, on page 241.

12. A quotation from Tennyson's 'Locksley Hall':

> I the heir of all the ages, in the foremost files of time.

13. A major earthquake had occurred on 28 October 1891. *Japan as We Saw It* by M. Bickersteth includes an eye-witness account of how that earthquake struck Osaka. Nagoya was among the worst affected places.

14. It does indeed deserve recording, though 'yesterday' and 'today' are misleading: the earthquake was on 3 June, the financial crash on 9 June. This bank failure had the direct effect on the Kiplings of curtailing their extended honeymoon trip round the world, and sending them back to the United States in what were temporarily very reduced financial circumstances. Certainly the timing of the move to Vermont, and very possibly the actual move itself, were direct consequences. The Kiplings were to spend the next four years there, a period which saw the production of *The Jungle Books*, *Captains Courageous*, *The Day's Work*, and other works.

15. In the words of the *Japan Weekly Mail* of 11 June 1892:

> Another financial catastrophe has occurred. The Agent of the New
> Oriental Bank Corporation in this port on Thursday announced that,
> in accordance with instructions from London, the Bank was obliged

to suspend payment. The news has been received with universal regret. During a period of over thirty years the Oriental Bank has been connected with this settlement. In the old days No 11 was virtually the centre of the Settlement, and when evil times and ill fortune compelled the much respected institution to close its doors, people felt as though they had lost a valued friend. Then followed the resuscitation of the Bank under bright auspices and in the hands of men universally liked in the East. For their sakes no less than for that time-honoured corporation, it was hoped that success would crown the new venture. But in these times when operations of international finance are complicated by a factor that defies all calculation, the shrewdest and most careful men may at any moment encounter failure. Such seems to have been the case with the New Oriental Bank ... But when the names of the men controlling the Bank's business in London are recalled, it seems reasonable to predict that depositors will ultimately be paid in full ...

The same newspaper reported on 25 June on a private meeting which had been called in Yokohama to discuss the position. There had been a general feeling in favour of supporting the bank 'in its attempt to resume business', and a resolution was passed to the following effect:

> that the creditors present at this meeting are in favour of converting 25% of their deposits into 5% Preference Stock, and agree not to withdraw their deposits – fixed or current – for the term of twelve months from the resumption of business.

We know from Mrs Kipling's diary that Kipling attended that meeting, on 24 June. Moreover, we know from Carrington's biography of Kipling that it was he who proposed the 25% arrangement. His losses were of the order of £2,000, and the sole resources he and his wife had left were a return ticket to Vancouver and $100 in a New York bank.

16. 'Pidgin-Japanese' was much in use among foreigners, and came to be called 'Yokohama dialect'. The words 'It is shut' are Kipling's anglicization of whatever the one Chinese said to the other.

17. The Peninsular & Oriental Steam Navigation Company, first incorporated in 1840, had run regular passenger services from Europe to Japan since the 1860s.

18. Baring Brothers, the famous British merchant bankers, were founded in 1770 and long enjoyed immense influence and prestige. In 1818 the Duke of Richelieu said of them, 'There are six Great Powers in Europe: England, France, Prussia, Austria, Russia and Baring Brothers.'

In 1890 a default on the part of the Argentine government brought the firm into a financial crisis from which they were rescued by the Bank of England and principal British joint stock banks, which took over responsibility for their liabilities: Barings was then reorganized, but remained in private hands. The crisis had been sensational, one of the most profound shocks in the history of the City of London.

19. The metaphor is military, implying the alignment of the companies within an infantry battalion.

20. From Carrington's biography of Kipling it is clear that during the two and a half weeks between the bank crash and their departure by the *Empress of China* for Vancouver, the Kiplings 'faced the world with equanimity, even with gaiety . . . danced at a ball . . . and went about as though nothing had happened'. They were indeed helped by the Thomas Cook agency in Yokohama, which handsomely refunded what they had spent on further travel bookings in the Pacific.

From Something of Myself

(1937)

EDITORIAL NOTE

In late 1935, during the last months of his life, Kipling was writing his autobiography, *Something of Myself*. In January 1936 he died, so the book came out posthumously. As far as it goes, it is a most valuable record, highly readable and in parts fascinating; but it is disappointingly sketchy and inaccurate and tantalizingly reticent.

In it, the visit to Japan in 1889 is never mentioned. Only a page is devoted to the longer stay in 1892. However, the earthquake and bank failure which Kipling experienced in June of that year are both briefly described, so as to throw one or two thin shafts of lateral light on the much fuller account in Letter Three of 1892 ('Some Earthquakes'). For instance, from that Letter no reader would have guessed that Kipling himself was one of the casualties of the crash of the New Oriental Bank Corporation, losing £2000 which was virtually all the money he had (though he much later recovered £500 of it). Only in *Something of Myself* is it made clear what impact the event had on the plans he had laid in London for 'a voyage round the world . . . all arranged beyond any chance of failure'.

His account of Japan is in the fifth chapter of the book. The narrative follows on from his marriage in London on 18 January 1892 to an American, Caroline Balestier, and touches on the programme for the honeymoon – if that word is appropriate to so prolonged a worldwide journey. The itinerary began with a passage from Liverpool – where the couple were seen off with something of a literary flourish by the novelist Henry James, the critic Edmund Gosse and the publisher William Heinemann – to their first destination, New York. Kipling's reference to a 'magic carpet which was to take us round the earth, beginning with Canada deep in snow', is misleading, since at least six weeks were spent in the United States, including two visits to Caroline's family's property near Brattleboro, Vermont, where Kipling bought land from his brother-in-law. Then in late March they crossed into Canada and headed for Vancouver to board the *Empress of India*, which was leaving on 3 April for Yokohama. By the time they landed there, Caroline was pregnant.

Apart from the obvious tourist merits of staying in Japan in springtime, there may have been other reasons for going to Yokohama and for staying there so long. Charles Carrington, in his official biography of Kipling, says that both the Kiplings 'had friends in Japan' – but does not identify them. Certainly they were accommodated for at least part of their stay by a Mr and Mrs Hunt, probably the Mr and Mrs H. J. Hunt who were listed with the Kiplings among the passengers on the *Empress of India*. Carrington also reveals that Caroline Kipling had a family link of some note with the country, in that her grandfather 'was well remembered as legal adviser to the Mikado who broke down the barriers that had closed Japan against the world'. This was Judge Erastus Peshine Smith, who served between 1871 and 1876 as the first consultant on International Law whom the Japanese Foreign Ministry employed – at the very high salary of $10,000 a year – to advise on treaty revision.

It was thus under favourable auspices that they disembarked from the *Empress of India*, seeing Japan as an agreeable stage on an onward journey. A few weeks later, after their sudden impoverishment, they recognized that it was the furthest point they were going to reach. There ensued the embarrassing return to Brattleboro. On the page opposite, Kipling refers to the 'heels of the melting snows' in Canada. This was hardly so: it was well into July.

As to whether they would have gone to Vermont in any case when their journey was over, and built their house there and settled in it as they did, no sure evidence exists. What the débâcle in Japan ensured was that their timing was precipitated, and funds for the immediate construction of their house were lacking. In the event, Kipling's earning power was so phenomenal that within weeks of reaching Brattleboro they were able to begin building, and within months they were financially secure again. Meanwhile, however, they rented a primitive cottage for ten dollars a month. There, in conditions of stark simplicity, Kipling began to work on material that would turn into *The Jungle Books* and *Kim*. There too, 'in three feet of snow' at the end of 1892, his first child was born.

KIPLING'S TEXT

Then to Yokohama, where we were treated with all the kindliness in the world by a man and his wife on whom we had no shadow of any claim. They made us more than welcome in their house, and saw to it that we should see Japan in wistaria and peony time. Here an earthquake (prophetic as it turned out) overtook us one hot break of dawn, and we fled out into the garden, where a tall cryptomeria waggled its insane head back and forth with an 'I told you so' expression; though not a breath was stirring. A little later I went to the Yokohama branch of my Bank on a wet forenoon to draw some of my solid wealth. Said the Manager to me: 'Why not take more? It will be just as easy.' I answered that I did not care to have too much cash at one time in my careless keeping, but that when I had looked over my accounts I might come again in the afternoon. I did so; but in that little space my Bank, the notice on its shut door explained, had suspended payment. (Yes, I should have done better to have invested my 'capital' as its London Manager had hinted.)

I returned with my news to my bride of [five] months and a child to be born. Except for what I had drawn that morning – the Manager had sailed as near to the wind as loyalty permitted – and the unexpended [Thomas] Cook vouchers, and our personal possessions in our trunks, we had nothing whatever. There was an instant Committee of Ways and Means, which advanced our understanding of each other more than a cycle of solvent matrimony. Retreat – flight if you like – was indicated. What would Cook return for the tickets, not including the price of lost dreams? 'Every pound you've paid, of course,' said Cook of Yokohama, 'These things are all luck and – here's your refund.'

Back again, then, across the cold North Pacific, through Canada on the heels of the melting snows, and to the outskirts of a little New England town . . .

'To the Dancers'

Whether we waltz in Kensington,
    Whether we dance in Ispahan,
London, Paris or Timbuctoo,
Cairo, Suez or Kalamazoo, –
    Love is as old as Fuji-san!

Whether we leave on the stroke of one,
    Or kitchen-polka the white stars wan,
Go to supper or go before,
Stay in the card-room or take the floor,
    Love is as old as Fuji-san!

If with the old, old tale we've done,
    Others are starting where we began –
Never was ballroom that did not hold
More than ever was written or told;
    Love is as old as Fuji-san!

Who shall speak of the thoughts that run,
    Deep in the hearts of maid and man?
Let them take for their edification
Maxim of commonest application!
    Love is as old as Fuji-san!

COMMENTARY

This poem has never been re-published since its first private appearance. We are indebted to Professor Andrew Rutherford, an authority on Kipling's early verse, for locating it for us in Kipling's scrapbooks (book 5, page 50); to the University of Sussex Librarian, custodian of these and other Kipling Papers, for sending us a copy; and to the National Trust for letting us reprint it. The original is on a decorated printed card which may have been part of a dance programme. At the foot, with the letters R.K., is a simple coloured sketch of fishing junks moored near a waterfront. On the reverse is a sketch of Mt Fuji – which in Japanese is normally called Fuji-San. ('San' here is the Sinico-Japanese reading of the Chinese character for 'mountain', which is also read in Japanese as 'Yama', whence the popular but incorrect western name 'Fujiyama'.)

Though the inference that Kipling wrote this in Japan is unavoidable, there are not many clues as to the date. His visit in 1889, relatively short and closely recorded, appears not to have included dancing. Nor do the verses, and the accompanying sketches, suggest a shipboard occasion. However, the longer visit of 1892, when he was on an extended honeymoon and spending weeks in and around the social hub of Yokohama, from where Fuji-San can be seen, is much more likely. We know from Charles Carrington's notes on Mrs Kipling's diaries that the Kiplings were at a dance at the Yokohama residence of their friends the Hunts on 14 June 1892. We may reasonably guess these verses mark that event.

As poetry, 'To the Dancers' is slight, but the lilt of the rhythm is pleasant, and the rhyme-pattern that links the four verses is typically ingenious. 'To the Dancers' belongs to the large category of ephemeral but often felicitous verse which Kipling produced with remarkable facility all his life, often tossing it out on the spur of the moment to amuse his friends. Scores of such pieces have been preserved: most of them, including this one, never passed the author's discriminating test for inclusion in his published work.

243

1892: Letter Four

HALF-A-DOZEN PICTURES

Goe, cool your feavers and you'll say
The dog days scorch not all the year;
In copper mines no longer stay,
But travel to the west, and there
The right ones see
And grant all gold's not alchemie.[1]

'Some men, when they grow rich, store pictures in a gallery.'[2] Living, their friends envy them, and after death the genuineness of the collection is disputed under the dispersing hammer.

A better way is to spread your pictures over all earth; visiting them as Fate allows. Then none can steal or deface, nor any reverse of fortune force a sale; sunshine and tempest warm and ventilate the gallery for nothing, and – in spite of all that has been said of her crudeness – Nature is not altogether a bad frame-maker. The knowledge that you may never live to see an especial treasure twice teaches the eyes to see quickly while the light lasts; and the possession of such a gallery breeds a very fine contempt for painted shows and the smeared things that are called pictures.

In the North Pacific, to the right hand as you go westward, hangs a small study of no particular value as compared with some others.[3] The mist is down on an oily stretch of washed-out sea; through the mist the bat's-wings of a sealing schooner are just indicated. In the foreground, all but leaping out of the frame, an open row-boat, painted the crudest blue and white, rides up over the shoulder of a swell. A man in blood-red jersey and long boots, all shining with moisture, stands at the bows holding up the carcase of a silver-bellied sea-otter, from whose pelt the wet drips in moonstones. Now the artist who could paint the silver wash of the mist, the wriggling treacly reflection of the boat, and the raw red wrists of the man would be something of a workman.

But my gallery is in no danger of being copied at present. Three years since, I met an artist in the stony bed of a brook, between a line of 300 graven, lichened godlings and a flaming bank of azaleas, swearing horribly.[4] He had been trying to paint one of my pictures – nothing more than a big water-worn rock tufted with flowers and a snow-capped hill for background. Most naturally he failed, because there happened to be absolutely no perspective in the thing, and he was pulling the lines about in order to make some for home consumption. No man can put the contents of a gallon jar into a pint mug. The protests of all uncomfortably-crowded mugs since the world began have settled that long ago, and have given us the working theories, devised by imperfect instruments for imperfect instruments, which are called Rules of Art.

Luckily, those who painted my gallery were born before man. Therefore, my pictures, instead of being boxed up by lumbering bars of gold, are disposed generously between latitudes, equinoxes, monsoons, and the like, and, making all allowance for an owner's partiality, they are really not so bad.

'Down in the South where the ships never go' – between the heel of New Zealand and the South Pole, there is a sea-piece showing a steamer trying to come round in the trough of a big beam sea.[5] The wet light of the day's end comes more from the water than the sky, and the waves are colourless through the haze of the rain, all but two or three blind sea-horses swinging out of the mist on the ship's dripping weather side. A lamp is lighted in the wheel-house; so one patch of yellow light falls on the green-painted pistons of the steering-gear as they snatch up the rudder-chains. A big sea has got home. Her stern flies up in the lather of the freed screw, and her deck from the poop to the break of the foc's'le goes under in grey-green water level as a mill-race except where it spouts up above the donkey-engine and the stored derrick-booms. Forward there is nothing but this glare; aft, the interrupted wake drives far to leeward, as a cut kite-string dropped across the seas. The sole thing that has any rest in the turmoil is the jewelled, unwinking eye of an albatross, who is beating across wind leisurely and unconcerned, almost within hand's touch. It is the monstrous egotism of that eye that makes the picture. By all the rules of art there should be a lighthouse or a harbour pier in the background to show that everything will end happily. But there is not, and the red eye does not care whether the thing beneath the still wings stays or staves.

The sister-panel hangs in the Indian Ocean and tells a story, but is none the worse for that.[6] Here you have hot tropical sunlight and a foreshore clothed in stately palms running out into a still and steamy sea burnished steel blue. Along the foreshore, questing as a wounded beast quests for lair, hurries a loaded steamer never built for speed. Consequently, she tears and threshes the water to pieces, and piles it under her nose and cannot put it under her cleanly. Coir-coloured cargo bales are stacked round both masts, and her decks are crammed and double-crammed with dark-skinned passengers – from the foc's'le where they interfere with the crew to the stern where they hamper the wheel.

The funnel is painted blue on yellow, giving her a holiday air a little out of keeping with the yellow and black cholera flag at her main. She dare not stop; she must not communicate with any one. There are leprous streaks of lime-wash trickling down her plates for a sign of this. So she threshes on down the glorious coast, she and her swarming passengers, with the sickness that destroyeth in the noonday eating out her heart.

Yet another, the pick of all the East rooms, before we have done with blue water.[7] Most of the nations of the earth are at issue under a stretch of white awning above a crowded deck. The cause of the dispute, a deep copper bowl full of rice and fried onions, is upset in the foreground. Malays, Lascars, Hindus, Chinese, Javanese, Burmans – the whole gamut of race-tints, from saffron to tar-black – are twisting and writhing round it, while their vermilion, cobalt, amber, and emerald turbans and head-cloths are lying under foot. Pressed against the yellow ochre of the iron bulwarks to left and right are frightened women and children in turquoise and isabella-coloured[8] clothes. They are half protected by mounds of upset bedding, straw mats, red lacquer boxes, and plaited bamboo trunks, mixed up with tin plates, brass and copper *hukas*,[9] silver opium pipes, Chinese playing cards, and properties enough to drive half-a-dozen artists wild. In the centre of the crowd of furious half-naked men, the fat bare back of a Burman, tattooed from collar-bone to waist-cloth with writhing patterns of red and blue devils, holds the eye first. It is a wicked back. Beyond it is the flicker of a Malay *kris*.[10] A blue, red, and yellow macaw chained to a stanchion spreads his wings against the sun in an ecstasy of terror. Half-a-dozen red-gold pines and bananas have been knocked down from their ripening-places, and are lying between the feet of the fighters. One pine has rolled against the long brown fur of a muzzled bear. His owner, a bushy-bearded Hindu, kneels over the animal, his body-cloth thrown clear of a hard brown arm, his fingers ready to loose the muzzle-strap. The ship's cook, in blood-stained white, watches from the butcher's shop, and a black Zanzibari stoker grins through the bars of the engine-room-hatch, one ray of sun shining straight into his pink mouth. The officer of the watch, a red-whiskered man, is kneeling down on the bridge to peer through the railings, and is shifting a long, lean black revolver from his left hand to his right. The faithful sunlight that puts everything into place, gives his whiskers and the hair on the back of his tanned wrist just the colour of the copper pot, the bear's fur and the trampled pines. For the rest, there is the blue sea beyond the awnings.

Three years' hard work, beside the special knowledge of a lifetime, would be needed to copy – even to copy – this picture. Mr. So-and-so, R.A.,[11] could undoubtedly draw the bird; Mr. Suchanother (equally R.A.) the bear; and scores of gentlemen the still life; but who would be the man to pull the whole thing together and make it the riotous, tossing cataract of colour and life that it is? And when it was done, some middle-aged person from the provinces, who had never seen a pineapple out of a plate, or a *kris* out of the South Kensington, would say that it did not remind him of something that it ought to remind him of, and therefore that it was bad. If the gallery could be bequeathed to the nation, something might, perhaps, be gained, but the nation would complain of the draughts and the absence of chairs. But no matter. In another world we shall see certain gentlemen set to tickle the backs of Circe's swine through all eternity. Also, they will have to tickle with their bare hands.[12]

The Japanese rooms, visited and set in order for the second time, hold more pictures than could be described in a month; but most of them are small and, excepting always the light, within human compass. One, however, might be difficult. It was an unexpected gift, picked up in a Tokyo bye-street after dark.[13] Half the town was out for a walk, and all the people's clothes were indigo, and so were the shadows, and most of the paper lanterns were drops of blood-red. By the light of smoking oil-lamps people were selling flowers and shrubs – wicked little dwarf pines, stunted peach and plum trees, wistaria bushes clipped and twisted out of all likeness to wholesome plants, leaning and leering out of green-glaze pots. In the flickering of the yellow flames, these forced cripples and the yellow faces above them reeled to and fro fantastically all together. As the light steadied they would return to the pretence of being green things till a puff of the warm night wind among the flares set the whole line off again in a crazy dance of dwergs,[14] their shadows capering on the house-fronts behind them.

At a corner of a street, some rich men had got together and left unguarded all the gold, diamonds, and rubies of the East; but when you came near you saw that this treasure was only a gathering of goldfish in glass globes – yellow, white, and red fish, with from three to five forked tails apiece and eyes that bulged far beyond their heads. There were wooden pans full of tiny ruby fish, and little children with nets dabbled and shrieked in chase of some special beauty, and the frightened fish kicked up showers of little pearls with their tails. The children carried lanterns in the shape of small red paper fish bobbing at the end of slivers of bamboo, and these drifted through the crowd like a strayed constellation of baby stars. When the children stood at the edge of a canal and called down to unseen friends in boats the pink lights were all reflected orderly below. The light of the thousand small lights in the street went straight up into the darkness among the interlacing telegraph wires, and just at the edge of the shining haze, on a sort of pigeon-trap, forty feet above ground, sat a Japanese fireman, wrapped up in his cloak, keeping watch against fires. He looked unpleasantly like a Bulgarian atrocity or a Burmese 'deviation from the laws of humanity,'[15] being very still and all huddled up on his roost. That was a superb picture and it arranged itself to admiration.

Now, disregarding these things and others – wonders and miracles all – men are content to sit in studios and, by light that is not light, to fake subjects from pots and pans and rags and bricks that are called 'pieces of colour.' Their collection of rubbish costs in the end quite as much as a ticket, a first-class one, to new worlds where the 'props' are given away with the sunshine. To do anything because it is, or may be, new on the market is wickedness that carries its own punishment; but surely there must be things in the world paintable other and beyond those that lie between the North Cape, say, and Algiers. For the sake of the pictures, putting aside the dear delight of the gamble, it might be worth while to venture out a little beyond the regular circle of subjects and – see what happens. If a man can draw one thing, it has been said, he can draw anything. At the most he can but fail, and there are several matters in the world worse than failure. Betting on a certainty, for instance, or playing with nicked cards is immoral, and secures expulsion from clubs. Keeping deliberately to one set line of work because you know you can do it and are certain to get money by so doing is, on the other hand, counted a virtue, and secures admission to clubs. There must be a middle way somewhere, as there must be somewhere an unarrived man with no position, reputation, or other vanity to lose, who most keenly wants to find out what his palette is set for in this life. He will

pack his steamer-trunk and get into the open to wrestle with effects
that he can never reproduce. All the same his will be a superb failure,
and afterwards (nothing this side of the grave can change most of us),

> When Earth's last picture is painted
> and the tubes are twisted and dried,
> When the oldest colours have faded,
> and the youngest critic has died,
> We shall rest, and, faith, we shall need it –
> lie down for an aeon or two,
> Till the Master of All Good Workmen
> shall put us to work anew.
>
> And those that were good shall be happy:
> they shall sit in a golden chair;
> They shall splash at a ten-league canvas
> with brushes of comets' hair.
> They shall find real saints to draw from –
> Magdalene, Peter, and Paul;
> They shall work for an age at a sitting
> and never be tired at all!
>
> And only The Master shall praise us,
> and only The Master shall blame;
> And no one shall work for money,
> and no one shall work for fame,
> But each for the joy of the working,
> and each, in his separate star,
> Shall draw the Thing as he sees It
> for the God of Things as They are![16]

1892: LETTER FOUR
COMMENTARY

1. This verse heading did not appear when the Letter was published in *The
   Times* (20 August 1892), but was in the New York *Sunday Sun* (28

August). It is from a poem by William Habington (1605–64). The 'dog days' were days of great heat, and the term was derived from the ancient Roman theory that particularly hot weather was induced on days when the position of Sirius, the Dog Star, was such as to add to the heat of the sun. The verse as a whole, though slightly obscure in its language, clearly supports the theme of 'Half-a-Dozen Pictures', itself a mixture of the literal and the allegorical. Kipling uses in the Letter the metaphor of painting pictures to convey characteristic ideas on the importance of work, the value of realism, the advantage of travel, the integrity of art; and in the mood of expansionism that marked the earlier letter, 'Our Overseas Men', he deplores the parochialism of those whose horizon is bounded by Europe.

2. We have not identified this quotation.

3. This is the first of the half-dozen 'pictures', or vivid memories, that Kipling chooses to describe out of his own experience. It would appear that on his westward journey from Vancouver to Yokohama in April 1892 he saw a sealing schooner and some such scene as this. Here, and in each of the other five 'pictures', it should not be assumed that Kipling's meaning is confined to the inadequacy of art: there are undertones of commerce, politics and adventure.

4. This second 'picture' is from Kipling's visit to Nikko in 1889 and his account of meeting an artist who was frustrated at his inability to depict the scenery, at least to the likely satisfaction of critics in Europe. See Letter Ten of 1889, Note 20, page 163.

5. The third 'picture' is derived from a rough passage which Kipling made between Bluff (at the southern extremity of South Island, New Zealand) and Melbourne, in a small steamer in November 1891. He described this much later in his autobiography: 'For the better part of a week we were swept from end to end, our poop was split, and a foot or two of water smashed through the tiny saloon . . .'

6. The fourth 'picture' has not yet been identified from Kipling's experiences at sea. The 'leprous streaks of lime-wash' would be from lime used as a disinfectant on the cholera-ridden ship. The concluding sentence quotes from Psalm 91 in the *Book of Common Prayer*, verses 5 and 6: 'Thou shalt not be afraid . . . for the pestilence that walketh in darkness . . . nor for the sickness that destroyeth in the noonday.'

7. This extremely vivid fifth 'picture' has likewise not yet been identified from letters or other records. However, it will be no coincidence that the 'cause of the dispute', a spilt bowl of cooked rice and onions, was similar to the shipboard provocation that led to a murder in Kipling's short story of 1889, 'The Limitations of Pambé Serang' (in *Many Inventions*). There is also a 'black Zanzibari stoker' in both accounts.

8. Isabella-coloured means greyish-yellow. There are at least two theories about the derivation of this. One, from Isaac D'Israeli's *Curiosities of Literature*, with which Kipling was familiar, describes the colour as 'the yellow of soiled calico', and explains that Isabel of Austria, daughter of

Philip II, at the siege of Ostend in 1601 vowed not to change her linen till the place was captured – which took three years. Another, mentioned in a letter to *The Times* on 12 February 1988, more plausibly attributes the word to the colour of a prized breed of horses, 'creamy chestnuts', the product of a stud established by Queen Isabella of Castile.

9. A *huka* (or *hookah*) is an oriental tobacco pipe with a long tube: its smoke is drawn through water in an attached vase.

10. A *kris* is a Malay or Indonesian dagger.

11. R.A. stands for Royal Academician. This passage, not least in its bitter conclusion, is an attack on the artistic establishment and the critics; but an attack on the literary establishment (which had grave reservations about Kipling's unorthodoxy, uncomfortable realism and sudden extreme popularity) may well be implied. In the *Academy* of 4 April 1891 Lionel Johnson had criticized Kipling's cult of the exotic: 'A writer may be intimate with Valparaiso and Zanzibar without being superior to the reader who knows only Bloomsbury and Kensington ...' In the *Contemporary Review* of March 1891 J. M. Barrie had accused Kipling of 'ignorance of life', and of believing that 'because he has knocked about the world in shady company he has no more to learn'. He also likened him to one of his own characters, the luridly realistic painter in *The Light That Failed*: 'if Dick Heldar had written instead of painted, or Mr. Kipling had painted instead of written, it would have been difficult to distinguish the one artist from the other.'

12. Though the allusion to back-tickling is rather obscure, there is no doubt about Circe. She was a sorceress in Greek mythology, and had the ability to turn those who drank her magic potions into swine: she practised this disagreeable trick on the followers of Odysseus, and he was lucky to get them back again in human shape.

13. This sixth 'picture', another of great vividness, could have come from Kipling's experiences in 1889 or 1892.

14. Dwerg: the Dutch word for dwarf. It is very close to the Anglo-Saxon form *dwerugh*.

15. The term 'Bulgarian atrocity' had been much publicized by William Gladstone in 1876 in his protests against the barbarous methods employed by the Turks in suppressing a rebellion in Bulgaria. In Burma, 'deviations from the laws of humanity' was a typical phrase employed in reporting atrocities committed by bandits and rebels in the prolonged guerrilla aftermath of the Third Burmese War (1885).

16. As it appeared in *The Times*, this Letter ended with the words 'superb failure', and did not include the poem. In the New York *Sunday Sun* another thirteen words of prose (as shown here) were published, together with the poem, though in that version the first line of the third verse was 'And only Rembrandt shall teach us, and only Van Dyck shall blame'. We have chosen the amended version, as published in 1896 in *The Seven Seas*, where Kipling placed this poem in the concluding position, as 'L'Envoi'.

1892: Letter Five

'CAPTAINS COURAGEOUS'[1]

From Yokohama to Montreal[2] is a long day's journey, and the forepart is uninviting. In three voyages out of five, the North Pacific, too big to lie altogether idle, too idle to get hands about the business of a storm, sulks and smokes[3] like a chimney; the passengers fresh from Japan heat wither in the chill, and a clammy dew distils along the rigging. That grey monotony of sea is not at all homelike, being as yet new and not used to the procession of keels. It holds very few pictures[4] and the best of its stories – those relating to seal-poaching among the Kuriles and the Russian rookeries[5] – are not exactly fit for publication. There is a man in Yokohama[6] who in a previous life burned galleons with Drake.[7] He is a gentleman adventurer of the largest and most resourceful – by instinct a carver of kingdoms, a ruler of men on the high seas, and an inveterate gambler against Death. Because he supplies nothing more than sealskins to the wholesale dealers at home, the fame of his deeds, his brilliant fights, his more brilliant escapes, and his most brilliant strategy will be lost among sixty-ton schooners, or told only in the mouths of drunken seamen whom none believe. Now there sits a great spirit under the palm trees of the Navigator Group, a thousand leagues to the south, and he, crowned with roses and laurels, strings together the pearls of those parts.[8] When he has done with this down there perhaps he will turn to the Smoky Seas and the Wonderful Adventures of Captain ———.[9] Then there will be a tale to listen to.

But the first touch of dry land makes the sea and all upon it unreal. Five minutes after the traveller is on the C.P.R.[10] train at Vancouver there is no romance of blue water, but another kind – the life of the train, into which he comes to grow as into life aboard ship. A week on wheels turns a man into a part of the machine.

[*The rest of this letter mainly concerns North America, and the evidence of expansion and development that Kipling observed there. The general theme is adequately conveyed by the following excerpts from its concluding paragraphs.*]

By the time that a man has seen these things and a few others that go with a boom he may say that he has lived . . . He has heard the Arabian Nights retold and knows the inward kernel of that romance, which some little folk say is vanished. Here they lie in their false teeth, for Cortez is not dead, nor Drake, and Sir Philip Sidney[11] dies every few months if you know where to look. The adventurers and captains courageous of old have only changed their dress a little and altered their employments to suit the world in which they move . . .

. . . It is the next century that, looking over its own, will see the heroes of our time clearly.

Meantime this earth of ours – we hold a fair slice of it so far – is full of wonders and miracles and mysteries and marvels, and, in default of being in the heart of great deeds, it is good to go up and down seeing and hearing tell of them all.[12]

1892: LETTER FIVE
COMMENTARY

1. The phrase 'Captains Courageous' was used again by Kipling in 1896 for the title of his famous novel about fishermen on the Grand Banks off Newfoundland. He derived it from the first verse of a once popular ballad, 'Mary Ambree', about the exploits of an English heroine who in 1584 took part in the siege of Ghent, held by the Spaniards:

   When captains couragious, whom death could not daunte,
   Did march to the siege of the citty of Gaunt,
   They muster'd their souldiers by two and by three,
   And the foremost in battle was Mary Ambree.

2. Sailing from Yokohama on 27 June 1892, the Kiplings disembarked at Vancouver on 8 July, and continued by rail across Canada (breaking their journey at least once, to fish at Banff, Alberta). When they reached Montreal on 19 July they found a telegram from Mrs Kipling's mother

in Vermont, confirming arrangements for them to go at once to Brattleboro where, in the event, they stayed till 1896.

3. 'Smokes': the reference here is to fog. See also comments on smoke and fog in Notes 5 and 9 below.

4. 'Pictures': a reference to the theme of the preceding Letter.

5. For an earlier note on the Kurile Islands see Letter Two of 1892, Note 18. Large numbers of seals had been found around these islands, and they had been much reduced by hunting. The Japanese name for the archipelago is *Chishima* ('Thousand Islands'), but Kurile is derived from the Russian *kurity* (to smoke), on account of the live volcanoes on the islands. Since the entire Kurile chain had been Japanese since a Russo-Japanese treaty of 1875, 'Russian rookeries' implies Russian-controlled sealing areas, particularly the westernmost extension of the Aleutian Islands, the Komandorskiye or Commander group east of Kamchatka. (A 'rookery', originally a collection of rooks' nests in trees, by the mid-nineteenth century also meant a breeding place for sea-birds and for marine animals such as seals.)

6. The 'man in Yokohama', seemingly from the context a captain or former captain of a sealing vessel, has not been identified. However, see notes on the likely sources of 'The Rhyme of the Three Sealers', pages 260–5.

7. Sir Francis Drake, c.1540–96, the great English privateer, explorer and naval hero, noted for exploits against Spain.

8. The Navigator Group: a name formerly applied to Samoa and its archipelago: it dates from the visit in 1768 of the French explorer Louis de Bougainville, who named the group Les Isles des Navigateurs. The 'great spirit under the palm trees' there was Robert Louis Stevenson, who lived in Samoa from 1890 till his death in 1894. Kipling was a strong admirer of Stevenson's writings. He had twice planned to go on to Samoa to see him, once from New Zealand in 1891 and then from Japan in mid-1892, but on both occasions found it impossible to arrange.

9. The 'Smoky Seas' (as is made clear from the use of the term in 'The Rhyme of the Three Sealers') here means the waters around the Aleutians where, to quote the *Encyclopaedia Britannica*, 'the fog is almost constant'. See Notes 3 and 5 above.

10. The C.P.R. was the Canadian Pacific Railway. Kipling's imperial reputation was by now such that on this return journey he crossed Canada as the official guest of the autocratic and formidable William Cornelius Van Horne, Chairman of the C.P.R.

11. Hernando Cortez (1485–1547), the Spanish conqueror of Mexico. Sir Philip Sidney (1554–86), remembered especially for his heroic death at the siege of Zutphen in the Netherlands.

12. In the New York *Sunday Sun* of 27 November 1892 (but not in *The Times* of 23 November), 'Captains Courageous' was accompanied by two poems. One was the first thirteen lines of what later became known as 'The Rhyme of the Three Sealers', which follows next as a whole; the other was a high-flown tribute to pioneers and explorers, 'The Voortrekker', which, since it has no connection with Japan, we are excluding.

'The Rhyme of the Three Sealers'

Away by the lands of the Japanee
  Where the paper lanterns glow
And the crews of all the shipping drink
  In the house of Blood Street Joe,[1]
At twilight, when the landward breeze
  Brings up the harbour noise,
And ebb of Yokohama Bay
  Swigs chattering through the buoys,
In Cisco's Dewdrop Dining Rooms
  They tell the tale anew
Of a hidden sea and a hidden fight,
When the Baltic *ran from the* Northern Light,
  And the Stralsund *fought the two.[2]*

Now this is the Law of the Muscovite, that he proves with shot and
   steel,
When you come by his isles in the Smoky Sea you must not take the
   seal,[3]
Where the grey sea goes nakedly between the weed-hung shelves,
And the little blue fox he is bred for his skin and the seal they breed
   for themselves.[4]
For when the *matkas* seek the shore to drop their pups aland,
The great man-seal haul out of the sea, aroaring, band by band.[5]
And when the first September gales have slaked their rutting-wrath,
The great man-seal haul back to the sea and no man knows their
   path.
Then dark they lie and stark they lie – rookery, dune, and floe,
And the Northern Lights come down o'nights to dance with the
   houseless snow;
And God Who clears the grounding berg and steers the grinding floe,
He hears the cry of the little kit-fox and the wind along the snow.
But since our women must walk gay and money buys their gear,[6]
The sealing-boats they filch that way at hazard year by year.
English they be and Japanee that hang on the Brown Bear's flank,

And some be Scot, but the worst of the lot, and the boldest thieves, be Yank![7]

It was the sealer *Northern Light*, to the Smoky Seas she bore,
With a stovepipe stuck from a starboard port and the Russian flag at her fore.[8]
(*Baltic*, *Stralsund*, and *Northern Light* – oh! they were birds of a feather –
Slipping away to the Smoky Seas, three seal-thieves together!)
And at last she came to a sandy cove and the *Baltic* lay therein,
But her men were up with the herding seal to drive and club and skin.
There were fifteen hundred skins abeach, cool pelt and proper fur,[9]
When the *Northern Light* drove into the bight and the sea-mist drove with her.
The *Baltic* called her men and weighed – she could not choose but run –
For a stovepipe seen through the closing mist, it shows like a four-inch gun
(And loss it is that is sad as death to lose both trip and ship
And lie for a rotting contraband on Vladivostok slip).[10]
She turned and dived in the sea-smother as a rabbit dives in the whins,
And the *Northern Light* sent up her boats to steal the stolen skins.
They had not brought a load to side or slid their hatches clear,
When they were aware of a sloop-of-war, ghost-white and very near.
Her flag she showed, and her guns she showed – three of them, black, abeam,
And a funnel white with the crusted salt, but never a show of steam.

There was no time to man the brakes, they knocked the shackle free,
And the *Northern Light* stood out again, goose-winged to open sea.
(For life it is that is worse than death, by force of Russian law,
To work in the mines of mercury that loose the teeth in your jaw.)[11]
They had not run a mile from shore – they heard no shots behind –
When the skipper smote his hand on his thigh and threw her up in the wind:
'Bluffed – raised out on a bluff,' said he, 'for if my name's Tom Hall,
'You must set a thief to catch a thief – and a thief has caught us all!
'By every butt in Oregon and every spar in Maine,
'The hand that spilled the wind from her sail was the hand of Reuben Paine![12]
'He has rigged and trigged her with paint and spar, and, faith, he has faked her well –

'But I'd know the *Stralsund's* deckhouse yet from here to the booms o' Hell.

'Oh, once we ha' met at Baltimore, and twice on Boston pier,
'But the sickest day for you, Reuben Paine, was the day that you came here –
'The day that you came here, my lad, to scare us from our seal
'With your funnel made o' your painted cloth, and your guns o' rotten deal!
'Ring and blow for the *Baltic* now, and head her back to the bay,
'And we'll come into the game again – with a double deck to play!'

They rang and blew the sealers' call – the poaching-cry of the sea –
And they raised the *Baltic* out of the mist, and an angry ship was she.
And blind they groped through the whirling white and blind to the bay again,
Till they heard the creak of the *Stralsund's* boom and the clank of her mooring chain.
They laid them down by bitt and boat,[13] their pistols in their belts,
And: 'Will you fight for it, Reuben Paine, or will you share the pelts?'

A dog-toothed laugh laughed Reuben Paine, and bared his flenching-knife.
'Yea, skin for skin, and all that he hath a man will give for his life;
'But I've six thousand skins below, and Yeddo Port to see,[14]
'And there's never a law of God or man runs north of Fifty-Three:[15]
'So go in peace to the naked seas with empty holds to fill,
'And I'll be good to your seal this catch, as many as I shall kill!'

Answered the snap of a closing lock – the jar of a gun-butt slid.
But the tender fog shut fold on fold to hide the wrong they did.
The weeping fog rolled fold on fold the wrath of man to cloak,
As the flame-spurts pale ran down the rail and the sealing-rifles spoke.
The bullets bit on bend and butt, the splinter slivered free
(Little they trust to sparrow-dust that stop the seal in his sea!),[16]
The thick smoke hung and would not shift, leaden it lay and blue,
But three were down on the *Baltic's* deck and two of the *Stralsund's* crew.
An arm's length out and overside the banked fog held them bound,
But, as they heard or groan or word, they fired at the sound.
For one cried out on the Name of God, and one to have him cease,

And the questing volley found them both and bade them hold their
    peace.
And one called out on a heathen joss and one on the Virgin's Name,
And the schooling bullet leaped across and led them whence they
    came.
And in the waiting silences the rudder whined beneath,
And each man drew his watchful breath slow-taken 'tween the teeth –
Trigger and ear and eye acock, knit brow and hard-drawn lips –
Bracing his feet by chock and cleat for the rolling of the ships.
Till they heard the cough of a wounded man that fought in the fog
    for breath,
Till they heard the torment of Reuben Paine that wailed upon his
    death:

'The tides they'll go through Fundy Race, but I'll go never
    more
'And see the hogs from ebb-tide mark turn scampering back to
    shore.[17]
'No more I'll see the trawlers drift below the Bass Rock ground,[18]
'Or watch the tall Fall steamer lights tear blazing up the Sound.[19]
'Sorrow is me, in a lonely sea and a sinful fight I fall,
'But if there's law o' God or man you'll swing for it yet, Tom Hall!'

Tom Hall stood up by the quarter-rail. 'Your words in your teeth,'
    said he.
'There's never a law of God or man runs north of Fifty-Three.
'So go in grace with Him to face, and an ill-spent life behind,
'And I'll be good to your widows, Rube, as many as I shall find.'
A *Stralsund* man shot blind and large, and a warlock Finn was he,
And he hit Tom Hall with a bursting ball a hand's-breadth over the
    knee.
Tom Hall caught hold by the topping-lift, and sat him down with an
    oath,
'You'll wait a little, Rube,' he said, 'the Devil has called for both.
'The Devil is driving both this tide, and the killing-grounds are
    close,
'And we'll go up to the Wrath of God as the holluschickie goes.
'O men, put back your guns again and lay your rifles by,
'We've fought our fight, and the best are down. Let up and let us
    die!
'Quit firing, by the bow there – quit! Call off the *Baltic*'s crew!
'You're sure of Hell as me or Rube – but wait till we get through.'

There went no word between the ships, but thick and quick and loud
The life-blood drummed on the dripping decks, with the fog-dew
from the shroud.
The sea-pull drew them side by side, gunnel to gunnel laid,
And they felt the sheer-strakes pound and clear, but never a word
was said.

Then Reuben Paine cried out again before his spirit passed:
'Have I followed the sea for thirty years to die in the dark at last?
'Curse on her work that has nipped me here with a shifty trick
unkind –
'I have gotten my death where I got my bread, but I dare not face it
blind.
'Curse on the fog! Is there never a wind of all the winds I knew
'To clear the smother from off my chest, and let me look at the blue?'
The good fog heard – like a splitten sail, to left and right she tore,
And they saw the sun-dogs in the haze[20] and the seal upon the shore.
Silver and grey ran spit and bay to meet the steel-backed tide,
And pinched and white in the clearing light the crews stared
overside.
O rainbow-gay the red pools lay that swilled and spilled and spread,
And gold, raw gold, the spent shells rolled between the careless dead –
The dead that rocked so drunkenwise to weather and to lee,
And they saw the work their hands had done as God had bade them
see!

And a little breeze blew over the rail that made the headsails lift,
But no man stood by wheel or sheet, and they let the schooners drift.
And the rattle rose in Reuben's throat and he cast his soul with a cry,
And 'Gone already?' Tom Hall he said. 'Then it's time for me to die.'
His eyes were heavy with great sleep and yearning for the land,
And he spoke as a man that talks in dreams, his wound beneath his
hand.

'Oh, there comes no good o' the westering wind that backs against
the sun;
'Wash down the decks – they're all too red – and share the skins and
run.
'*Baltic*, *Stralsund*, and *Northern Light* – clean share and share for all,
'You'll find the fleets off Tolstoi Mees,[21] but you will not find Tom
Hall.
'Evil he did in shoal-water and blacker sin on the deep,

259

'But now he's sick of watch and trick and now he'll turn and sleep.
'He'll have no more of the crawling sea that made him suffer so,
'But he'll lie down on the killing-grounds where the holluschickie
    go.
'And west you'll sail and south again, beyond the sea-fog's rim,
'And tell the Yoshiwara girls to burn a stick for him.[22]
'And you'll not weight him by the heels and dump him overside,
'But carry him up to the sand-hollows to die as Bering died,[23]
'And make a place for Reuben Paine that knows the fight was fair,
'And leave the two that did the wrong to talk it over there!'

Half-steam ahead by guess and lead, for the sun is mostly veiled –
Through fog to fog, by luck and log, sail you as Bering sailed;
And if the light shall lift aright to give your landfall plain,
North and by west, from Zapne Crest you raise the Crosses twain.[24]
Fair marks are they to the inner bay, the reckless poacher knows,
What time the scarred see-catchie lead their sleek seraglios.
Ever they hear the floe-pack clear, and the blast of the old bull-whale,
And the deep seal-roar that beats off-shore above the loudest gale.
Ever they wait the winter's hate as the thundering boorga[25] *calls,*
Where northward look they to St. George, and westward to St. Paul's.[26]
Ever they greet the hunted fleet – lone keels off headlands drear –
When the sealing-schooners flit that way at hazard year by year.
Ever in Yokohama port men tell the tale anew
   Of a hidden sea and a hidden fight,
    When the Baltic *ran from the* Northern Light,
And the Stralsund *fought the two.*

'THE RHYME OF THE THREE SEALERS'

Explanatory Background

The first thirteen lines of 'The Rhyme of the Three Sealers' originally
appeared in November 1892 as a part of the Letter entitled 'Captains
Courageous'. The poem as a whole, however, was not published
until December 1893, when it was printed, with illustrations, in a
London magazine, the *Pall Mall Budget*. In 1896 it was collected in

The Seven Seas, and thereby became a regular part of Kipling's collected verse. How much of it was initially written in Japan in 1892 cannot be determined, but it certainly stems, in inspiration and in content, from Kipling's Japanese experiences.

In rhythm, style and narrative shape it is a 'ballad', being based on the traditional anonymous heroic ballad form which had hardly been composed, as verse of any quality, in the preceding two hundred years, but to which several of Kipling's striking ballads of the 1890s gave powerful modern expression. Sir Arthur Quiller-Couch, in his preface to the *Oxford Book of Ballads* (1910), after giving credit to Sir Walter Scott and to Samuel Taylor Coleridge (for 'The Ancient Mariner') as successful imitators of the ballad, added that 'If any poet now alive can be called a ballad-writer of genius, it is [Kipling] the author of *Danny Deever* and *East and West*.' To these he might have added 'The Rhyme of the Three Sealers', though perhaps it does not attain to the same standard of excellence.

Its subject, seal-poaching, was of significant contemporary relevance, as would have been recognized by any educated reader. It had been an intermittently sensitive issue since the purchase from Russia, by the USA, of Alaska and the Aleutian Islands in 1867; and it was initially brought to prominence by the audacious American policy of claiming the right to control all seal fishery not just within the orthodox three-mile limit off the mainland and islands, but throughout the entire eastern Bering Sea. In 1886 an important case in this regard arose from the capture by the US authorities of three British sealers, the *Thornton*, the *Onward* and the *Carolena*, with serious diplomatic consequences, leading to pressure in 1887–90 for a joint British/American/Russian Convention to regulate sealing. This became bogged down by legal arguments over international rights in the Bering Sea, and over distinctions between 'pelagic' sealing (carried out at sea) and the land-based hunting. In April 1892, while Kipling was in Yokohama, the Americans agreed to take the matter to an arbitration tribunal: this duly sat in February to August 1893, and decided in favour of Britain, against the USA. The matter at issue had been American claims in the Bering Sea, and had not related to Russian prohibition of intrusion in their own sealing areas to the west, where causes of friction were frequent.

It was against this background of public interest that Kipling wrote 'The White Seal', published in magazine form in August 1893 and included in 1894 in *The Jungle Book*. 'The White Seal' and its accompanying poem, 'Lukannon', were inspired, as Kipling informs the reader, by information picked up on his voyage to Yokohama in April 1892, but they are outside the scope of this book.

Not so 'The Rhyme of the Three Sealers', the relevance and realism of which would be obvious to any authority on late nineteenth-century Japan. One such, in two letters written to Basil Hall Chamberlain in early 1894 just after the appearance of 'The Rhyme of the Three Sealers', declared that he was 'astonished at the immense power of the thing', which was 'above all praise', and 'gains with every reading'. It was 'queer how he hits the local colour and the exact human tone always. I used to chat ... in Yokohama with just such men as the sealers ... They can tell you wonderful things; and their talk is never dull. But to use it like Kipling one must have worked with them, lived their life...' – (from *The Japanese Letters of Lafcadio Hearn*, Constable, 1911).

Kipling indeed possessed an uncanny flair for drawing accurately on such source material; but precisely who his informants were in the matter of seal-poaching will probably never be known. Two clues, however, suggesting separate sources, one oral and the other written, have come to our notice.

In February 1984 a tentative identification, headed 'Did Solomon meet Kipling?' was published in *Spotlight*, the monthly English-language magazine of the Kobe Club, in one of a series of short articles on 'Solomon the Sealer' by H. S. Williams, OBE, a very long-established British resident. According to him, the man who could have given Kipling his material for 'The Rhyme of the Three Sealers' was one Stuart (or Harry) Solomon (1857–1907), a 'burly but genial sea-dog' who had a colourfully disreputable past and 'looked a perfect buccaneer'.

By the time of Kipling's visits, Solomon had adopted Japanese nationality, married a Japanese wife, changed his name to Hoshino Yoshiharu, and settled down to respectability in the hotel business at Lake Shoji, seventy miles west of Yokohama. The supposition is that he had been over to Yokohama when Kipling had been there, and that he was just the type of man whom Kipling would have been pleased to meet. This speculation is supported by the fact – as alleged by Williams – that long before Kipling wrote 'The Rhyme of the Three Sealers' Solomon used to tell much the same bloodstained story when gossiping about the past with old shipmates in the waterside taverns of Yokohama. Moreover, he had claimed to have been himself a participant, adding that when the fight was over scarcely enough men had survived to work the three ships back to port. (A few others of the survivors were possibly in Yokohama during Kipling's time there. This emerges from *The Death of Old Yokohama* (Allen & Unwin, 1965), a book by a former long-term

American resident, Otis Manchester Poole, who had known the city since his first arrival there as a boy in 1888. Poole described Bloodtown, a notorious area on the fringe of Chinatown which had acquired that name owing to the frequency of the sanguinary brawls that broke out there. He was sure that it would have been in a Bloodtown saloon that 'Kipling first heard the yarn spun in his "Rhyme of the Three Sealers", by no means a mythical tale. The writer himself [Poole] knew two of the participants in that battle.')

Given the poem's opening stanza, we here have a reasonably plausible theory as to where Kipling derived his knowledge of the fight in the fog – either direct from Solomon, or else indirectly (since according to Williams it was an 'oft-told tale') from others who had heard the epic story. Sailors were in abundance during Kipling's visit in April to June 1892: it was the off-season when sealers congregated in Yokohama, in many cases spending all their recent takings in prodigal living, until the onset of the next sealing season, in about September, should take them to sea again.

However, there is a second and entirely separate clue to the sources. From it the conclusion is inescapable that Kipling drew much supporting evidence – not about the earlier fight, nor about the precise *locale* where it took place, but about the day-to-day risks and realities of seal-poaching – from a conspicuously reported court case involving three sealers, which occurred in Yokohama while he was there in 1892.

The case opened on 27 April 1892, before R. A. Mowat (1843–1925), a former consular official who had become the Judge in 'Her Britannic Majesty's Court in Japan', and who heard extra-territorial cases in Yokohama. The plaintiffs were James Carey and Captain James Curtis, respectively owner and master of the British schooner *Mystery*. The defendant was Captain Walter Pyne, owner of the British schooner *Arctic*. A third vessel, the *Diana*, commanded by Captain Petersen, had been involved in the incidents in question, but was not a party to the litigation. All three sealers had been operating in October 1891 in the Sea of Okhotsk, more precisely off the eastern shore of Sakhalin – an island of which the northern part had been Russian, the southern Japanese, until the Treaty of 1875, which had given the Kuriles to Japan and southern Sakhalin to Russia.

The plaintiffs' case had been as follows. The *Mystery* had fallen in with the *Arctic* and the two captains had reached an agreement to co-operate for the rest of their voyage and to share equally such seals as they should kill. (The *Diana*, also in the neighbourhood, had at first been associated with the contract, but had later withdrawn.) The

Mystery had then proceeded, ahead of the *Arctic*, to Robben Island, an islet a dozen miles off the Sakhalin coast and a well-known haunt of seals. While sealing there, the *Mystery* was intercepted by a Russian warship, and all her crew afloat and ashore were arrested and taken to Vladivostok, where their ship was impounded. Captain Curtis had protested, but unavailingly, that he had no knowledge that Robben Island was Russian territory. On being handed over in November 1891 to the British consul in Nagasaki, Captain Curtis had gone to Yokohama to ask the owner of the *Arctic* for the agreed half-share of that ship's profits, but had been refused, even though the *Arctic* had returned to Yokohama with the 1500 seal skins which the *Mystery*'s crew had obtained and been forced to abandon on Robben Island when they were arrested.

A point which emerged in cross-examination was that the chief hunter aboard the *Mystery*, John Kearnan, when sailing with Captain Curtis two years earlier in another ship, had played a trick on Captain Pyne; he had hoisted Russian colours and had stuck a stove-pipe out of a port-hole as a dummy gun, so as to simulate an armed Russian vessel and frighten Captain Pyne away from his poaching.

The defendant's case was that no long-term contract had been agreed. There had at first been a short-term agreement between all three ships, to work jointly on one extended beach, so as the more effectively to drive the seals to slaughter, but even this had been revoked when the *Diana* withdrew from it, and it had never extended to sharing the catch. The *Arctic*, after a brush with a Russian warship, from which she had escaped in a gale-force wind, had indeed visited Robben Island when the coast was clear, and had hunted seals there, but her crew had not removed any skins belonging to the *Mystery*, as these were by then no longer in a fresh and usable condition. (From this arose much technical argument as to what period would elapse before fresh seal skins would deteriorate.) The judge eventually found for the defendant.

These proceedings were extensively reported in the *Japan Weekly Mail* of 30 April, 7 May and 14 May (the last issue being the one in which Kipling's speech at the Tokyo Club was also reported). Editorial comment was very scathing: the poachers were disreputable and shameless, the contract if it existed was improper, the skins were stolen property, Robben Island was unquestionably Russian territory and was self-evidently subject to an official Russian proclamation of 1881 forbidding unlicensed sealing in the territorial waters of the Russian Empire.

This editorial viewpoint, however, was fiercely opposed by a correspondent calling himself 'Kotik'. In two letters, dated 5 and 10 May, in the issue of 14 May, he made an eloquent case for the sealers as a class, claiming that their activities were widely misrepresented and were not analogous to theft. Robben Island, a 'bare flat-topped rock a few score yards in extent, surrounded by a sand beach', lay well off the coast of the formerly Japanese part of Sakhalin, and was not indisputably Russian territory, and despite the pretensions of the Americans in the Bering Sea controversy no state had a legal right to ownership of animals such as seals outside its three-mile limit.

From this case, Kipling picked up a large number of points which he used in the different context, and the altogether different geographical location, of his 'Rhyme of the Three Sealers'. His borrowings are listed in the footnotes that follow. One other derivation, which it is tempting to see in the certainty that Kipling read the *Japan Weekly Mail*, is the name 'Kotik', which, as Kotick, he gave to the White Seal in the *Jungle Book* story of that title. (The suffix *-ik* is a diminutive, and *kot* is an old word for 'cat' – the modern word being *koshka* – so *kotik* means 'little cat', or 'puss'. *Kot* however can also mean 'fur seal', or 'seal skin'.)

Notes to the poem

1. 'Blood Street Joe': this has been rather unspecifically identified by H. S. Williams (cited above) as 'one of many grogshops in Yokohama', and one where the original story underlying Kipling's poem was often recounted. 'Bloodtown' was a disorderly area of the Foreign Settlement, described by Williams as 'along Honmura Road, as far as Cock-Eye the tailor's shop'. There is a vivid description of Bloodtown in *Terry's 'Japanese Empire'*, a guidebook published in 1914:

   Land-sharks of varying skill prey upon the sailor-folk who wriggle through the meshes of the safe-guarding net cast by the Salvation Army. Conspicuous features are the cheap and lurid saloons ... where vitriolic 'Jack-rabbit' whiskey is sold to the feverish and thirsty. Here considerable canned music is dispensed by bedizened foreign harpies with cheeks enameled like tropical sunsets, and with bella-donna eyes whose lids nictitate instinctively at passing masculinity ...

   'Cisco's Dewdrop Dining Rooms' have not been identified.
2. The ship's name *Baltic* is an echo of the *Arctic* in *Curtis & Carey v. Pyne*. This would not be convincing on its own, but it acquires cumulative support from many other such echoes listed below.

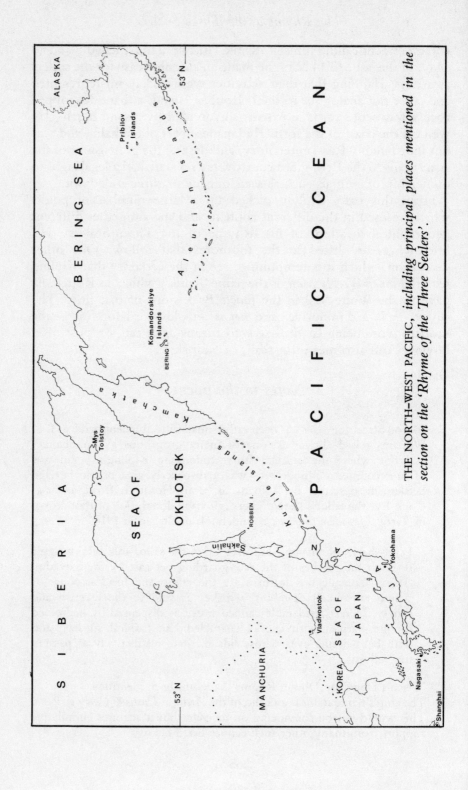

THE NORTH-WEST PACIFIC, including principal places mentioned in the section on the 'Rhyme of the Three Sealers'.

3. The 'Law' is a reference to the 1881 proclamation, as described editorially in the *Japan Weekly Mail*: according to 'Kotik', it was no more than a local police regulation promulgated under pressure from the Alaska Commercial Company which enjoyed the sealing monopoly.

   The geographical point is significant. The 'Smoky Sea' is the Bering Sea, and these islands are undoubtedly the Komandorskiye Islands between the Aleutians and Kamchatka. This is the first of numerous pointers in the poem which make it clear that the action is set far away from the scene of the episode of the *Mystery* and the *Arctic*, which had taken place in the Sea of Okhotsk.

4. The blue fox, a variant of the Arctic fox (*Alopex lagopus*) which unlike others in the category does not turn white in winter, has for many years been bred in the Bering Sea islands for its fur. It is distinct from the kit fox (*Vulpes velox*) mentioned a few lines later.

5. *Matka* is Russian for 'mother' and is here used for the she-seals. (Spelt *Matkah*, the word recurs in the *Jungle Book* as the name of Kotick's mother in 'The White Seal'.) Since all the Bering Sea islands were Russian till 1867 there is a certain logic in this. Likewise the word *holluschickie*, by which Kipling means the young unmated male seals, is from the Russian; as is *see-catchie* (in the final stanza), meaning the mature bull seals; these words also occur in 'The White Seal'. The references to the bull seals 'hauling' out of and back to the sea, is technically correct; one of the letters from 'Kotik' in the *Japan Weekly Mail* asserts that when the Russians learnt that Robben Island was a 'hauling ground' for seals, they laid territorial claim to it, even though it lay off what was at that time the Japanese end of Sakhalin.

6. As to the economic inducements to the seal-poacher, one skin might fetch over five yen or four dollars; seal fur was a very fashionable item of dress, whether for export abroad or sale in Japan. Within living memory, to quote the articles on Solomon the Sealer by H. S. Williams, 'every Japanese gentleman – and many who were not gentlemen – had a seal-skin collar on his winter cape or coat'.

7. This comment on the exceptional audacity of the American pirates would have had a political undertone in 1892/93, when the American posture in the Bering Sea dispute was one of seal conservation and injured innocence. In this poem Reuben Paine is clearly, and Tom Hall probably, American. In *Curtis & Carey v. Pyne* Captain Curtis, together with his senior hunter Kearnan (who was responsible for the trick with the flag and the stovepipe), were Americans.

8. See the last sentence of Note 7. This is straight from *Curtis & Carey v. Pyne*.

9. The figure of 1500 skins recurs several times in *Curtis & Carey v. Pyne* as the number that the hunting party that had landed from the *Mystery* had been forced to abandon when the Russian warship appeared. The

parallel is unmistakable. The 'coolness' of the pelts also featured in the court case as a measure of their condition: if left too long unsalted they deteriorated. Giving evidence on the way the pelts of the seals skinned on Robben Island were 'scattered about', Kearnan said that 'if left in a heap they would have got heated and gone bad'.

10. In *Curtis & Carey v. Pyne* Curtis and his crew were taken in custody to Vladivostok, and their ship was impounded there.

11. The implication is that the convicted poacher might be consigned to labour in a mercury mine in Russia, where over-exposure would render him liable to mercurialism or chronic poisoning. The symptoms of this would include first a tenderness of the gums, then a loosening of the teeth accompanied by great outpourings of saliva; for want of treatment, death could result. However, there is a distinction to be drawn. Imprisonment would be the penalty for poaching in the indisputably Russian territory of the Komandorskiye Islands, but when it came to poaching on Robben Island, where the Russian claim was arguably weaker, Captain Curtis merely lost his ship: he and his crew were repatriated within weeks to Japan. This point was emphasized by 'Kotik' in his defence of poachers in the *Japan Weekly Mail*: in his view it confirmed the legal fact that the poached seals were not the property of the Russian state.

12. Paine: one of the captains in the court case was called Pyne.

13. 'Bitt and boat': a *bitt*, usually one of a pair, was a heavy timber post bolted to the deck beams and used for fastening cables, etc. There are many nautical technicalities in this poem, enough to bewilder Lafcadio Hearn, who wrote, in a letter already cited:

> But what are 'sheer strakes,' 'chocks,' 'bends and butts,' 'cleats,' and 'topping-lifts'? You will confess that, though mysterious to the landlubber, there is a blocky, bumping, raking force, even in the sound of them ...

To deal with these in order, a *sheer strake* is the top strake, or plank, of a wooden vessel, next below the gunwale, running from stem to stern. A *chock* would be a block of wood, placed to retain a movable object in its proper position. *Bends* are the thickest planks in the side of the hull, from the waterline upwards. A *butt* is the end of a plank, cut square and secured to e.g. the timbers of the hull frame. *Cleats* are pieces of wood or metal with two arms, to which ropes can be made fast. A *topping-lift* is a rope tackle by which the end of a spar is hoisted or lowered.

14. *Yeddo* is an old spelling of *Edo* or *Yedo*, the modern Tokyo. Although there is and was a port at Tokyo, sea-going shipping tended to use Yokohama, because of its easier access.

15. The 53rd line of latitude, running just south of the Komandorskiye Islands, confirms the location of the setting of this poem.

16. The meaning is that for shooting seals a heavier shot is needed than the light shotgun pellets, sometimes called dustshot, that are adequate for shooting small birds.

17. The Bay of Fundy is an inlet of the Atlantic, between Nova Scotia and New Brunswick. Its tides are exceptional, reaching a height of seventy feet.

18. There are two Bass Rocks that are possible in this context: both are on the coast of Massachusetts.

19. There was a steamer service between Fall River in southern Massachusetts and New York; it went by Long Island Sound.

20. A sun-dog, also called a mock sun or parhelion, is an effect of light which may resemble a halo or small rainbow near the horizon.

21. 'Tolstoi Mees': a *mys* is a cape, in Russian. There is a Mys Tolstoi on the northern coast of the Sea of Okhotsk, but from the context and sense it is likelier that Kipling was referring to a less well-known cape of that name in the Pribilov Islands, at that time a great focus of sealing.

22. The Yoshiwara was the red light district of Tokyo (though the same word, literally 'Reed Plain', was used to describe other such districts in other cities). Lafcadio Hearn, in a letter to Basil Hall Chamberlain already cited, expressed strong admiration for this line – 'the very first time that any Western writer ever succeeded in making infinite poetry with that much befouled word'. He described the simplicity and the pathos, the awareness of sin and impending death, all concentrated in the dying man's thought of a joss-stick and a prayer for him, supplied by the prostitutes he had known, as 'sheer magic. One word more would have spoiled the effect. One word less would have rendered it impossible.'

23. This supplies another clue to the location of the fight. The great Danish navigator Vitus Jonassen Bering (1681–1741) served for many years in the Russian navy, and his explorations of the far north of the Pacific were conducted for Russia. His last voyage was a disaster, and he died on the island in the Komandorskiye group now called Bering Island. It is somewhere here that the story in the poem is set.

24. Zapne is presumably a contraction of *zapadnyy*, meaning west; Crest, or *Krest*, means headland. One extremity of Bering Island is called Mys Severo-Zapadnyy, or North-West Point. Kipling could be using a sailor's abbreviation of that term. However, an exact geographical pinpointing of the place where the two captains were buried, with the crosses over their graves serving as a landmark, is hardly to be looked for in a poem.

25. A *boorga*, properly *boorya* in Russian, is a violent storm.

26. St Paul is the north-western, and St George the south-eastern, island of the Pribilov Group. The names date from the visit to the islands of Gerasim Pribilov in 1786. St Paul is so called because Pribilov's second-in-command landed there on the feast day of St Peter and St Paul; St George is named after Pribilov's ship.

Appendix 1

KIPLING'S LATER COMMENTS ON JAPAN

(A) Miscellaneous References

After sailing from Yokohama for the second time, in June 1892, Kipling maintained for the rest of his life the habit of travel. However, though his journeyings in the next forty-three years took him far, he never again saw Japan – nor, despite invitations to go there, India. But whereas Indian themes recurred frequently in his later books of prose and verse, and can also be found in his speeches, letters and newspaper articles, Japan rarely featured at all – apart from references already noted such as the evocative use of 'Buddha at Kamakura' in *Kim*, and the brief account of his 1892 visit in *Something of Myself*.

Yet Kipling's lifetime saw the steady rise of Japan to the status of a world power. It is inconceivable that so observant a political commentator, having so trenchantly described the emergent nation he had known in 1889 and 1892, would fail to be impressed, for better or for worse, by the portentous manner in which her destiny unfolded in later years. When the great mass of Kipling's surviving personal letters, which number some seven thousand and are currently being selected and edited by Professor Pinney of the United States, reaches the stage of publication, it may well be found to contain interesting comments on Japan. Meanwhile, in the corpus of Kipling's standard works and published letters, there is surprisingly little on the subject.

Politics apart, it might have been confidently expected that a writer with so developed a taste for the exotic, after substantial exposure to the colour, the variety and the individuality of Japan, might have drawn upon that country for more in the way of short story material than the slight farce of 'Griffiths the Safe Man' which he had dashed off on his travels in 1889. However, for some reason, any such ideas Kipling may have had failed to mature. There is a hint of one in a letter he wrote on 28 July 1894 to Robert Barr, joint editor with Jerome K. Jerome of an illustrated literary magazine, the *Idler*. Writing of ideas in hand which might develop into short stories, Kipling said he was working on 'a sort of nest of notions in the complicated absurdity line'. One of these was 'the tale of a Japanese riddle which undermined the peace of two Clubs in Yokohama and Tokyo'. All three, 'short tales – not over 7000 at the outmost', would prove to be 'full of the purely male horseplay and schoolboy rot that women-folk, bless 'em, find so hard to understand. I'll send 'em along as they transpire and eventuate ...' From hints in the letter one of these embryo plots can be tentatively identified in a later story, but the Japanese one cannot: it was presumably never completed to the author's satisfaction.

In that same year, 1894, he published a long and powerful poem, 'McAndrew's Hymn'. This is a brooding monologue reflecting the thoughts of a Scots engineer looking back over his life at sea. It contains one fleeting reference to Japan, in a passage where McAndrew prays to his Calvinistic God to be forgiven his youthful 'steps aside' from virtue in the seaports where his ship had called.

> Blot out the wastrel hours of mine in sin when I abode –
> Jane Harrigan's an' Number Nine, The Reddick and Grant Road!

'Number Nine', also called 'The Nectarine', was a well-known Japanese brothel for foreigners, at Eirakucho, Itchome, Yokohama. It was a competitive trade, and Number Nine contrived to circumvent official prohibitions on advertising by placing its cards in the sitting-rooms of hotels, and urging potential clients to eschew other inferior premises which had copied its name. A visitor to Yokohama in the late 1890s noted that brothel tariffs ranged from thirty sen (about sevenpence-halfpenny in British currency of the day) to three yen (six shillings), according to quality. The ladies of Number Nine, which claimed to be 'the only first-class house in Japan', would have been at or above the top end of that scale.

Years later, on 2 September 1903, in a letter to an old naval friend, W. J. Harding, Kipling made some passing references to the Chinese and the Japanese, apprehensive in respect of the former, disparaging in respect of the latter and expressed in terms which echo what he had picked up from expatriates in Japan about Japanese business methods, both in 1889, as reflected in Letter Five of that year, and in 1892:

> ... Glad you feel about the Chink as I do. Frankly I'm afraid of him. he has more guts than the Jap; and is honest. Remember how in Japan all business was done through a Chinese comprador.
>
> The Jap is a shifty little beggar about contracts and some day he'll be sorry he ever stirred up the sleeping whale. But I think he may make the Muscovite unhappy. I've been hearing details of the Russian fleet that are rather quaint. They seem to have all the makee-look but very little of the makee-do aboard their vessels ...

Written as they were five months before the outbreak of the Russo-Japanese War, the last sentences were prescient. One certainty about the Russian fleet which laboured round the world to be annihilated by the Japanese in the straits of Tsushima is that it was unfit to put to sea. In any case, it is likely that the startling outcome of that war finally removed any political condescension there may still have been in Kipling's view of a people who by military determination and courage had firmly established themselves as a factor in the world's uncertain balance of power. A Treaty of Alliance, albeit of limited application, had existed between Britain and Japan since January 1902, and shortly after the Battle of Tsushima in the summer of 1905 it was renewed for a further ten years.

Not surprisingly, in 1912, in a short story called 'As Easy as A.B.C.' which was a futuristic science fiction piece descriptive of an imagined World Government of the 21st century, a Japanese, Takahira, is a prominent member of the eponymous 'Aerial Board of Control' which dominates the planet.

In 1914 the Japanese entered the first World War as allies of the British. In August 1918, after the collapse of Russia, a Japanese expeditionary force participated actively in allied operations against the Bolsheviks in eastern Siberia. It was a critical and still uncertain stage of the overall war that provided the background for a frank letter from Kipling to his old friend ex-President Theodore Roosevelt on 21 October 1918, in which he expressed characteristically strong misgivings about the inept high-mindedness of President Wilson:

> One sometimes wonders how much blood that man might have saved while he was so busy saving everybody's soul. And God and the Government alone know how much he is hampering us in regard to Japanese action in Siberia, and our own in Ireland!

The young man who in 1889 had so sweepingly judged that the Japanese, incomparable artists though they were, lacked 'the last touch of firmness in their character' which would qualify them for the rough-and-tumble of the world's political arena to which they so wrong-headedly aspired, had been wrong, as he now recognized. Within three decades of that judgement, their formidable troops were providing the key contingent, associated with British, American and other forces, in a counter-revolutionary invasion of collapsed Russia. While those ultimately ill-fated operations lasted, the Japanese played a dominant part, and they far outstayed their allies, not leaving eastern Siberia until 1922.

(B) On Japanese in Canada, 1907–8

Though, in 1907, those events in Siberia lay far in the future, memories of the recent Russo-Japanese War were fresh. In the popular British view of that conflict, 'gallant little Japan' had stood up manfully against Russia, and prevailed. As for the decisive naval battle of 1905, the British, in the words of Richard Storry (*A History of Modern Japan*), had 'felt almost as pleased about it as the Japanese, for the victorious navy had been largely built and equipped at Barrow, Elswick and Sheffield; and most, if not all, of the Japanese officers had been trained or professionally advised by Englishmen'.

In September to October 1907 Kipling spent a month touring Canada, with a busy programme of travel, receptions and speeches. After his return to England he turned his notes into a series of newspaper sketches describing what he had seen and heard in Canada. These appeared in the *Morning Post*, also in *Collier's Weekly* and the *Vancouver World*, in March to May 1908 and, as 'Letters to the Family', were collected in 1920 in his *Letters of Travel*.

One of those articles, entitled 'Labour' and devoted to immigration policy, focuses on the hostility of organized Canadian labour to Japanese immigrants, notably in British Columbia. This hostility was engendered partly by racial prejudice but more, it seemed to Kipling, by fear of the sheer determination and industriousness of Japanese immigrants, with which those of British stock seemed unable to compete. Though Kipling himself would have strongly preferred to see many more Britons going to Canada, and deplored the myopia of those in Canada and Britain who did not do all they could to further that desirable aim, he had no time for the timid disparagement of the Japanese that he everywhere encountered. The following are relatively brief excerpts from that article:–

One cannot leave a thing alone if it is thrust under the nose at every turn. I had not quitted the Quebec steamer three minutes when I was asked point-blank: 'What do you think of the question of Asiatic Exclusion which is Agitating our Community?

. . . I had to temporise all across the Continent till I could find someone to help me to acceptable answers. The Question appears to be confined to British Columbia. There, after a while, the men who had their own reasons for not wishing to talk referred me to others who explained . . .

The Chinaman has always been in the habit of coming to British Columbia, where he makes, as he does elsewhere, the finest servant in the world. No one, I was assured on all hands, objects to the biddable Chinaman. He takes work which no white man in a new country will handle, and when kicked by the mean white will not grossly retaliate. He has always paid for the privilege of making his fortune on this wonderful coast, but with singular forethought and statesmanship the popular Will, some few years ago, decided to double the head-tax on his entry. Strange as it may appear, the Chinaman now charges double for his services, and is scarce at that. This is said to be one of the reasons why overworked white women die or go off their heads; and why in new cities you can see blocks of flats being built to minimise the inconveniences of house-keeping without help. The birth-rate will fall later in exact proportion to those flats.

Appendix 1

Since the Russo-Japanese War the Japanese have taken to coming over to British Columbia. They also do work which no white man will; such as hauling wet logs for lumber mills out of cold water at from eight to ten shillings a day. They supply the service in hotels and dining-rooms and keep small shops. The trouble with them is that they are just a little too good, and when attacked defend themselves with asperity . . .

The objection is all against the Japanese. So far – except that they are said to have captured the local fishing trade at Vancouver, precisely as the Malays control the Cape Town fish business – they have not yet competed with the whites; but I was earnestly assured by many men that there was danger of their lowering the standard of life and wages. The demand, therefore, in certain quarters is that they go – absolutely and unconditionally. (You may have noticed that Democracies are strong on the imperative mood.) An attempt was made to shift them shortly before I came to Vancouver, but it was not very successful, because the Japanese barricaded their quarters and flocked out, a broken bottle held by the neck in either hand, which they jabbed in the faces of the demonstrators. It is, perhaps, easier to haze and hammer bewildered Hindus and Tamils, as is being done across the Border, than to stampede the men of the Yalu and Liaoyang [battles in the Russo-Japanese War].

A man penned me in a corner with a single heavily capitalised sentence. 'There is a General Sentiment among Our People that the Japanese Must Go,' said he . . .

'Quite so. Sentiment is a beautiful thing, but what are you going to do?' He did not condescend to particulars . . .

Another man was a little more explicit. 'We desire', he said, 'to keep the Chinaman. But the Japanese must go.'

'Then who takes their place? Isn't this rather a new country to pitch people out of?'

'We must develop our Resources slowly, sir – with an Eye to the Interests of our Children. We must preserve the Continent for Races which will assimilate with Ours. We must not be swamped by Aliens.'

'Then bring in your own races and bring 'em in quick,' I ventured.

This is the one remark one must not make in certain quarters of the West; and I lost caste heavily while he explained (exactly as the Dutch did at the Cape years ago) how British Columbia was by no means so rich as she appeared . . . and that whatever steps were necessary for bringing in more white people should be taken with extreme caution . . .

'But didn't the Salvation Army offer to bring in three or four thousand English some short time ago? What came of that idea?'

'It – er – fell through.'

'Why?'

'For political reasons, I believe. We do not want People who will lower the Standard of Living. That is why the Japanese must go.'

'Then why keep the Chinese?'

275

'We can get on with the Chinese. We can't get on without the Chinese. But we must have Emigration of a Type that will assimilate with Our People. I hope I have made myself clear?'

I hoped that he had, too . . .

A little later I had occasion to go through a great and beautiful city between six and seven of a crisp morning. Milk and fish, vegetables, etc., were being delivered to the silent houses by Chinese and Japanese. Not a single white man was visible on that chilly job . . .

*   *   *

When 'Labour' was published, Canadians were disturbed by Kipling's frankness, which was also resented by the political left, which he had blamed for orchestrated and selfish discouragement of increased immigration from Britain. However, his account of anti-Japanese sentiments in British Columbia was accurate and relevant: these had led to a fishery strike in 1900 and ugly riots in Vancouver in 1907. Eventually, recourse was had to diplomatic negotiation between Britain and Japan, with the result that from 1909 Japanese immigration into Canada was considerably reduced.

Its volume needs to be put into due proportion. The scale was at one time substantial, and in 1905–08 it reached a peak. In those four years alone, some forty per cent of all Japanese immigrants into Canada in the whole period 1900 to 1941 arrived. Kipling's observations of hostile reaction were therefore focused on the precise time when a backlash among Canadians of European stock was at its predictable height.

However the available figures are inexact for the earlier years, and require to be qualified throughout by the fact that most of the Japanese who came to Canada from Japan did not stay permanently but later made their way south into US territory. This, too, is reflected in Kipling's article, where he took note of Canadian comments to the effect that anyone introducing unacceptable or unduly competitive labour into British Columbia was liable to intimidation by union militants on the American side of the frontier. As one small employer had told him:–

'I can't afford to take any chances fighting the Unions.'

'What would happen if you did?'

'D'you know what's happening across the Border? Men get blown up there – with dynamite.'

'But this isn't across the Border?'

'It's a damn-sight too near to be pleasant. And witnesses get blown up, too. You see, the Labour situation ain't run from our side the line. It's worked from down under. You may have noticed men were rather careful when they talked about it?'

'Yes, I noticed all that.'

'Well, it ain't a pleasant state of affairs . . . I suppose they've told you that little fuss with the Japanese in Vancouver was worked from down under, haven't they? I don't think our own people 'ud have done it by themselves.'

*　　*　　*

The first Japanese settler in Canada, according to Kodansha's *Encyclopedia of Japan*, arrived in 1877, after which there was 'sparse but steady migration ... with a heavy yet transitory migration in the last years of the 1890s ... The 1901 census found fewer than 5,000 Japanese in Canada, most of them in British Columbia.' In the next forty years 25,000 more had arrived, more than 10,000 of whom had come in 1905–8. At that peak period, because of the Anglo-Japanese Alliance of 1902, Canada as a British Dominion was inhibited from passing discriminatory legislation against Japanese immigration, as it had done against the Chinese, who were virtually excluded by a prohibitively high head-tax – on which Kipling had commented ironically.

Appendix 2

RUDYARD KIPLING, 1889–92

The outline chronology of four formative years

1888 31 December. Kipling's 23rd birthday. In India since 1882, he moved in 1887 from the *Civil & Military Gazette* (Lahore) to the *Pioneer* (Allahabad). He lives in Allahabad as paying guest in the home of Professor and Mrs Hill.

1889 January/February. Final two months as a staff journalist. Miscellaneous prose and verse for the *Pioneer*. Farewell visit to his parents in Lahore.

9 March to 15 April. Leaving India with the Hills, he travels from Calcutta to Nagasaki, via Rangoon, Moulmein, Penang, Singapore, Hong Kong and Canton. (A record of his journeys from March to September appeared in the *Pioneer* as a series of some forty Letters. With many cuts, they were re-published in 1899 in *From Sea to Sea*.)

15 April to 11 May. In Japan: itinerary as covered in Part One of this book.

11–28 May. Yokohama to San Francisco.

28 May to 25 September. Travelling extensively in the USA with two short visits to Canada (Victoria/Vancouver and Toronto). Parts from the Hills in San Francisco: rejoins them in Pennsylvania: is briefly engaged to be married to Mrs Hill's sister Caroline Taylor (broken off in early 1890).

25 September to 5 October. New York to Liverpool.

October to December. In London, meeting editors and publishers. Negotiates the reissue in England of his Indian books: has new prose and verse items accepted. Rents a flat in Villiers Street. His impressions of London are sent to the *Civil & Military Gazette*, as part of a series of sketches sent to India since March. (In 1909 they were re-published with other miscellanea in *Abaft the Funnel*.)

278

Appendix 2

1890 January to March. In London, writing intensively for periodicals: verse and short stories (to be incorporated later in *Barrack-Room Ballads* and *Life's Handicap*). Begins on a novel, *The Light that Failed*. Has suddenly achieved sensational popularity.

25 March. Subject of a leading article in *The Times*.

April to December. Mainly in London, though with visits to Paris in May and Italy in October, and around England. Completes the first version of *The Light that Failed*; and in collaboration with Wolcott Balestier starts another novel, *The Naulahka*. Kipling's parents join him in London in May. He meets Wolcott Balestier's sister Caroline (his future wife).

1891 January to April. In London. A revised version of *The Light that Failed* is published. Work proceeds on *The Naulahka* (complete by August, serialized from December).

May/June. Visits New York.

July. *Life's Handicap* published. Kipling now under considerable strain from overwork. Decides on a sea voyage to recharge his batteries and broaden his area of knowledge.

22 August to 10 September. Southampton to Cape Town via Madeira. Writing or revising the poem 'The Long Trail'.

10–25 September. In South Africa.

25 September to 18 October. From Cape Town to Wellington.

18 October to 6 November. Touring in New Zealand. Prevented by steamer schedules from visiting Samoa to see R. L. Stevenson.

6–12 November. A rough passage in a small ship from the Bluff (New Zealand) to Melbourne.

12–29 November. Touring in Australia.

29 November to 10 December. From Albany (Western Australia) to Colombo.

10–18 December. By sea and rail from Colombo to Lahore.

18–27 December. With his parents in Lahore. Receives news of Wolcott Balestier's death in Germany. By train to Bombay.

27 December. Sails from Bombay. The end of his final visit to India.

1892 10 January. Back in London after a very fast journey from India (by rail from Trieste across Europe).

18 January. Marries Caroline Balestier at All Souls' Church, Langham Place.

18 January to 2 February. In London, writing. *Barrack-Room Ballads* sent to press (published in late March).

3–11 February. Liverpool to New York. Working on the final stages of *The Naulahka*.

11 February to 6 April. Mainly in USA, briefly in Canada. Buys a site on his wife's family's land in Vermont. (A record of his impressions between February and July 1892 appeared in a series of eight Letters published in *The Times*: they were republished in 1920 in *Letters of Travel*.)

6–20 April. Vancouver to Yokohama.

20 April to 27 June. In Japan. Principal events covered in Part Two of this book.

27 June to 8 July. Yokohama to Vancouver.

8–19 July. Across Canada by rail to Montreal, as guests of the Chairman of the Canadian Pacific Railway. A few days fishing en route, at Banff, Alberta.

Late July. To Vermont.

August to December. Living at Bliss Cottage, Brattleboro, Vermont.

September. Preliminary work on the site of their future house near Brattleboro (completed in September 1893).

October. Working on a first draft of *Kim*.

November. Working on an early story for *The Jungle Book*.

29 December. The first child (Josephine) born.

31 December. Kipling's 27th birthday. Writes in his wife's diary, 'The Good God be thanked for the ending of the happiest year in my life.'

Appendix 3

GLOSSARY

Note 1. Where fuller explanations of words or phrases are provided in the Commentaries accompanying the text, we have shown it accordingly; e.g. *1889.L6.n20* indicates the 1889 series, Letter 6, Note 20.

Note 2. Kipling's generation of expatriates in India used the term *Hindustani*, now regarded as unscholarly. However, any attempt to be more specific calls for careful explanation, as follows. When the language is written in Arabic script it is properly *Urdu*: when in Devanagari script, *Hindi*. Learned people and purists, when speaking it, tend to emphasise its different linguistic origins, selecting a vocabulary that reflects one or other of its divergent classical roots. Thus 'mullahs' or 'maulvis' will incline to the *Persian* sources of *Urdu*, whereas 'pundits' prefer the *Sanskrit* sources of *Hindi*. Nevertheless – as in the case of English with its mixture of origins, Latin, Teutonic, etc – many ordinary people use the language freely, without undue heed to its derivations. The hybrid nature of Kipling's *Hindustani* is well reflected in the definitions below, where it is not always helpful to distinguish between an *Urdu* and a *Hindi* source, and for simplicity we have preponderantly referred to *Hindi*.

★　★　★

auto-da-fé (from Portuguese, lit. 'act of faith'). Term applied to the burning to death of heretics condemned by the Inquisition.

Babu (Hindi, from Sanskrit). Formerly a title of respect, particularly in Bengal, it came to be used by the British in an ironic sense, for an Indian clerk with a veneer of English culture.

Bakufu (Japanese). A term used to mean the government of the *Shogun*. (Its first use in Japan dates from about 1190, but the characters read by the Japanese as *Bakufu* were originally used in China for the headquarters of the Commander of the Imperial Guard.)

bandobast (Hindi from Persian, lit. 'tying and binding'). A common word loosely used for 'arrangements', 'organisation', etc.

banto (Japanese). The Japanese equivalent of *comprador*, *q.v.*

Belaitee or *Belaiti* (from the noun *Belait*, also *Wilayat*, Hindi from Arabic). A common term meaning 'European' (or 'Europe', as in 'Europe clothes').

beloo (from Burmese). A giant or ogre.

biwa (Japanese). A musical instrument resembling a lute.

Bodhisat (from the Sanskrit *bodhi*, enlightenment, and *sattva*, essence). A term which could either mean a potential Buddha or the Buddha himself before enlightenment. [*1889.L10.n17* and *1892.L1.n18.*]

bund (from Persian). A word commonly used in India for an embankment, dyke, causeway; at a port, an embanked quay. [*1889.L1.n9.*]

bunnia (variously spelt, indirectly of Sanskrit origin). A common term for an Indian trader or shopkeeper.

byle (from Hindi). An ox or bullock.

comprador (from Portuguese *comprar*, to buy). A term used in China and Japan for the Chinese manager or agent of an expatriate business firm.

chubara (Hindi). A summerhouse or pavilion in a garden. [*1889.L3.n8.*]

Cryptomeria japonica. A coniferous tree of China and Japan.

dacoit (from Hindi). A bandit, armed robber.

Daibutsu (Japanese, lit. 'Great Buddha'; also abbreviated, *Daibutz*). The famous bronze statue at Kamakura [*1892.L1.n14*]; also used for other large statues of Buddha.

Daimyo (Japanese, lit. 'great name'). Feudal lord(s).

dak (Hindi). A stage or relay on a journey. [*1889.L8.n7.*]

dasturi (Hindi, lit. 'what is customary'). A commission on a transaction.

dekhne ke waste. A common Urdu phrase meaning 'for appearances'. [*1889.L6.n24.*]

dun (Hindi, also *doon*). A term in northern India for a plateau among hills. For Dehra Dun see *1889.L5.n8*.

Edo. The former name of the city that became Tokyo in 1868.

ekka (Hindi, from *ek*, 'one'). A common one-horse springless conveyance.

exempli gratia (Latin). Literally 'for the sake of example', 'e.g.'.

Fudai (Japanese). A hereditary vassal or retainer. In Tokugawa times, a term used for Daimyo owing special loyalty to the Tokugawa. Cf. *Tozama*.

fukoku-kyohei (Japanese, lit. 'rich country, strong army'). A slogan adopted in the Meiji era to describe the policy to be pursued by Japan.

ghari (Hindi, variously spelt, e.g. *gharri*, *gari*). A generic term for a cart or carriage.

ghat (Hindi, variously spelt, e.g. *ghaut*). A landing place, quay or steps on a river bank.

godown (from Malay, *gudang*). A warehouse or store.

hara-kiri (Japanese, lit. 'belly-cutting'). Ritualised suicide. [See further in *1889.L12.n18.*]

hatoba (Japanese). A pier or jetty.

Hong (from Chinese, *hang*, a row or rank). A house of business, warehouse, etc. Whence, via 'Hong-Merchant', it came to mean a foreigner permitted to trade in China; whence, a leading expatriate merchant in Japan.

hti (from Burmese, also *htee*). The gilded 'umbrella' at the top of the dome of a pagoda in Burma.

hyoshigi (Japanese). Twin pieces of wood, clapped together in a Japanese theatre to indicate the end of a scene, or a highlight of the plot.

id est (Latin). Literally 'that is', 'i.e.'.

inro (Japanese). A medicine case.

jhampani (Indian usage but uncertain derivation). One of the team of men who carried a *jhampan* or sedan chair. [*1889.L9.n9.*]

jinrickshaw. See *rickshaw*.

Jiyuto (Japanese). The Liberal, or Radical, Party in Japan.

kabari (Hindi). A second-hand furniture dealer.

Kabuki (Japanese). A traditional form of Japanese popular drama. [*1889.L3.n2.*]

kago (Japanese). A light palanquin, basically made of bamboo.

ken (Japanese). An administrative district or prefecture in Japan.

Khattri (from the Sanskrit *kshatriya*). For a note on this military caste, and Kipling's misuse of the term, see *1889.L4.n34*.

khud (Hindi from Sanskrit). A common word in Himalayan hill stations, meaning a precipitous hillside. [*1889.L9.n8.*]

koku (Japanese). A traditional unit of measure, used for rice and similar commodities. [*1892.L1.n12.*]

kris (Malay). A Malayan or Indonesian stabbing or slashing knife.

kul (Hindi, otherwise *kal*). 'Tomorrow'; also, confusingly, 'yesterday'.

lakh (Hindi). One hundred thousand.

maidan (Hindi, from Persian). The common term for a planned open space (cf. *piazza*) in or adjoining a town in India.

makan chor (Hindi). Literally 'butter-thief', an epithet of the god Krishna.

Marengo. The recipe *à la Marengo* is for cooking chicken with mushrooms and various other accessories. It was apparently served to Napoleon by his chef after the French defeated the Austrians at Marengo in 1800.

Maru-Maru Chimbun. The title of a Japanese magazine; for its derivation see *1889.L8.n5*.

Meiji (Japanese, lit. 'enlightened government'). The name given to the reign of the Emperor Mutsuhito (1868–1912).

Mikado (Japanese, lit. 'Noble Gate'). A title for the Emperor of Japan, much used by foreigners in the 19th century. [*1889.L1.n12.*] Also the title of an opera by Gilbert and Sullivan (1885).

mofussil (Hindi). A term widely used in British India, meaning 'up-country', 'rural district', etc. [*1889.L12.n22.*]

Mon (Japanese). Heraldic escutcheon. The Imperial Mon are a sixteen-petal chrysanthemum and the Paulownia flower (*Paulownia imperialis*). The Tokugawa Mon is three leaves of asarum in a circle.

Nakasendo (Japanese, lit. 'road through the mountains'). The inland route between Kyoto and Tokyo. [*1889.L8.n6.*] Cf. *Tokaido.*

napi (from Burmese, sometimes spelt *gnapi* or *ngapi*). A strong-smelling fish delicacy in Burma. [*1889.L1.n26.*]

nautch (Hindi). A formal display of dancing. [*1889.L7.n1.*]

netsuke (Japanese). A carved ornamental toggle.

No (Japanese). Form of Japanese classical drama. [*1889.L3.n2.*]

nota bene (Latin). Literally 'note well', 'n.b.'.

numdah (Hindi, from Persian). A felt rug or saddlecloth.

o-hayoo (Japanese). Greeting equivalent to 'good morning'.

obi (Japanese). The Japanese woman's long sash, worn round the stomach with the 'bow' at the back.

Om mane padme hum. A mystical Buddhist invocation: see *1889.L12.n14* and *1892.L1.n27.*

pahari (Hindi). A common term in northern India for a hillman.

peepul (Hindi, also *pipal*). The sacred fig tree of India, *Ficus religiosa.*

pice (from Hindi, *paisa*). A term used either literally for a quarter-anna coin, or generally for 'money'. [*1889.L5.n17.*]

pikdan (Hindi). A spittoon.

pro re nata (Latin). 'In the circumstances'. [*1889.L8.n4.*]

pukka (Hindi). 'Thorough' or 'proper'. [*1889.L9.n6.*]

R.A. Royal Academician.

rajbahar (Hindi, also *rajbaha*). A main channel in an irrigation system.

Rajput (from the Sanskrit, *rajaputra*, 'king's son'). For a note on this great Hindu class, with its hereditary profession of arms, see *1889.L4.n33.*

rickshaw (also *'rickshaw* and *jinrickshaw*, from the Japanese *jinrikisha*, lit. 'man-power-vehicle'). For the origin of this conveyance see *1889.L1.n13.*

Rikken Kaishinto (Japanese). The Progressive Party in Japan.

ronin (Japanese, lit. 'wave-man', i.e. 'wanderer'). A *samurai* who lacked the master to whom he should owe allegiance.

ryot (Hindi, from Arabic *raiyat*). An Indian peasant or cultivator who was liable to taxation.

sagar (Hindi). A lake.

sahib (Hindi, from Arabic). A word with various implications in India, e.g.

'gentleman' and 'master'. During the Raj it came to be applied to Europeans generally. [*1889.L2.n14.*]

sake (Japanese). Rice wine, normally served hot in small cups.

samisen (Japanese, lit. 'three strings'). A stringed musical instrument.

sambhur (from Hindi). A species of large Indian forest deer. [*1889.L1.n26.*]

samurai (Japanese). The fighting class, in Japanese feudal society.

sayonara (Japanese). Equivalent to 'goodbye'.

seer (Hindi). An Indian unit of weight [*1889.L9.n13.*]

Seinan (Japanese, lit. 'south-east'). Name given to Satsuma rebellion, 1877.

Shi-no-ko-sho (Japanese). A way of expressing the division of feudal society into four classes: fighting men, farmers, artisans, merchants.

shikar (Hindi, from Persian). Hunting, or shooting.

Shinto (Japanese, lit. 'way of the gods'). Indigenous Japanese religion.

Shogun (Japanese, lit. 'generalissimo'). Military ruler.

Shri (from Sanskrit). Holy. [*1889.L12.n14.*]

sitar (Hindi). A type of stringed musical instrument in India.

Sonno-Joi (Japanese, lit. 'revere Emperor, expel barbarians'). Slogan of the anti-Shogun Daimyo in the 1860s.

tan (Japanese). A measure of land, 0.245 acres.

tehsildar (Hindi, also *tahsildar*). A native tax collector or revenue officer in India.

tiffin (common among British in India, but of uncertain origin). Lunch.

Tirthankars (from Hindi). Saints of the Jain religion. [*1889.L2.n11.*]

Tokaido (Japanese, lit. 'eastern sea road'). The coastal route between Tokyo and Kyoto. [See *1889.L8.n1*, and cf. *Nakasendo.*]

tokonoma (Japanese). A recess in a Japanese room, artistically its focal point. [*1889.L1.n28.*]

Tokugawa. The period of Japanese history named after Tokugawa Ieyasu lasted from 1600 when he defeated his rivals, till 1868.

torii (Japanese). The standard formal gateway of upright and horizontal beams, leading to a Shinto shrine.

Tozama (Japanese, meaning 'outsider'). A term applied to Daimyo who submitted to the Tokugawa after the battle of Sekigahara in 1600. [Cf. *Fudai* for the Daimyo who were vassals of the Tokugawa or fought on their side in the battle.]

tulsi (Hindi, from Sanskrit). A plant related to the Basil family, venerated by Hindus and commonly grown in pots near their temples and dwellings.

wallah (Hindi). For a note on this common term see *1889.L5.n27*.

Yeddo or *Yedo*. Variant of *Edo*, *q.v.*

zushi (Japanese). A case, e.g. for holding a small figure of the Buddha.

Index

Index

Index

Gaiety Theatre (Simla), 142, 149.
Garden Parties, Imperial, 178, 214, 221.
Gay, V., 181.
Gaya, xii. *See* Buddh Gaya.
geisha, 150.
Germany / Germans, 77, 83, 102, 129, 198, 231, 279; Germans & art, 106, 157, 180; German influence, 5, 36, 185, 212, 213.
Gladstone, W.E., 170, 176, 251.
Gosse, Edmund, 239.
Grand Hotel (Yokohama), 129, 138, 146.
Grand Trunk Road, 125, 135.
'Griffiths the Safe Man', 15, 23, **109–14**, 271.
guides, 71, 74, 76, 92, 94, 101, 120, **146**, 152, **154**, **156–9**, 185. *See also* Y-Tokai; Yamaguchi.
Gurkhas, 73, 165, 166, 174.
Gwalior, xii, 81.

Habington, William, 250.
Haggard, Sir Rider, 151, 160, 227.
Hakodate, xiv, 2, 6, 228, 235.
Hakone, 7, 127, 128, 135.
Hamamatsu, xiv, 137.
Hankow, 85.
hara-kiri, 181, 187, 188, 282.
Harashima, Yoshimori, 25.
Harding, W.J., 272.
Hearn, Lafcadio, x, 14–15, 175, 262, 268, 269.
Heinemann, William, 239.
Hill, Professor S.A., **12–13**, 18, 20; as 'the Professor' *passim* throughout Part One; the Professor & photography, 33, 41, 64, 89, 99–100; in a tea-house, 43–5, 99; at the theatre, 59, 61; at Osaka Castle, 72–3; on art, 102, 104–6; on the USA, 52–3, 152; on China, 54–5; on the Japanese, 56, 69–71, 77–8, 81, 100–1, 122, 129, 178–80, 190; sightseeing, 68, 84, 92–4, 115, 116, 118, 145, 156, 158–9, 168, 184–5; as travelling companion, 121, 131, 134, 141–2, 154; as 'Griffiths', 113.
Hill, Mrs E., **12–13**, **18**, 20, 34, 78.
Himalayas, xii, 82, 128–9, 138.
Hindus / Hinduism, 38, 58, 62, 82, 118, 155, 187, 203, 209, 246, 275.

Hindustani, 28, 114, 146, 170, **281**.
Hirobumi, Prince Ito, 5, 220.
Hobson-Jobson, 49, 80, 149.
Hokkaido, xiv, 2, 219, 235.
Hokusai, Katsuchika, 45, 147, 148, 150, 181.
Holtham, E.G., 79.
Hong Kong, 12, 18, **33**, 34, **41**, 47, **53**, **57**, 81, 90, 152, 174, 185, **211**, 218, 233, 278.
Honshu, xiv, 3, 57.
Hooghly, xii, 13.
Horace, (Q. Horatius Flaccus), 236.
Hoshiarpur, xii, 126, 137.
hotels:– Japanese hotels (general), 7, 110–2, 113, 117–8, 120–2, 133–5, 154, 197, 212, 232, 272. *See also* Charleville; Fujiya; Grand; Imperial; Jutei's; Oriental (Kobe); Oriental (Penang); Peliti's; Raffles; Victoria; Yaami's.
hot springs, 127, 132–5, 140–2, 149.
Hunt, Mr & Mrs H.J., 240, 243.
Huntington Library, xi, 18, 20, 45.
Hyogo, 3.

Imari ware, 102, 107, 131.
Imperial Hotel (Tokyo), 164, 173.
In Black and White, 11.
'Incarnation of Krishna Mulvaney, The', 224.
India, xii; general references *passim* throughout; Kipling's Indian background, 9–15, 18, 26, 28, 34, 72, 76, 107, 137–8, 226, 271, 278–9; comparisons with Japan, 36, **38**, 40, 41, **53**, 63, 73, 81, **86**, 116, 127–8, 169, **172–3**, 192, 195; India & Russia, 47; Indian enamelware, 104; Indian tea, 85, 96. *See also* place names and *Civil & Military Gazette*; *Pioneer*.
India Office Library and Records, xi, 19.
Ingles, Captain John, RN, 224, 226.
Inland Sea, xiv, 51–2, 184.
Iquique, 63, 67.
Ireland, 128, 215, 273.
Irving, Sir Henry, 60, 66.
Itagaki, Count Taisuke, 176.
Italy, 106, 131, 279.

Jain, 55, 58.
Jaipur, xii, 104, 108.
James, Henry, 239.
Japan Weekly Mail, 23, 28, 136, 150, 204, **219–21**, **224–6**, **236–7**, **264–5**, 267, 268.
Jerome, Jerome K., 271.
Jesuits, 39, 48, 63. *See also* missionaries.
jhampan/jhampani, 94, 142–3, **149**. *See also 'rickshaw*.
Jharipani (Jerrapani), 84, 95.
Jingoro, Hidari, 163.
jinrikisha. See under 'rickshaw.
Jizo (Khsitigarbha), 162.
Jodhpur, xii, 72, 81.
John, King, 171, 176.
judo techniques, 198, 205.
Jungle Books, The, 236, 240, 261, 265, 267, 280.
Jutei's Hotel (Osaka), 71, 72, 80.

Kabuki theatre, 59–61, 66, 283. *See also* theatre.
Kaga, 102, 107, 131.
Kagoshima, 3.
Kali, 63, 67.
Kalka, xii, 133, 139.
Kamakura, x, xiv, 184, 189, **201–4**, **205–9**. *See also* 'Buddha at Kamakura'.
Kamchatka, 219, 254, 266, 267.
Kamti falls, 84.
Kanagawa, xiv, 2.
Kannon, 66.
Kano school of painters, 83, 90–1, 95, 96.
Kaoru, Prince Inoue, 226.
Kearnan, John, 264, 267, 268.
Keats, John, 46.
Khattri (also *Kshatriya*), 77, 81–2, 283.
Kim, 26, 47, 207, 208, 240, 271, 280.
Kinchinjunga/Kangchenjunga, xii, 128, 138.
'King Euric'. *See* 'For hope of gain'.
Kipling, Mrs Caroline (*née* Balestier), 15, 237, 239–40, 243, 279, 280.
Kobe:– general, xiv, 36, 45, 51, **52–6**, **62–5**, 66, 71, 76, 115, 184, 185; as a Treaty Port, 3, 6, 57, 79; and railway system, 4, 68, 69, 78–9, 118, 144.
Kobe Club, 262.

Kodansha (*Encyclopedia of Japan*), 277.
Komandorskiye Islands, 266–9.
Korea, xiv, 223, 266.
'Kotik', 265, 267, 268.
Krishna, 63, 67.
Kulu, xii, 70, 80.
Kundoo, F., 121–2, 124.
Kurile Islands, xiv, 119, **124**, 212, **219**, 252, **254**, 263, 266.
Kutani ware, 107.
Kyosai, Kawanabe, 146–7, 150.
Kyoto:– general, xiv, **1–3**, 14, 68, 70, 76, **77–8**, **82–91**, 94, 95–7, 98, 100, 110, 112, 113, **115–7**, 184; and railway system, 4, 7, 124, 125, 136; and manufactures, **101–5**, 131.
Kyushu, xiv, 1–3, 47, 107, 144.

'Labour' (Japanese in Canada), 24, 274–7.
lacquer, 101, 154, 156, 157; frequently mentioned *passim*.
Lahore, xii, 9, 11, 62, 66–7, 79, 97, 278–9. *See also Civil & Military Gazette*.
Legros, Alphonse, 75, 81.
Letters of Travel, ix, x, **16**, 17, **22**, 24, 25, 207, 219, 274, 280.
'Letters to the Family', 22, 24, 274.
Lettres du Japon, 17, 24.
Liaoyang, 275.
Liberal. *See* Radical.
Life's Handicap, 15, 108, 227, 279.
Light that Failed, The, 15, 251, 279.
'Limitations of Pambé Serang, The', 250.
Liverpool:– destination, 11, 13, 192, 279; port of departure, 204, 239, 279.
London:– general, 133, 168, 216, 226; the City, 85, **211–2**, 231, 238, 241; Kipling in London, 15, 278, 279.
'Long Trail, The', 279.
'Lukannon', 261.

'McAndrew's Hymn', 190, 272.
Madeira, 198, 205.
Malays, 49, 246, 275.
'Man Who Would Be King, The', 113.
Mandalay, xii, 48, 50, 141, 148.
Manila, 185, 212.
Many Inventions, 15, 250.

Index

'Rikki-Tikki-Tavi', 12.
Robben Island, 264, 265, 266, 268.
Roberts, Lord, 77, 81–2.
Rokumeikan, 224, 226.
Roman Catholic Church, 63, 88–9, 190.
Rome, 51, 57.
Ronin, Forty-Seven, 180, 187, 284.
Roosevelt, Theodore, 273.
Royal Academy / Academician (R.A.), 247, **251**.
Royal (Regiment of) Artillery, 141, 149.
Royal Geographical Society, xi, 57.
Royal Society for Asian Affairs, ix, xi.
Russia:– and Japan, 2, 47, 272–3, 275; as a menace, **36**, **47**, **106**, **108**; and sealers, 212, 219–20, **254–5**, 261, **263–5**, 267–9.
Rutherford, Professor Andrew, xi, 12, 243.
ryot, 93, 97, 179, 187, 284.

Saharunpur (Saharanpur), xii, 69, 79.
sahib, 40, 56, **58**, 76, 83, 122, 143, 146.
St Cyr, 215, 222.
St George Island, 260, 269.
St Paul Island, 260, 269.
sake, **44**, 76, 84, **93**, 116, 117, 150, 182, **189**, 285.
Sakhalin, xiv, 263–6.
Salvation Army, 265, 275.
samisen, 66, 98–9, 106, 215, 285.
Samoa, 15, 254, 279.
samurai, 2–5, 39, 66, 77, 96, 174, 215, 221, 285.
San Francisco, 11, 12, 18, 33, 131, 132, 136, 185, 186, 190–2, 278.
Sanskrit, 155, 162, 187, 207.
Sapporo, xiv, 228, 235.
Sarun (Saran), xii, 100, 107.
Satsuma, xiv, 3, 4, 222, 285; ware, 101, 102, 107, 131.
Saturday Review, 151, 161.
Scindia / Sindhia, 73, 81.
Scott, Sir Walter, 261.
sealing, 119, 120, 212, 252, 254, **255–69**.
Seaside Library / Publishing Company, 151, 152, **159**.
Seinan war, 4, 285.
Sekigahara, 1.
Seven Seas, The, 251, 261.

Shakespeare, William, 66, 106, 130, 138.
Shanghai, 47, 211, 233, 235, 266.
Shiba Park (Tokyo), 180, 187.
Shimabara, xiv, 1.
Shimonoseki, xiv, 3.
Shinto, 8, 62, 118, 123, 155, 285.
Shogawa, 144, 150.
Shogun / Shogunate, 1, 2, 47, 77, 82, 158, 162, 187, 221, 235, 285. *See* Tokugawa.
Shoji, Lake, 262.
Shway (Shwe) Dagon, 40, 43, **49**, 50, 203, **208**.
Siberia, 41, 266, 273. *See also* Russia; Vladivostok.
Sidney, Sir Philip, 253, 254.
Simla, xii, 43, 48, 57, 99, **107**, 133, 139, 142.
Simon's Town / Simonstown, 211, 218.
Singapore, 12, 33, **53**, **57**, 76, 152, 185, 195, 226, 233, 278.
Siwaliks, The, 78, 82, 84, 95.
'Smoky Seas, The', 252, 254–6.
Soldiers Three, 11, 81, 224, 227.
'Solomon the Sealer', 262, 263, 267.
Something of Myself, 23, 27, 188, 236, **239–41**, 271.
South Africa, 190, 210, 279. *See also* Cape Town.
Southsea, 10, 11, 79.
Spain / Spanish, 77, 106, 114, 146, 182, 224, 253.
Spotlight magazine, 262.
Stalky & Co., 11, 26.
Stephen, J.K., 227.
Stirling, Admiral Sir James, 47.
Sterne, Lawrence, 178, 186.
Stevenson, Robert Louis, 15, 151, 160, 254, 279.
Storry, Richard, 273–4.
Story of the Gadsbys, The, 11.
Strid, The, 155, 163.
Sun / Sunday Sun. See New York *Sun*.
Sussex University Library, xi, 23, 243.

'Takahira', 273.
Takao, 84, 96.
Tamils, 275.
tariffs, Japanese, 170, 175.
taxes, Japanese, 192, 199–201.